D1429051

DAUGHTERS OF EVE

DAUGHTERS OF EVE

*A Cultural History of French Theater Women
from the Old Regime to the Fin de Siècle*

Lenard R. Berlanstein

HARVARD UNIVERSITY PRESS

Cambridge, Massachusetts

London, England

2001

Library of Congress Cataloging-in-Publication Data

Berlanstein, Lenard R.
    Daughters of Eve : a cultural history of French theater women from the
    Old Regime to the fin de siècle / Lenard R. Berlanstein.
        p. cm.
    Includes bibliographical references and index.
    ISBN 0-674-00596-1
    1. Women in the theater—France—History—19th century.
    2. Women in the theater—France—History—18th century.
    3. Actresses—France—Biography.   I. Title.
PN2622.W65 B47 2001
792′.028′082094409033—dc21   2001024841

In memory of my father,
David K. Berlanstein

CONTENTS

Acknowledgments   *ix*

Introduction   *1*

1 Setting the Scene   *10*

2 Theater Women and Aristocratic Libertinism, 1715–1789   *33*

3 Defining the Modern Gender Order, 1760–1815   *59*

4 Magdalenes of Postaristocratic France, 1815–1848   *84*

5 The Erotic Culture of the Stage   *104*

6 The Struggle against Pornocracy, 1848–1880   *135*

7 Imagining Republican Actresses, 1880–1914   *159*

8 Performing a Self   *182*

9 From Notorious Women to Intimate Strangers   *209*

Conclusion   *237*

Notes   *243*

Index   *295*

ACKNOWLEDGMENTS

I can remember the day, sitting in the Library of Congress, when the notion of writing on French theater women popped into my head. I had been seeking a new research project, and this idea immediately seemed plausible. Where it came from I am not sure, but reading Robert Herbert's *Impressionism: Art, Leisure, and Parisian Society* might well have been the stimulus. In any case, a great deal of help—financial, editorial, scholarly, emotional—was necessary to take me from the idea to the finished work. A Sesquicentennial Grant from the University of Virginia allowed me to take the spring semester of 1996 off to complete my research in Paris. Funding from the National Endowment for the Humanities and the John Simon Guggenheim Memorial Foundation permitted a crucial leave during the 1999–2000 academic year. Committee work at the university being what it is, without this generous support I would, no doubt, still be writing chapters.

It is humbling to reflect on how much my work has benefited from friends and colleagues' willingness to take time out from their busy schedules to assist. Vanessa Schwartz applied her fertile mind to all my chapters and pushed me in fruitful directions. Sarah Maza was consistently generous about sharing her research on the French bourgeoisie and helped me to shape my argument. Joyce Seltzer's line-by-line editing tightened the manuscript in innumerable ways. Edgar Newman took the trouble to send me dozens of references about stage women from his worker-poets; I always found these communications helpful for contextualizing my study. Patrick Fridenson brought me to the Ecole des Hautes Etudes en Sciences Sociales in 1996 and gave me a chance to lecture on my preliminary ideas and receive excellent feedback; Alain Corbin's seminar was particularly helpful in this regard. Invitations to give talks from William Weber, Timothy Tackett, and Patrice Higonnet also provided valuable opportunities to refine my thoughts. It has become a ritual for me to pass my penultimate manuscripts to Jack and Jane Censer for a reading, and I greatly appreciate their having undertaken the task once again. Cissie Fairchilds assisted on the chapters about the Old Regime and the Revolution. Elinor Accampo and Jo Burr Margadant, readers for Harvard University Press, provided excellent ideas for my final revisions.

The list of colleages whom I need to thank goes on: Matthew Affron, Barry Bergen, Linda Clark, Alon Confino, Michael Cooper, Rachel Fuchs, Scott Haine, Ran Halévy, Janet Horne, Lynn Hunt, Gay Gullickson, Susan Lancer, Theresa McBride, Ted Margadant, Rene Marion, Ann Martin-Fugier, John Merriman, Clair Goldberg Moses, Philip Nord, Jeffrey Ravel, Donald Reid, Mary Louise Roberts, Sophie Rosenfeld, Mary Lynn Stewart, Elizabeth Thompson, Victoria Thompson, and Whitney Walton. Their stimulating conversations, shared ideas, archival tips, and suggestions for revisions have made this study far better than it would otherwise have been. I am deeply grateful to all of them.

I dedicate this book to my father, David K. Berlanstein, who, before he passed away, was never quite sure why I was studying French actresses but was nonetheless proud of his son.

ILLUSTRATIONS

Alceste at the Opéra, 1776 and 1861. *Le Journal amusant,* no. 315 (January 11, 1862), p. 3.   *12*

Gentlemen dining with actresses. *Le Journal amusant,* no. 270 (March 2, 1861), p. 1.   *40*

Actresses and aristocrats plotting with the king. *Les Révolutions de France and de Brabant,* no. 45 (October 4, 1790), p. 253.   *77*

Reading committee at the Comédie-française, 1830s. Courtesy of La Bibliothèque nationale de France.   *94*

The eroticism of the stage. *Le Monde illustré,* no. 477 (June 2, 1866), p. 349.   *105*

Reading committee at the Comédie-française, post-1848. *L'Illustration,* no. 33,060 (October 19, 1901), p. 249.   *146*

The professional ballerina. *Fémina,* no. 275 (July 1, 1912), p. 401.   *163*

The actress Rachel reciting "The Empire Means Peace." Courtesy of La Bibliothèque nationale de France.   *201*

Sarah Bernhardt endorsing beauty products. Courtesy of La Bibliothèque nationale de France.   *232*

DAUGHTERS OF EVE

Introduction

What could be more ordinary, more natural, than women appearing on stage, pleasing audiences with their gracious movements and convincing role playing? Of course, in fact, such pleasure was forbidden for centuries in much of Europe and was highly contentious even after its legalization. A great deal of cultural work was necessary to make women on stage an unremarkable fact of life. This book is about how the French, from the years of royal absolutism to republican democracy, incorporated women performers into their culture. The French, to be sure, have an enviable reputation for a worldly attitude of tolerance toward sexually transgressive women. Yet this turns out to be one of their recently invented traditions, built on partial truths (and deployed particularly at times of scandal in the English-speaking world). Placed in comparative perspective, the French path to accepting theater women was, in fact, unusually traumatic, protracted, and discontinuous.[1] French culture gave actresses greater prominence than elsewhere at the same time that it withheld respectability more resolutely. This pattern raises far-reaching questions about the interplay of gender and politics.

The celebrated eighteenth-century diva Sophie Arnould provided the key idea behind this book when she quipped, "The whole art of being an actress consists of locking the door securely"—so that one lover will not take the performer and another lover by surprise.[2] This study is much more about loves and lusts of Frenchmen for female players than about the quotidian practices of theatrical life. I treat actresses as cultural sites where social, class, political, and gendered forces intersected in such a way as to produce meanings that helped explain social organization. To

1

a large degree, the representations of actresses entailed conflicts about female and male identities.

The outstanding quality of theater women in France was their inimitable place in the erotic imagination of Frenchmen as daughters of Eve. Actresses were uniquely desired women. The great novelist Stendhal, as a twenty-three-year-old in 1806, noted: "I passionately desired to be loved by a melancholy, thin, woman—an actress."[3] Starting in the era when most studies date the quickening pace of "modernity," the end of the seventeenth century, actresses became the preeminent consorts of men at the top of the social hierarchy and remained so at least up to the First World War. The pursuit of theater women as mistresses was something of an obligation among elite men of France. Commentators did not bother to inquire whether the kept actress was typical or not; they wanted to characterize every actress as a goddess of illicit love. One literary critic disparaged Edmond de Goncourt's biography of the famous eighteenth-century thespian Mademoiselle Clairon on the grounds that "the lives of all actresses are the same."[4] The uniformity that the critic had in mind was that they were all unruly women who had their way with important men.

I use the terms *theater women* and *actresses* in a broad sense to include performers of most sorts—thespians, ballerinas, modern dancers, opera singers, popular songstresses, and so on. To be sure, each of these categories has its own history. Yet their commonality in the minds of the French makes their collective treatment desirable. Contemporaries did not hesitate to group them together, so I do not consider the usage artificial. What I do regret is having been unable to use gender-neutral language. Referring to both female and male performers as "actors" would have been too confusing, since my study demands attention to gender specificity.

At the most general level, this work examines how a culture formulates controversial social perceptions and reshuffles collective identities over time. Representations of theater women merit attention from this perspective because they were significant figures in defining the balance of power between the sexes. Their physical appeal made them quintessential strong women in the French social imagination, and they had to be contained in one way or another. Conventionally in French culture, men had power and women had *powers*.[5] There was an acceptable way for women to influence men, identified by *Le Journal amusant* in

1854 when it quipped that "a woman's strength consists precisely in not needing to be strong."[6] The caricaturist Gavarni presented a vastly different idea of female powers in his cartoon portraying the troubled Orléanist regime of the 1830s as an actress, Mademoiselle Monarchy, who enslaved men by giving them pleasure.[7] Some of the most influential thinkers in modern French history, including Jean-Jacques Rousseau, Jules Michelet, and Hippolyte Taine, were all certain that women were too strong in France, that the complementarity of the sexes did not work within the Hexagon. This issue resonated through French culture. It was debated, and temporary solutions were devised, around the subject of theater women. Peter Gay has noted that "no century depicted women as vampires, as castrators, as killers so consistently, so programmatically, so nakedly as the nineteenth century."[8] Actresses certainly did receive this sort of treatment. However, panic over unruly women was only part of the story. There were moments in French history when representations of actresses were considerably more consistent with current ideals for women, and I shall seek to explore the reasons for these shifts.

Two interrelated types of perceptions dominated discourses on theater women, and they are particularly interesting for the way they illuminated the social order producing the representations. The first was how much danger theater women, with their powers over men and their ties to the male elite, posed for society. Would men possess the strength of character to resist actresses' wiles? There was no consistent answer to this question across the two hundred years covered by this study. Instead, I find eras when theater women were repeatedly and noisily perceived as threats (the prerevolutionary decades and the mid-nineteenth century) alternating with eras when the sense of danger subsided (between the Revolutions of 1789 and 1848 and after the establishment of the Third Republic, around 1880). In the first set, actresses' sexuality was seen to pervert men's judgment. In the second, actresses evoked sympathy as creatures who could charm men but not enough to subvert masculine self-control.

The cycles of fear and sympathy had little to do with changes in actresses' actual conduct (about which we know only through observations made from within the prevailing and self-reinforcing discourses). Like all other students of this field, I had to come to grips with sexually charged women serving as a code or substitute for other concerns.[9] The scholarship on French gender history has drawn mainly on women's political activism, cultural unease about the market economy, and fears about falling birth rates to explain denunciations of unruly women.[10] While I recognize the power of these forces, they play only a secondary role in this study. The controlling issue, I claim, was the way French people understood the workings of their political order.

While theater women often haunted French public life through their sexuality and strong will, public life continuously haunted theater women—in the sense of determining how they would be perceived. Shifts in theater women's representation coincided with new forms of political organization—absolute monarchy, parliamentary liberalism, authoritarian democracy, and liberal democracy. Moreover, the perceptions changed suddenly with the new political cosmology and maintained an overwhelming uniformity within each regime. Collective amnesia about previous representations quickly set in. These findings lead me to conclude that political organization and ideologies determined representations of theater women. I seek to demonstrate in this study that the nature of the political realm produced nuances in notions of masculinity and femininity that, in turn, set the terms in which theater women would be imagined. In those regimes that required an active public sphere and a dynamic civil society for their legitimacy, the culture accepted men as rational and self-disciplined in their relationships with women. By the early nineteenth century, those self-disciplined men were identified with a class, the bourgeoisie (or later, more vaguely, with the middling social strata). However, in authoritarian regimes with elites designated as ornamental, the culture figured men, particularly those of the ruling class, as emasculated and dominated by women. Civil society constituted the crucial link between political organization and notions of manhood and womanhood.[11] It transformed ideology into lived experience via public debate, political parties, voluntary associations, and parliamentary life, all of which brought men together, empowered them, and accentuated the exclusion of women from the public sphere.[12]

Readers who are skeptical about social constructionist explanations might be reassured by the fact that I did not come to the material with any particular predisposition for this model. I might even have been more comfortable with explanations based on what historians now call "experience."[13] Yet the coincidence of changes in political order and representations of actresses, on the one hand, and the extraordinary degree of intracyclical consistency, on the other hand, inevitably pushed me to the understanding just outlined.[14] The state of civil society must have been especially relevant to the ways theater women were imagined because of their role as courtesans to France's most important men.[15]

The second vital perception of theater women was how close to the feminine ideal they were. Jean-Jacques Rousseau projected the critical vision by defining women as modest, self-sacrificing, and domesticated by nature. He constructed actresses in opposition, as vain, artificial, and corrupt. The Rousseauist view endured but was challenged at different times by other claims: that actresses, though morally flawed, might yet have a hidden core of purity, or even that there was nothing inherently unwomanly about them. Men projected on theater women the qualities they hoped or feared to find in woman in general. As such, female performers served as a sensitive index of possibilities for women's publicness and personal autonomy over time. One of the values of examining gender through the prism of actresses is that they drew such intense reactions and thus revealed sensibilities, collective psychological states, and unconscious assumptions that are otherwise difficult to detect.

The understandings that emerged from measuring actresses by the standards of women, and women by the standards of actresses, had a cyclical pattern, too. When confidence in men's potential for self-governance was low, there was widespread despair that women were not the selfless beings that they needed to be. When confidence was high, the public was more generous in setting the boundaries of gender orthodoxy. In the latter case, shifting attitudes toward theater women traced the outer limits of possibilities for women in general. For much of the century, the principles of complementarity held, and the most to which actresses could aspire was to be self-sacrificing and devoted to their men. By the fin de siècle, however, domesticity was not the only standard by which stage performers might be measured. A breakdown of complementary thinking was occurring, and those women who stole the limelight with their talent were no longer abhorrent models for women in general.

The evidence about theater women comes from newspapers, professional writing on theater life, official reports, public rituals, and fiction in which these women were central characters. My use of the last source requires some elucidation. I read every fictional work that I could find— some ninety-eight of them—that had actresses as principle characters.

The treatment of actresses in plays and novels during the nineteenth century turns out to be highly patterned. During the entire first half of the century, actresses were heroines or victims of oppression—which often amounted to the same thing. For the three decades after the Revolution of 1848, they were almost always villains who tried to ruin good men and tear families apart. After 1880, theater women were once again sympathetic figures, though in more complicated ways than earlier. My reading of the fiction was quite intentionally straightforward, giving much attention to the plot device. Literary critics might object that I read too little into the stories and that readers, not the texts, determined meanings. Yet I would counter that the vast bulk of the theater fiction was melodramatic and employed familiar stereotypes. Since reading is a culturally informed act, the public of the day did not have much difficulty or discretion in deciding whether the protagonist was a heroine or a monster.[16] Moreover, the cyclical patterns derived from the belletristic evidence is well corroborated by nonfictional writing and by shifts in public policy. For example, during the Second Empire, when fictional stage women were depicted as predatory, the government took steps to reduce actresses' decision-making authority at the Comédie-française. Just before World War I, when the theater woman was once again a heroine, the government restored actresses to positions of authority within the troupe.

One of the most intractable problems for this study is defining whose culture is at its center. The safest answer would be that of urban (especially big-city) people of above average wealth and education. These were the readers of the newspapers that had the most abundant coverage of theatrical life, journals like *Le Figaro,* which had a large circulation without being a mass-circulation daily. The well off also made up the bulk of theater audiences, which were cross-class in composition but weighted toward the upper end. The fashionable authors of the Grand Boulevard, who provided most of the record on theater women, wrote for this group. Finally, this was the milieu in which the domestic imperative for women was most venerated and observed.[17] I strongly suspect that much about upper-class culture would have resonance in "mass," "popular," and even "working-class" culture, but I will leave that for other scholars to verify.

Inevitably, men's voices dominated the discourses about these famous women. For most of the era under discussion, actresses were under the male gaze. Women were generally denied the right to comment openly about theater performers, on grounds of decency.[18] Actresses did eventually come under the female gaze, but only as part of a wider process in which performers' political significance became more limited.[19]

The male (and, whenever possible) female voices were by no means transparent when they discussed actresses. Representing women's powers inspired peculiar habits of mind, and the French reputation for enlightenment on this score has not always been earned. Dishonesty, dissimulation, and contradiction bathed the perceptions of theater women. On the one hand, French culture produced recurrent fantasies of purifying national life by removing women from the stage à la Rousseau. On the other, there was a proud defense of French theater culture, including its erotic elements, as the epitome of elegance and sophistication, especially in contrast to British and American standards of propriety. Actresses' comportment evoked such controversial concerns about gender, morality, and public order that there was a pressing need for those who spoke about them publicly *not* to tell the truth. Even seemingly guileless issues (for example, Did husbands or wives most want to attend the theater? How much did the audience pay attention to the fare? What sort of women enrolled in the Conservatory?) were freighted with ideological implications. Consequently, useful fictions surrounded theater women. Males projected on actresses behavior they feared in themselves; bourgeois projected on aristocrats conduct that was scandalous but all too tempting. The voluminous literature discussing theater women, though light in tone, was nonetheless ideologically informed. To deconstruct it is to engage in peeling back the obfuscation that prevents us from seeing how patriarchy created its authority and its categories of understanding.

When I began this study, I presumed that a good deal of it would consider female performers' subversion of womanhood as conventionally understood. However, I eventually discovered that the issue was not at all a simple one. The deviations from gender orthodoxy that actresses lived out could just as easily confirm biases. Moreover, society rewarded actresses handsomely for sustaining stereotypes, and many did. They lacked the feminist consciousness that might have provided the will to combat prejudices. Ultimately, *the culture* had to change before actresses would become effective models of emancipation. That did happen eventually, and I have tried to trace the path by which it did.

Finally, I wish to claim for this study national significance, although most of the institutions and figures that I follow were settled in Paris. People throughout France thought about theater in Parisian terms. It is meaningful that not more than one or two of the many novels about stage life were set outside the capital. Performers who were successful in the provinces migrated to Paris. Provincials received much of their theater from the visiting troupes of the capital. Moreover, the representations of Parisian theater life in periodicals, society columns of newspapers, and fiction circulated nationally. While I do not doubt that scholars could and will uncover regional variations, the scope of this study is nationwide.

Examining theater women as a site where upper-class culture debated and temporarily determined the balance of power between the sexes leads to a rethinking of modern French gender history. In general, the literature posits a growing intolerance for all sorts of "exceptional" women as equality replaced privilege as the basis of social organization.[20] The radical phase of the Revolution (1792 to 1795) takes its place as a moment when the dangerous powers of women weighed heavily on revolutionaries' minds as a result of Jacobin ideology or women's organizational success.[21] Yet I find that the fear theater women inspired, which had been on the rise across the eighteenth century, diminished substantially after 1789, and it was because the new revolutionary order made the rule of male reason appear the natural and inevitable result of social progress. Louis-Napoleon Bonaparte's Second Empire, between 1852 and 1870, is another period that needs reexamination. It has generally not engaged historians of gender as particularly interesting, but I show that it contained a serious crisis of femininity. Men charged actresses and even married women with subverting the ideals of womanhood on which the social order depended, and with seeking to dominate men. Through a vilification of theater women, the culture expressed a virulent strain of misogyny the significance of which scholars have not sufficiently explored. In contrast, the misogyny of the pre-1914 Third Republic has been intensely explored in recent years through the prism of a crisis of masculinity. This focus has led scholars to emphasize the angry reaction against demands for expanded rights for women.[22] Urgent and important as this theme is, the gender history of the period seems to have been too complicated to fit a single schema. While some Third Republic men did put women who demanded more rights on the defensive for betraying the nation, there were many others who had the courage to admit actresses to true womanhood. My findings cut against the grain of a historiography featuring the shortcomings of the Third Republic by showing that a liberating breakthrough occurred. There was a greater acceptance of women who were ambitious, achieving, and public. We see this, for example, in the way actresses' celebrity at the end of the nineteenth century reflected a more individualistic culture for women and for men. These observations point to the need to reexamine in fundamental ways the history of women's place in the public sphere.

Representations of theater women do provide a serious index of the balance of sexual power in the French past, and historians must take account of them in order to understand the evolution of masculinity and femininity. The present work is a first attempt to advance this project.

Setting the Scene

Audiences of stage spectacle were a remarkable social mix during the eighteenth century and much of the nineteenth.[1] Well before and after the Revolution of 1789, foreign visitors often noted the mania for stage productions that reigned throughout French society. The novelist Henry James, a correspondent for the *New York Tribune* in 1875, remarked, "That the theater plays in Paris a larger part in people's lives than it does anywhere else is a fact too well established to need specific comment."[2] However, maintaining this broad appeal in the face of late-nineteenth-century social and cultural change was a daunting challenge.

Scanning the Audience

About 5,000 people regularly attended the theater and another 10,000 attended occasionally in Paris during the first half of the eighteenth century, when the capital had a population of about 400,000 inhabitants.[3] The doubling of theater seating capacity during the second half of the century (from 6,000 to 12,000 seats) suggests a proportional increase in the audience.[4] Another large leap in attendance occurred in the mid-nineteenth century. The distinguished critic Francisque Sarcey, lamenting in 1868 that tickets had become hard to obtain, observed that the number of habitués (a term he did not define) had grown from 20,000 or so at midcentury to "hundreds of thousands."[5] When the journalist Pierre Giffard wrote a book on theater mores in 1889, he asserted that 500,000 people went to the theater once a week and that 1 million to 1.2 million went once a month. His estimate was probably highly exaggerated, but the claim that Parisians "lived with theater, by theater, and for theater" at least captured the importance of the stage in French cultural life of the time.[6]

Stage presentations in France had come to transcend the level of the medieval itinerant troupes through royal patronage during the seventeenth century. Louis XIV made the Opéra, the Comédie-française, and the Comédie-italienne into royal companies. The players became "the king's actors" and were placed under the supervision of the First Gentlemen of the Bedchamber. In exchange for subsidies from the crown and monopolies over specified repertories, the royal theaters were obligated to uphold the highest standards of taste, as set by such playwrights as Jean Racine, Jean-Baptiste Molière, and later, Voltaire. The political domination and grandeur pursued by the Bourbon kings favored the creation of a rich theatrical life by incorporating plays into the spectacle of royal power and by fostering a centralized aristocratic culture.[7] The boxes, lobbies, and backstage of the royal theaters became extensions of the Versailles court. The members of the beau monde displayed themselves at the theater and, through conversation and gesture, carried out the social functions of an elite.[8] Audiences were not exclusively aristocratic, however. Members of high society, known as Le Monde (the World), did not occupy the pit, or parterre, the area on the floor between the stage and the first boxes. In the pit were men (the area was exclusively for men) mostly on the fringes of Le Monde: younger sons of noble families, servants, impecunious artists, and so on.[9] The king also allowed his subjects to enjoy light diversion during the seasonal fairs of Saint-Laurent and Saint-Germain. The temporary theaters at the fairs attracted large audiences, and there titled lords did not seem to mind mixing with the rabble.[10]

Three crucial moments of transition prepared French theater for the revolutionary social and cultural changes that arose after the mid-eighteenth century. The transitions occurred under the impact of a growing commercialization of the theater and entailed, initially, a fusing of high and low taste, and then a separation of the two. The first breakthrough took place in the 1760s, when the royal government allowed permanent commercial theaters to open. Louis XV probably did not realize that he was abetting the fusion of classical and plebian taste when he permitted the well-known fair director, Jean Nicollet, to open the Gaieté, a year-round stage that would not depend on royal subsidies and direct state supervision, in 1760. More such theaters followed, both the Ambigu-comique and the Associés in 1769, and the Délassements-comiques in 1785. The government showed its desire to shield the royal theaters from commercial competition and to maintain the boundary between high art and popular diversion by placing severe restrictions on the fare at the new theaters—for example, forbidding them to use spoken dialogue or to have more than two players on stage at one time.[11] Very quickly, however, the new "little theaters," as they were called, were evading the restrictions or using them so creatively that the royal troupes became jealous of their success. The bastions of high art, the royal playhouses, found it necessary to incorporate elements from the lower forms of entertainment at an accelerating pace to keep their houses full. Some farces originating at the little theaters were even performed at court.

With the expansion and commercialization of the theater industry in the nineteenth century, women's costumes became considerably more revealing, as this comparison of two productions of *Alceste,* in 1776 and 1861, at the Opéra points out. Regardless of the era, however, male spectators did not lack for erotic stimulation.

The location of the new commercial theaters, on the boulevard du Temple in eastern Paris, was significant. That thoroughfare had developed into the premier space for plebeian leisure by the end of the seventeenth century. It was a permanent fair, filled with street entertainers of all sorts, especially on Sundays. The rustic cafés and dance halls attracted a very mixed crowd. When lords and prosperous commoners came to the boulevard du Temple, they did so to escape the constraints of their normal milieux for the bawdiness and exuberance of life on the street of popular pleasures.[12]

A middling sort of production, between the classics and popular fair performances emerged from the intense interchange of authors, genres, and stage techniques between the royal and commercial playhouses. As the spirit of the boulevard du Temple found its way into the bastions of classical taste, higher doses of sentimentality, action, and emotion seeped into the fare of the royal theaters. So too did the elaborate scenic effects and greater historical accuracy in costuming found in eastern Paris. New genres that were to have a brilliant future, drama and operetta, emerged in the little theaters.[13] The aristocracy, inclined to relax the formalities that had structured their code of conduct in the decades just before 1789, supported these innovations with their patronage.[14]

When, in 1791, the revolutionary government removed all restrictions on the opening of theaters, the explosion of new playhouses—dozens were founded—confirmed the popularity of commercial theater.[15] Napoleon, fearing the eclipse of the classical stage by popular fare, eventually closed most of them and reimposed a strict system of theater licensing.[16] Yet just as Bonaparte was assuming power in the last year of the eighteenth century, the boulevard du Temple was producing one of its most influential cultural innovations. Melodrama partially replaced the farcical and scatological content of popular theater. Audiences in the wake of the Revolution and the Terror flocked to dramatic enactments of virtue triumphing over vice. The spectators enjoyed the clearly drawn heroes and villains on stage and responded to the high emotional pitch of the conflicts. The street became known as the "boulevard of crime" because of the graphic plots presented on stage. Romantic dramatists in the following decades would appropriate melodramatic effects (surprise, alternation of comedy and pathos, profuse sincerity) in their more serious art forms.[17]

The declining allure of the boulevard du Temple for the upper classes

in the 1830s—one sign among many of deepening class divisions—
marked the onset of a new era in the social history of French theater.[18]
The publishers, playwrights, critics, and directors who formed the theatrical establishment no longer looked to popular theater for direction. Instead, their commitment was to preserve theater as an upper-class form
of entertainment characterized by conventional good taste and displays
of elegance. This meant reviving or inventing traditions that associated
the theater with the aristocratic past. Popular spectacle would continue
to flourish, but in café-concerts (pubs offering musical entertainment),
dance halls, and the streets, rather than in playhouses.

Abandoning eastern Paris, the well off in the decades after the Revolution of 1830 sought more elegant surroundings in the western portion of the thoroughfare, known as the Grand Boulevard, that continued
beyond the boulevard du Temple, through central Paris, to the Madeleine Church.[19] The theater distict itself moved westward, too. By the
mid-nineteenth century, the boulevard Saint-Martin was home to the
Porte Saint-Martin, Folies-dramatiques, Ambigu, and Renaissance theaters. Further to the west were the Gymnase, the Variétés, the Vaudeville, the Casino de Paris, Olympia, and the Opéra-comique. Not far off
were the Bouffes-parisiens, the Déjazet, Gaieté, Anthénée, and Palais-
Royal theaters and the Comédie-française. In 1875, the Opéra moved
from the nearby rue Le Peletier to the western end of the boulevard des
Italiens, in the magnificent building designed for it by Charles Garnier.
The luxury café-concerts also situated themselves in the district. The
Alcazar was on the rue du Faubourg Poissonnière; the Eldorado, La
Scala, and Eden Concert on the boulevard de Strasbourg, and the Folies-
Bergères on the rue Cadet (near the Conservatory of Dramatic Arts).[20]

The new theaters were splendid edifices, designed to impress. Codes
of dress for an evening at the theater became uniformly demanding. It
was not only at the Opéra and the Théâtre-italien that white tie and tails
were de rigueur on opening nights. That was also the expected dress at
the Bouffes-parisiens, the Variétés, Palais-Royal, Gymnase, Renaissance,
and Vaudeville theaters.[21] While attending plays during the warm season
had always been unpleasant, it was only in the mid-nineteenth century
that most theaters adopted the summer closing, tying themselves to the
migratory pattern of Parisians wealthy enough to have secondary resi-
dences in the countryside.[22] In 1857, the director of the Porte Saint-Martin theater seized the opportunity to use his lobby to market luxury merchandise, and other directors followed the lead.[23]

With most theaters projecting a fashionable aura, popular theater suffered a devastating blow in 1862 when the seven remaining theaters of the boulevard du Temple were closed and demolished for urban renovation. They were never replaced. The boulevard du Temple had been where spectators could find alternatives to the literate, fashionable plays of central Paris. According to elite accounts, spectators in the modest playhouses of the eastern boulevard had carried the odor of varnish (the woodworking industry was centered in the neighboring Faubourg Saint-Antoine) and pipe smoke. Tickets had generally cost less than two francs, with many under one franc. The more stylish theaters to the west did have tickets in the upper balconies for under a franc, but most seats cost a worker's full day of pay or more.[24] At the Variétés theater during the 1870s, for example, the most expensive box seats went for eight and a half francs; orchestra seats, between five and seven francs.[25]

The resolutely fashionable face of theater life after 1830 was the result of its complete integration into the sociability of the Grand Boulevard. The boulevard des Italiens and its extension along the boulevards Montmartre and Bonnes Nouvelles had become during the July Monarchy the center of elegant leisure for which Paris was famous among Europe's rich and powerful. Honoré de Balzac was one of many who referred to these streets as "the heart of Paris."[26] The men who set fashion and the women who were part of their pleasure-centered lives frequented its posh restaurants and cafés, which became legendary. To mention the Café Tortoni, Café Anglais, Maison d'Or, Bignon, or Café Riche was to invoke the ultimate in European worldliness. Up to mid-century, the Boulevard remained relatively serene by most accounts, the preserve of sybarites.[27] However, a commercialization of its elegance and fashion ensued during the prosperous middle decades of the century, with Baron Haussmann's renovation of the capital and with the new railroad system, which brought hoards of visitors. Crowds seeking a taste of *la vie élégante* strolled on the boulevard des Italiens. Window shopping outside luxury stores became a pastime for the wealthy and those who dreamed of being so. This street was not for "slumming," as the boulevard du Temple had been. Banks, insurance companies, department stores, and newspapers placed their headquarters nearby so as to acquire an aura of grandeur. Hotels with modern conveniences for well-heeled tourists completed this center of commodified elegance.[28] Never before had one thoroughfare so monopolized the industries and spectacles that defined Paris as a world capital.

As the heart of a world capital and as Europe's center for pleasure seeking, the Boulevard had a complex cultural impact. On the one hand, its commercialism led to a certain social inclusiveness. This feature came to the fore most prominently at the end of the nineteenth century. For most of the century, though, the Boulevard stood for fashionableness and exclusiveness. It opened itself discreetly to those with money and scorned the vulgar multitudes who came to admire the chic face it showed to the public. The Boulevard was central to French cultural life because it fused a backward-looking worldliness with a forward-looking urge to publicize and commercialize. The publishing industry concentrated itself on the Boulevard and took on the aura of its surroundings. Many writers considered themselves at home on the Boulevard; these were not the sort who dreamed only of serving art regardless of the sacrifices, but rather those who longed for, or had already achieved, fame and fortune by reaching a large audience. They had accepted the literary marketplace and intended to prosper from it. Newspaper publishing became a major Boulevard industry.[29] The papers had taken steps toward widening circulation without yet reaching for the masses. In the 1830s a number of journals, led by Emile de Girardin's *La Presse,* had cut subscription prices in half (to 40 francs a year) and started to depend more on advertising revenue.[30] They did not, however, sell single copies at an attractive price for laboring people, and they continued to write for the educated reader.

The Boulevard had risen to prominence as the public gathering spot of choice for high society. The most fashionable Parisians occupied townhouses near it, and some elegant gentlemen professed not to know any other part of the city. By midcentury, though, the Boulevard did not so much host the social elite as replace it as the arbiter of taste and elegance. High society had become too small and fragmented to impose itself on a wider world, while the number of important people had become too large for everyone to know one another firsthand. The communicative powers of the Boulevard were needed to integrate the expanded elite of wealth and celebrity, to define what upper-class values were, and to demonstrate worldliness to a broad audience. The high born found themselves compelled to fall in line behind values propagated in their name.

The prominent figures of the Boulevard represented high society to the rest of France. Duke Ludovic de Gramont-Caderousse, who made the rounds of the elegant cafés and had a highly public affair with the diva Hortense Schneider, was the acknowledged leader of Boulevard society until his death in 1865.[31] Most blue bloods of the Faubourg Saint-Germain avoided such visibility, and the duke's fellow pleasure seekers were more likely to be foreign lords, like Paul Demidoff and his son, Anatole, fabulously wealthy Russian industrialists on whom the czar had conferred the title of prince. The Prince de Sagan held court at the Café Anglais and had a grand townhouse just off the Boulevard. The yearly income of 400,000 francs he drew from his Silesian duchy was barely enough to keep him out of debt.[32] In a postrevolutionary France that had emphatically rejected birth as a the sole criterion for elite status, the Boulevard was open to wealth and talent—particularly the talent to draw attention to oneself. Upstarts managed to become social leaders in their own right, not just tolerated inferiors who were there to entertain the high born. Enterprising writer-journalists, like Nestor Roqueplan, Aurélien Scholl, and Arsène Houssaye, placed themselves among the "kings of the Boulevard" and contributed mightily to the publicizing of elegance in the second half of the nineteenth century. They did so by combining the qualities of sybarite, man of letters, impressario, and prince charming. They developed the model of the writer in white gloves. Their sparkling conversation, literary fame, and ostentatious lifestyle won for them the epithets "fashionable" and "dandy."[33] On the Boulevard, a newspaper magnate like Emile de Girardin (whose family origins were not only obscure but also dubious) could impress socialites as an "elegant cavalier."[34] The lifestyles of prominent Boulevard writers linked theater, the beau monde, publishing, journalism, and politics.[35]

Much of the intertwining of Boulevard and theater was a matter of the growing importance of the press in representing opinion and commercializing elegance. The actor Edmond Got, just at the beginning of his distinguished career at the Comédie-française, noted in 1845, "The newspapers! Journalism! These are the powers of the moment." He went on to say that "the greatest preoccupation of theater is what will be said on Monday [the day reviews appeared]."[36] The few thousand habitual theatergoers of the mid-eighteenth century needed only the rudiments of an impersonal press to connect viewers and the stage. Direct contact and word of mouth at dinners or in salons provided much of the publicity. A century later, however, filling tens of thousands of seats required performers to draw attention to themselves through the press. In 1874, the theater columnist of Le Figaro described a technique theater directors were using to manage a rising star. The director would remove her from public view on the pretext of a serious illness. Daily news bulletins on her health followed, so as to keep her name before the curious public. Once suspense had built, the thespian would return for a while, only to find another pretext for a dramatic departure (a reported marriage or retirement to a convent, perhaps).[37] Performers came to regard getting their name into newspapers as an essential career-building activity. Having close connections to the Boulevard writers was helpful for this purpose.

The journal Le Figaro was illustrative of the Boulevard press that covered theater extensively. Its founder, Hippolyte de Villemessant, was part of the elegant crowd at the Café Riche.[38] Foreigners were often amazed by how much theatrical coverage there was in Le Figaro: a review column each for drama and music, a column on theater life, a column on Parisian society events, and a list of spectacles. Altogether, a sixth of the paper was about the stage.[39] Le Gaulois, Gil Blas, L'Echo de Paris, and L'Eclair were other Boulevard newspapers, and Le Temps also offered substantial coverage of theater life. They were joined by the early illustrated weeklies (featuring engraved illustrations, not photographs) like L'Illustration, La Vie parisienne, and Le Monde illustré. None of the theater-rich newspapers followed the lead of the first mass-circulation journal, Le petit journal, which started in 1863 to sell individual copies and was available for purchase on the street. The Boulevard press was too costly for workers, but the journals did sell to a broad stratum of the propertied and educated French. That is why their readership was substantial for the day. Le Figaro and L'Echo de Paris achieved circulations of more than 100,000 copies.

The apogee of glory for the Boulevard playhouses undoubtedly occurred with the Universal Exposition of 1867 in Paris, which Emperor Louis-Napoleon used to highlight the achievements of his reign and the splendor of his capital. Box office receipts had doubled between 1850 and 1864 (from 8 to 16 million francs). The completion of the railroad system had facilitated an invasion of tourists, and a booming population of potential theatergoers had moved into the luxury apartments constructed on the boulevards that Baron Haussmann had created in midcentury Paris. During the exposition, the French capital seemed to play host to the world. Visitors were eager to enjoy French operetta, which was at the height of its inventiveness with such composers as Jacques Offenbach and Hervé. The divas Adélina Patti at the Opéra, Hortense Schneider at the Variétés theater, and Thérésa at the Alcazar café were among the most famous people in Europe. Their photographs were everywhere, and hawkers sold souvenirs adorned with their pictures. Otto von Bismarck and the crowned heads of Europe, including the czar of Russia, rushed to the Variétés theater to see La Schneider in Offenbach's *La grande duchesse de Gérolstein.*[40] To a writer for *L'Illustration*, it seemed that "this little stage [the Variétés] is the beam of light that guides the entire world."[41]

The excellent box office results of midcentury did not, however, continue beyond the early 1880s. In the first year of that decade, playhouses earned 17.7 million francs; while the totals moved up and down a bit in subsequent years, theaters took in only 18.2 million francs in 1899.[42] Theater attendance was lower during the Exposition of 1900 than it had been at the Exposition of 1889.[43] The end to steady advances at the box office marked the commencement of still another transition in the social history of French theater, characterized by greater competition from mass culture. Significantly, the stagnating revenues occurred during an era of rising prosperity for the laboring population. As a result of falling commodity prices and slightly rising incomes, working French people enjoyed one of the most notable gains in disposable income in centuries.[44] Yet these potential patrons did not spend that income on stage plays. The tastes that they had developed led them to other commercial spectacles.

Early mass culture, which made everyday life into spectacle, emerged in Paris during the 1880s. Forms of diversion that featured everyday life or current events took off just as theater attendance stagnated. Panoramas, for example, had existed for most of the century, but an "o-rama craze" arose after 1880. Crowds lined up to view enormous circular paintings that enveloped the spectator, giving the illusion of being at a particular battle site or immersed in a landscape. Eventually, developers of the panoramas added props and learned how to created a sense of motion, making them precursors of the cinema.[45]

Café-concerts proved to be another popular alternative to stage productions.[46] These spectacles charged no admission fee, and for the price of a half-franc drink, a patron could get up to an hour of entertainment.

(Continuous drinking was required to remain in the hall.) The typical show comprised several acts: circus performers, tunes played by an orchestra, an exhibition of pretty girls singing, and the featured artist, who might sing up to forty songs in an evening. Street dress was the rule, except at the luxury cafés (the Eden, Eldorado, Alcazar, and Scala). Patrons had the freedom to smoke, roam around, and speak with companions. The average patron spent two francs or more for an evening at a café-concert and might have purchased a theater ticket for that amount. Yet many people judged the café-concert more worthwhile than attending a stage play, with all its constraints. From a few scattered cafés at midcentury, the number of such establishments grew to at least 360 by 1885.[47]

Legitimate theater did remain a favored leisure activity for the upper classes even as the lower strata lost their taste for it. It was telling that, year after year, the state-supported theaters, the Opéra, the Comédie-française, the Opéra-comique, and the Odéon, took in the most revenue. These were the most expensive and socially exclusive spectacles. Seasonal subscriptions were still the rule, and people attended to fulfill their social duties or out of family tradition. These four theaters (out of a total of forty-five to fifty-five, depending on the year) accounted for a third of total ticket revenue up to the First World War.[48]

Since theater remained so important to upper-class culture, the Boulevard press, which was sold by subscription mostly to well-off and educated readers, continued to provide extensive coverage of the stage. By contrast, the treatment of the stage in the "Big Four" mass-circulation dailies (*Le petit journal, Le petit parisien, Le Matin,* and *Le Journal*) was insubstantial, with theater columns that were little more than lists of current offerings and with intermittent reviews. The prestigious critics remained with the Boulevard press, which was also far more likely than the mass-circulation dailies to present bulletins on stage stars. The subscription press, along with the photographic magazines that began to appeared around 1900, pioneered the "star interview."[49]

The hold of the Boulevard elite on the theater industry was such that word of mouth remained just as important as print publicity for attracting audiences. In 1875, thirty years after Got had extolled the power of the press, Alexandre Dumas, Jr., expounded on a subject he knew well, how to make a play a success. His opinion was that "the composition of the opening night crowd is capital," and he particularly underscored the importance of the men-about-town who belonged to the exclusive clubs.[50] The relevance of his advice was still strong at the turn of the century, according to a convincing authority, Camillo Antona-Traversi, the business manager for the star Réjane. He insisted on the need to invite the right people to the final dress rehearsal. He claimed that the fate of a play was decided before the reviews appeared. The decisive factor was "the opinion of the invitees, who broadcast the word of the success or failure at the family table, in the café, in their social clubs [*cercles*], on the Boulevard and a little everywhere."[51] The exclusive crowd still mattered enormously in what was becoming the circumscribed world of legitimate theater in republican France.

So intertwined were theater and the elegant life of the Boulevard that the emerging mass culture had its impact on both of them simultaneously. Just as playhouse revenues went flat, Boulevard men perceived the "decline" of their formerly chic milieu. "Decline" had a specific meaning, because the thoroughfare remained busy, even prosperous. In fact, at the very moment observers spoke of the decline, the Boulevard was taking on a new life as a center of early mass culture.[52] What was diminished was the aura of glamour and elegance. It no longer reigned as the center of upper-class pleasure seeking, as the Champs-Elysées took over that role. A series of articles in *L'Illustration* in 1894 lamented the "democratizing" trends on the formerly "aristocratic" Boulevard. Cheap restaurants for office clerks had replaced the grand ones where George Sand, Ernest Renan, and Théophile Gautier had once held listeners spellbound with literary conversation. "I regret with all my heart the gay Paris of yesterday," wrote the columnist, for "I find the new one rowdy."[53] The prosperity of wax museums and panoramas on the Boulevard signaled decay, not renewal, from this perspective. The educated were losing their cultural leadership. Ordinary working people, including the throngs of white-collar employees, increasingly stayed out of theaters and preferred frequenting their own modest eateries to glimpsing from the sidewalk the rich dining in their glamorous restaurants.

By the late nineteenth century, the cultivated classes had consolidated their hold over legitimate theater but could no longer count on deference to their taste. The theater industry was not yet in a precarious position, because its patrons still dominated French politics and economic life. The loss was a matter of narrowing the resonance of stage productions. Average French people were eager to attend other sorts of entertainments to see everyday life portrayed in an engaging manner. Henceforth, performers who appeared on screen would capture the public imagination.

Making a Career

Actresses began to appear with some regularity on the Parisian stage during the first years of the seventeenth century, assuming the roles previously played by cross-dressed boys.[54] The new performers quickly became central attractions. Salon gossip and the early theatrical press of the eighteenth century lavished attention on them. Alluring female performers became crucial to the success of theater as a business and an artistic enterprise. The novelist Félicien Champsaur, writing in 1889, asserted that most plays of his day had hackneyed plots that numbed the spectators' minds; it was only the presence of popular actresses that drew large audiences and made theater a thrilling experience.[55] However, despite the prominent place actresses had in the theater world, young aspirants to stardom had to begin their career by stepping gingerly around the question of being a proper woman. When asking for a favor from officials, even young women far from the centers of power realized that a semblance of gender orthodoxy was required. Whereas young male supplicants could boast about their talents, accomplishments, and ambitions, the female supplicant had to pose as a modest woman. Her best strategy was to justify seeking a stage career by presenting it as a sacrifice of her domestic dreams for the sake of her needy family. Thus, a student named Mathilde Savreux was savvy enough to turn her petition for late admission to the Conservatory of Dramatic Arts into a melodrama. She wrote to Emperor Napoleon III about coming across her mother in tears. Her mother had invested the entire family fortune of 39,000 francs in a local railroad and had lost it all. Savreux, suddenly seeing her duty, reported herself as saying, "Console yourself, good mother. I am young and will work, if you permit me, on stage. I have been told that I have a disposition for comedy." Her mother had taken a long time deciding to allow her daughter to enter the dreaded career—hence, the late application.[56] Similarly, a ballet dancer, Pauline Santi, assumed that she should not dwell on her professional credentials, though they were substantial, when petitioning for an audition at the Paris Opéra. Santi had already performed at the Théâtre lyrique in

Paris, at the Viennese opera, and at Convent Garden in London. The petitioner stressed, instead, her family responsibilities. Her father, a former caterer, had lost everything, and Santi described herself as the sole support of her parents and siblings.[57]

The necessity of claiming the qualities of proper womanhood was disingenuous and, perhaps, even cruel, for it forced the young women to confront the fact that their aspirations were quite unwomanly by the reckoning of the day. The stage hopefuls had to prostrate themselves before standards of respectability that would long stigmatize them as outcasts. Becoming an actress brought shame to an individual, her parents, and her community, because the woman put herself on public display. For centuries, the French church had treated such women as sinners who, by virtue of their profession, were outside the community of Christians, for it was assumed that men lusted after actresses and often kept them as mistresses. So strong was this prejudice up to the twentieth century that the French state dared not recognize the achievements of theater women who had distinguished careers and carried French glory around the world.[58] By asking petitioners to pose as virtuous and modest daughters, the authorities seemed to want the girls to acknowledge that female ambition and sensuality were troubling to the rest of society, even though these were qualities that an actress needed in order to make a career.

The directors and playwrights who served as gatekeepers to working on stage would not have welcomed aspirants who sincerely intended to live by the precepts of true womanhood. A more honest petition, and maybe even a more effective one, came from one Baroness de Valézieux, who wrote to the director of the Opéra to help a young protégée get an audition. "Although I know from experience that the recommendation of a pretty woman counts for something to men like you, Monsieur, whose gallantry exceeds your kindness," the baroness affirmed, "I know it is not enough." She invited him to her home to consider the matter further. It is hard to miss the suggestion that the impresario could hope to deploy his gallantry (a term that implied libertinism as well as chivalry) if he accepted.[59]

The nineteenth-century registration records at the state-sponsored Conservatory of Dramatic Arts show that the stage aspirants' family backgrounds were humble. They were mostly daughters of big-city workers, artisans, and shopkeepers.[60] Their career choice was, in part, an uphill struggle for fame and fortune. Whereas acting became more respectable for males during the nineteenth century, it continued to be perceived as a deviant path for women. Many hopefuls had already differentiated themselves from most working girls whose family background they shared, by having led sexually adventurous lives before heading for the stage. Their youth had often involved running away from home, living on the streets, earning money in prostitution, or being kept. This pattern was established well before the Conservatory was founded in 1786, as the family background of Henriette Saint-Marcel shows. Born around 1732 in Rouen, her father, a sailor, was found guilty of smuggling and was hanged. Her mother, also implicated in the crime, was sentenced to life in the Hôpital Général, where prostitutes were incarcerated, and Henriette was raised there. She escaped at the age of thirteen, only to work as a prostitute. She eventually made her way to the capital, where a wealthy American kept her and found her a position in the chorus line of the Opéra.[61] The life of Mademoiselle Mirot, a singer at the mid-eighteenth-century Opéra-comique, resembled the plot of a fin-de-siècle family drama. Her mother was an actress who had been kept by a Monsieur Dauizy, a magistrate in the distinguished Parlement of Paris. It so happened that Dauizy's son, though newly married, fell passionately in love with his stepsister, not knowing her paternity. The elder Dauizy did all he could to have his illegitimate daughter incarcerated or even transported à la Manon Lescault. However, the beautiful Mirot had a bevy of important men protecting her, so she never spent a long time in prison. The family dilemma resolved itself only when the young Dauizy fell out of love with Mirot and took another actress as his lover.[62]

Nineteenth-century actresses also had their adventures. Andrée Mégard-Gémier, for example, was born to a family of well-off peasants in eastern France. She claimed that even as a child she had displayed a "shocking coquetry" and was strong-headed as well. These traits were to propel her into the theater by an indirect route. Her parents rushed her into an apprenticeship with a stern aunt, who ran a dry-goods store in a nearby town. The aunt tried to break her coquettish habits, and the girl ran away because of the harsh punishment. The fifteen-year-old found herself on the streets of Paris for the next three years. Nineteenth-century codes of propriety prevented Mégard-Gémier from specifying how she survived except for a stint in a department store. At the age of eighteen, a well-known painter of the day, Auguste Toulmouche, took her in as a model and mistress. It was then that she received her first exposure to the theater.[63]

Inevitably, girls came to the decision to make a career on stage through a circuitous route. The conservatory's archives contain information on the professional experience of seventy-six females admitted between 1819 and 1821. Less than a third of the girls could cite any meaningful sort of professional background. (Seven had already worked on the stage; another seven had had acting lessons; eight claimed to have played in amateur theater.)[64] The autobiographies of theater women offered two basic accounts of their career decision. The majority advanced the notion of the "sacred flame": from the moment they had been exposed to theater, they had known that they were intended to be on stage. The girls had resisted all the objections from parents, kin, and friends, who were often appalled, and had dared to follow their dream. The alternative narrative stressed serendipity: the actress had had no contact with theater and had never considered the career. The opportunity to be on stage had simply come along, and the woman had seized it, almost on a whim.

An underlying consideration in both narratives was the aspirant's confidence that she belonged on stage because she was physically attractive. This was the sine qua non of a stage career for females. The future music hall star Mistinguett learned the lesson as a child in the 1880s, when she was first seized by the "sacred flame." She visited a singer, Anna Thibaud, who had settled near her home, for career advice. Thibaud's counsel was categorical: "To succeed in the theater . . . you must be pretty. You must excite men." Mistinguett sought clarification by asking if Thibaud meant exciting "the crowds." The adviser corrected her, "No. The men!"[65] Even the professors who sat on the admission committee of the conservatory tacitly agreed with the principle. They were well known to admit female candidates on the basis of two qualities, a sonorous voice and fine physical features. The committee dismissed the actual performance at the audition as immaterial. Indeed, the judges of the seventy-six accepted students mentioned above had rated seventy-three as having a pleasing figure, and did not have many other reasons to praise them. Beauty sufficed to give an actress a career even at the most venerated theater in France, the Comédie-française. The ministerial report on a Mademoiselle Juliette claimed that she was "an extremely pretty woman with little talent." However, the director of this temple of dramatic art thought that her appearance was an asset in the minor roles she took.[66]

Because of the overwhelming predominance of men in powerful theatrical positions and the habit of thinking about women as weak and dependent, it was common to portray actresses as clay in the hands of influential men. Arsène Houssaye, as director of the Comédie-française, was characteristically egotistical. "Give me ten women, and I'll make ten actresses. The only art is to put women in their suitable frames."[67] Women's career decisions did lie almost entirely in the hands of men, because men monopolized positions as government officials overseeing the theaters, as directors, and as playwrights, who had the right to cast the roles in their plays. Women had run theaters in the eighteenth century and would do so again at the end of the nineteenth, but none did so in the intervening period, during which the required licenses were given only to men.[68] Just a few female playwrights were exceptions to the rule, and none belonged to the exclusive circle of male writers who came close to foreclosing the trade to others by the end of the century.[69] Under the Old Regime, the First Gentlemen of the Bed Chamber had been in charge of the royal theaters. Strictly speaking, a thespian was not hired but rather "ordered" to perform. The eighteenth-century First Gentlemen were active—and in some cases, celebrated—ladies' men.[70] One way to get their attention was to accord them sexual favors. In the commercial theaters of the eighteenth and nineteenth centuries, the director took the place of the First Gentlemen and was all-powerful on hiring decisions.

Gossip about "casting couch" practices—extorting sex for career advancement—did surface from time to time, but was ultimately rather rare. This was not necessarily because the extortion was infrequent but because actresses were assumed to be implicated in more significant patterns of sexual subordination. The social imagination figured theater women as mistresses of powerful men. That role was seen almost as an official position. Instead of focusing on a director's priapic demands, the interest was in what influential protectors could do for their lovers. Ministers, great lords, and diplomats were supposed to advance their lovers' careers. Their efforts carried more cultural meaning in France than the momentary demands for favors on the part of directors or dramatists. In British or American theater cultures, where actresses were held to more conventional moral standards, obsession with the casting couch loomed larger than it did in France.

Acting was nevertheless a difficult, competitive career requiring more than beauty and the astute management of influential men. Beyond talent, theater women had to display persistence, resiliency, courage in the face of disappointments, and the pluck to take advantage of opportunities. There were certainly no formulas for success, but theater women did well to keep three guidelines in mind. First, they had to cultivate intelligently their contacts in the small, personal community of directors, playwrights, and newspaper columnists who made up the theater world. The stage was an appendage of the Boulevard, and its socialites and writers were ubiquitous. Even theater critics (who were simultaneously playwrights and directors) remained enmeshed in face-to-face relations with the professionals they evaluated in print. That is why poor performances generally brought silence rather than negative comments. (Reviews consisted mainly of plot summaries, in any case.) At the same time, praise was a personal favor for which the critic expected gratitude. Thus the late-nineteenth-century star Eve Lavallière apologized to the journalist Edouard Gauthier for taking so long to thank him for an appreciative piece he published in *La Revue théâtrale*. She had heard through friends that Gauthier had been peeved at not having received a word of thanks from her.[71] A second worthwhile measure was to keep one's name before the public. Though the modalities of celebrity evolved across the century, the public's curiosity about performers' private lives was a constant. Patrons would come to see even a miserable play to watch a performer who captured their interest.

The third guideline for a performer was to do whatever she could to procure the role that might give her a breakthrough. Nothing was so important to a beginner than to find that special part that would resonate with the public. It had to accord perfectly with her physical appearance, tenor of voice, and range of gestures. The part also had to be universal enough to build many plays around, for the actress would thenceforth have to make her career by personifying the type. Unfortunately, finding the breakthrough role was an unpredictable process. Even the superb theatrical intuition of Sarah Bernhardt let her down on this score. Bernhardt told interviewers that she had reluctantly taken the part that brought her to the attention of the public, that of the lute-player Zanetto in François Coppé's *Le Passant* (presented at the Odéon in 1869).[72]

The critic Francisque Sarcey underscored the importance of the right role in his exceptionally candid newspaper column on Maria Favart's career of the mid-nineteenth century. She had been languishing as a tragic actress at the Comédie-française even though she possessed all the desirable qualities that she should—an aura of grace, a sonorous voice, good diction, and a statuesque appearance. These assets, however, failed to establish an emotional rapport between her and the spectators. Quite by chance, Favart took the role of Camille in Alfred de Musset's *On ne badine avec l'amour,* and her career took off. She was able to move audiences. Favart proceeded to make a solid career by playing "serious girls, capable of tender, pure, and noble sentiments." The public identified her with that type.[73]

Having established the stage persona, sticking with it was the best advice. Even one of the most accomplished artists of the century, Julia Bartet, refused roles that were outside her type. "However regrettable the situation is," Bartet explained to a disappointed playwright, "the public sees us in the theater through our dramatic past; all artists who risk a new role that differs from ones to which spectators are accustomed run the danger of disappointing."[74]

The advice to stay true to a character type, useful though it was, could take an actress only so far. As Sarcey noted in the case of Favart, "She ranked as a great actress, but she was not a star."[75] Stardom required stirring the interest and emotions of the public to an exceptional degree. At root was the mystery of charisma. With charisma, a star could make up her own rules.

Because in France theaters were not just halls that producers rented for mounting a single production but rather fixed companies of thespians bound together by long-term contracts, professional success entailed moving up within a troupe from bit parts to major roles. The most thoroughgoing model of the troupe organization was the Comédie-française. Following a successful probationary period, salaried performers would become partners (*sociétaires*) in the Comédie and receive a share of the profits. Being a partner at the Comédie had enormous prestige in the theater world. One could remain there for an entire career and get a pension on retirement.[76] The commercial theaters used the troupe system as well (giving their players three- or five-year contracts) because the government licensing system required them to have a full range of actors on hand to present a designated repertory.

The trials and tribulations of advancing within a troupe, the subject of much theatrical lore, posed a distinctive set of challenges. Backstage was known to become a snake pit of intrigue as company members maneuvered for choice parts.[77] A powerful protector was supposed to help his actress-mistress obtain good roles. At the state-supported theaters, even ministers intervened in role distributions. Seniority customs worked against younger performers, and probably, the best hope for a beginner was to do so well in a minor part that another director would hire her away and put her in better roles.

Though aware of the ugly aspects of the troupe system, the theatrical establishment in the second half of the nineteenth century lamented the "rise" of the star system, in which productions were organized around a crowd-drawing name instead of the company as a whole. The troupe system came to stand for art and community values; the star system, for greed on the part of artists and low artistic standards on the part of audiences.[78] The idealized version of the troupe system, in which all company members had a chance to show their talents by cycling through the best of the repertory, was based on memories of the eighteenth-century Comédie-française. In truth, the star system had not suddenly emerged in the mid-nineteenth century. Since the time that royal theaters had to compete with commercial ones, the two systems had been intertwined. The star system had formed within troupe organization, not as a later alternative to it.

The star system adapted troupe organization to its needs throughout the entire nineteenth century. When a particular performer appealed to audiences, the house playwrights wrote scripts featuring her. Although theater columnists liked to imagine a golden age when billing was based strictly on seniority and no player had the hubris to demand her or his name at the top of the poster, this vision was bathed in nostalgia. Whenever audience appeal gave stars the power to insist on top billing, they took it.[79] Even the Comédie-française, rich in troupe tradition as it was, had to put up with the practice. Mademoiselle Mars, for example, had successfully imposed her will to see her name above a play's title numerous times in the 1820s and 1830s, decades before the star system had presumably triumphed.[80]

While theater companies had been making adjustments to audience preference all along by taking advantage of star appeal, the foundations for the troupe system fell away in the second half of the nineteenth century. In 1864, the state freed theaters from regulation. Anyone could open a theater and mount any sort of production. The troupe system limped along on inertia but was increasingly marginal to theatrical life. Directors hired fewer thespians on multiyear contracts. Promotions within a troupe became much less important than jumping from one to another. Hiring players for just one production, a proletarianization of the profession, became more common.[81] Rachel, in the 1840s, had shown she was a towering figure by bending the Comédie-française to her will.[82] Sarah Bernhardt, thirty years later, showed that she dominated the stage by leaving the Comédie altogether and making a career on her own. She and Réjane took the star system to its culmination at the end of the century by running their own theaters and headlining in their own productions.

The long development of the star system at the expense of the troupe system reinforced a polarization of financial rewards between the haves and have-nots. The commercialization of the stage was the key to rising salaries for the better-known performers. During the first half of the eighteenth century, actors were paid more like royal bureaucrats than people who generated box-office income. Even at the Opéra, which continuously set the ceiling on pay, at midcentury the leaders of the troupe earned 3,000 francs a year or less, barely the income of a modestly successful lawyer. Once the monarchy allowed permanent commercial theaters to establish themselves, competitive pressure forced salaries up, at least for name performers. By 1784, the Opéra paid its leaders more than twice as much. Madame Saint-Huberty earned 9,000 francs.[83] International competition among the great opera houses of Europe continued to push the pay of star singers and dancers into the stratosphere. In 1848, the Paris Opéra gave Carlotta Grisi a contract for 44,000 francs, and Sophie Cruvelli earned 150,000 francs for eight months of performances in 1855.[84]

Considering the sub-subsistence pay characterizing most women's work at the time, the compensation for actresses generally was not abysmal. Those lucky enough to be hired by a troupe in the mid-nineteenth century started out earning about 150 francs a month, which would have been a common starting salary for male white-collar workers. Because rich, free-spending men were so well integrated into the theatrical milieu, salary expectations were high. Thus, the critic Sarcey expressed a great deal of sympathy for Céline Chaumont because she earned only 350 francs a month while her husband was ill.[85] Sarcey did not consider that the majority of Parisian workers and clerks would have been pleased with such an income. The theatrical milieu measured success by the standards of a Grisi or Cruvelli.

During the 1830s, the most popular players, like Marie Dorval or Virginie Déjazet, commanded 20,000 to 25,000 francs a year. In 1862, the Ambigu-comique theater paid the leader of its troupe, Marie Laurent, 24,000 francs, and she was not really a performer of the first order.[86] The box-office boom of the middle third of the century had at least doubled the salaries of the best-paid actors. Rachel's pay increases may have provided the psychological breakthrough. She earned only 4,000 francs in 1838, but the sensation she caused allowed her to negotiate an income of 60,000 francs in 1841.[87] Bernhardt, a rising star at the Comédie in the 1870s, thought of 30,000 francs as the proper pay for a competent performer who intended to spend her career within the troupe.[88]

The base pay was only part of an actress's compensation, and as always, the bigger the star, the larger her share of the ancillary earnings. Performers in demand could negotiate a supplemental fee for each performance or rehearsal (called the *feu*). When a director had to compete for a player, he might agree to pay for her costumes, which was ordinarily an expense she bore, and a heavy one. Finally, actresses could request time off to tour. Organizing a tour would make an actress into a temporary theatrical entrepreneur who assumed the risks and reaped the rewards of a traveling troupe. Though circumstances beyond a performer's control could transform a tour into a financial disaster, tours must have been lucrative enough, because many performers accepted the risks.[89] Reporters dared to ask Bernhardt how much she would earn in her American tour of the 1890s, and she was pleased to announce the fabulous figure: 3,000 francs per performance plus a third of the box-office receipts.[90]

Though even moderate success had never been easy, the thespians of the late nineteenth century who did not break through to stardom were in an increasingly hostile environment. While theater revenue stagnated, the headliners were taking an ever larger share of it, leaving less for the many bit players. A proliferation of small theaters made for more intense competition for audiences, which were not expanding. Ruthless theatrical agencies took advantage of beginners by keeping a larger portion of their pay as commission. Social reformers, viewing the situation, claimed that actresses were becoming part of the exploited working class.[91]

The analogy was misleading, though, because being a stage performer did not much resemble "women's work" as it had been constructed during the nineteenth century.[92] Poverty was not inevitable. Being an actress held the possibility of becoming rich and consequential. This was one of the features of the career that so troubled the male-dominated society. To be sure, only a few female aspirants realized their dreams. Yet it is hard to imagine any actress starting out as most female workers did, knowing that their life would inevitably be harsh without a man to help support them.

The commercialization of spectacle, the rise of a star system, and the emergence of mass culture were the long-term forces shaping the actress's professional fortunes. Ironically, these processes, far from undermining hierarchy as "modernizing" forces are supposed to do, reinforced the exclusiveness of the stage. The French social imagination situated actresses at the heart of an elite libertine sociability that epitomized worldliness and glamour. This was a tradition that took root by the early eighteenth century.

2

Theater Women and Aristocratic Libertinism, 1715–1789

The pursuit of pleasure, including sexual pleasure, was a central activity of the high society that dominated Old Regime France. This was not a hidden pursuit. The court aristocracy assumed the right to engage in it, and the public, though definitely growing more critical as the eighteenth century progressed, was accustomed to it. Few themes were more common in novels of the eighteenth century than extramarital affairs and the keeping of mistresses among the high born—called "aristocratic libertinism" since the Regency.[1] Novelists like Claude-Prosper Crébillon, Charles-Pinot Duclos, Claude Dorat, Pierre Marivaux, Denis Diderot, Abbé Antoine-François Prévost, and Choderlos de Laclos bequeathed to later generations a riveting—and seemingly truthful—portrait of an elegant, idle, polished high society that systematically indulged in sexual intrigue. However, the novelists did not really address the realities of eighteenth-century libertinism. Their most glaring omission was the failure to describe the central role played by theater women. Actresses were responsible for the features of fashionable adultery that had to be hidden. They had made libertinism more a matter of scandal than of worldliness. The novelists might have hoped to fool posterity by ignoring stage women, but they surely knew that contemporaries would see through their embellishments, for the role actresses played in aristocratic licentiousness had become all too visible by the early eighteenth century.

A Public Sexuality

The novels of libertinism that numbered in the hundreds during the course of the century set the practice of mistress keeping rigidly within

33

the most exclusive milieu of the day. This cultural sphere, Le Monde, was perceived by novelists and their readers to comprise titled lords and ladies who appeared, or might have appeared, at the royal court. Le Monde was an exclusive, self-enclosed entity, and the novels portrayed libertinism as being bounded by it in two ways. All the actors in the drama of seduction belonged to Le Monde; the worldly did not imagine going outside their circle for partners. Furthermore, libertinism had increased appeal and meaning because it took place among Le Monde. The worldly players did not care what those outside knew or thought of their habits, but what those in Le Monde knew and thought was all-important to the lords and ladies who were part of it.[2]

A fundamental convention of the novels of libertinism was that the participants were vying for personal reputation among their own kind. To seduce a lover could give fleeting physical satisfaction, but the lasting pleasure was having the rest of Le Monde know that the seducer had been successful. Publicity about the success was essential. A secret tryst with a desirable partner was a trifling victory, according to the novelists; the victor would do what he could to make the meeting known. Vanity was the supreme value to which the characters devoted their lives. No wonder that the most common metaphor for Le Monde was the theater: the lords and ladies were performers seeking the admiration of a knowing and often critical audience of peers.[3]

With reputation the goal, seduction was far more a matter of reason and will than passion. The novelists depicted elaborate strategies for success that entailed competition, calculation, and deception. There was never a hint of buying sexual favors. Planning an affair was like preparing for a military campaign, making it worthy of male intellect. The love that emerged from the affairs was, at best, brief and lighthearted. Grand passions were undesirable, since they were an obstacle to successful conquest. Ideally, a lover needed to start planning his next affair from the moment of his conquest. Authentic emotions seemed to be banished from the libertinism of the eighteenth century.[4]

Although the novels granted highborn women much sexual freedom, they were unequal players in the game of seduction. Women did not acquire prestige from a conquest and were closer to pawns in a struggle for reputation among men than autonomous players in their own right. A lady's appeals to propriety were assumed to be a ruse, but if she gave herself to a man it was *his* victory and her capitulation. The novels, such as

Laclos's *Dangerous Liaisons* (1782), in which the female characters were as good at the game of seduction as the male characters were the most critical of the practice as a whole.[5]

The fiction that codified libertinism in this way have long been read as a sort of "twilight literature," the expression of an aristocracy that had been excluded from power, reduced to a supernumerary status. It is not difficult to find in the background a nostalgia for an age in which more meaningful love and more purposeful activity were possible.[6] Certainly after the emergence of a Rousseauist cult of sincerity and intimacy in the 1760s, the novelists of libertinism were ever more critical of the practice they described. Laclos's *Dangerous Liaisons* carried libertinism to its logical conclusion to demonstrate how self-destructive it was. Though readers even today often take these novels as a reliable description of a particular time and milieu, they were, in fact, grand examples of myth making and idealization.[7] They elevated certain codes of behavior into authentically aristocratic and worldly practices. They provided for posterity a definition of aristocratic individualism: the pursuit of reputation in a closed and exclusive milieu that insisted on its values as if no others counted. However, the novels are highly misleading as descriptions of eighteenth-century libertinism. Titled ladies were no longer the exclusive objects of seduction, the game was not a matter of cold calculation and reason, and reputation was not always the supreme end. Libertine lords had in fact shifted their sights from aristocratic women to theater women, and that shift changed the rules of the game. An aristocratic debauchery centered on theater women was too sordid for the novelists to depict.

The amorous life of Louis de Bourbon (1709–1771), Count de Clermont, a prince of the blood, abbot of Saint-Germain des Près, and sometime marshal of the royal armies, may not have been typical in all respects, but it reveals a good deal more about libertinism as practiced in the eighteenth century than the novels do. Just out of his teen years, the young lord had the experienced duchess of Bouillon for a lover. She, however, was the last court lady with whom he had anything more than a passing liaison. The stage, in which he had a deep interest as an amateur actor and playwright, became his field of conquest. In 1737 he was linked with one of the most sought-after women of her day, the dancer Mademoiselle Camargo. Rather than admiring her from his seat at the Opéra and having the rest of the aristocracy bear witness to his conquests from their boxes, Clermont made her retire and, according to a police inspector, even saw to it that the neighbors did not catch a glimpse of her through a window. He spent so much satisfying her whims that he had to will his duchy of Châteauroux to the king to clear his debts. He had two children with her, and the monks of Saint-Germain complained that their real abbot was "a whore of the Opéra." In 1742 Clermont put Camargo aside and stole the dancer Leduc from Président de Rieux (son of the fabulously rich financier Samuel Bernard) of the Paris Parlement.[8] When Leduc gave birth to his child eighteen months later, the count had grown so emotionally attached to her that he set her up as the official mistress of his estate at Berny. Eventually he bought her the marquisate of Tourvoie. Police reported that Leduc was "absolute in the household" and that "the people, even of quality, who compose the prince's court have all the deference that one should have for an honest woman."[9] Leduc had come a long way, considering she was the out-of-wedlock daughter of a soldier and had spent her early years as a common prostitute.[10]

The sexual adventures of one of the few military heroes of eighteenth-century France, Maurice, Count de Saxe (1696–1750), also belie the accounts of seduction contained in the novels. Marshal of the French armies, hero of the battle of Fontenay (1745), son of the elector of Saxony, Maurice was a great ladies' man even though he lacked the Herculean body nineteenth-century writers liked to attribute to him.[11] As a young man in the 1720s, he was involved in a love triangle with the duchess de Bouillon and the tragic actress Adrienne Lecouvreur.[12] The thespian's sudden, mysterious death stirred rumors that the duchess had poisoned her to end the rivalry for Maurice's heart. If true, Bouillon was still unable to keep his love, for Maurice shared his bed with one theater woman after another. The marshal was a patron of the theater and even took an accomplished acting group along with him on military campaigns. The writer Jean-François Marmontel explained that Maurice de Saxe believed that "the French never behave so well as when one brings them diversion, and what they fear most in warfare is boredom."[13] The actresses in his troop kept Maurice from experiencing boredom, but the marshal was rarely able to keep them faithful. Marmontel had affairs with two of Maurice's mistresses, Mademoiselles Navarre and Verrière (with whom Maurice had a daughter, who became the grandmother of George Sand). Although it was considered unseemly for great lords to show jealousy, the marshal complained to Louis XV about "that insolent poet who takes all my mistresses." He also complained, on another occasion, that his mistress Mademoiselle Beauménard gave him "more torment than all the soldiers of the queen of Hungary."[14] Later, the marshal wanted to make Madame Favart the mistress of Chenonceaux, the Loire Valley chateau that the king had given him for his victories, but had to use intimidation and even incarceration to make her submit to his will.[15] Clearly, the theater women who so troubled the great warrior were not mere pawns in the libertinism of the court.

These examples begin to suggest that the worldly, male-dominated game of seduction, described in such intimate detail by the novelists, was a sideshow to another style of mistress keeping. Theater women did not let noblemen establish the rules of libertinism as a reflection of the patriarchal, hierarchical values at court and did not let the gaze of those in Le Monde constrain them at all. The actresses gave their bodies and affections to whom they chose, on their own grounds, whether for money, passion, or whim. The performers risked offending even the greatest lords by leaving them for men of lesser status. Mandatory monetary payments were a central aspect of the relationships, and so was passion, on the part of the men, the theater women, or both. In the libertinism that developed after the reign of Louis XIV, actresses had at least as much control as the men who paid their bills. One can trace certain elements back to seventeenth-century courtly precedents, but there is an important discontinuity in the history of mistress keeping when actresses became the preferred lovers.

Though the great lords (*les grands*) of the royal court had always arrogated the right to bend Christian injunctions and live by their own rules, the ideology and elementary practices that were to bring theater women to the center of aristocratic amorous life took shape in the mid-seventeenth century. This was a formative moment for the French aristocracy. *Les grands* were being tamed by strong monarchs and were seeking to redefine their social role, which could no longer be justified in terms of warrior virtues. Titled lords turned more to birth (hereditary legal status) to support claims to superiority, supplemented by an ethos and a stylized way of life that was supposed to typify the polished gentleman.[16] Courtiers invented a new aristocratic tradition to accompany estate owning and being a warrior, the obligation to live a worldly life centered around the highest pleasures, including sensual ones.[17] *Galanterie* was the current term, and since its English cognate means something very different, we can translate it as "libertinism" or "amoral worldliness."

In making the pursuit of pleasure one of the fundamentals of aristocratic existence, courtiers singled out love as the greatest of pleasures. The love that was so extolled was experienced in short and uncommitted relationships. Since great passions were thought not to endure, conjugal affection could not rank among the ultimate pleasures. Theorists of *galanterie* even argued that marriage and love had to be antithetical. Matrimonial vows of fidelity were to be taken lightly on these grounds. Gallants assumed that the pleasures of love were emotionally cost free, that jealousy did not have to be part of amorous adventures. Though often criticized even in its own day for superficiality and excessive frivolity, amoral worldliness became the dominant code of conduct among Louis XIV's courtiers.[18]

The libertinism of the seventeenth century was played out among the titled men and women. Male aristocrats presumed that court ladies would be their partners in love. Up to midcentury, great lords, male and female, were hardly more delicate than peasants about hiding bodily functions. Courtiers were just beginning to internalize higher standards of language, gesture, and sexual behavior.[19] Although seventeenth-century aristocrats did not attribute a purer sexual nature to women, a double standard was, nonetheless, at work.[20] While lords gained in reputation as a result of a conquest, ladies lost their respectability, even in the eyes of libertines. There was no such thing as a *femme galante.*[21]

Jean-Baptiste Molière's *Bourgeois Gentleman,* depicted the prototypical social climber of the seventeenth century, who believed that he must seduce a court lady to gain entry into the aristocracy; he did not consider an actress appropriate. Yet when the play was first performed in 1670, theater women were already gaining a foothold in libertine practices. Actresses had made their appearance in Parisian society during the first quarter of the century as permanent members of resident acting troupes. Almost at once there were sexual encounters between them and courtiers—the first complaint about actresses' bad morals was made in Gédéon Tallemant de Réaux's *Histoirette de Mondory,* which was written sometime before 1659.[22] However, these were merely "adventures" dictated more by the will of the flesh than the pursuit of amoral worldliness. Louis XIV inadvertently prepared the way for actresses' more central involvement in libertinism by making theater such an integral part of court ritual, before his turn to piety after 1680.[23] When the Sun King's piety forced the worldly members of his court to migrate to "the city" for their pleasure and to escape his minute regulation of their behavior, male aristocrats were free to select partners other than highborn women. Under the Regency they readily did so, with the duke d'Orléans setting the example.[24] Between roughly 1680 and 1720, theater women replaced court ladies as the principal female participants in aristocratic libertinism. French actresses thus joined the geisha of Japan, the hetaerae of ancient Greece, the xiaochu of Imperial China, and the courtesans of Renaissance Venice as a category of women expected to provide pleasure to the male elite.[25]

Stage women had several clear advantages over court ladies as mistresses. Actresses had gone through a selection process that almost assured their exceptional beauty and charm. Theater women had the opportunity to shine, to establish a reputation for desirability before the assembled court. Actresses also benefited from the psychological appeal of being exotic to lords, because so often they came from the lower depths of society and had tarnished, titillating reputations. Moreover, whatever freedoms the ideology of *galanterie* had offered court ladies, they still had to be more cautious in their behavior than actresses because they were married women or could expect to marry. Their libertinism was limited for the sake of appearances. Not so for actresses. They could easily outmaneuver highborn women when lords pursued the pleasures of the flesh.

The transformation of worldly amoralism from court-centered to theater-centered was not just a matter of substituting one category of woman for another. Lords were making different kinds of choices, and the rules governing libertinism were no longer the same. Actresses changed the costs and consequences of having affairs and imposed their own agenda on the practice. Amoral worldliness, as conceived at the Sun King's court, had been an ideology of male empowerment. It was a reaction against an older code that had idealized women and made them worthy of male sacrifice for their honor. The libertinism of the second half of the seventeenth century had removed women from the pedestal but bestowed only a spurious sexual liberation on them. It encouraged court women to yield their bodies but did not ensure their respectability.[26] Theater women were well positioned to shift the balance of gender power in their favor.

Actresses would not have betrayed public expectations very much if they had simply sold their sexual favors. Some had spent a part of their life as common prostitutes, but most followed the example of the most celebrated courtesan of the era, Ninon de Lenclos, who elevated the selling of her body to a refined art that also provided her with a good deal of autonomy and infinitely raised the prestige of vice. Lenclos (imitating the courtesans of Renaissance Italy before her) made sexual pleasure into an art. No longer primarily about bodily appetites, lovemaking became in her charge a matter of delicate gestures and language. To be worthy of Lenclos, a gentleman had to be skilled in the rituals of love. She was known to reject suitors even when they offered generous sums

The bacchanalian late-night supper with actresses became de rigueur for worldly aristocratic men early in the eighteenth century. This engraving shows mid-nineteenth-century gentlemen carrying on the tradition in all its decadence.

to sleep with her, if they did not please her. The result was to render the courtesan more exclusive and more valued, at the same time that it raised her far above the common prostitute. It also presented men with the obligation to give pleasure to their lovers. In return, the men could add the certification of being an enthralling lover to their accomplishments.[27]

Theater women had the opportunity, and certainly the interest, to perfect this strategy. They would demand a certain minimal financial commitment from their lovers, but beyond that, they could insist that the successful suitor please them. When an actress was "fashionable," she could impose ruthless competition in her circle of admirers. Expensive gifts conferred nothing more than the right to consideration. Lenclos had shown the value of having on hand a gentleman who was willing to pay to be part of a woman's entourage but did not get sex in return. Such a suitor taught a salutary lesson to the actual lovers by acting as a threat and potential replacement.[28] Actresses also abandoned the practice of having a single lover. According to Grimond de la Reynière, writing just before the Revolution, actresses were entitled to three lovers. If they had more, they were cheating; if they had fewer, they were being foolish.[29] Already by the time of the Regency, kept women were expected to have a hierarchy of lovers. There was an "official lover" (*amant en titre,* or Monsieur), who set up the mistress's household, bore her expenses, and received in exchange liberal rights of visitation. There were also one or several "unofficial lovers" (*greluchons*), who gave the woman gifts and were more in the shadows. They could presumably see the mistress when the official lover did not. There might also be a "true love" (*ami de coeur*), who did not pay for attentions and was present to amuse the mistress.[30] It is worth noting that the hierarchy was defined in terms of monetary obligations and rights, not in terms of the sincerity of the relationship with the mistress. The presumption was that jealousy among the males would not be an issue. Indeed, one of the great libertines of the eighteenth century, the duke of Richelieu, observed that to be concerned about a wife's infidelities was to behave like a commoner. Guiseppi Casanova, however, had claimed that Frenchmen were not jealous of their wives but rather of their mistresses.[31] As we shall see, the relationship among the multiple male lovers of a mistress never was a settled issue. It was a principal cause of tension, anger, and broken relationships.

The courtiers' choice to consort with performers instead of highborn women was part and parcel of a major cultural reorientation among the

French aristocracy during the age of Louis XIV. The change had a para-
doxical quality. On the one hand, family, state, and church were imposing greater discipline and constraint on individuals. On the other hand,
the demands resulted in an intensified sense of the self and one's private
needs. Religious authorities were more active in opposing the sins of the
flesh. Court etiquette reached its apex of intricacy under Louis XIV;
courtiers had to observe higher standards of delicacy and refinement in
gestures and language. The state exacted obedience, and the demands of
lineage became increasingly pressing as aristocrats sought a viable basis
for privilege.[32] Yet at the same time, and in response, noblemen forged
personal careers for themselves and accepted the right to and need for
personal ambition. Their enhanced sense of self found expression in
higher expectations for affection and intimacy within a privatized sphere
of domestic life.[33]

The rising desirability of theater women reshaped the contours of
libertinism and hastened the privatization if not the disciplining of the
will. Actresses enticed lords into a market where beauty, charm, and
sexual appeal were sold, and the lords were all too happy to follow. Although the gentlemen of Le Monde were willing to do their duty to family and lineage by marrying appropriately, and even to limit their number of offspring so as to conserve the patrimony, they needed to carve
out an area of freedom where they could express their passions and im-
pulses. Within their affairs with actresses, they pursued their own happiness, disregarding formal social obligations. Aristocrats were developing a distinct, private sphere of life ever more separate from their public
role. Their amorous behavior became more individualized. This change
in their own code of conduct prepared them for the upsurge of sentimentality and domesticity in the second half of the eighteenth century.[34]

From Ritual to Passion

So central had stage women become to the amoral worldliness of the
mid-eighteenth century that the Parisian police, charged with keeeping
vice in check, thought to draw up a chart of their participation.[35] With
Cartesian clarity, the inspectors listed performers (from the Comédie-
française, the Comédie-italienne, the Opéra, and the Opéra-comique,
but not from the theaters of the fairs) in one column and their official
lovers in the other. The table contained entries for 105 performers (54

thespians and 51 dancers). The police did not link any performer under the age of seventeen with a protector. Half of the actresses over forty had lovers; the other half lived with husbands or alone. Of the 78 actresses between seventeen and forty, all but 3 had lovers. The police agents proposed that "ugliness" was the explanation for two of the unattached artists. The other was said to be engaged in the "retail trade"; that is, she took any man with the money for the night (and did so while wearing men's clothing, according to the marginal notes on the chart). On the list of male lovers were some of the great names of the kingdom—Conti, Soubise, Orléans, Luxembourg, Montmorency, Grimaldi, Gramont, Villeroy—and foreign princes, too. Financiers and, particularly, farmers-general (men who leased the state's tax collection machinery) were also a visible presence. In fact, a profile of the mistress keepers mentioned in the midcentury police reports makes clear that libertinism was a practice of the very cream of French society.[36] Dukes, counts, marquises, foreign lords, and holders of the most lucrative financial offices made up a majority of Messieurs. One-third were military officers; sometimes these were young men who might not yet have had a great fortune, but who certainly cut a dashing figure in the society of their day. The noble judges of the sovereign courts of Paris, often very wealthy and descended from financiers, accounted for another fifth of the libertines.[37] The fact that at least a third of the protectors were under thirty years of age and that 45 percent were single suggests that libertinism was as much a prelude to marriage as a violation of it. A certain settling down appears to have occurred as lords aged. Possibly the financial costs, which were considerable, limited the duration of the practice, or theater women simply rejected older, less attractive aristocrats who did not offer exceptionally generous support to compensate for their physical deficiencies.

What the lovers could each expect from a relationship, and what sort of compromises were necessary, is well illustrated by the sexual affairs of Rosalie Astrodi, an artist at the Comédie-italienne. The police reports picked up her adventures in 1750, when Astrodi was in her early twenties. She was in the midst of a stormy affair with Count d'Egmont, a married military officer twelve years her senior. The police inspector reported the couple as being very much in love. The count's carriage took Astrodi to the theater and brought her back to a love nest outside Paris, in Chaillot, every night. Within six months, however, there were reports that the actress was secretly seeing other men and had accepted a regular income from a banker. By 1752, the inspector thought Astrodi ready to break with Egmont. The lover beat her when he found her with another man; she complained of neglect. He promised to be more attentive and was, in fact, prepared to bestow a 2,000-livre income on her. However, he tore up the document in her face when a servant alerted him to the presence of a young nobleman hidden in Astrodi's bedroom. That was the last straw for Egmont. For the next several months, Astrodi had several short-term affairs, including a few weeks with the fabulously wealthy financier Lenormand. He was generous to her, but she shared him with other mistresses. Suddenly, in the summer of 1753, the actress seems to have inspired a passionate love in a young ensign, Leferon, the son of a deceased president of the Parlement of Paris. To the horror of his family, the youth proposed marriage, but despite an offer of bribes, priests would not wed them because Astrodi, as an actress, could not receive Christian rites. Leferon's family prevailed on the government to have him incarcerated for a few weeks, long enough for Astrodi to reassess her marriage plans.

While the fiancé was under lock and key, the actress was already seeing the recently married duke de Montmorency, who belonged to one of the most illustrious families in the kingdom. His new wife was very upset by the liaison and asked her father-in-law, the duke of Luxembourg, to break it up. Luxembourg visited the actress and threatened to have her arrested as a prostitute. On hearing of the interference, Montmorency ran to his father's mistress, the dancer Mademoiselle Vestris, and tried to seduce her as an act of revenge. In the meantime, Leferon had been released and was more madly in love with Astrodi than ever. Unfortunately for him, their separation had made the actress indifferent to him. Even his threat to fall on his sword did not sway Astrodi. The police reports do not relate how Leferon dealt with the emotional blow. Astrodi's affair with Montmorency was brief, in any case. The dancer Mademoiselle Retz took the duke away. Astrodi, who had been seeing three other lovers anyway, took her revenge by forming a liaison with Retz's lover, the count d'Egreville, a rich and handsome military officer. Within six months, though, the police reported a more serious liaison between Astrodi and Pajot de Villiers, a financier.[38] The reports ceased at this point.

Whereas Astrodi had a series of affairs, some serious, some ephemeral, Mademoiselle Dallière, a singer at the Opéra, had a long-standing though turbulent relationship with one man, the noble magistrate Président de Tourmont of the Cour des monnaies, or Coinage Court. Dallière was in her mid-twenties when the relationship began, and the president was in his fifties, married and the father of three children. The actress was not sexually faithful to the judge, but she was loyal to him in her own way. She took the lucrative income that Alexandre Le Riche de la Popelinière, a farmer-general, gave her, but she allowed Tourmont into her bed, too. Not limiting herself to an official lover and a true love, Dallière also slept with a German baron as well as a nobleman named Villeclos, with whom she had a child.

Perhaps to stir Dallière's jealousy, Tourmont took another mistress, Mademoiselle Delorme. The strategy worked for a while, for Dallière resisted the advances of Vicomte de Chabot and gave herself solely to Tourmont. Despite having suspicions, the magistrate lived tranquilly for a while with his lover. Eventually her expensive tastes must have overcome her sense of loyalty, for she took a secret lover, one of the president's colleagues, so that he could share the bills. (Tourmont was not particularly rich.) When the actress became pregnant, and not with his child, Tourmont left her, and she took up with a Venetian diplomat. Debts (run up for Dallière?) made the diplomat flee Paris, and he left her pregnant. Tourmont returned to nurse the singer through the pregnancy and reportedly wept when the infant died. Tourmont and Dallière were still together a year later. The actress was once again pregnant, and this time with Tourmont's child. The police reports end on this domesticated note, but it would require a leap of faith to assume that the relationship continued as Tourmont would have wished.[39]

If these cases make any general point at all, it is that libertinism had no one pattern, no one meaning. It was a practice that revolved around three poles of uneven and variable importance: reputation, money, and sentiment. Sometimes these goals reinforced one another but often they did not. In many cases, the two lovers were guided by different goals, with the result that the liaisons were often stormy. Libertinism, as practiced in the eighteenth century, was anything but a source of undisputed pleasure and prestige for the male aristocracy.

The pursuit of personal honor was the motivation that novelists placed at the center of the libertine code of conduct, making mistress keeping an exercise in aristocratic individualism. There was, inevitably, a public aspect to keeping a theater woman, a sign of privilege and prestige. It symbolized the unification of exalted status with masculine prowess. The protector of a widely admired woman sought the aura of being a "great lover." Thus, Count de la Marche bragged about having had intercourse with Mademoiselle Deschamps (of the Opéra) twelve times in one evening by inscribing the number on the buttons of his trousers.[40] The quest for a virile reputation was also why two of the greatest lords of the realm, Prince de Conti and Prince de Soubise, went to the expense of keeping what were called "harems" of lovers. The police reported the number of women Conti kept as being as high as twenty.[41] An official lover had the right to expect a public acknowledgment of the liaison from the stage, and the more obvious the gesture the better. The performer on stage might, for example, direct her character's declarations of love to her protector's box, ignoring the actor next to her. It is well known that the requirement that actresses wear their lovers' gifts of dresses and jewels retarded the development of historically accurate or realistic costuming. Monsieur de Curin gave his lover Madame Vestris a shepherdess's hat covered in diamonds.[42] When the celebrated dancer performed in it, she certainly did not resemble any shepherdess one was likely to find with a flock, but she did inform the assembled Monde that she belonged to Curin.

Understanding eighteenth-century libertinism as a public display of grandeur, a source of vanity, however, tells only part of a complex story. The privatizing of the relationship between a protector and his mistress was a more pronounced trend, even as early as midcentury. Far from insisting that a mistress display herself on stage as the keeper's conquest, protectors often wanted the artists to retire to the privacy of a retreat. The count of Clermont was not the least bit eccentric in forcing Camargo and then Leduc into retirement for the sake of the relationship.[43] On occasion lords did use their contacts to get their mistress into a royal theater (as an extra, for example), but the motive was not display, it was prudence. This was a means to escape from harassment by parents or police, since entering a royal troupe put an end to parental rights, as the youths came under the supervision of the First Gentlemen, who habitually turned a blind eye toward debauchery. A protector also helped the career of his mistress not to give her greater visibility, but to please her. To win Mademoiselle Pinet as a mistress, the marquis de Villeroy promised to place her in the Comédie-française. He claimed to be able to do that because his brother's mistress, Mademoiselle Clairon, was the premier performer at that theater, and she would train Pinet and use her great influence over the troupe.[44]

As a public act, keeping a theater woman offered as many occasions for scandal, even ridicule, as it did for the show of grandeur. Theater women were not duchesses; they were moral outcasts, and even when presented in grand style, they carried the taint of sin. In 1742, the count of Clermont allowed Leduc, her sister, and several other actresses to come to a royal outing at Longchamps in his elegant carriage, wearing his colors, blue and silver. A member of the royal guard insulted them, and a melee almost broke out. The king expressed his displeasure to Clermont, and a biting satire, "The Triumph of Vice on the Stage of Longchamps," circulated, making the count regret his lack of prudence.[45] Although lords might have hoped to demonstrate their masculine prowess through mistress keeping, it was just as much an open invitation for wits to mock their sexual failures, and the occasions for ridicule were all the more frequent because actresses rarely had just one lover. One can imagine that the marquis de Brancas did not win much prestige when his lover, Mademoiselle Pouponne, openly showed her passion for her dance partner while performing at the Opéra.[46] The communication of venereal disease, so common in these sorts of affairs, also provided frequent opportunities to deflate egos and skewer the haughty. The ballerina Mademoiselle La Chanterie was so beautiful that Louis XV inquired about her. Yet one of her lovers, the duke de Montmorency, might have regretted his affair with her because he became infected and then Sir Maupeou wrote a satirical song that mocked the duke.[47] When Mademoiselle Brillant (of the Opéra) was imprisoned at the request of her lover's family, the marquis de Virbrary took the trouble to get her released, but rumors soon spread that the reward for his efforts had been a case of the clap. This incident, too, became the subject of a song that, according to a police agent, "long made the rounds of all the entertainment spots in Paris."[48] Venereal disease lent itself admirably to satire in these cases because it countered the demonstration of masculine prowess with suggestions of cuckoldry and the loss of sexual mastery. So, too, did another source of ridicule, disputes over the paternity of out-of-wedlock children. Far from being a convincing display of potency, the eighteenth-century practice of mistress keeping usually resulted in charges and countercharges about who was the father of such a

child, as the mother tried to find one lover who would bestow an annuity on the offspring. A pregnancy only reminded a lover that he shared
his woman with others, and it was usually the occasion for a quarrel.

Thus, keeping a theater woman may have enhanced personal honor
occasionally in Le Monde, but it also had much potential to cause a loss
of face. In any case, lords often lost sight of the quest for reputation and
allowed passion (or infatuation) to guide their affairs. Liaisons took
place *despite* what anyone thought. The affection that protectors felt for
their mistresses often led them to privatize the relationship and remove
it from the gaze of Le Monde. Unlike liaisons with aristocratic women
who may have been married or whose status conferred responsibilities
that placed limitations on affairs, many instances of libertinism with theater women effectively became exercises in domesticity and entailed the
establishment of a second home.

It is clear that the Monsieur of the eighteenth century was displeased
with the actresses' practice of having multiple lovers and became resigned to it only with reluctance. The police once reported on the three
lovers of Mademoiselle Favier who came to the Opéra to applaud their
mistress and decide, in a cooperative spirit, which among them would
take her home that night.[49] However, jealousy and attempts to exclude
other lovers were far more often the rule. The aunt of the singer Mademoiselle De Metz, who supervised her niece's liaisons, acknowledged
that protectors did not wish to share their mistresses, and she was happy
to keep second lovers away so long as Monsieur showed his appreciation
financially.[50] Gentlemen usually had to rely on their own methods for
keeping a mistress faithful, and they sometimes hired spies to keep
an eye on her or paid a servant in the household to do so. Two different lovers had the home of the actress Caroline under surveillance at
the same time in 1755, and seeing so many strangers lurking in alleys
made neighbors nervous enough that they complained to the police.[51]
Le Riche de la Popelinière, taking advantage of his wealth as a financier,
offered to pay his mistress more than the usual sum if she remained
faithful. (She took the money but did not uphold her end of the bar-
gain.) The army officer De Lowit simply announced to Mademoiselle
Beauchamps (a dancer at the Opéra) that he would kill any other man
who became her lover.[52] The writer Marmontel might have expected
great lords to be above jealousy, but they were not, and multiple lovers
created endless discord among couples. When the count de Coubert laid

down the law to Mademoiselle Romainville (a singer at the Opéra) about taking other lovers, she retorted that he was asking her to live as his "slave," and she refused to obey. Very soon thereafter, she became the mistress of the count de Caraman.[53] It is not surprising, in the end, that one gentleman told a police agent he intended to have affairs only with aristocratic ladies because they were easier to acquire as mistresses and they cost less.[54]

A principal reason why more gentlemen did not come to that conclusion is that their affairs were based on passionate sentiment and commitment rather than on convention. They were in love with a particular woman (for the moment, at least), not just guided by the idea of having a mistress. The rituals and gestures framing the relationships allowed for, and came to be centered around, intimacy and domesticity rather than public display. A protector, if he could afford it and arrange it, kept his mistress in a love nest, often secluded in the suburbs of the capital. His comings and going were discreet, not open announcements of possession. A gentleman usually stationed his carriage away from his mistress's door when visiting and approached on foot.[55] Messieurs reserved publicized arrivals for special occasions—for proclaiming, for example, that a disrupted affair was on again. The exchange of portraits was a frequent gesture of sharing between protectors and mistresses. Official lovers also accepted the obligation to support the woman's family. A police inspector reported on the confusion the marquis de Villeroy experienced when his mother and his "mother-in-law"—the term used for his mistress's mother—died at the same moment, and he had to plan and attend both funerals.[56] A protector recognized his mistress's children and had them raised decently—sometimes even under his personal attention—so long as he could be sure they were his offspring.

There were, certainly, a good number of long-term affairs. If they were not in the majority, this may have been because the theater women insisted on multiple lovers in the realization that their career and their ability to attract wealth lasted only as long as their youth did. Even in short-term affairs, signs of caring relationships were frequent. Mademoiselle Duplessis of the Opéra owed her name to the army captain who kept her and made her take the name of his manor.[57] The duke d'Olonne placed Mademoiselle Amédée in a love nest outside Paris, with her mother running the kitchen. He took the actress back to his estates and even taught her how to hunt. When his family obtained a royal order that he stay away from the woman, Olonne defied it.[58] Even a ne'er-do-well like Sir Darbonne, a twenty-four-year-old nobleman who had no occupation but gambling, had an affair with De Metz that was still passionate after three years, according to the police agent.[59] When Sir de Marsay had to return to his regiment, he wrote to the ballerina Mademoiselle Courant every day and begged her not to appear on stage; she returned his commitment by not leaving her home except to attend Mass.[60]

The depth of passion in some affairs was demonstrated by the acts of jealousy and vengeance that filled the annals of libertinism. The marquis d'Hautefort, France's ambassador to Vienna, found that his mistress, Mademoiselle Montfort (of the Opéra-comique), had been having a secret affair, and he threatened to have her locked up for the rest of her life as a prostitute. He knew, however, that he could not carry out the threat without making himself look ridiculous.[61] When Marshal Lowendal learned that Brillant had been sleeping with his aide-de-camp, he took back the 10,000 livres in silverware, 15,000 in diamonds, and the portrait he had given her.[62] Count d'Egmont went to his mistress and, before her eyes, tore up a document bestowing an annuity on her in order to express his resentment over her betrayal. Resorting to violence was uncommon, because publicity would only bring humiliation, but occasionally a lover's emotions led to desperate plans. After putting up with a number of infidelities, the farmer-general Daugny learned that his mistress, Mademoiselle Coupée (a dancer), was sleeping with a magistrate named de Bauche. He hired three men to attack his rival as the couple was returning from a concert at Versailles. De Bauche managed to repel his attackers, and the only revenge Daugny could take was to use his authority as a tax officer to imprison Coupée for a while. What the financier did not realize was that his mistress and de Bauche had been emotionally tied for some time. When Coupée had a child in 1750, Daugny assumed it was his and gave it a pension, but de Bauche also gave it a pension and even saw to it that the child was nursed near his estate so that he could supervise its care. Apparently both men made themselves the father of the love child.[63]

The novelists of libertinism who contrasted the game of seduction within Le Monde with the sincere love expressed in lesser milieux were imagining a false opposition. The writers seemed intent on constructing the distinctiveness of an aristocratic caste just when important differences were being effaced. French culture in the prerevolutionary decades displayed growing respect for a private sphere centered on the caring family and for men's personal autonomy within that sphere. Sentimentality, sincerity, and intimacy became ideals for personal and familial relations.[64] The shift toward more domestic, private lives and the pursuit of individual satisfaction did not pit aristocrat against commoner. Lords wanted to relate to lovers as both intimate companions and grand protectors. Noblemen made correct marriages but followed the promptings of their heart outside matrimony and sometimes found the joys of domesticity away from home. Moreover, they did not necessarily make a distinction between the quest for reputation, on the one hand, and the pursuit of feeling, on the other, because, in their eyes, becoming the true love of a beautiful, admired performer was prestigious *and* pleasurable. What they rarely did was initiate an affair just for the sake of appearances in Le Monde. They seemed willing to pay for love and sexual pleasure, or were resigned to it, but resented mistresses who imposed restrictions on their affection.

Theater women, too, were capable of loving sincerely, but until they accumulated a substantial fortune, the monetary aspect of their relationship with Monsieur was usually central to them. They negotiated in a hard-headed manner, and only after getting what they wanted did they cover the affair with a fig leaf by pretending that they were giving themselves freely and getting gifts as an afterthought. Keeping a mistress was expensive in the eighteenth century. An official lover had to shoulder several sorts of costs. Initiating an affair could easily cost 40,000 livres or more. The protector had to set up the mistress in a new household and bestow an agreed-upon income on her. Twelve hundred livres in yearly pocket money (which required purchasing a 24,000-livre annuity) was a common figure at midcentury. A lord would be able to recover some of the expenses on furnishings when an affair ended, but the annuity was retained by the mistress. If a gentleman had to win an actress away from other lovers, a bidding war would inflate all the costs.[65] Mademoiselle De Metz, the most sought-after woman in Paris in 1751, commanded 10,000 livres in cash from the duke de la Vallière in addition to extravagant spending on an apartment and 4,000 livres of pocket money.[66]

A liaison had to be maintained, as well. The protector could expect to pay his mistress's debts, support her family, and, above all, offer a steady stream of gifts. Increasingly, kept women did not defer to court ladies in fashion but rather expected to set the standards for splendor in carriages, dresses, jewels, and furnishings.[67] Denying luxuries led to quarrels, and making up required an expensive present, too. Monsieur de Courtenvaux had to give a 30,000-livre note to Mademoiselle Saint-Germain (of the Opéra-comique) to get back into her good graces.[68]

Actresses casually spurned the formal hierarchy of rank and took lovers based on personal inclination or, more often, the best offer. One result was the growing prominence of financiers and tax farmers, men with prodigious resources, in the competition for desirable women.[69] At midcentury, there was still a sense that such men were not grand enough to play the aristocratic game of debauchery. Minister-Cardinal de Fleury could warn Le Riche de la Popelinière that "a publically maintained mistress [was not] a permitted luxury for a financier." By the end of the Old Regime, however, a scandal sheet reported that an actress, lecturing a police agent who had dared to question her morality, explained that her "behavior depends solely on a financier's strongbox and the face of a handsome man."[70] The libertinism dominated by theater women did not observe the ideals of a society based on inherited rank.

Thus, what noblemen gained as men of passion and will, they sacrificed as great lords of the realm. Making actresses, outcast women, the object of their personal desire did not, in the end, reinforce the legitimacy of hierarchical society based on inherited privilege. Rather, the pursuit of popular beauties for passionate liaisons often robbed aristocrats of their wealth and honor and even raised questions about their right to rule. The quest for reputation such as novelists advanced would have been more sensible. No doubt the aristocrats wanted their affairs with actresses to bring them both passion and honor—but that was often impossible in a society where a separate and active "public sphere" could expose the contradictions.

Celebrated Outcasts

In 1753, the count de Clermont held a grand celebration in honor of his mistress of ten years, Mademoiselle Leduc. Of course, it included performances in the famous private theater at his chateau of Berny. Among the paid professionals was Madame Lekain of the Comédie-française. She disrupted the conviviality of the evening by demanding to sit at the head table, apparently because her colleague Mademoiselle Gaussin was seated there. The prince rejected her request, stating (according to the police) that "he admitted to his table only the women he had the honor of admitting to his bed," and bluntly told Lekain to leave.[71] Another dispute over precedence occurred two years later during the festivities that the financier Le Riche de la Popelinière held at his pleasure palace in Passy. The usual guests at these evenings were highborn men and kept women. That night, however, some titled women were present, and their informal dress seemed to authorize more social mixing than usual. Yet when Mademoiselle Coupée dared to sit at the table of the court women, they protested and sent her running from the room in tears.[72] The first scene of exclusion might have been morally troubling to those who knew about it. Clermont had arranged his gathering, at least in part, as a display of his own sexual prowess and had assembled his male courtiers to pay him homage. Certainly the second instance of rejection was more reassuring in a moral sense. Even society ladies who were bold enough to visit Passy drew the line at dining with theater women. Such rituals of exclusion were a principal line of defense against stage women who tried to invade respectable society and usurp the privileges of titled women.

The irate aristocratic ladies of Passy were not alone in drawing a line. They were, in fact, acting on the same principles as the worldly novelists who presumed the necessity of excluding theater women—erasing them—from representations of high society. Though the novels of libertinism were hardly models of moral uplift, the writers exercised a collective prohibition on bringing the scandals associated with actresses into the world of the high born. The novelists believed, apparently, that it was more acceptable to portray court women as being involved in sexual intrigue than to highlight the links between Le Monde and stage women.

The erasure that the novelists practiced was informed by the inevitable association of theater women and vice. One account of theatrical scandal relates a conversation between two well-bred people. Madame notices that a particularly ugly man always has women about him and assumes these women are "those one pays and who roam the streets like carriages." Her partner informs her that these are theater women, and Madame replies, "That is more or less the same thing."[73] When a court lady asked the count de Tilly to explain the difference between a common prostitute and a woman like Adeline Colombe of the Comédie-italienne, he told her: "Without education and taste, the prostitute is a danger only to your lackey; the other, armed with a thousand seductions, infects your friend, your brother, your husband."[74] The noblewoman could not have found the distinction reassuring. Charles Collé, a writer close to the duke d'Orléans, proposed another dark, but similar, association in 1765. When an entrepreneur was selling a medallion in honor of Mademoiselle Clairon, Collé immediately recalled a medal struck in honor of the farmer-general Bouret. The actress and the financier seemed linked in his mind to highly visible abuses: both accumulated vast, ill-gotten wealth.[75]

Excluded from representation in the respectable literature of the day, theater women were frequently portrayed in the forbidden publications, scandal sheets, and pornographic fiction that circulated secretly. When nineteenth-century writers expressed amazement at how openly their eighteenth-century counterparts had reported on shocking details of performers' lives, it was this underground literature they really had in mind. Scandal sheets printed abroad and smuggled into France did not hesitate to name names and make very specific accusations of vile behavior. The actor François Mayeur de Saint-Paul wrote several popular brochures about his female colleagues at the Ambigu theater (on the boulevard du Temple) in which he did not hesitate to label them "whores" and to demonstrate why. He wrote, for example, that Mademoiselle Julie was "a charming little brat whose affairs and keepers were too numerous to mention."[76] Another popular revelatory account was François Chevrier's *Le Colporteur* ("The Tattler"). The preface promised "daring truths that authors should reveal when they are unmasking the foolish and the wicked."[77] *Opéra* and *actress* were standard keywords in the titles of forbidden books.[78]

Probably the most widely read scandalous account about a performer was the apocryphal autobiography attributed to Mademoiselle Clairon during her early days at the theater of Rouen, actually written by Pierre Gaillard de la Bataille.[79] Editions appeared in 1730, 1740, 1752, 1772, 1782, and 1783. The work, filled with sexual adventures, begins with the actress being thrust into prostitution by her mother. Clairon maintains a genuine love for the young, handsome Ridhills (who dies and returns to life more than once in the long and disjointed narrative). True to Ridhills in her fashion, the actress sleeps with dozens of other men out of need, lust, and the pressures of the moment. The tale reads much like the reports the police made on libertine relationships. Had respectable novelists not attempted to render theater women invisible, their books would have resembled this one.

Only one openly circulating novel of the eighteenth century contained the term *actress* in its title, and even then she was not precisely its subject.[80] Written by a little-known author, de Sainte-Croix, and published in Brussels in 1756 (but set in Paris), *La Comédienne* ("The Actress") tells of the coming of age of a noblewoman. Her father has wronged her in two ways: first by ordering her to marry an elderly financier whom she despises, and second by having had an affair with an actress whom he then made his daughter's governess. The father receives his punishment when the daughter, on the advice of the governess, runs away with her true love and becomes an actress herself. The theater world is a distant but threatening presence in the novel.

The effort to exclude theater women and to erase them from representations of society occurred because they were, in fact, all too visible and close to the centers of power and respectability. Theater women occupied a large and growing place in elite sociability and in the social imagination of the mid-eighteenth century. Their coverage in the society newsletters of the day shows that the emerging public was intensely curious about them.[81] Stage performers received more mention than any other women, including the queen and the great court ladies. Only such towering male figures as Voltaire or Jean-Jacques Rousseau enjoyed the amount of coverage that actresses received. The reports mixed theatrical business (debuts, failures, and such) with sexual adventures. Readers of the *Mémoires secrets,* an important source of worldly gossip, received news on the state of Mademoiselle Raucourt's virtue and loss thereof; her lust for other women, labeled tribadism, was also a well-developed topic.[82] Le Monde, along with the artists and writers permitted to mix with the elite, focused avidly on theater women, on what they did on stage and off.

Fashion was another channel by which theater women invaded respectable society. Sartorial practices were going through profound changes during the mid-eighteenth century. Clothing evolved from an expression of status to an enhancement of appearance. As such, it became more feminized than ever before; it was increasingly perceived as a woman's concern, reflecting her "natural" inclination to please men. Moreover, fashion was penetrating more deeply into the social order, with more people spending the cash to keep up with the latest taste.[83]

Theater women's influence on style was openly acknowledged. Indeed, the stage was not too far from challenging the royal court as the primary influence. The dancer Marie Guimard was a "goddess of taste" in the 1770s, according to poems published by her admirers. A dress à la Guimard became high fashion, and Marie Antoinette herself was influenced by her wardrobe.[84] In the next decade, the diva Madame Saint-Huberty became a model of chic. Mayeur de Saint-Paul hailed her as the "sovereign of dress." Her feathers and hats (à la Marlborough) defined what the well dressed should wear.[85] The trend was morally troubling because it reminded society of its fateful addiction to luxuries and particularly of women's weakness for them. Fashion journals cited actresses as models but warned of the need to exercise moderation in adopting dress from the stage, in that "the least affectation will give you the air of a *fille* [whore]."[86] At the same time, the growing fashion press did connect, in an explicit manner, actresses' success in seduction with their influence on style.

Rituals of exclusion did not keep theater women even from the sacred center of the social order, the monarchy. Officially designated as the "king's performers," actresses at the royal theaters had a certain claim on the attention and solicitude of the crown. On stage, the performers were participants in the royal public sphere, charged with representing the splendor of the monarch and with giving diversion to his subjects. However, royal attention was not limited to this official realm. The dauphin (the future Louis XVI) and dauphine (Marie-Antoinette) decided to honor the memory of Marshal de Saxe by having his daughter, Aurore, raised at royal expense. The dauphin was not deterred from the good deed by the fact that the child had been born out of wedlock, to the actress Mademoiselle Verrière.[87] It was by no means accidental that the two most hated royal consorts, Madame de Pompadour and Marie-Antoinette, involved themselves too much for the sake of propriety in backstage intrigues.[88] While it was true that personnel questions at royal theaters were affairs of state, the public did look askance at contacts between performers and the crown that were too intimate. Marie-Antoinette did not hesitate to offer her support to Mademoiselle Raucourt, whose scandalous liaisons, debts, and tribadism counted heavily against her. In 1778, Raucourt's debts were so huge that she had to flee the capital. The queen intervened personally in the effort to make her return possible. She offered to pay 200,000 livres toward her debts. She even worked to restore the actress's respectability by attempting to marry her to the actor Fleury (undeterred, it seems, that rumors of his homosexual relationships might have added to the scandal). The merchants of Paris were angered by a royal decree limiting the liens on performers' salaries, the timing of which appeared to make it a favor for the unsavory Raucourt.[89] The rising chorus denouncing the queen's extravagant dress (symptomatic of deeper vices) at the end of the Old Regime linked it to the influence of theater women, especially Guimard.[90] Even Marie-Antoinette's mother, Empress Maria-Theresa, was concerned, returning a painting of her daughter to her ambassador with the remark that "this is not the portrait of a queen of France; this is the portrait of an actress."[91]

Theater women were developing a quality that did not yet have a name—celebrity.[92] It grew in tandem with the public sphere. The theatergoing public and the underground reading public knew a good deal about theater women's personal lives and were eager to know more. What actresses did, said, and wore stirred interest—and imitation. A certain glamour and excitement adhered to them beyond the achievements that brought them to attention in the first place. Against this strong current of interest, rituals of exclusion and moral condemnation were impotent.

Anyone who cared to chart the advances theater women had made since the early seventeenth century might have written it as a history of extraordinary conquest. From a position of moral censure and social taboo, they had by the mid-eighteenth century won the eyes and hearts of lords, who created a privatized sphere devoted to libertine pleasures, even domestic bliss, at their behest. The actresses' invasion of respectable society was unstoppable because the public found them intriguing and attractive. Spectators elevated them into "celebrities" before the term existed.

These conquests stirred as much anxiety as awe. Count Alexandre de Tilly contrasted scandal-ridden Paris, where hundreds of courtesans lived in splendor, with what he identified as the healthier situation in London. In the British capital, he claimed, gentlemen visited prostitutes, but they did not set them up in conspicuous luxury.[93] Theater women in eighteenth-century France contributed to the sense that the follies of the elite would corrupt the rest of society. Social critics were concerned about the visibility and the moral implications of actresses' celebrity. Yet rituals of exclusion did not erode their powers, and even the excommunication of performers enforced by the Gallican church seemed anachronistic to many.[94] Reformers sought either to moralize the actresses who were so prominent or to inoculate men from their perfidious influences. Such concerns were easily assimilated into broader fears about the legitimacy of absolutist society and calls for a new and morally regenerated political order.

3

Defining the Modern Gender Order, 1760–1815

Many actresses did very well in the century before 1730 because kings incorporated them into royal spectacle and because it became de rigueur for highborn men to compete for their favors. Instead of becoming ever more accustomed to the visibility of theater women, however, political thinkers and reformers were increasingly troubled by them as the eighteenth century progressed. Misgivings about actresses' sexual conduct deepened as Enlightenment thinkers sought the causes of moral and political corruption. The critics' searching questions seemed particularly urgent because French society was shedding its absolutist political culture and taking on aspects of a civic order in which favorable public opinion and the consent of the nation were required to legitimize government action.[1] When grave economic, political, and fiscal crises hit France in the late 1780s, widespread but diffuse discontent turned into revolution. The leaders of 1789 then had to deal with the problems that actresses posed for a sovereign people.

Fantasies of Containment

Louis Riccoboni, one of the great actors at the Comédie-italienne, wrote a treatise on theatrical reform in 1743, forty years into his career. He believed that his beloved profession suffered from grave moral problems and came to the heart of them in a chapter on "Theater Women" (there was no chapter on men of the stage).[2] Riccoboni began by noting that female performers had been a source of anxiety since antiquity. He looked back nostalgically to the sixteenth century, when troupes were all male, but he did not think banishment of women from the stage was possible in his day. Instead, he proposed several reforms that would diminish significantly the "inconveniences of women" and restore "good morals" to theatrical performances.

Riccoboni's proposals were by no means modest and practical, even though he offered them as a sensible alternative to removing women from the stage. First, he asked the king to transform patterns of recruitment of actresses by requiring them to come from good families and to present a certificate of good conduct when seeking jobs. Next, the author called for a drastic change in the nature of plays: they should no longer be about love. In a history of the Comédie-italienne that Riccoboni published in 1723, he had documented the emergence of romantic love as a theme in dramatic literature, attributing it to the Corneillan tragedy.[3] He asked for a return to the innocent scripts of earlier years, but was willing to permit romance on stage if the playwright provided valuable moral lessons. A third reform was to allow on stage only women who were married and living with their husband. To this he joined a measure borrowed from Holland, that of fining actresses who caused scandals and confiscating their pensions. Riccoboni was not concerned about male actors' potential for causing scandal and did not propose any sanctions against them. He predicted that his most unpopular reform would be a prohibition on female dancers. Because dancers wore short dresses and had exposed throats, "the most scabrous comedy was a thousand time less dangerous than women dancing on stage."[4]

Riccoboni's fears about theater women inflaming spectators' passions had been heard many times before. Seventeenth-century clergy who denounced the stage as it had become an integral part of court culture had often made this case as part of their argument justifying the condemnation of the acting profession enforced by the French (Gallican) church. The church's position was that theater itself was inherently corrupting. Female and male performers were, in effect, victims of their profession. They could save their soul only by renouncing their career.[5] Riccoboni's originality was to add gender specificity to the ancient condemnation by making actresses' licentiousness the central issue. The renewed problem of women as spectacle, now taken out of a Christian discourse and secularized, was a telling sign of the emergence of the modern gender order in eighteenth-century France.[6]

The modern gender order was not more sexist than older patterns of discrimination, but it was configured differently. The construction and consequences of women's subordinate position took new forms. Modern patriarchy emphasized the complementarity of the sexes rather than women's lesser status. The qualities of the sexes were patterned such that the strengths of one sex compensated for the deficiencies of the other. The male qualities were considered to be mental vigor, bodily strength, and reason. Female qualities were sensitivity, weakness, emotionality, and an instinct for self-sacrifice. Imagining women as the mental equals of men, debated as a serious possibility in the mid-seventeenth century, no longer seemed conceivable. Authorities were basing their assessment of women's intellectual capacity on the female body, which nature now seemed to have designed for motherhood. The recently identified sex-specific attributes were made to appear part of the natural order of things by being connected to biological foundations.[7] Until the early eighteenth century, scientists did not stress physiological differences between male and female bodies and did not even give female sex organs distinct names. Thereafter, experts increasingly insisted on separate body types with opposite psychological, moral, and physical capacities.[8] A consensus was emerging that women had a natural instinct for morality. Whereas male reason might be the instrument of self-interest and self-assertion in the public sphere, women's superior capacity for love, tenderness, and pity operated in intimate settings. Women were by nature dependent on male strength and reason, while men were intended by nature to be autonomous individuals.[9]

These reconfigured assumptions about sexual difference took shape gradually and mingled with older notions until the caesura of the Revolution clarified the situation.[10] The modern gender order grew out of the increased importance of the autonomous individual, who was gendered male.[11] Rationality was the essence of this individual. As the Enlightenment advanced universalistic claims about human equality and liberty, thinkers established "natural" grounds for applying the beliefs to men but not to women. Here was the cultural impetus for the eighteenth-century medical profession to discover physiological differences between the male and female bodies.[12] Likewise, the acceptance of an implicit contract theory as the basis of government necessitated bipolar thinking about gender to dispense with the need for women's consent.[13] Women's dependency and passionate nature precluded their being autonomous citizens. New assumptions about economic life that started to

gain sway in the early eighteenth century also fostered the modern gender order. Self-interest and market forces as legitimate sources of economic organization promoted the gender-based understanding of men
competing against each other while women supplied their tender and
intimate escape from the rough-and-tumble world.[14] The rational and
secular order sought by enlightened thinkers had the effect of providing
an arsenal of new arguments for women's subordination.

Rank, order, and degree made less sense in the face of the growing prestige of the (male) individual. What was taking the place of these
hierarchical categories was the powerful, life-organizing vision of a civil
society bifurcated into gendered public and private spheres. One of the
most significant changes in eighteenth-century French political culture
was the rise of the public sphere—that is, the practice of referring issues
to private citizens who spoke in the name of the public good.[15] As a cor-
ollary to this active male sphere, the domestic sphere of family emerged
as the repository of the sense of sacredness that had formerly surrounded monarchy and the church.[16] Roger Chartier identifies the privatization of behavior as a profound eighteenth-century cultural trend.
He also notes the erection of "strict divisions between conduct that was
allowed or required to be public and conduct that had to be removed
from the community's sight."[17] In this shifting context, what remained of
the courtier's public sexuality became increasingly odious. In contrast
to aristocratic libertinism, the autonomous individual was called to a
"higher" form of sex, domesticated, tempered by emotional attachment,
and exercised with self-control.[18]

Jean-Jacques Rousseau crystallized these changes in political culture
and brought them to bear on the questions Riccoboni raised about
women as spectacle. This is why Rousseau initiated a significant debate
about actresses' place in French society of the second half of the eighteenth century. His 1758 Lettre à Monsieur D'Alembert sur les Spectacles
("Letter to D'Alembert on Theater") laid out the modern and secular
case against theater and especially actresses as sources of social and
moral corruption. Intervening in the dispute about opening a theater in
his native Geneva, Rousseau cast the Swiss republic as a polity in which
the public and private spheres were not only well developed but also still
virtuous. He took it as a lesson from antiquity that the separation of the
sexes was a necessary condition for continued morality and public virtue. Rousseau feared that opening a theater would harm the republican

virtue of Geneva by increasing the influence of women and weakening the powers of reason that men needed to govern themselves. The stage, he feared, would make the republic more like France, where men were too effeminate, women too powerful, and morality too sullied to allow for self-government.

Rousseau placed women at the center of his analysis of public and private morality. He formulated a paradigm that would reverberate for more than a century in discussions of relations between men and women: When women were strong, men were inevitably weak.[19] He found women in France too strong, too much like actresses, whom Rousseau depicted as blatantly contradicting nature's plan for women. The female sex was, in his view, inherently modest, self-sacrificing, and submissive. Yet, in France, Rousseau found that women exercised too much behind-the-scenes influence, mixed too freely with men, and had too much hold on cultural and literary activity. Under these conditions, men's capacity for reason and virtue was undermined. Rousseau connected this dissipation and effeminacy directly to the prominence of theater in France. Parisian playwrights put female characters in the unnatural situation of being superior to the male characters. The effect, he claimed, was to "extend the empire of the Sex [women], to make women the public's moral tutors" and "to give them the same power over spectators as they have over lovers." The theater also encouraged the mixing of the sexes in public and replaced innocent pleasures with licentious ones. Rousseau jumped easily from theater to salon because both were dominated by women. He drew a fearsome portrait of Parisian-style salons, where "each woman gathers in her drawing room a harem of men more feminized than she." He contrasted the emasculating salon with the Genevan social circle, an all-male institution that encouraged virile mores. Rousseau feared that the theater would destroy the taste for the healthy pleasures developed within these circles.[20]

Rousseau argued that the moral failings of theater were so inherent that they could not be corrected. He did not see how plays could teach any lessons but the irresistable power of the passions. Rousseau also presumed that the behavior of thespians would inevitably be deplorable. "To forbid performers from being depraved," he proclaimed, "would be like forbidding men to be ill." He cited the condemnation of actors in Roman law with approval. Unlike Riccoboni, Rousseau was evenhanded in condemning actors and actresses. Both were careless about money and about respectable appearances. Of course, he viewed the social consequences of actresses' unruliness as more serious because of their influence over men.[21]

Rousseau's *Lettre* struck a responsive chord in France because of his ultimate concern with how the immorality of theater infected government and society. French thinkers were drawn to his discussion of the civic underpinnings of a people capable of governing themselves wisely. The changes in French political culture, particularly the emergence of a public sphere, made Rousseau's discussion provocative and also disturbing. His French readers did not want to accept the vision of a virtuous (if threatened) Geneva and an irretrievably feminized France. With different degrees of urgency, they argued that France might become, and should become, more like Geneva. Moreover, French thinkers rejected Rousseau's despair about the moral effect of plays. Some defended the classics, but more commonly they placed hope in a new style of play, the drama. Written in prose, this genre would revolve around the domestic and intimate lives of the characters. Denis Diderot, one of its principle advocates, believed that such plays would allow authors to create on stage a moral universe of honest, authentic, and virtuous emotions rather than the base passions Rousseau described.[22] Having affirmed that plays could improve public morality, French thinkers were left with performers' deplorable conduct as the central drawback of theater. Like Riccoboni, they presumed that the performers who really mattered in this regard were the female ones, and all writers on French theater deplored actresses' behavior. However, they did not agree on how to assess actresses' culpability. Were they the *cause* of moral decay in France or more a symptom, revealing that France was not serious about seeking private virtue?

In his tract *Du Théâtre* ("On the Theater") of 1773, the eclectic writer, journalist, and playwright Louis-Sébastien Mercier called on playwrights to be "legislators" of the public good. Rather than denouncing plays, Mercier wrote that he hoped the moral impact of the drama would teach sincere and authentic values. He did accept Rousseau's definition of woman's nature, even though he had been editor of the *Journal des dames* and had advocated education for women.[23] He also accepted Rousseau's vision of unruly women corrupting male reason. Indeed, Mercier identified actresses' licentiousness as the most intractable obstacle in making theater a school of morality. Their corruption would ruin the effect of even the most edifying drama. Mercier was firm in urging society to protect itself against actresses' depravities. He recognized that "the prestige that surrounds an actress makes her the most dangerous woman the imagination can grasp and embellish." Domestic virtue was in peril so long as actresses exercised their spell over spectators. Virtuous women could not compete for men's attention against actresses' beauty, sensuality, and fame. No family patrimony was safe from the depredations of these Messalines.

Such fears made Mercier undertake a controversial defense of the French church's centuries-old excommunication of performers, which fellow *philosophes* widely denounced as a benighted remnant of medieval obscurantism. Recalling favorably the Roman custom of making theater women appear on stage nude "either to efface the impression that their veiled charms had made or to confirm the opinion one had of the profession," Mercier supported excommunication as the only weapon France had at the time to counter actresses' threat to chastity and marital fidelity. Downplaying the Catholic theology and morality behind the church's position on performers, he promoted the condemnation as a necessary civic act in support of public morality.[24]

Nicolas Rétif de la Bretonne, another writer and disciple of Rousseau, was so troubled by the deleterious impact of theater women on men's conduct and reasoning powers that he indulged his imagination to produce utopian schemes of containment. His corpus of writing often referred to the erotic impact of the stage on male spectators.[25] *La Mimographe* of 1770 (subtitled "Ideas of a Virtuous Woman on the Reform of the National Theater") proposed a radical restructuring of the private lives of performers. His book outlined a plan for replacing professional players with citizen-actors. Schools would inculcate a love of drama, and citizens would specialize in one role and come to identify with it to such an extent that they would imbibe the noble sentiments of their characters. Performers would be under the close supervision of twelve directors and directresses, chosen among citizens of irreproachable conduct. A director could never summon an actress to his home for a consultation; contact would occur through the performer's parents. The theater wings, rather than being open to debauchery, would become tightly controlled environments. Men and women would be segregated and, even then, only parents would be permitted backstage. Rétif's work appealed to Rousseau's sense of citizenship as an all-consuming calling.[26]

Toward the end of *La Mimographe,* Rétif fretted that he had not gone far enough in undermining the physical enticements that performers exercised over spectators and proposed a strategy for a still more thoroughgoing containment. Rather than having citizen-actors, he now called for recruiting actors among the children of the foundling homes and making them slaves. They would live in segregation from the rest of society, under draconian discipline. Rewards would depend on obedience to a severe code of conduct as well as on the quality of performances. To ensure that both the public and the players understood the outcast quality of the profession, there would be an annual ritual of humiliation like the one eighteenth-century thinkers attributed to ancient Rome. Artists would appear on the stage bound in chains, and an official would denounce their faults. The ritual would be intended especially for female performers, "whose faces and talents might inspire vanity and whose attractiveness might have caused ravages among the spectators."[27] Even more than Mercier, Rétif followed Rousseau in supposing that a society in which the people ruled themselves needed to take extraordinary measures to protect itself from the depredations of theater women.

Discontent with the moral state of womanhood was rife in prerevolutionary France.[28] However, many thinkers did not see the repression of actresses as a useful measure. An optimist like Jean-François Marmontel held that the crown could restore moral authority to theater simply by removing the taint of excommunication. Then, he reasoned, respectable women would be more inclined to enter the career.[29] For others, the scandalous comportment of theater women was characteristic of a deeper problem, the lack of commitment to domestic virtue among those who established moral values in France. Jean D'Alembert argued, in effect, that France had the sort of actresses it deserved. They behaved deplorably because society gave them no reason to behave otherwise. Since the public would not reward them for virtuous behavior or punish them for immoral conduct, they had no incentive to renounce lovers. Moreover, D'Alembert dared to point out that women of Le Monde behaved similarly without a loss of respect. Actresses were notorious because they were so visible, but vice was just as widespread among titled women. D'Alembert advocated improving women's upbringing as a solution. He described women's current state as "slavery." Once properly trained for roles as wives and mothers, women would raise moral standards in France, and scandalous actresses would lose favor.[30]

An L. H. Dancourt, who claimed to be a French actor working in Berlin, agreed that France had the actresses it deserved. He conceded that theater women committed moral outrages, but he said it was in part because they were victims of poverty and society's neglect. Dancourt proposed improving their economic situation through a complicated formula that would raise salaries by taking money from male actors' pensions and compensating the latter through a special tax on tickets. If the licentiousness persisted once poverty was no longer an excuse, then Dancourt was willing to employ harsh repression. Actresses should be incarcerated "like prostitutes, to cry over their infamy without hope of ever returning to the stage." Their diamonds would be sold to support the poor house. Dancourt shifted some of the blame for actresses' misbehavior to the governmental authorities, who left them entirely free of supervision and abandoned them to "barbarism." By tolerating immoral behavior, officials were encouraging vice. Like D'Alembert, Dancourt pointed out that the current depravity of theater women demonstrated mainly that France had not taken the necessary steps to ensure private virtue.[31]

Rousseau explained in political and philosophical terms what Riccoboni had intuited: that actresses' public sexuality was dangerous. French thinkers recognized that the civic qualities Rousseau prescribed for Geneva were needed in France, where absolutist political culture was crumbling and something new was arising. French opinion was groping its way toward demanding morally purified public and private spheres. Public women, among them actresses, posed a problem with which reformers would have to grapple.

Women with Power

Appalled or simply amused by the impertinent luxuries that theater women extracted from their rich lovers, the French public could easily find illustrations of Rousseau's warning that when women were strong, men were weak. Any visit to the Opéra or the Longchamps promenade would confirm the lesson as actresses displayed themselves, their possessions, and their powers over great men. Actresses also deployed their power by participating in the absolutist public sphere. At two theaters, the Comédie-française and the Comédie-italienne, they had the very same privileges male performers did to engage in corporate decision making.[32] Though the presuppositions of the modern gender order were penetrating French culture by the mid-eighteenth century, it was still not "natural" to find life organized around the ideal of a male public sphere and a female private sphere. French society was at an early stage of assimilating the implications of male autonomy. The Old Regime, influenced by royal absolutism and biblical patriarchy, offered a different paradigm for women.[33] Men and women shared the same destiny—as superiors and inferiors—within a workshop, the royal court, the theater, or any other institution. Traditional patriarchy infused early modern culture with a profound suspicion of women's influence over men. Women became disorderly by escaping their divinely ordained subordination to a master and exerting undue influence. In practice, it was often impossible to distinguish modern from biblical patriarchy. Until 1789, the agenda of the modern gender order had to be articulated through the political language of the Old Regime. Political reformers, and eventually revolutionaries, would move toward an understanding of the new gender order, in part by examining the legitimacy of actresses' place in the public sphere.

State building and absolutism in France since the Renaissance had laid the foundations for a private sphere in which husbands had legal authority over wives and women were excluded from rights vested in feudal practices (including the inheritance of property). The crown's goal, however, had not been to empower men and ensure the subordination of women, but rather to break the influence of clans and to confirm the authority of the French state over men.[34] In fact, far from confining women to the household, kings offered certain groups of privileged women visible roles in their absolutist public sphere. The French monarchy was based on repeated displays of its splendor, exalted roots, and solemnity, and women had a place in the spectacle.[35] No one would have thought to describe the royal court as a male institution in which women were to be as inconspicuous as possible. Royal theater was an analogous institution. Under Louis XIII, the crown started to encourage the kinds of plays that needed female performers and to permit women on the stage, even making them a part of royal companies.[36] It did so to shape courtly culture. During the formative era of the royal troupes, theater was one of the ceremonies that made visible the imaginary body of the king, which was the incarnation of the French nation in the seventeenth century. Even before the Sun King's reign had come to an end in 1715, the royal body had been absorbed into the machinery of state.[37] Theater became less a matter of sacred spectacle and more a matter of the king's giving art and diversion to his people. Actresses also served the crown in this public capacity.[38]

The regulations governing the Comédie-française, France's first theater, adhered to the accepted Old Regime paradigm for women. Men and women were part of the same institution, in this case, a general assembly that met weekly to consider all the matters that concerned the troupe. A distinctive feature of the Comédie was that female thespians had as much right as males to vote and express their opinion. The expected subordination of women took the form of the troupe's theoretical control by the First Gentlemen of the Bedchamber, who ran the theater in the king's name. Although the Comédie was organized according to this conventional pattern of authority in absolutist France, the theater did have a well-deserved reputation for gender disorder because in practice, troupe members, and particularly the female ones, did not remain in their proper place. Royal officials had to struggle to maintain even a modicum of control over the thespians.

Large egos abounded at the Comédie. The king himself had to accept with good humor Madame Dangeville's refusal to perform at court because the travel tired her.[39] Frequently putting orderly administration to the test was the highly contentious matter of selecting the new plays. Even well-disposed observers admitted that the assembly did not always judge plays on their own merits. Performers paid more attention to their own roles than to the quality of the plays. Troupe members used their influence to accept plays that had the sole merit of giving them a pithy part, and they were known to vote against scripts that gave rivals good roles. In addition to this source of disputes, performers did favors for friendly playwrights, and protectors interfered to get desirable roles for their lovers. Regulations issued in 1719 noted that assembly meetings were quarrelsome and that "sharp comments" were often made.[40] Such deliberations became only more tumultuous as the century progressed.

The female players were just as strong headed, stubborn, and self-assertive as the actors. Denis Papillon de la Ferté, the royal officer (*intendant des menus plaisirs*) charged with daily oversight of the troupe, would have described *all* his underlings as impossible to govern. However, he thought about female and male performers in different terms, and the differences had more to do with the cultural filter he applied than with actual behavior. Both men and women formed strategic alliances, brought in powerful protectors, threatened disruptions, and appealed to emotional principles in order to prevail. Nonetheless, actresses' disturbances loomed larger in his vision. Their power plays were likely to be described as the sexual manipulation of influential men and, hence, particularly heinous. Ferté complained that the First Gentlemen had liaisons with women in the troupe, with the result that actresses had "lost all sense of subordination." Not only Ferté but the actors, as well, lamented that actresses used their bodies so effectively that there was no way to control them.[41]

Squabbles over desirable roles were not the only occasions for actresses to exercise their power within the general assembly. Mademoiselle Clairon, one of the great tragic actresses of the eighteenth century, demonstrated that a theater woman could advance serious ideological principles and lead "public opinion" in righteous protest. Clairon was amazingly resourceful and a charismatic personality. She had risen above a sordid past to become an admired figure on stage and within Le Monde. She was respected by the most celebrated writers of the day, among them Voltaire, for her intelligence. During the 1760s, Clairon became not only the outstanding member of the troupe but also an enlightened reformer. She forced the royal administration and the public to focus on the injustice of actors' excommunication because of their profession.[42]

Clairon started working behind the scenes in 1761 to throw doubt on the legal basis for the church's condemnation of performers. She urged other players and her writer friends to speak out on the issue. Several years later, she led the troupe to fight for its dignity in the incendiary Dubois affair. Dubois was an actor who had dishonored himself by lying in court testimony. Aroused by Clairon, the troupe refused to work with him. However, one of the Gentlemen was sleeping with Mademoiselle Dubois, and he insisted on including the miscreant in the cast. Clairon and several colleagues were incarcerated for their disobedience. The events moved beyond being one more confrontation between the troupe and the Gentlemen to become a cause célèbre. The public was moved by the punishment, and society ladies even visited Clairon in her cell. When the king indicated that he was willing to meet the troupe halfway by eventually dismissing Dubois after the artists had obeyed his orders, Clairon opposed the compromise.[43] She decided to put her career on the line for the sake of her cause by informing the Gentlemen that she would not return to the stage until the king ameliorated the church's harsh position on thespians. Clairon did win several concessions from the crown, including permission to reprint letters patent from Louis XIII (dating from 1641) that removed moral blame from actors, but she was not satisfied and ultimately retired from the stage in protest.[44] Clairon had used her crucial position within France's first theater to make herself a voice of conscience and reason. She contributed to the emergence of "public opinion" by using conflicts at the Comédie to express opposition to royal policy.[45]

Clarion's protests of the 1760s were among the last instances in which the troupe of the Comédie was viewed as being on the side of enlightened reform. As a privileged royal theater that guarded its position jealously, the Comédie could easily be seen as a beneficiary of indefensible regulations and of ministerial despotism. Controversy increasingly focused on the theater in this light because of growing public displeasure with the performances and because playwrights resented the autocratic treatment they received from the troupe. Since the Comédie was France's most prestigious stage, authors urgently wished to place their scripts there. Yet men of letters had little confidence that they would get a fair reading. They deplored the intrigues within the general assembly and were upset that there was no court of appeal.[46] It undoubtedly occurred to some writers that actresses' sexual liaisons played far too large a role in decision making. Even an actress, Madame Gaussin, accused Clairon of having seduced a playwright to get a part she wanted.[47] Despite the suspicions of female intrigue, makers of public opinion did not yet question the fundamental legitimacy of women exercising power within the Comédie. The reformers contested the privileges of the troupe as a whole.

Starting in the 1770s, authors began to make their resentments known by appealing to the tribunal of public opinion for redress. When Louis XVI came to the throne in 1771, he opened an era in which the crown seemed ready to listen to complaints against ministerial despotism. A group of "Frondeur journalists" took advantage of the moment to attack the Comédie-française as one of the corrupt institutions of the day. Among these reformers were playwrights whose scripts had been rejected. They raised their personal grievances to a higher plane by portraying themselves as "Romans" and "patriots" defending the public good. The writers argued forcefully that the Comédie was not the school of morality that it should be and did not serve the nation well.[48]

Mercier, who was involved in a lawsuit against the Comédie, was among the Frondeur journalists. His protests against the actors' abusive treatment of authors appeared not only in the opposition press but also on stage. His one-act play of 1777, Les Comédiens ("The Actors"), used sarcasm to expose the injustices. Early on in the play, a thespian informs a young, promising playwright that the troupe will get around to reading his script—in three or four years. Ultimately, the troupe's laziness, arrogance, and indifference to the public good compel the ghost of its venerated founder, Jean-Baptiste Molière, to return and rebuke his successors. Molière warns them that the public is angry and will cease attending if their misbehavior continues. However, Mercier was too cynical to present the players as chastened. In the final line of the play, an actor recalls that the Comédie still has its privileges to protect it from public wrath.[49]

It is telling that Mercier's play failed to single out actresses as particularly pernicious. At one point, Molière's ghost chides the female performers, "who waste their time in bedrooms and often are illiterate," and instructs them to "act with justice rather than get involved with intrigue."[50] However, Mercier saw actresses as only part of the problem. He condemned the entire troupe and did not specifically call for eliminating female influence. Neither did Rétif when he thought about reforming the process of selecting plays. Rétif proposed a selection committee that included actors or actresses based on the quality of their judgment rather than on their gender.[51]

Another controversy in the mid-1770s gave reformers an opportunity to examine actresses' participation in decision making within theaters. Charles Palissot de Monteroy submitted a play, Les Courtisanes, ou l'école des moeurs ("The Courtesans, or School for Morality") to the Comédie in 1774.[52] The troupe rejected the script twice for being scandalous, but its author was able to put enough pressure on the royal administration to get the play produced. By transforming his rejection into an indictment of the moral character of the Comédie-française, Palissot created a serious public issue. He claimed to have exposed the troupe's indifference to the sacred task of moral instruction.[53]

The power of actresses within the Comédie was at the center of this controversy; they were rumored to be behind the rejection of the play because they were afraid of being associated with the immoral characters. Palissot and his lawyer, Nicolas François de Neufchâteau, pointedly reminded the female thespians that the public would scorn the prudery they feigned in finding the play too bold.[54] However, the conflict did not escalate into an attack specifically on the actresses' authority within the troupe. Palissot and his supporters addressed their grievances to "Messieurs, les Comédiens," used the political language of the Old Regime, and did not question the legitimacy of actresses' making decisions for the theater. The conflict produced only gendered accusations. For example, the writer Alexandre du Coudray supported Palissot by likening the general assembly to "10 or 12 women just freed from the arms of their imperious lovers who . . . suddenly remember that they are at a reading. And without understanding anything, protest that the play is detestable, the comedy is indecent."[55] Although "patriot" reformers might portray the entire troupe as feminine in its deceitfulness, they did not grasp fully the implications of the modern gender order, which would have authorized removing women from positions of authority for the sake of good government.

Efforts to reduce female influence within the Comédie came more from the crown than from the public. In 1766, a royal decree began to remove power from the general assembly by creating a committee, composed only of male actors, with the task of screening scripts and submitting the worthy ones to the full assembly. A more exclusionary step came in 1780, when a committee composed of six actors and two actresses received the right to evaluate scripts previously in the hands of the entire assembly.[56] Actresses still had a presence, but the female artists were singled out for a reduced role in running the theater. The crown's policy was probably guided more by the Old Regime paradigm of giving women a subordinate place within the public sphere than by the modern notion of women in the public as unnatural. Before 1789, France did not have to face the gender implications of the transfer of sovereignty to the people. Once the nation became sovereign in 1789, it suddenly and urgently needed the same civic virtue as Geneva. The revolutionary change made actresses' participation in the public sphere highly problematical.[57]

Actresses Face the Sovereign Nation

That theater women would be capable of participating in the sacred task of national regeneration facing the French people in 1789 was called into question even before the Bastille fell. As France drew up its grievance lists (*cahiers de doléances*) in anticipation of the meeting of the Estates-General during the spring, a satirical one claiming to speak for the personnel of the royal theaters appeared.[58] The pamphlet portrayed performers as being perverse enough to select actresses as their officials, and the theater women went on to confirm their intractability by making blatantly irresponsible demands. The actresses claimed for the royal actors the right to do whatever they wished, when they wished, without any accountability to the public. The pamphlet showed theater women—and anyone under their influence—to be egregiously out of step with a France needing patriotism and good citizenship.

Among the ways that the French Revolution created modern politics was by establishing new relations between women and power.[59] So long as the sacred monarchy remained the fundamental organizing principle of public life, reformers characterized corruption and ministerial arbitrariness as feminine but did not reject a place for women in the royal public sphere. Once the acceptance of a social contract between the state and the people became the foundation of public life, the role of women in decision making became threatening. Male reason had to prevail over womanly wiles, and female instincts for morality had to be channeled into domesticity. For the Comédie, where actors struggled to keep actresses from being more than their equal, the gendering of power meant that actresses had to come firmly under male guidance or be excluded entirely from decision-making roles. They could not be trusted to reform the theaters of France.

The male actors at the Comédie began to confront the nature of modern gender roles as the troupe met to draft its grievance list. A new and pressing reform came into focus: excluding female members from the general assembly. Even though the majority of the thespians would eventually regret the disappearance of the Old Regime, they were in tune with the hopes of national regeneration in the spring of 1789. Their deliberations took place in an atmosphere of crisis for their theater. The troupe members knew that public distrust was strong, that they had a reputation for arrogance and indifference to the general welfare, and that authors were intent on having the troupe's privileges revoked. No wonder that the actor Saint-Phal opened the meeting with the promise that "the French people will be able to come en masse to the theater for grand lessons in *patriotism* [his emphasis] and virtue."[60]

The urgency of teaching lessons in virtue had implications for actresses' publicness. The male artist Naudet, who would be pro-Revolutionary in the future, opened a heated debate by proposing to remove women from the assembly. He did so on the grounds that "they are excluded by the law from all virile functions."[61] Whether Naudet meant the laws of nature or French law as understood through a Rousseauist gloss is not clear. In any case, no such effort at exclusion had arisen before, even though actors had often deplored the excessive influence actresses wielded. In this moment of national regeneration, governance became a virile function, and women's presence was intolerable to some. Mademoiselle Raucourt, an actress unlikely to be associated with virtue in the public mind, immediately defended her rights. Claiming that laws excluding women were "absurd, unjust, and tyrannical because in letters, art, and combat a women is worth a man," she refused to leave. Other actresses seconded her protest. In the end, by a vote of nineteen to eight, the assembly decided to allow actresses to participate. However, the vote was not so one-sided as it seemed, because the balloting was confused by a second issue, whether one actor who claimed to be noble could be present at this meeting for members of the Third Estate.[62] The new notion of excluding women was appealing enough that it would have carried if actresses had not lined up against their male colleagues.[63]

The assembly then proceeded to take a stance that Riccoboni, four decades earlier, would have found congenial: placing the onus for grievances against the theater on actresses.[64] Dugazon, one of the actors who would actively support the Revolution, blamed his female colleagues for the odious reputation of the profession. Though Dugazon, himself, had once been the cause of scandal by speaking familiarly to the queen at the Opéra ball of 1778, he now insisted that the assembly must punish actresses' scandalous behavior for the sake of national regeneration. The only way to improve conduct would be by "showing inflexibility in dismissing all unwed actresses who become pregnant," he said. Dugazon also proposed firing any married actor who allowed his wife to misbehave. The proposal took aim at actresses' public sexuality.[65] Once an inconvenience or occasional embarrassment, actresses' participation in aristocratic libertinism now was unacceptable to Dugazon. Madame Vestris, his sister, answered that the sanctions would undermine artistry, for "a woman who must constantly restrain the urging of the heart would soon extinguish the sacred fire that allows the abandon, the delirium of passion, that produces grand effects on stage." Vestris's defense of actresses' exceptionalism would be repeated throughout the next century, but 1789 was not an opportune moment. The assembly voted sixteen to thirteen to expel all unmarried actresses who became pregnant and to "urge" all husbands to keep close guard over their wives.[66]

This was a significant reversal of opinion for the troupe. A variation on the issue of single motherhood had arisen just a few years earlier, in March 1782. The Gentlemen had fined Louise Contat for missing performances because she was pregnant. The assembly protested with vehemence against the sanction. Molé, an actor who would later embrace the Revolution, called the fine "an act against the laws of nature." Mademoiselle Doligny called for "according [women] the liberty to make children." Even Dugazon had denounced the punishment. It looked to him like a "a law against nature and against decency."[67] Though the two incidents were separated by only seven years, the new political culture organized around popular sovereignty made the difference. Actresses' special role as courtesans to the great ones had still appeared legitimate before 1789. Even Dugazon had not yet perceived one universal model of comportment for womanhood. These assumptions fell away once the nation recovered its sovereignty and a Rousseauist notion of public virtue came to seem necessary.

The debate within the Comédie over women in the public sphere suggests that the French Revolution was masculinist from its inception. It was not the case that the revolutionaries opened political possibilities for women only to reverse themselves later because groups of females proved to be too potent a political force.[68] In 1782, the laws of nature seemed to protect theater women who gave birth out of wedlock, but in 1789, single parenthood for women became scandalous. Purifying the troupe through male governance, excluding women, and putting females on a pedestal all flowed from the revolutionary ideology of popular sovereignty.

Put on notice that they must defer to male citizens, theater women did not have to experience the Revolution as a threat to their way of life. In

Having excluded women from the public sphere in 1789, revolutionaries no longer dwelled on the dangers posed by theater women, but individual performers could still raise suspicion. Actresses, dressed as harlots, line up with aristocrats and prelates to plot with the king in this cartoon published in a radical journal in 1790.

fact, one crescendo of outrage against them had already passed by 1790. Just because the new regime succeeded in laying the foundations for the modern gender order, stage women stirred less anxiety than before. No political leader seriously proposed applying the utopian plans to regenerate theater women along the lines laid down by the Merciers or Rétifs of prerevolutionary France. By exercising prudence, actresses might have carried on much as before behind the scenes, but some brought suspicion on themselves by supporting the enemies of those in power.

Despite its willingness to deal sternly with public women at the Comédie, the troupe put itself on a collision course with the Revolution from early on. This was partly because the theater was one of the privileged monopolies that the new order promised to eliminate. It was also because many of the artists identified so strongly with their highborn patrons and protectors that the ideal of equality held little attraction. The troupe tried at first to treat the revolutionary authorities with the same high-handedness it had used with the royal administration. Tensions arose in the fall of 1789, when the National Assembly transferred governance of the Comédie from the king to the city of Paris. The troupe members voted defiantly in December to retain the title "actors of the king." Mademoiselle Raucourt, who was about to add counterrevolutionary to her unsavory reputation, declared, "Never will I take orders from a municipal officer who is my candle maker or dry goods merchant."[69] By the end of the first year of the Revolution, relations between the Comédie-française and the new authorities were in a state of crisis. The immediate cause was the "*Charles IX* affair," a deadlock over performing a notorious play by Marie-Joseph Chénier that had strong antiroyalist overtones. Revolutionaries wanted *Charles IX* on the program, while the majority of players refused. One of the troupe's rising stars, François Talma, sided with revolutionary opinion, while Mademoiselle Raucourt and Louise Contat (the latter was notorious for having been the mistress of the king's brother, the count d'Artois) led the opposition.[70] A cartoon in Camille Desmoulin's radical newspaper, *Les Révolutions de France et de Brabant,* represented the troubles in early October 1790. It depicted two indecently dressed actresses (Contat and Raucourt, no doubt) presenting the keys of the theater to Louis XVI. The legend, "Sire, we close," was a double-entendre linking sexual scandal to counterrevolutionary plot.[71]

Although theater women were adding counterrevolution to their other manifestations of unruliness, the fears of disorder that actresses inspired were no longer great by the time of the *Charles IX* affair. Even the radical journalists, though ideologues imbued with Rousseauist anti-feminism, refused to attribute much gravity to the actresses' intransigence. Jean-Paul Marat's *L'Ami du peuple* did not consider the affair worth covering. Desmoulin's *Revolutions de France* treated the actresses' royalism only in a letter to the editor, which reviewed the conflict in bland terms and described the speeches made by Raucourt and Contat in support of the Old Regime as "frivolity."[72] Though another radical newspaper, Louis Prudhomme's *Révolutions de Paris*, followed the *Charles IX* affair in greater detail, it did not express outrage either. The two actresses particularly created controversy the night (in early November 1790) they read a letter denouncing Talma to the audience. "This ceremony was performed," noted the reporter, "with all the pomp and dignity due to these erotic highnesses." The writer mocked Contat for her insolence in telling the audience that it must submit to her will. Yet the journal claimed that the reaction of the spectators in the pit and balcony, *le peuple,* was subdued. The sovereign people were indifferent to this female display of perfidy. When Contat mentioned her sense of morality, laughter arose from the pit. After hearing the letter, the spectators shrugged their shoulders, settled down, and the evening went on as if nothing significant had happened.[73]

By contrast, Prudhomme was capable of outrage when male performers engaged in counterrevolution. Just a few weeks after Contat and Raucourt were featured, the radical newspaper reported a royalist demonstration at the Opéra. Some members of the audience had encouraged the chorus to repeat a verse that praised the queen. The male singer, Lainez, had stepped forward and told the audience, "Gentlemen, all good Frenchmen ought to love their king and queen." This affair did not meet with indifference. Prudhomme claimed that when word spread, all the neighborhoods of Paris were indignant. Patriots attended the next performance and booed Lainez. The audience forced him to cast aside the crown of laurels he had received on the previous night, and *le peuple* stomped on it.[74] Prudhomme's accounts of the two events show the gendering of politics that had occurred since the opening days of the Revolution. Actresses' support for counterrevolution was no longer worthy of outrage. Prudhomme had not even connected Raucourt and

Contat to the aristocratic plot; their sin was to confound the will of the people, who wanted to see the Chénier play. The male singer, however, was dangerous, and patriotic Frenchmen had to discipline him.

Even the radicals had lost their ability to perceive theater women as (in Mercier's words) "the most dangerous women the imagination can grasp." This was because the Revolution had etablished male governance by giving adult men (at least those who had some property) full citizenship. The separate spheres were on their way to being realized, "restoring" men and women to their rightful places. The new institutions of the nation offered hope that unruly women could not easily pervert male reason. Furthermore, the regime of equality would presumably put an end to aristocracy, theater women's special area of domination. The high born now had to assimilate into the nation. The aristocrats' public sexuality and extravagances would become a disgrace, not a mark of prestige. The events of 1789 had presumably created a new elite, defined by reason, responsibility, and public virtue. The reign of Liberty, Equality, and Fraternity appeared to have rendered actresses' bodies harmless.

Though the radicals who led France during the Terror were committed to a rhetorical war of virtue against vice, actresses who could avoid the taint of counterrevolution had little to fear, even when their sexual conduct was scandalous.[75] Theater women applied for and received certificates of good citizenship from the Jacobin authorities. Even Mademoiselle Guimard, remembered for her ties to Marie-Antoinette, obtained one, though not on the first try.[76] However, in the summer of 1793, the troupe members (male and female) at the Theater of the Nation did go too far by performing a play that offended militants. The performers were arrested and were slated for the guillotine when a clerk saved them by purposely misplacing their papers. Ultimately, the radical leaders of the Republic of Virtue did not pursue rigorous measures for moralizing theater women and did not even give the problem much attention.

Female performers during the Revolution did not so much change their behavior as adapt to new circumstances. The circle of highborn men who had once been their lovers was in disarray as a result of emigration and persecution. However, libertinism did not disappear. The national political and economic elite thrust forward by the Revolution stepped into the void. A gathering at the home of Julie Talma, a former actress and wife of the actor who had earned Raucourt's enmity, showed that republican deputies had replaced courtiers. Leading Girondin politicians (republicans who opposed the more radical Jacobins), including Pierre Vergniaud, Jacques Brissot, and Jean Boyer-Fonfrède, attended the reception, intended to celebrate the military victories of General Charles Dumouriez in Belgium. Their female companions were stage women. Suddenly, Jean-Paul Marat, voice of Jacobin virtue, burst into the drawing room with members of the Committee of General Security. The Friend of the People thundered at Dumouriez, around whom rumors of an anti-Jacobin coup swirled, that he "was hoping not to find [the general] in such a house, in the midst of such a collection of concubines and counterrevolutionaries." The next day, the radical press denounced the conspiracy Marat had uncovered.[77] That segment of the press would have been loathe to acknowledge that Jacobins, themselves, were not always innocent of keeping mistresses.[78]

When the Terror ended in 1794, the surviving republican leaders felt comfortable reviving an elegant sociability. They allowed actresses not only to recover their position in worldly sociability but to improve it. Theater women advanced out of the shadow of opprobrium into a new role, that of society ladies.[79] Once relegated to mostly male sociability, theater women could now mingle with respectable ladies. The rich and powerful of the post-Terror Republic paid little heed to Rousseau's ideal of a gender-segregated society. Instead, actresses hosted salons and balls. Before the Revolution, they had presided over only late-night *soupers*, and though the gatherings may occasionally have had a literary quality, they were still associated with debauchery. Now the elite of the new regime found themselves tolerating and even participating in the renewed practice of libertinism, but in a way that was less public than earlier.[80] Republicans resorted to separating appearances from practice. They deemed it sufficient to uphold the priciple of domestic virtue through words and did not count it a grave fault (for men) to violate the principle through deeds. By insisting on the sanctity of the private sphere, revolutionaries had created a realm in which family virtue should be practiced and in which covert deviations only honored the ideal.

When Napoleon Bonaparte took charge of the Republic in 1799 with the intention of shaping it to his will, he continued the policy of tolerating theater women in high society. Indeed, Napoleon took the seemingly incongruous position of promoting actresses as fashionable ladies *and* encouraging the revival of aristocratic libertinism. Actresses, particularly Louise Contat, retained their place as salon mistresses. She and Mademoiselle Lange appeared at dinner parties attended by Joséphine and other female members of the Bonaparte family.[81] When Mademoiselle George, a beautiful newcomer to the Comédie-française and a student of Raucourt, excited audiences, the wily minister Charles Talleyrand thought it perfectly appropriate for her to open a salon. He urged on her the role of salon mistress despite her youth and lack of any pretense to sophistication. Talleyrand may have been hoping that her salon would eclipse Contat's, which was too royalist.[82] During the Hundred Days, when Napoleon was struggling to retain power, he invited Mademoiselle Mars, a rising star at the Comédie-française, to take a seat on his reviewing stand. His indiscreet glances in her direction had the public buzzing. Some observers suggested that he was trying to co-opt some of her popularity.[83]

The revival of court life under Napoleon renewed the Old Regime display of public sexual prowess by prominent males. With approval from the head of state, titled men reestablished liaisons with theater women. The battle-tested officer corps pursued performers at the Opéra with such zest that Napoleon had to recruit nubile young girls from the provinces as energetically as he conscripted soldiers.[84] Napoleon even promoted the keeping of theater women by example. He had ephemeral affairs with Mademoiselle Branchui of the Opéra; Louise Rolandeau of the Théâtre-italien; Guiseppina Grassini, a singer from Milan; and Joséphine Duchesnois, a tragic actress at the Comédie-française.[85] His most enduring sexual adventure, which was an open secret for the public, was with Mademoiselle George. When writing her memoirs under the Second Empire and hoping for a pension from Napoleon's nephew, George described the affair as a model of patriarchal relations. She, virginal and naive, agreed to the liaison at first out of duty and awe for the nation's leader but soon came to love him for his tenderness. In spite of her growing love, she never forgot how insignificant she was in the life of her master, who was necessarily preoccupied with affairs of state. Therefore, every act of attentiveness filled her with gratitude.[86] In reality, the affair, which lasted two years, was nothing like the model. After the Consul decided to sleep with the beautiful actress, he had to send her current lover, a foreign prince, packing. Both Napoleon and George had other lovers between their trysts. Reports from spies made Napoleon well aware that he shared George with several other men.[87] The example that came down from on high was not much different from the courtly libertinism of the Old Regime.

Whenever Napoleon perceived that the Revolution jeopardized his high standards of patriarchal control, he was capable of acting decisively to rectify the situation.[88] However, he was content to allow theater women to remain in high society. Rather than fearing their potential to rule men and infect the rest of society with disorder, Napoleon shared the hope of most Frenchmen for the general domestication of women. A few women out of their proper place and serving men's pleasure did not alarm him.

Emerging public opinion in the prerevolutionary decades was alarmed by the way women's bodies corrupted men's capacity to reason. The public was also troubled by women's participation in royal institutions but found it harder to articulate the dangers of it within the political language of the Old Regime. Once the French people made a revolution and proclaimed themselves sovereign in 1789, they had to clarify their position on public women and quickly found them profoundly unnatural. The Revolution made self-government plausible by creating a new kind of public sphere, characterized by male suffrage (often limited to the qualified few), open debate, and freedom of civic activity.[89] With the establishment of the institutional and ideological bases for the rule of male reason, fears of disorder from theater women remained low through the next two regimes. The public was prepared in the first half of the nineteenth century to explore the ways that theater women might exemplify the ideals of true womanhood.

4

Magdalenes of Postaristocratic France, 1815–1848

During Napoleon's final captivity on the isle of Saint Helena, he came to interpret his personal involvement with theater women as incompatible with the legacy he wanted to leave. He wished posterity to believe that there had been only one liaison with an actress, the affair with Mademoiselle George, and he presented it as nothing more than a passing adventure.[1] Isolated on Saint Helena, Napoleon could not have been aware of developments on the Continent; yet his retreat into denial coincided with a closing down of options for theater women. France's dominant political groups between Napoleon's downfall and the Revolution of 1848, however bitterly divided they were on many issues, could agree on returning theater women to outcast status and segregating them from respectable women.

Nonetheless, the symbolic exclusion of theater women was inherently problematical because society in the first half of the nineteenth century was no longer fearful of actresses' powers to subvert the civic order. The Bourbon and Orleanist constitutional monarchies, with their active public spheres and with suffrage limited to France's wealthiest 100,000, then 300,000 men, continued the expectation, born of the Revolution, that men would be strong and reasonable. Since theater women were not deemed threatening, ostracizing them was a contentious matter. Opponents of the ruling elite fastened on the contradiction to charge it with hypocrisy. Even those who supported the status quo could not be bothered to defend the exclusion with conviction.

The Politics of Domestic Virtue

The Old Regime aristocrats who came back from exile with the re-stored Bourbon monarch in 1815 were chastened and insecure. They were determined to do what was necessary to reinvigorate respect for social hierarchy and privilege. Central to their strategy was support for the authority of the Catholic Church, including a conspicuous display of conformity to its moral laws. Aristocratic women, contrite about the ways their own prerevolutionary liberties might have contributed to the fall of their caste, were ready to accept domesticity and piety as essential to good order in the kingdom.[2] A renewal of the spiritual values of the Old Regime implied a condemnation of theater women and meant returning them to their old status as outcasts. The effort to do so, however, exploded into public disorder when the notorious actress Raucourt died in 1816. The priest in her parish, supported by ultraroyalist court-iers, refused to give her a Christian burial. Forgetting her early and courageous support for the counterrevolution, ultraroyalists used her as a symbol of the debauched actress whose excommunication was an ancient church practice. On the other side, anticlericals and liberals conveniently forgot about her brazen sexuality and saw the incident as a challenge to principles of liberty and citizenship established by the Revolution. Stirred by anger over clerical fanaticism and Bourbon despotism, a crowd stormed the parish church that would not admit Raucourt's casket. In the end, Louis XVIII had to allow the burial for the sake of maintaining public order.[3] The royal government could afford the concession, anyway, because society was becoming markedly less tolerant of theater women mixing freely with respectable ladies.

Had it not been for the aggressive stance of the clergy, the liberals would have been embarrassed to rise in defense of a Raucourt. In fact, they were just as offended as the ultraroyalists to see theater women in contact with respectable ladies. Liberals had to make actresses into pari-ahs to validate the conception of domestic womanhood consolidated by the Revolution (and on which their individualistic conception of manhood depended).[4] When the Revolution of 1830 drove the Bour-bons from the throne and gave liberal political leaders the levers of power, theater women continued to be relegated to the world of the backstage, midnight suppers, and discreet trysts. Memories of thespians having served as salon mistresses during the Directory and the Empire became so effaced that Sophie Gay's 1837 history of salons placed Louise Contat's into a distorted historical context. Gay began her account of Contat's salon by acknowledging that the very idea of an actress serving as a hostess seemed absurd and that her readers would surely assume she was describing a "boudoir."[5] To explain what now appeared to be unseemly, Gay resorted to a most peculiar rewriting of history. She described the Contat salon as a prerevolutionary phenomenon, arguing that the mixing of highborn and theater women was possible only before the Revolution had instituted formal equality; afterward, fears of social contamination were too high. In her own day, during the July Monarchy, Gay claimed, "society women would be embarrassed to appear in the drawing room of our leading actresses." Furthermore, Gay did what she could to dissociate Contat, the salon mistress, from the performer. "Nothing in this salon," the writer insisted, "recalled a theater woman, not the guests, nor the mistress, nor the home."[6] She noted that Mademoiselle Mars, still young and virginal at the time, was the only other actress admitted. When an older and more notorious Mars gave balls, male courtiers were delighted to attend, but their wives and daughters dared not cross the performer's threshold.[7]

Theater women's identity between the Restoration and the Revolution of 1848 was deeply enmeshed in the formation of two classes vying for leadership of the nation—"the bourgeoisie" against "the aristocracy." Female performers took on a political meaning as markers of difference between the two constructed groups. Stage women provided an arsenal of arguments establishing the moral deficiencies of the aristocracy and the self-control of the bourgeoisie. The arguments were all the more effective in that they were taken as definitional rather than needing substantiation.

The bourgeoisie as a ruling class was to have a unique hold on the social imagination of modern France—and on the writers who crafted the history of the nation. The bourgeoisie and its related category, the middle class, were not the outcome of centuries of economic development. There had been a "bourgeoisie of the Old Regime," but this was not a group of entrepreneurs and individualists who would one day be strong enough to challenge the aristocracy. It was defined by its imitation of the nobility.[8] When Rousseau wrote in his widely read *Lettre* on theater of 1758 that "a bourgeois would refuse to frequent the very performers that

the Great Ones have at their table every day," he was inventing a constit-
uency for his populist ideas (as later polemicists would also do). The
bourgeoisie neither made the Revolution of 1789 nor was made by it. In
fact, the Revolution failed to produce a distinctive "bourgeois" identity,
and the category was not current in the political discourse of the Revolutionary-Napoleonic era. The bourgeoisie was born after the Bourbon
Restoration, as a result of political and ideological conflict over how to
rule postrevolutionary France.[9]

The ruling class that the French Revolutionary-Napoleonic era actually bequeathed to the nation was "the notables." This was an amalgam of individuals and families with recognized local power. Some of
the families had roots in the Old Regime, and others did not. Landed
property was the most common source of wealth, but some notables had
achieved their prominence through commerce, manufacturing, or state
service. The notables were divided politically between liberal supporters
of the revolutionary reforms and conservatives who despised the Revolution.[10] Because of this division, they experienced internal conflict at
moments of political strife, such as under the Bourbon Restoration.
Then, the notables temporarily put aside what they had in common and
divided into factions under the labels "bourgeois" versus "aristocrat."

The bourgeoisie developed its self-awareness and foundational myths
out of the political contention with the ultraroyalists between 1815,
when parliamentary politics reemerged in France, and the Revolution
of 1830.[11] The struggles for and against the political influence of the
church, civil liberties, and constitutional guarantees of freedoms came to
be defined in class terms. The idiom of the bourgeoisie as a class con-
tending with the aristocracy for the leadership of French society entered
French political life. The struggle included a liberal rewriting of national
history, with François Guizot, Adolphe Thiers, and François Mignet
placing the accomplishments of the bourgeoisie at the center, as the
source of all material and moral progress. Like Rousseau before them,
the historians were claiming a social base for their liberal ideology by
imagining a progressive, prosperous, and masculine middle class, opposed to a backward-looking and feminized aristocracy.[12]

The Revolution of 1830 was the crucial moment in creating "bourgeois society" in modern France. Though there may not have been a significant transformation in the social composition of the ruling elite, the
departure of the Bourbons came to signify the victory of the bourgeoisie

over the aristocracy because of the prior cultural work on class formation.[13] To its supporters, the bourgeoisie had earned the victory by re-
affirming the accomplishments of 1789 and winning once again the
Rights of Man for the nation through its firmness and resolve. After
1830, the most self-evident group to qualify as "the ruling class" was the
bourgeoisie. The idiom was a means of making sense of the triumph of
marketplace values and liberal notions of equality as the new guiding
principles of social organization, now that the counterrevolutionary opposition had been vanquished.[14]

The cultural change that 1830 crystallized is, perhaps, best seen in the
completion of a sartorial revolution in the years following the ascent of
the Orléanists. Upper-class males gave up their flamboyant wardrobes,
decorations, and knee breeches for somber-colored suits and minimal
ornamentation. This mode of dressing had its roots among those paragons of sobriety, the English Puritans and Quakers.[15] The sartorial code
pointed to the new configuration of gender and class relations. It natu-
ralized the polar opposition between male and female attributes that had
been under construction since the late seventeenth century. Women
would continue to be objects of display and observation, while men's
clothing referred to an inner worth that could not be perceived with a
casual gaze.[16] The gendered meaning of dress also had implications for
the struggle among elites. The faction associated with the splendor of
the Old Regime aristocrats was stigmatized as feminine and weak because it had the same frivolous mode of dress as women. Moreover, the
sartorial principles that became hegemonic after 1830 announced a new
kind of individualism, superior to the sort attributed to the aristocracy
of the Old Regime. The old mode was about aristocrats competing for
reputation on the basis of appearances within a close, privileged world
that applied its particularistic standards. The new brand of bourgeois individualism called for outward conformity and modesty as achievement
took place out of sight, the result of hard work and character.

Since the bourgeoisie was born through political contention, in opposition to the aristocracy and the Bourbon monarchy, it had to advance
justifications for its own superiority. Self-control was one of the most
prized badges of identity and one of its most earnest appeals. It was
through the association with self-mastery that theater women became
part of bourgeois class-consciousness. Well before the Revolution, an
ethos of domesticity was forming in contrast to court morality and aris-

tocratic libertinism.[17] Aristocrats' hold on masculinity was something of a lost cause by the end of the Old Regime. The practice of keeping mistresses had exposed lords to ridicule for being under the control of strong women, and ideas of virile self-discipline and civic mindedness took hold. The liberals of the Restoration had everything to gain by representing titled lords as addicted to sexual self-indulgence and profligate spending on disgraced women. The bourgeoisie, in contrast, claimed to display the worthiness to rule through the discipline it exercised at home and at work.[18]

Actresses were a particularly dangerous model for the bourgeois woman. When a newspaper columnist described preening actresses at the Longchamps racetrack, for whom "neither God, nor father, nor mother, nor child, nor friend mattered, but only the [male] public," he was intentionally offering a representation that his readers would understand as the negation of the true nature of women.[19] Forging a bourgeois identity entailed engagement with theater women as Others, as a threat to the bourgeois way of life. Unlike aristocrats, the common people, and workers, the bourgeoisie was expected to resist actresses' enticements.

To a remarkable degree, the nineteenth-century organs of public opinion went along with the presumption that bourgeois men (or, more generally, men of the middling ranks) were too strong and rational to fall prey to theater women. Almost precisely a century after Rousseau ascribed the correct moral position to the bourgeoisie, a columnist for *L'Illustration* asked, "What is an actress in the eyes of a bourgeois?" The answer was that she was "the most charming creature under the sun, but for whom there is only scorn regarding her private life." The bourgeois, it seemed, was "convinced that even the ostensibly well-behaved actress has ruined many a young man," and he "supposes that acting is a cover for another sort of profession." A columnist for *Le Monde illustré,* diagnosing the wild passion for an actress that overtook some men as a mental disorder, presumed that the "monomania" victimized aristocrats and what he called the "the vulgar multitude," leaving those in the social middle unlikely to be affected.[20] Confirming this observation, *La Revue illustrée* found that a play featuring the beautiful Blanche Pierson and Céline Montaland "produced a sensation in the world of princes, diplomats, gentlemen, and artists," all of whom sent bundles of love poems and flowers to the stars.[21] One writer for *Le Figaro* described with wonder the adulation that French actresses received from audiences in Saint

Petersburg: the Russian princes lavished extraordinary sums of money on their heroines. The columnist noted that French audiences could not behave so impulsively, since the nation had become "too bourgeois."[22] An incident in Félix Pyat's 1832 novel *Les Filles d'actrices* ("The Daughters of Actresses") makes clear how the Revolution of 1830 had defined France as bourgeois and had changed the relation between theater women and their fans. An aspiring actress's mother tells her daughter that the Revolution has ruined her chance to acquire wealth: "The good times are over for theater women, the time of great lords, marshals of the Empire, the men in elegant carriages . . . Today bankers marry women and no longer keep them." The mother advises her daughter to fit into the new times by making herself into "a good bourgeois woman."[23] Extravagant behavior over theater women signified an earlier stage of social development.

The representation of middle-class restraint in the press was not based on observation of actual behavior and was not even meant to be. Rather, the comments drew on powerful political fictions. The struggle over the legacy of the Revolution's policies exaggerated the divergence in behavior and values between the upper and lower factions of the notables. Differences were accentuated in times of political contention, but when the press shifted from the language of class to one of masculine identity, it celebrated the erotic appeal of actresses. Nonetheless, the issue of domestic virtue, who did and did not have it, became an outstanding marker of class difference. As such, representations of theater women helped French people make sense of their postaristocratic social and political experience.

The construction of "bourgeois society" made the ostracism of theater women necessary from one perspective and arbitrary from another. The bourgeoisie was defending its own liberal order when it made actresses into the enemies of family and respectability. At the same time, with a ruling class like the bourgeoisie, society had nothing to fear from theater women. It would even be tempting to wax sentimental about the "charming creatures" and assimilate them into true womanhood. The many oppositional groups would seize on actresses' victimization to expose the deficiencies of the new ruling class.

Once the Revolution of 1830 installed the bourgeoisie as the ruling class (or so it was imagined and endlessly repeated), spokesmen for the class

no longer needed to affirm its superiority and could return to rebuild-
ing the integrity of the notables as a whole. Defining what the bourgeoisie stood for passed mainly to its critics—members of Le Monde,
bohemian writers, and eventually, the working class and feminists.[24]
The first two sorts of critics, in particular, used the bourgeois disdain for theater women to disparage the sensibilities of the new ruling
class. The bourgeoisie proved itself hypocritical because its individualism and respect for the virtues of womanhood did not extend to actresses. Except for certain key values relating to property and family, the
critics' antibourgeois views may well have reflected the outlook of most
French people between 1830 and the Revolution of 1848.[25]

Le Monde could tolerate bourgeois rule, but only grudgingly. The
bourgeoisie, in doing battle with the aristocracy, did not define itself as a
worldly class; it could not command the respect of the fashionable, who
scorned the bourgeoisie for lacking the blood, bearing, and indulgence
of a true ruling class. The bourgeoisie appeared drab and uninspiring.
Many who inhabited Le Monde, or were happy to speak for it, also
lacked blood and bearing, but they erected themselves into a spiritual aristocracy based on taste and refinement. Defenders of Le Monde used
"aristocratic" as a metaphor for the finest things in life.[26] Their disdain
for the pragmatic outlook ascribed to the bourgeoisie produced what has
been called "the antibourgeois bias of bourgeois culture."[27]

By the 1830s, Le Monde fused the titled, the talented, and the wealthy
into a fashionable elite. Its members defined their superiority in terms of
luxury, leisure, celebrity, and worldly intelligence *(esprit)*.[28] The combi-
nation of exclusiveness and relative openness allowed the notables to accept bourgeois values at an unacknowledged level but still extol the elegance associated with the ancient aristocracy as the highest mark of
personal distinction. Under the July Monarchy, Le Monde carved out a
conspicuous space for itself in the center of the capital, the Boulevard,
and shaped it into the antithesis of Louis-Philippe's bourgeois monarchy.[29] The dandies, young men who dressed with ostentatious and inten-
tional elegance in violation of the new functional code of male dress,
displayed themselves as a rebuke to bourgeois practicality. Dandies considered themselves self-created aristocrats.[30] One of the most observed
of the sort, Charles de Morny, wore a studied air of nonchalance and arrogance as he strolled the Boulevard. Worldly young men admired his
attitude of elegant discontent and imitated it. That Morny had made a

fortune growing sugar beets did not reduce his disdain for "the bourgeoisie."[31]

Demonstrations of bourgeois restraint were not welcome on the exclusive Boulevard of the July Monarchy. The newspaper *L'Illustration* presented a portrait of the Boulevard in 1845 and found it to be the "province of young Parisian aristocrats." The author of the article clearly understood the values of the Boulevard as the antithesis of the dominant bourgeois ones: "The Parisian displays himself like an actor who plays his role for an elite audience and condemns himself to a gaze that is difficult to satisfy."[32] The description was a denial of the deepest meaning of the bourgeois sartorial revolution. The Boulevard seemed to reaffirm the sense of the externalized, aristocratic individuality inherited (or so it was imagined) from the Old Regime. It returned men to the elegant, if effeminate, role of being performers before an exclusive audience.

Those "actors" on the Boulevard frequently met genuine actresses there. Stage women participated in the male-centered, late-hour sociability of the cafés and restaurants. In addition to physical propinquity, there were spiritual ties. Theater women provided links to a tradition of aristocratic display and self-indulgence. Liaisons with theater women continued to confer prestige, and they were among the liveliest subjects of gossip in Le Monde. Actresses created an aura of excitement that allowed Boulevard men to escape what they took as the dullness of bourgeois life. As such, theater women symbolized hierarchies of taste and display in an age when fashionable people worried that social distinctions were disappearing because of postrevolutionary equality and market rationality.

Another center of concerted protest against aspects of bourgeois culture was bohemia. Indeed, the historic struggle between artists and bourgeois first appeared in Paris during the second quarter of the nineteenth century.[33] Striving artists held the bourgeoisie responsible for the grayness and conformity of the July Monarchy. They considered themselves to be the first to confront the exigencies of the marketplace in all its harshness and recalled an aristocracy of old that had been more generous to talent.[34] Many writers found the bourgeois promise of individualism and freedom filled with hypocrisy. The liberal order demanded conformity to social convention for its own sake, whereas the artists dreamed of the quest for passion and happiness, defined in intimate terms. In this conflict of values, even the legitimacy of the family came

into question. Writers rehabilitated the courtesan by making her capable
of admirable behavior.[35] Their fiction approached being sympathetic to
adultery.[36] Male writers, influenced by George Sand, gave female characters a certain freedom to pursue personal fulfillment, but they also filled
the heroines with remorse for violating society's norms. In these themes
of liberation, actresses' beauty and passion offered a sublime challenge
to bourgeois manners. Bohemian writers saw in stage women the promise of lighting a sacred fire that could scorch hypocrisy and awaken both
life and art.

Disdain for bourgeois convention easily coexisted with a contempt for
bourgeois selfishness inspired by political radicalism. Faith in *le peuple*,
revived by the Revolution of 1830, was one of the chief sources of idealism of the day. Radicals drew attention to the short-circuited nature of
the revolution, which benefited the bourgeoisie and failed to bring any
benefits to the common people. The recurrent periods of intense material hardship after 1830 engaged the sympathy of bohemians for the laboring poor, whose misery they sometimes shared.[37] In casting about for
noble symbols of the oppressed people, writers drew on actresses and
prostitutes, who made their living by indulging male sensuality. These
outcasts, like *le peuple*, incurred the scorn of proper bourgeois, but were
depicted as capable of noble conduct by artists seeking escape from conventional views.

When Le Monde and bohemia excoriated the bourgeoisie for oppress-
ing theater women, they were distorting a complex situation for their
own ideological purposes. The critics actually received a respectful hearing from a public they might have considered perfectly "bourgeois."
This was partly because a large portion of middle-class people shared the
sense of grievance against bourgeois society. If nothing else, the notorious oversupply of educated young men without jobs ensured a ready audience for protest.[38] More generally, the French population perceived
liberal institutions as falling far short of their ideals.[39] The bourgeois
population was inclined to dwell as little as it had to on actresses' evils.
Confident that the balance of power between the sexes favored men,
bourgeois leaders were not motivated to maintain strict vigilence against
strong women. Public opinion wanted to believe in the natural goodness
of womanhood and was pleased to find examples of generous behavior and womanly vulnerability among actresses. Conflicting ideological
needs produced a compromise with which the public of the July Monar-

Actresses' authority was tolerated within the Comédie-française during the 1830s, as shown by the women's inclusion in the reading committee.

chy was comfortable: keeping theater women outcasts and sympathizing with them as victims. When writers undertook to excuse actresses' moral failings and reveal their virtues, the public was ready to accept this.

Feminizing the Actress

Pierre-Joseph Proudhon argued in a tract written in the 1860s that the French Revolution had been preceded by a disastrous feminization of society and that 1789 had "remasculinized" it. Though a radical social critic, Proudhon was expressing a commonplace about the national narrative.[40] The revolutionaries' reordering of public life in 1789, confirmed by 1830, had "returned" women to their proper place in the private sphere. Even a woman of ideas who had escaped domestication, Germaine de Staël, recognized that the Revolution had given women a diminished role by substituting public opinion, a male institution, for indirect influence, at which women had excelled.[41] Confidence that male reason controlled the reins of power was much higher than it had been before 1789 and would be after 1848.

Michelle Perrot has argued that the exclusion of women from the public sphere produced a "huge investment of masculine imagination and symbolism in representing women."[42] Her insight may account for the surge of fiction featuring that problematical category of women, actresses, after the Bourbon Restoration. One must suppose that theater women became more interesting—more urgent, even—to the French social imagination as citizens of postrevolutionary France absorbed the shift in gender understandings that had occurred. These characters allowed authors to pose important questions about the place of strong women in "bourgeois society."

The plays and novels written between 1815 and 1848 that featured theater women were overwhelmingly sympathetic to them—there is hardly a counterexample to cite.[43] Certainly, female performers were portrayed as being outside respectable society. However, the authors insisted that theater women had instincts for self-sacrifice that would redeem their past sins. The confidence in male, bourgeois authority of the era relieved writers from having to warn against the depredations theater women could cause. Instead, they explored the ways in which actresses approached true womanhood.

François Andrieux's *La Comédienne* ("The Actress") was probably the earliest play at the Comédie-française to have a stage woman as the central character. It opened in 1816, the same year as the scandal over burying Raucourt, and it ridicules the prejudice against actresses' circulation in high society. The protagonist, Madame Belvale, is not only "the first actress of Bordeaux" but also a gracious society lady who has the elite of the city to her table. In the course of the play, she must teach reason to Monsieur de Gourgnac, who has forbidden his nephew to marry a charming ingenue. Gourgnac describes himself as the "declared enemy" of theater women because they are "sirens." The nephew, as he sees it, is "hopelessly attracted to actresses' flesh." Belvale exposes Gourgnac's prejudices by having him fall in love with her and then revealing her profession. He begs to marry her even so; she agrees to it—without promising to retire from the stage—if he proves that he can correct his poor judgment by permitting his nephew to wed, too.[44] Andrieux's script involves a strong woman plotting against a foolish man—a situation that might have been, and later would be, offensive to the bourgeoisie—but in this case the plotting is condoned by the triumph of reason over prejudice.

Casimir Delavigne's *Les Comédiens* ("The Troupe") of 1820 treats the indignities that playwrights suffer at the hands of performers.[45] The subject might have offered an occasion to berate actresses for their indifference to art, but Delavigne was characteristically sympathetic to them. Victor, a poet in love with the virtuous actress Lucile, needs a theatrical success to consolidate his position, and then he can marry his beloved. Unfortunately, the players raise one obstacle after another to performing his play. Finally Victor is able to trick the players into working with him, and he weds Lucile. A review in the *Journal des théâtres,* commenting on the character of Lucile, noted that it was a "ridiculous prejudice" to deny that theater women could be virtuous and that "we are beginning to admit that actresses are capable of sincere attachments and a pure love [*amour désintéressé*]."[46]

The fiction following the Revolution of 1830 confirmed the turn toward a reassuring view of theater women. Eugène Guerin's two-volume novel of 1833, *Une Actrice* ("An Actress"), mined two important literary themes of the July Monarchy, a fallen woman redeemed through love and an upright man in rebellion against hypocritical social conventions.[47] The actress Juliette has had many men willing to keep her, but she is not so corrupt as to be unable to differentiate between the heartless lords who pursue her and the virtuous commoner, Fernand, who truly loves her. Fernand, certain of his own love and willing to forgive Juliette ("Not all actresses aspire to be Messalenes.") for having yielded to temptation, begs her to marry him.[48] The actress is the one who understands how impossible it would be for her to become the wife of a respectable man. For a while the couple lives blissfully together, but poverty eventually takes its toll. With bill collectors hounding them and Juliette's luxurious habits hard to break, she leaves with a rich lover. At the very moment Fernand loses Juliette, his mother dies with a curse on her lips for her son. Fernand shoots himself fatally, and Juliette falls into a mortal fever when she learns of the suicide. The author indicts society for not allowing theater women to recapture their virtue and accept the love of a decent man.

The author Georges Touchard-Lafosse did not take a chance that readers would miss the lesson of his long (and clumsy) novel of 1834, *La Prudeur et l'Opéra* ("Prudence at the Opera"). First in the title and then in the conclusion, the author proclaims that decency can exist at the Opéra.[49] To teach that lesson, the author replays the social antagonisms of the recent revolution. The aristocrats are thoroughly evil. The hero, Louis Nicot, is a virtuous cabinetmaker, the kind of worker who fought on the barricades during the Trois Journées Glorieuses and did not resent the bourgeois victory. Louis falls in love with Victorine, a novice at the Opéra-comique, who has been endlessly pursued by roués. Victorine is weak and naive; noblemen's charms and elegant manners tempt her, but Louis keeps her on the straight and narrow path. The couple finally marries. Louis soon dies but leaves his widow with enough moral strength to resist the titled cads who lust for her. Perhaps what the author had in mind was to show how domestication of women moralized them even under the most difficult of circumstances.

By the time Victor Hugo wrote *Angelo, tyran de Padua* ("Angelo, Tyrant of Padua") in 1835, the actress as a fallen woman still capable of pure love and noble conduct was a familiar figure.[50] Hugo portrayed La Tisbe, "an impoverished actress," as a heroine who sacrifices her life to passion and duty. She is the mistress of the ruler Angelo, but really loves Rodolfo. Unfortunately, Rodolfo cares for Catarina, a Venetian noblewoman who is Angelo's wife. Tisbe comes to hold Catarina's fate in her hands when she catches her with Rodolfo. Informing Angelo would get rid of a rival and deliver Rodolfo to her. However, Tisbe martyrs herself for Rodolfo out of the purest love, and for Catarina, out of gratitude for her mother's having saved Tisbe's mother's life years earlier. Just before her martyrdom, the heroine decries her impoverished childhood, made especially bitter because "all pity went to the great ladies."[51] Tisbe's end is all the more tragic because she dies fully aware that her self-sacrifice replicates the injustices society inflicts on the low born.

Eugène Scribe, the most prolific playwright of the time, professed to despise the excesses of romantic fiction and, in return, received the scorn of romantic writers.[52] Yet when he joined with Ernest Legouvé in 1848 to adapt the life of the great eighteenth-century actress Adrienne Lecouvreur, their tale had much in common with *Angelo*. Lecouvreur's life was familiar to the educated public because, when she died mysteriously in 1730, she had been denied a Christian burial, and her friend Voltaire had used the incident to denounce the excommunication of performers. The playwrights chose not to develop this aspect of her biography and instead focused on Lecouvreur's rivalry with the duchess de Bouillon for the love of the great general Maurice de Saxe. In the Scribe-Legouvé version, the actress is the true woman, and the duchess is the virago. Beauty, graciousness, and a desire to please are the virtues Lecouvreur has to offer Saxe. Bouillon has her powerful position, and Saxe, a soldier in search of a crown, needs her support for his ambitions. Saxe gives his love to the actress, and Bouillon has her revenge by poisoning her rival before the wedding can take place. As in *Angelo*, the actress is the admirable woman and the victim of a society lady.[53]

In Gérard de Nerval's *Sylvie,* the protagonist's uncle, designated as a man of the eighteenth century, tells his nephew that "actresses are not women, and nature has forgotten to give them a heart." The young man, however, is skeptical and suspects that theater women are no longer the same as they were in the Old Regime.[54] Here, Nerval poses the central issue for authors of the first half of the nineteenth century who wrote about theater women. The writers affirmed overwhelmingly that actresses were, indeed, true women and that they did have hearts capable of genuine love. Novelists and playwrights were exploring the universal category of "woman" through the ostensible exception of the actress and finding that she was not really an exception at all.

The reviewer of Delavigne's play who conceded in 1820 that social attitudes were changing and that it was possible to believe actresses capable of sincere love was correct about his times. In fact, the writers of the day were expressing values that were not just peculiar to bohemia or to the Boulevard. They had a much wider societal resonance. There was an inclination to dismiss actresses' threatening, emasculating qualities and, instead, to perceive their womanly qualities, despite their moral failings. In this era of confidence in the authority of male reason, men could control actresses, resist their wiles, and even raise them up to their true vocation as women. Though kept apart from the females who deserved society's respect for their upright behavior, theater women were more admired than feared in the first half of the century.

Stage women were sufficiently assimilated into the dominant ideals for womanhood that the postrevolutionary era saw the birth of a new gesture for feting, honoring, and proclaiming them—presenting them with flowers. Associating performers with the beauty, delicacy, and fertility of flowers was a way to celebrate their female nature and to sentimentalize them. Flowers evoked sexuality, to be sure, but it was rooted in the natural order; they suggested maternal fertility rather than carnality. The practice of offering flowers quickly came to seem a natural and timeless act of chivalry. Yet it was actually a tradition invented at the same time the bourgeoisie was being recognized as a rising class.

Under the Old Regime, the theatergoing public had given little, if any, attention to floral gifts, and admirers did not think them appropriate tokens of esteem. Jewels, clothing, and furniture were expected from a protector. These were the marks of carnal relations between the actress and her keepers. They declared to the public both the power of Monsieur and the accessibility of the recipient. These gifts were features of a society in which the sexuality of the great lords was still public spectacle. In contrast, the nineteenth-century image of flowers raining down on a performer from adoring audiences and lovers belonged to an age that had fully assimilated the complementary natures of men and women. Female corruption had become a much uglier fact after the Revolution, and women's power over men was also more painful to acknowledge. The prestige of public sexuality had been abandoned in favor of a regime of privacy and respectable appearances. The downfall of any woman, even an actress, was now a distressing sign of social disorder. Flowers exalted the feminine qualities of the actress, those qualities they shared with respectable women. Although a gentleman could spend huge sums on rare flowers, the gift lacked the carnal implications of jewels and furnishings. The emergence of flowers as the appropriate tribute thus signified the will to disguise actresses' moral disgrace. Rather than requiring conspicuous luxuries, an actress now accepted accolades to her feminine qualities. More than ever, theater women became enmeshed in rituals that marked them as passive objects of male adulation.

Flower vendors became increasingly visible outside theaters during the First Empire, according to the actress Corvée Flore, but it is not clear from her account if the blooms were intended for performers or women in the audience.[55] The first throwing of a bouquet in a Parisian theater occurred in the summer of 1827, at the conclusion of a performance by Marie Taglione. By some accounts, the bouquet landed on the stage accidently, but the gesture sent the audience into such a rapture of approval that imitations proliferated.[56] Pressmen soon cooperated in presenting the gesture as timeless and natural. A columnist for Le Monde illustré noted in 1864 that the saying, "Diamonds are the flowers of opulent men" was a commonplace at the Opéra.[57] The aphorism showed how much flowers had become the preeminent gesture for celebrating a performer.

Even though protectors continued to give dresses and jewels to lovers on the stage, nineteenth-century society columnists gave their moral support to the floral tokens of esteem. To lavish jewels (not to mention cash) on a theater woman was to pass into the realm, if not of vulgarity, then of opulence and aristocratic excess. One writer noted that men in Italy and Spain still gave jewels to performers but that Frenchmen now disdained the practice. Even the boyars of Russia, holdovers from feudal society, were developing the good taste to hide their gems in bouquets of flowers.[58] Now Arthur Bertrand, the son of a Napoleonic marshal and a young man who captured the hearts of several celebrated performers (including Rachel, who bore him a child), could establish a reputation for being consummately fashionable by spending more than anyone else on flowers and white gloves.[59] The writer Oscar Méténier, although short of cash, did not hesitate to spend 600 francs on flowers for actresses at the premier of his play in quest of the "reputation as a stylish man [his emphasis] one acquires in Le Monde through these floral generosities."[60] The Boulevard press portrayed the gift of flowers as an enlightened choice. The tribute allowed the gentleman to recall aristocratic libertinism while affirming verities about women's naturalness and purity.

So much had the feminine qualities of actresses come to the fore that

it was even possible to sentimentalize an infatuation with them under certain circumstances. Increasingly after 1789, young (bourgeois)
men, usually students at lycées, had cultural permission to fall in love
with an actress—and not just in a restrained manner, but passionately.
This was a development that Mercier or Rétif de la Bretonne would not
have understood at all. The eighteenth-century writers could see nothing but dangerous, sexualized contacts between young men and theater women.[61] Nineteenth-century social commentators lost the sense of
threat entirely. Actresses' stirring a schoolboy's first heterosexual yearn-
ings now seemed nothing short of the natural order of things.

In the nineteenth century, falling in love with a stage lady came to
have the status of a rite of passage in the progression from sexual in-
nocence to manhood among upper-class men (the elite who attended
secondary schools). The claim of one writer that "just about all our
school boys [*collégiens*] have desired a theater woman" rings true, if not
in actual experience then in expectations.[62] Chateaubriand, Stendhal,
Gustave Flaubert, Alphonse Lemonnier, Maxime Du Camp, Robert de
Flers, Gaston Jollivet, Henri Rochefort, and Ernest Daudet were among
the many prominent men who left testimony of having experienced
their first passion sitting in a theater and gazing upon an actress.[63] One
novel of the 1830s described the strong sentiments at issue: for the nar-
rator, just out of high school, "the theater seemed to me to be the fantastic essence of all human happiness. To be admitted into the sanctuary
[of an actress] to see these privileged beings, these divine creatures up
close—this is the most ardent desire which torments a novice's heart."[64]

Having been smitten with love, the next step in the ritual was to de-
clare it, with the naive hope of having it returned. Declaring it properly
meant writing a passionate note—and, even better, verse—to the stage
goddess. Gaston Jollivet described how he fell madly in love with Madeleine Brohan during a visit to the Comédie-française at the age of sixteen. In a state of "delirium," all he could do was to retire to a cafe and
write poems to his beloved.[65] Boulevard writers sometimes mocked the
hopeless naïveté of these declarations (which they, themselves, had often written when they were young) in their works. Nestor Roqueplan,
for example, presented samples of love letters in *La Vie parisienne* because, when read by a sober adult, they were supposed to provide a
good laugh as well as a nostalgic moment.[66] Actresses expected to receive reams of love letters each year. The performers were sometimes

piqued over the banality of the sentiments and the presumption that they wanted to hear about the young man's lust.[67] However, the actresses always returned to good humor and indulgence on the subject. Eve Lavallière resigned herself to the stream of love letters by deciding they helped to keep actresses youthful; since players lived in a constant "bath of love," she said, they aged much more slowly than did society ladies.[68]

Commentators were quite willing to ascribe idealism to the youthful adoration for an actress. As the first love, it would be the most noble and selfless one.[69] They expected the boy not to be aware of all that stood between him and his beloved. As such, the love was a metaphor for the sweet promise of life. However, they presumed that disillusionment would follow as the boy learned that the actress was inaccessible and, perhaps, not even worthy of his devotion. This realization would bring wisdom along with pain. After his heterosexual awakening and then disillusionment, the young man might be ready to transfer his affection to a proper woman and, more generally, assume up his adult responsibilities.

By serving as a boy's first love, a theater woman had a positive role to play in the development of masculine identity. There was almost no consciousness of—and no corpus of medical thought about—prepubescent sexuality during the first half of the nineteenth century. The understanding was that boys and girls remained sexually undifferentiated until puberty. This meant that the first stirrings of manhood were not at all a gradual occurrence. Passion *exploded* in the youth, who had been incapable of any sexual longing until then.[70] Actresses had the important assignment of igniting the pubescent urges. Whereas statesmen had once engaged actresses to initiate their princes in the art of making love, actresses now played featured roles in an imaginary and democratized initiation for bourgeois boys. Having arrived at the threshold of manhood, a testing of it followed. Jollivet described how schoolboys often engaged in fistfights with comrades to champion their goddesses.[71] The fiery journalist and political agitator Henri Rochefort claimed to have fallen in love with Anaïs Fargeuil when he was five years old and saw her at the Opéra-comique. The incident was not just a tiny biographical fact; it was meant to signify Rochefort's precocious and powerful manliness.[72]

Schoolboys stirred by puberty knew what was expected of them. They attended the theater assiduously and made their favorite actress into an obsession. When students in Léon Daudet's lycée class had the assignment to write an essay on the death of an important person, no fewer than three took their inspiration from the death scene in Edmond de Goncourt's theater novel, *La Faustin*.[73] The cultural permission to fall extravagantly in love with a theater woman inevitably led to excesses. A delegation of students from Louis-le-Grand, one of the most distinguished lycées in Paris, asked Jeanne Granier and Réjane to be patrons of their charitable lottery to aid flood victims in Alsace. Photographs signed by the performers were used to promote the lottery, and the grand prize was a day in the company of each actress, including a visit to the dressing room. When the school officials decided the prize was inappropriate, some students rioted and were expelled. The public registered mixed feelings about the stars' involvement, and there were troubling rumors that the expelled boys were living at Granier's home. Newspapers also reported that the singer had taken the trouble to scold the boys for their foolish behavior.[74]

Men worthy of being citizens might express their masculinity by fantasizing about actresses as lovers, but they were also supposed to exercise reason. Falling extravagantly in love with theater women was what aristocrats of the past or Russian princes did, and it defined them as belonging to a earlier stage of social development. Well-brought-up youths, however, were authorized to make fools of themselves, to idolize actresses as goddesses. It was an act of generous idealism that defied the harsh realities of life and a rite that prepared them for adult responsibility in bourgeois society.

Public opinion of the first half of the nineteenth century scrutinized the actress as never before for signs of a womanly heart within her seductive body. The perception of one required indifference to the erotic associations and practices in actresses' lives. Even as the bourgeois ruling class insisted on its moral integrity, the public expected that theater women would inflame men's senses and challenge their reasoning powers. It was an act of idealism to hope for goodness from theater women, and one had to be inspired, even moved, when it was revealed.

5

The Erotic Culture of the Stage

A newspaper society column of 1867 described audience reaction to a play at the Gymnase theater featuring two attractive performers, Blanche Pierson and Céline Montaland:

> Women in the audience look at her [Pierson] and say, "That dress is evidently from Madam Laferrière [a noted dressmaker]. No one else could make such a skirt. And the hat! It is ravishing!" Men look through their glasses and murmur under their breath, "I don't know. The blonde is softer, but the brunette is more spirited. But maybe . . . Well, the blond has a stunning mouth. And the curls on her neck. Wow!"[1]

Was the columnist about to launch into an attack on the audience for having such superficial responses to the play? Not at all. Female attention to clothing and male attention to female anatomy seemed natural to the journalist. The responses accorded with the innate qualities of men and women and identified what was elegant and worldly about the theater. The theatrical press actually encouraged the male reaction through its obsession with actresses' stunning body parts and by making *delicious* one of the most common adjectives in descriptions of theater women.

Even though public opinion of the first half of the nineteenth century was inclined to feminize and sentimentalize theater women, it never assumed that they were other than impure. Rehabilitation was an abstract possibility but not necessarily a desired state. Indeed, for many, the impurity made the feminine side all the sweeter. A young and enthusiastic Stendhal confessed that actresses excited him so much because of "their

104

freedom of habits, that audacity in speech."[2] Bourgeois men, as *men,* wanted to gaze upon erotic actresses. They even granted that keeping a theater woman was the mark of aristocratic elegance conferring prestige. Only with the triumph of republican politics after 1880 would serious cultural work be applied to de-eroticizing theater women. And even then, the impact was ambiguous.

Male Fantasies

During most of the nineteenth century the theater was *supposed* to offer a strongly erotic experience to men—and theater was intended to be more meaningful to male than female spectators.[3] Even the critics and columnists, the opinion makers who might have been expected to emphasize the artistic glories of the stage, willingly allocated a dominant

The caption of this cartoon mocks the subterfuges used to disguise the eroticism of the stage. The women says, "My friend, you embarrass me. People will think you are a dentist if you stand up like that to stare at Mademoiselle Montaland's teeth!"

place to erotic responses from the male audience. The theatrical establishment understood the eroticism to be a component of a fashionable lifestyle for the upper classes. Thus, courtesans filling the boxes
were not a moral threat but rather a contribution to the elegance and
playfulness of an evening at the theater.[4] Theater columnists explored
the stage as a male, heterosexual experience, not just because, as men,
their perspective was narrowed by the optic of gender but also because
the female spectator in this erotic vision was problematical. When a few
reformers advocated moralizing the stage, the establishment defended
theater's carnality and devised clever arguments against its purification.
A theater that was not sexually charged would have been unfamiliar, undesirable, and even un-French.

Such was the opinion of Francisque Sarcey, the most respected theater
critic of his day, when he followed the Comédie-française on its historic
trip to London in 1879, the one that catapulted Sarah Bernhardt to her
place as France's most intriguing star. Attempting to explain the frenzy
of excitement Bernhardt inspired among British audiences, Sarcey cited
an English journalist for the *Times,* who claimed that English audiences
wanted to see on stage "the graces proper to women." Bernhardt, the
British reviewer claimed, projected "purity, tenderness, weakness, and
the need for protection; in short, all that distinguishes woman from
man." Sarcey realized how hopeless this description was when applied
to the formidable Bernhardt, who was not known for her purity or
frailty. Moreover, he perceived that the hypothesis said more about British values than about the star's appeal. All this was foreign to the French.
They sought other qualities; namely worldliness and wickedness. Sarcey
heaped contempt on the British outlook because he was so proud of the
French tradition of refined libertinism, which he took to be an integral
aspect of French theatrical culture.[5] When another critic, reviewing an
1878 revival of *La Dame aux camélias,* referred to the "natural penchant
in the French character for damaged heroines," he was adopting the
same frame of reference as Sarcey.[6]

Just as youths were culturally authorized to fall in love with actresses,
adult males in the audience, even bourgeois ones, were expected to lust
after them and dream of having them as mistresses. To a significant degree, the spectator's manly identity even depended on becoming sexually inflamed by an attractive woman on stage. Responsible, middle-
class men presumably did not act on these passions, but there was no

stigma at all against lecherous thoughts. To this extent, the aristocratic privilege of cutting a dashing figure with an actress was reworked in a democratic fashion and became the daydream of many a bourgeois man.

Jules Poignard, writing on "the women of Paris" in 1889, would have instinctively agreed with Sarcey on the priapic appeal of the theater. He firmly believed that the average male spectator was there to fantasize about sleeping with one of the actresses before him:

> However desirable our wives or mistresses are, actresses enjoy a sort of privilege, a prejudice, if you will, which makes them more desirable than the others . . . We consider actresses as women to conquer, to seduce, to take . . . Besides the pleasure that we find in the troubling and radiant nudity of their arms, shoulders, throats, we embrace the vague hope that all those parts could, perhaps, be ours. We do not believe in the virtue of theater women. We know them to be, for the most part, available for affairs [*intrigantes à l'amour*].[7]

Poignard went on to give the example of a friend who made a list of actresses and began to conquer them in turn. The friend rarely failed, according to Poignard, "because a certain artfulness and care are all that is needed."[8]

The point was made many times before and would be made many times again. Octave Uzanne, writing just before the First World War, noted that "the public is accustomed to the irregular life of an actress . . . and each spectator gives himself the pleasure of imagining a possible liaison with one of these queens of the footlights."[9] Nestor Roqueplan made the same claim for male viewers earlier in the century. He cited the crowds of clerks, students, and provincials who thought of actresses as always carefree, generous, and available for a joyous adventure. It made the theater in their minds a "Hades of voluptuousness and pleasure."[10] The journalist Pierre Giffard was certain that the situation was no different in the provinces during the 1880s. When a troupe came to town, he affirmed, "all provincial men" saw actresses as potential mistresses and bombarded them with letters, gifts, flowers, and visits. Even in small towns, the theater was a "school for old libertines." The management often sold tickets to enter the wings, where men could encounter actresses and try to arrange trysts.[11]

It is easy to understand, then, why Alphonse Lemonnier would claim to have known stagehands in the 1870s who grew rich from tips received from stage-door Johnnies for delivering love notes to performers' dressing rooms. He also knew wives of stagehands who earned money advising the men who crowded at the stage door on which actresses to pursue.[12] Other observers of the playhouse reported on provincials visiting Paris who surrounded stage doors for a glimpse of their idol after performances. Each tourist dreamed of escorting her to his carriage, for the act would confer on him the awe of the crowd.[13] This fantasy reminds us that men were dreaming not only of carnal pleasure but also of worldly prestige. Boulevard journals barraged their readers with provocative images of men behaving obsessively for the love of an actress—in order to be fashionable.[14]

There was, of course, a counterdiscourse that portrayed the stage as a moralizing experience. The government often justified its subsidies for theater in terms of its being a "school of morality."[15] That idea filled official documents about the stage and occasionally excited reformers. However, the theater establishment always opposed changes that would have diminished the theater as an institution of refined libertinism. Theater men could not openly challenge the idea that plays should promote morality, but they could and did argue that reform efforts would inevitably fail and that the theater was ineluctably an erotic experience.

One of the discourses defining the erotic culture of the stage concerned the possibility of actresses marrying and living as honorable wives while they pursued their careers. This was a model of quasi respectability that the British stage offered, but it was not one that the French theatrical establishment was the least inclined to accept.[16] Theater columnists and Boulevard writers walked a fine line between seeming to approve the crude prejudices against actresses as pariahs, on the one hand, and opposing marriages, on the other hand. They did so by emphasizing the difficulties of actresses' taking husbands. A writer for *L'Illustration* made the classic case against theater women becoming wives: "One might say that an actress who married commits a minor crime [*un petit larcin*]. When she is unattached, she is the fiancée of all spectators who gaze at her or applaud her. Married, she acts unfaithfully. This sentiment is rather complex and subtle but is easily explained. The public lives by illusions, and every spectator is an aspirant [for her love]."[17] Of course, the columnist assumed the viewpoint of the male spectator and used the more polite term *fiancée* instead of *mistress*.

Alexandre Dumas's play of 1876, *La Comtesse Romani,* tackled the subject of an actress who married into high society and stressed the disastrous consequences. The reviewer for *Le Figaro* summed up the moral lesson this way: "The actress is not made for a regular life. Domestic joys are forbidden to her. The eternal salamander, she is condemned to the flames of impure passion during her life and the flames of hell after death."[18] The play provoked a good deal of discussion in the Boulevard press about marriage to a theater woman. The reviewer for the *Journal amusant* was certain that such unions would inevitably verify the old adage: "Delighted at first, desolate thereafter, and dishonored in the end."[19]

An actress's husband was a figure of derision on and off the Boulevard. The presumption that the spectator's right to fantasize about theater women was primordial informed discussions of the fate that lay in store for the husband. Writers assumed that male theatergoers would not respect the sanctity of the marriage vows and would continue to shower the performers with lover letters and gifts. Pierre Giffard gave the man who would undertake the burden of wedding an actress two choices: either tolerate the admirers who would inevitably surround his wife or withdraw and give her "the most complete liberty."[20] Jeanne Samary's experience confirmed the problem. She found it difficult to attend social engagements because "creeps [*les fats*] assume from my being an actress that they can pursue me and make disgusting proposals and then treat me like a prude when I reject them." At the same time, if her husband accompanied her, she had the uncomfortable feeling of being chaperoned.[21] Beyond ridicule, actresses' husbands were subject to rumors that they managed their wives' love affairs for profit.[22] Actresses who were faithful wives were not of much interest to the French media until late in the century.

A second discourse that validated the erotic underpinnings of the stage concerned whether a disorderly life was *professionally* necessary for a theater woman. We have already seen that Madame Vestris had made the case in 1789 that the passions actresses drew upon to move audiences were likely to lead to (or follow from) libertinism. However, the more imposing argument in the eighteenth century, advanced by Rousseau and even Diderot, had been the opposite, that virtue in an actress was a professional asset and that depravity in her personal life was detrimental.[23] By contrast, observers of the theater between 1815 and 1880 did not make any case at all for womanly virtue as a professional asset. Instead, commentators repeatedly cited the opinion of the critic and poet Théophile Gautier: "I regret that there are actresses who claim to be virtuous . . . We prefer that they show spirit, verve, madness, and petulance. Domesticity, fine for the bourgeois woman, does nothing positive for the actress."[24] The sober critic René Peter elaborated by claiming that the actress's need to be on display all the time could never be put aside, with the result that "even offstage and involuntarily, she has an aptitude for seduction and coquetry." Moreover, Peter wondered how an innocent woman could possibly perform convincingly in a love scene with a stranger, believing that the psychological strain would be too much for one who was inherently chaste.[25] Arsène Houssaye expressed the mindset of the Boulevard writers when he affirmed that a passionate affair improved the talent of an actress.[26] Indeed, Edmond de Goncourt built much of his 1882 novel *La Faustin* around that idea. The book tells of an actress who searches for the emotions to rise to greatness in the role of Phèdre, considered the preeminent challenge for a tragic actress. She had been living an orderly life, supported by a financier who made few demands on her and did not sleep with her. The chastity had induced "coldness" in her soul, and Faustin realizes that she needs chaos in her love life to meet the artistic challenge. Fortunately for her art (though not for her happiness), she develops a passion for a handsome English lord. As Faustin's worldly sister recognizes, "A need for debauchery comprised in some way a part of her genius."[27]

Theater writers did not make the same argument about male actors. Illicit passion was not a professional requirement for them. Houssaye even affirmed that actors could be "excellent fathers and husbands," whereas their female comrades could not be domesticated.[28] There was not the least bit of curiosity about how male performers developed the passions to excel in their roles. By contrast, the expectations for womanhood seemed so contrary to what actresses had to do that modesty did not even seem desirable for stage women. It is also noteworthy that male commentators on the theater avoided the obvious objection to the argument: that actresses had to portray virtue at least as often as vice. The nineteenth-century theater establishment resisted qualifications to the argument that actresses had to be sexually unruly. It was one more defense of the carnal excitement that they believed should surround the stage.

The theater business over the course of the nineteenth century became, if anything, ever more dependent on the sexualized body of the actress as the industry grew more competitive, more market oriented. Beautiful bodies, leggy chorus lines, and skin-colored tights were indisputable aspects of the theater industry. Theater writers had no particular reason to disguise the exploitation of female flesh through a hypocritical focus on artistic issues. Indeed, critical coverage of actresses relied heavily on the evocation of sensual beauty. Julien Geoffroy, one of the early critics who established many precedents for the profession, recommended focusing on an actress's appearance: "Their natural deficiencies are subject to critical judgment," he claimed, "because they contracted the obligation to please and to put themselves on display [*font acheter la vue de leurs personnes*]."[29] That master of the operetta, Jacques Offenbach, understood the ethic as well as anybody, and bragged to his collaborators that he wrote his music so that it would not require trained or even pretty voices. His team could hire physically striking women and had to be concerned with singing talent only for the lead role.[30] The nineteenth-century theater establishment was eager to service male fantasies.

In addition to artistic arguments for the inevitable depravity of theater women, there was an economic one: that actresses were victims of impossible financial pressures. Performers had to pay for their own costumes when they were playing contemporary roles, and the standard argument was that audiences now expected such luxurious clothing that actresses' salaries could never cover the cost. Thus, if women wanted to make a career on the stage, they needed rich gentlemen to buy them fabulous wardrobes. Other presumed solutions to the predicament, either higher salaries or lower public expectations regarding costumes, seemed unlikely to the writers who explored the issue. The *Le Monde illustré* columnist Pierre Véron devoted considerable space to airing the issue in 1881 and called it a "question of major gravity and interest for the future of the art." He began by citing a lawsuit instituted by an actress at the Gymnase theater whose salary for two months was 4,200 francs, yet she had to spend 6,000 francs on costumes. The columnist claimed that a magistrate released her from her contract because the conditions were *"contrary to public morality"* (his emphasis).[31]

Véron lamented the situation because of its impact on art. The pressures made a theater woman either accept "gilded libertinism" or leave the stage. If she accepted, she inevitably performed below her capacity because she had to give most of her time and attention to Monsieur, who put her on display. Véron suggested even a Rachel would have been caught in the undertow because talent was no longer enough to please an audience. "Today," he asserted, "a Rachel who does not have a wardrobe designed by [Charles] Worth runs the risk of remaining disdained and ignored among the cheap chorus girls."[32] Véron did not express sympathy for the plight of the women themselves, and most commentators simply wrote about the dilemma as a fact of life in the profession for which there was no solution.

In the late 1870s, theater critics and columnists began to perceive a new threat to the erotic culture of the stage: a growing pressure to report on the details of actresses' private lives, to adopt an "up close and personal" approach to the coverage of theatrical stars.[33] While some columnists happily pursued the trend, many others complained about giving performers' homes, family lives, and daily routines undue publicity. In fact the distinction between the traditional, discreet journalism and the new, invasive one was more subtle than the establishment wished to admit. The Boulevard press had always given readers piquant details on actresses' private lives, but they took the form of anecdotes about unnamed or disguised individuals, whom insiders could identify. In 1835, a theatrical dictionary had already proclaimed that "the history of actresses' private lives is as well-known as Roman history."[34] The new directness about covering offstage life disturbed pressmen of the old school because they feared it would undermine the erotic appeal of the theater. It was not that reporters would have to devote themselves to divulging scandals but rather just the opposite. Forced to "reveal" how actresses lived, journalists would have to stress the respectable, uneventful aspects and leave aside any hint of unruliness. The concern was that theater women would lose their aura of sexualized glamour and take on a bourgeois ordinariness. The media would water down the ethos of fashionable libertinism that theater men wanted to preserve for actresses.

The wary columnists opposed the intrusion into performers' private lives with a number of high-minded arguments. Of course they evoked the right to privacy. Intrusion into domestic arrangements was so unworthy of respectable journalism, they claimed, that no reader would tolerate it. Given the enormous importance of preserving appearances for French families, the writers' defense of privacy undoubtedly struck a responsive chord—but not enough to still the public demand to get up close and personal with celebrities. A second line of defense was that private life was self-defeating as a proper journalistic subject. The public would soon learn all it could ever want to know about a person and find the reporting tiresome.[35] The defenders of privacy did not want to imagine that they were just at the beginning of an explosion of coverage of celebrities' private lives.[36] Finally, they raised the specter of declining standards of performance, for if the press was preoccupied with actresses' homes and children, how would it adequately cover their artistic achievements? A columnist for *L'Illustration* claimed that performers "lost their authority" when their lives where examined too closely, and cited the example of a picture of one actress in her sleeping gown.[37] The champions of the old ways were being disingenuous because they had long reported on far more mischievous comportment, though in an elliptical manner. The erotic aura was on the defensive after 1880, and the establishment believed that the theater would be diminished if that attraction were eroded.

The cutural expectations surrounding the stage included a set of identities that situated theater women as the "Other" in relation to bourgeois womanhood. The identities gave actresses a collective history along with distinctive gender and racial characteristics, all of which marked them as sexually arousing and perverse. Even as critics evaluated the artistic skill of actresses, they drew attention to them as sensually charged beings. The intention was to make them provocative for bourgeois society.

Theatrical writers endowed actresses as a category of womanhood with a distinctive past, mainly through repeated casual references to predecessors. The seventeenth-century courtesan Ninon de Lenclos was far and away the most frequently cited ancestor to the actresses of the nineteenth century.[38] Her ascent from prostitute to confidante for male courtiers seemingly offered a model for theater women later, and writers hoped to appropriate the charm and elegance of the legacy. When a young Yvette Guilbert (later a celebrated singer in café-concerts) met Sarah Bernhardt in the 1870s, she thought the rising star the very embodiment of the "romantic" actress, a grand courtesan in the style of those of Renaissance Italy or of Ninon.[39] A more wicked association slipped out when Virginie Déjazet's lover referred to Ninon as a whore (*fille*) in a love letter. The actress was upset because the press had so frequently compared her to the courtesan.[40]

The numerous biographies and biographical sketches featuring actresses of the eighteenth century also provided historical context for thinking about theater women. In almost all cases these books were light treatments of the subject, focusing on libertinism and its excesses. Authors quoted liberally from the extravagant love poems dedicated to theater women and cited case after case in which a lord dissipated his fortune for a mistress.[41] Nestor Roqueplan pointed out that these sketches had "romanticized" (poétisé) the lives of theater women and made their libertinism familiar to all.[42] Among the most frequently treated of the eighteenth-century stars were Sophie Arnould, Hippolyte Clairon, and Louise Contat. These women offered ample opportunities to regale the reader with scandalous detail about their ambitions and appetites. Yet they were also women of substance, well known for their sharp wit and broad ideas. Authors always treated them respectfully in spite of their sexual escapades. The biographical sketches reminded readers of actresses' traditional role as fashionable mistresses. They put theater women in the center of a supremely elegant, refined, and irreverent prerevolutionary society. Never very far from the surface, though, was the thought that this was a doomed society and that unruly women had hastened its collapse. Among the most commercially successful of Edmond de Goncourt's controversial works was his history, La Femme au XVIIIe siècle ("Women in the Eighteenth Century").[43] It developed a widely accepted thesis that women had dominated prerevolutionary society and had enjoyed an extraordinary amount of freedom from male control. Female ascendancy had been responsible for its polish as well as for its decadence and ultimate self-destruction. Thus, the historical context writers offered for theater women rendered them eternal mistresses who inevitably sowed disorder.

The frequent references to Lenclos, Arnould, Contat, and Clairon were symptomatic of the actress's challenge to the category of woman as constructed in the nineteenth century. Observers hinted that actresses entered into sexual affairs as much to satisfy unwomanly physical urges as to acquire wealth. At the very least, the consequence of a string of affairs was to render an actress mannish.[44] What was one to make of the opera singer Adélina Patti, whose many divorces made her appear to be a "Madame Blue-Beard"? Pressmen wondered in print whether even her marriage at the age of fifty-seven to a thirty-year-old he-man, a Swedish diplomat known for his gymnastic skills and "muscles of steel," would be able to satisfy her lust.[45] The will to dominate men was just as troubling. Moreover, the wit and intelligence of certain actresses made them both admired and unwomanly within the sophisticated circles of the Boulevard. (Victor Hugo once told Sarah Bernhardt, "If a woman who is beautiful begins to cultivate her intelligence, her dimples soon change to crow's feet."[46]) The contradictions brought writers to explore and explain theater women as an intermediate gender, with a woman's tempting body and a man's sex drive.

Many theatrical writers may have shared the assumptions about gender made by Edmond de Goncourt, who proclaimed to a feminist group in 1893 that if autopsies were performed on "women of talent" like George Sand or the singer Pauline Viardot, they would be found to have genitals resembling those of men.[47] In the same vein, Arsène Houssaye declared Augustine Brohan to be an "upright man" because she did not take gifts from her many lovers.[48] Had these writers been immersed in the medical literature of the fin de siècle or inclined to give their writings a scientific tone, they might have referred to actresses as "inverts."[49] However, a scientific understanding was not their intention, and they were willing only to play suggestively with alternatives to gender binarism.

Implying that actresses were a third gender made expectations of lesbianism inevitable. Indeed, rumors of same-sex affairs were ubiquitous for theater women. Lacking the concept of "sexuality" until the end of the nineteenth century, Boulevard writers drew on commonplace assumptions of the day that made gender the central organizing principle of sexual behavior. The characteristics adhering to manhood or womanhood were fixed, and sexual orientation followed from them.[50] Being assertive, intelligent, or libidinous identified theater women as something other than women. That female performers had a manly lust for women contributed to an understanding of their nature as a third gender. The highly publicized lesbianism of Raucourt, Clairon, Arnould, and Bernhardt, and the ubiquitous rumors about other same-sex affairs confirmed the association. Actresses displayed masculine traits when they jumped from affair to affair with men (or women). At the same time, the rejection of male advances could also arouse suspicion of lesbian interests, because actresses were perceived as more male than female in their passions.

No actress—perhaps no person of the late nineteenth century—did more to challenge the conventional two-gender model than Sarah

Bernhardt. The manner in which she overwhelmed categories of male and female preoccupied the press and the fashionable salons.[51] At a relatively early stage in her ascent, the journalist Pierre Véron wrote about her as "*Monsieur* Sarah Bernhardt" (his emphasis), awed as he claimed to be by her strength of will.[52] Observers characteristically opposed her "feminine" qualities—physical frailty, beauty, siren's voice—to her boundless energy and heroic will to achieve. Journalists shook their heads in wonderment as Bernhardt bore up under the strain of international tours, conquered the audiences of the New World, directed her own theater, and dominated the French stage with her artistry. The commentators were thrown back on analogies to Bonaparte and on military metaphors. Commenting on her seemingly endless pursuit of glory, *Le Monde illustré* proposed that Bernhardt "has one of the most extraordinary temperaments of our era. She has prodigious moments of glory succeeded by passing setbacks."[53]

Actresses' oddness, particularly their imputed sexual energy, also required the use of racial constructions. Popular anthropology recognized that women of "inferior" races displayed not only earlier stages of physical development (protruding buttocks) but also a weaker proclivity for modest behavior and domesticity.[54] Belonging to a more primitive race, or having degenerated to that state, might explain actresses's unwomanly sex lives. And the idea of a woman who was sexually appealing and yet had underdeveloped instincts to behave chastely could easily be an intoxicating one for men. Actresses even appropriated the mystique of the primitive to gain publicity. Léonide Leblanc created a stir by wearing a necklace of crocodile teeth rather than the usual (civilized) diamonds.[55] Julia Feyghine, finding her career languishing, reinvented herself as a "Russian bohemian," though her parents had raised her in the seventeenth arrondissement of Paris.[56] Mademoiselle Taillandiera was said to be "a half-savage from Tunis who consumed raw pigeon."[57] The cabaret-singer-turned-actress Polaire put on a nose ring during her American tour in 1913 and even had herself photographed wearing one. Yet when the caricaturist Sem took the implications a step further and drew her head (with nose ring) atop the body of an African woman, she sued him for libel for portraying her as "a Negro woman in heat." Sem defended himself by arguing that Polaire's "form and her charming neckline are so justly celebrated that they will not be confused with the allures of a Hottentot Venus."[58]

In the second half of the nineteenth century, actresses' identity as the exotic Other was bolstered by associations with geographical and temporal terms that took on potent meanings. Theater women became "Parisian" and "modern." The same qualities that signified actresses' regression to the primitive also signified their modernity, as that notion came into usage. Their presumed nervous activity, irregular love life, and open sensuality were characteristics that marked them as modern. The novelist Félicien Champsaur identified actresses as prototypes of the modern woman because they were "always in quest of sensations, extremes, elegant perversities."[59] A short story appearing in *La Vie parisienne* in 1887 described actresses from two generations. Madame de Bréda was content being kept luxuriously by a rich man. Her daughter, however, was a "modern" actress—she even worked at the Théâtre moderne—who had absorbed feminist theories and had more voracious ambitions. She sought and attained marriage to a titled gentleman, along with freedom from any of the normal constraints on wives.[60] By being unconventional or ambitious, theater women embodied fears about the direction women were taking in the late nineteenth century.

No label was more closely tied to theater women in the second half of the century than "la Parisienne." Columnists described nearly every young and pretty actress as "very Parisian" at some point in her career. Réjane, Jeanne Granier, Anna Judic, Louise Théo, and Cécile Sorel brought the title to the pens of writers repeatedly and superlatively: "The most Parisian of Parisian ladies." The prince of Wales (the future King Edward VII) bestowed the epithet on just about every one of his French actress-friends.[61] The idea of a woman's being particularly Parisian seems to have appeared in the 1820s, and it became more precise with the growth of the Boulevard as an entertainment district and with the embellishment of the capital during the Second Empire. La Parisienne personified the joyous, sophisticated city that outdistanced all its rivals as the high-society playground of the world. Just as Paris dictated the most refined way of life for Europe's rich and powerful, so la Parisienne led men to the sensual pleasures of life. As such, la Parisienne was the opposite of the domesticated bourgeois woman. Inevitably, not far beneath the surface of la Parisienne as the personification of pleasure lurked the primitive, the invert, and the modern degenerate. Even though theater pressmen meant to celebrate the charms of actresses by describing them as very Parisian, the label carried implications of danger. *L'Illustration* made beauty the key feature of la Parisienne but noted that "it is the beauty of the devil!"[62]

The theatrical establishment understood that the stage worked its magic, in part, by featuring supposedly loose women whose physical attractions made them worthy of consorting with France's important men. The average male spectator was to enjoy actresses vicariously. This erotic culture endured because it was so tied to the political arrangements favoring the power of notables and to deeply ingrained notions about womanizing as the measure of masculinity. By the end of the century, though, political and cultural changes would weaken the eroticism of the playhouse. Then, in addition to being descendents of eighteenth-century courtesans, creatures of a third gender, primitives, and Parisians, theater women might also become *bourgeoises*.

Recasting the Libertine Tradition

Prudence, the character in the 1848 novel by Alexandre Dumas, Jr., *La Dame aux camélias*, who was supposed to speak with the voice of worldly wisdom, declares, "We decry men who ruin themselves for actresses and kept women; what surprises me is that they do not commit twenty times as many follies for them."[63] Finding the proper balance between committing follies and avoiding ruin was very much a cultural dilemma for elite males of the nineteenth century. Indeed, Boulevard writers early in the century reconfigured the tradition of aristocratic libertinism that they understood to have existed before 1789 and recommended it to postrevolutionary elites as the model of worldliness dictated by the past. In contrast to the eighteenth-century novelist, they glamorized liaisons between theater women and lords, now leaving titled ladies out of the picture. In the nineteenth-century construction of aristocratic libertinism, keeping a female performer was not the debasement of courtly practices but rather the authentic tradition. Despite this revision, the Boulevard writers followed the lead of the eighteenth-century novelists in minimizing the place of passion in their ideal affair. The code of mistress keeping continued to be a quest for prestige in Le Monde.[64]

The reinvented tradition had a serious purpose, to reinforce hierarchy in a society shaken by revolutionary change. Like the eighteenth-century novelists of libertinism, Boulevard writers of the next century were constructing a code of comportment for elites—in a France much further along on its postaristocratic evolution. The code had to differentiate in this new context "aristocrat" from "bourgeois"; fashionable from philistine. The writers sought to preserve an aristocratic individualism in which men competed for reputation within a circumscribed high society.[65] They took care to enthrone personal honor as the highest value and left more practical virtues to the common man.[66] Since female purity was so much more important in the postrevolutionary era, the updated code would have to avoid implicating society ladies in scandalous conduct. Thus, nineteenth-century writers were pleased to put actresses at center stage.

The terminology and roles entailed in mistress keeping remained basically unchanged after the Revolutionary-Napoleonic era, even though their substance was shifting. There was still "Monsieur," the officially recognized lover, the person who furnished and supported the household. In principle, a mistress was obliged to receive him whenever he called. A kept woman could also have one or several second lovers, now called *amants en second* instead of *greluchon*. The seconds made certain financial payments and had specific visiting privileges, inferior to Monsieur's. Moreover, their relationship was not openly acknowledged. Finally, there was the lover (no longer "friend") of the heart. He was presumably there to amuse the mistress, and she took only small gifts from him. It would have been a violation of the accepted code to give him too much attention, but, at the same time, kept women could freely acknowledge their link with a lover of the heart (although not, of course, before Monsieur).[67]

Fashionable writers of the nineteenth century presumed that they were perpetuating authentic eighteenth-century practices when they insisted that the correct form of elite libertinism was a quest for reputation and prestige. The ultimate purpose of keeping a woman, they said, was not to enjoy intimacy with her but rather to have Le Monde know that she was under your protection and displayed your wealth. The Second Empire playboy Gaston Jollivet described with sympathy the case of Edmond de Langrené, a cultivated, charming, and well-off young man who suffered grievously because he was not rich enough to be Monsieur to the theater woman he desired. He had to *settle* for being the lover of the heart.[68] Roqueplan associated affairs based on mutual affection with social leveling and disorder. He noted that Jacobins during the Terror had taken from actresses what rich men had to purchase.[69] Even on the eve of World War I, Octave Uzanne could state categorically that "men of Le Monde who go in for a conspicuous liaison . . . do so in the passionless frame of mind in which one might sign a contract by which one's mistress undertakes to direct and organize a thoroughly correct establishment, the luxury of which will be a credit." In a description that was also a prescription for elite behavior, he claimed that men acquired mistresses as they did yachts and race horses. A Monsieur "requires of her everything that can augment the reputation of his fortune and improve his position in those circles where one is observed and esteemed." Ultimately, protectors sought a "consecration of their reputations as men about town."[70]

Mistress-keeping arrangements in the eighteenth century had not, as a rule, been so cold and calculating. And in fact they were still less so in the nineteenth century, when the cult of romantic love had made much headway. Even among royalty, Uzanne's description of libertinism did not necessarily obtain, as the case of Alexandre, prince of Württemberg, illustrates. His Highness fell in love with Esther de Bongars, a minor actress at the Variétés theater, after seeing her perform several times in 1840. The actress accepted him as Monsieur and allowed him to set her up in an apartment. Soon, her brothers and mother came calling on the prince for financial assistance. The prince, who signed his love letters to her as "Your Alexandre," using the familiar form as a child would, clearly based the affair on sentiment. Esther, on the other hand, steadfastly rebuffed his requests for fidelity and monogamy. In one letter, Alexandre declared that he had hoped that "a deep sincerity would develop between us," but that she had forced him to become bitterly disillusioned. His letters continued to insist on his love for her, but he dared call her feelings only "mutual sympathy." The prince suffered torment when he saw with his own eyes Esther admitting other men to her apartment after the maid had assured him that Madame was out. Esther did bear him a child, but the affair came to a painful end in 1842.[71] The recast code of libertinism, recommending a passionless pursuit of prestige, was rarely an accurate description of the practice of mistress keeping in the nineteenth century.

While society columnists lavished attention on foreign princes and titled lords, the center of gravity of libertine practices shifted down the social scale to include many artists, writers, and Boulevard bon vivants. Accordingly, the terminology that the press employed to describe

Monsieur underwent subtle changes, from one of rank to a language of fashionableness. The keepers of mistresses were now "men-about-town" (*viveurs*), "clubmen" (that is, men who belonged to exclusive groups like the Jockey Club), "fashionable men" (*hommes à la mode*), "stylish men" (*hommes chics*), and, after Alphonse Daudet's 1880 play of that title, "nabobs." In 1895, the worldly journal *La Vie parisienne* identified as the perfect lover for a famous actress not a great lord but a famous playwright. The author was worthy of shining in the eyes of Le Monde because he had "fame, prestige, and style."[72] As in the First Republic, politicians of the Third replicated the libertine behavior of the former monarchical courtiers. The journalist Pierre Giffard identified senators and deputies as the most common types who kept young dancers at the Opéra.[73] Edmond de Goncourt cited the case of the Paris municipal councilman Alphonse Humbert, who had a minor actress at the Théâtre lyrique as a lover. When he was elected to the Chamber of Deputies, he took a player at the Comédie-française as a lover because, said Goncourt, "the actress at the Comédie is the favored mistress, imposed on all men who have arrived in political life."[74]

During most of the nineteenth century, the Boulevard was the center of libertine activity and its lore. Sociability on the Boulevard was built to a considerable degree around a subculture of single men, bachelors, widowers, husbands who did not live with their wives, and (eventually) divorced men. Many Boulevard men, living on a limited budget, could not make the grand gestures required by aristocratic libertinism even if they wanted to. Presumably, Alexandre Dumas, Jr., spoke to their condition when he created the character of Armand Duval in *La Dame aux camélias*. He is the provincial law student who falls in love with the prominent courtesan Marguerite Gautier and takes her away from her gilded life without having the means to support her. Duval and Gautier engage in an idyllic intimacy, but bills pile up. The author has the aptly named Prudence, Gautier's confidante, dispense her worldly wisdom to Duval. She tells him that all but the supremely rich accept the fact that their mistress will have other lovers; the men know that they cannot afford to support a fashionable woman on their own. Rather than ruining themselves, they resort to face-saving appearances: "They don't ever say that they know. They just appear not to see anything."[75] While such hypocrisy was unacceptable to the fictional Duval, it probably served its purpose in the real world of the Boulevard.

The fashionable men of the Boulevard and their circle did not approve of passionate affairs—not openly, at least. They preferred to think in terms of the controllable liaisons recommended by the libertine tradition, but based them on male superiority more than the pursuit of prestige. Their subculture extolled male bonding and homosocial relations while fearing intimacy with females. Heterosexuality in this subculture provided an exciting and necessary diversion, but the men wished to think of sex as something men did to women, not shared with them. Edmond de Goncourt actually spoke for many in the Boulevard milieu when he argued that "men like ourselves require a woman with little breeding, little education, gay and natural, to charm and to please us, as would an agreeable animal."[76] The actor Edmond Got shared Goncourt's preferences for mistresses. He claimed that until the age of thirty, he had not been able to think of his mistresses as full human beings with their own needs and desires. He had regarded each one as "a simple female creature [femelle], so far below a man that her personality escaped me."[77] Paul Porel, the theater director and husband of Réjane, lectured his teen-age son on the centrality of homosocial bonds: "Don't give women much importance. Give priority to male friendships. They are all that count. Only they are solid."[78] It is worth recalling that nineteenth-century bourgeois men were content to let calculation of interest, rather than sentiment, guide them in choosing a wife.[79]

Boulevard sociability was mostly male, with a few women of ill repute included to provide an erotic and heterosocial focus. The sophisticated participants were by no means above priapic playfulness. In 1877, Guy de Maupassant presented a pornographic play at his home in which male players took female roles (a practice banished from the public stage since the beginning of the century). A central scene entailed a dance around a giant phallus.[80] At one of Maupassant's Sunday meals given at a suburban inn, attended by a crowd of men and a few theater women, guests arrived at the table to find plaster casts of penises, realistically painted, at each setting.[81] Similarly, at a party given by Nestor Roqueplan, the women present, mainly from the corps de ballet, played with toy penises that ejected milk. (Roqueplan had purchased the devices from the bordello next to his home.)[82]

Actresses were supposed to be the type of women who enjoyed such male sex play. La Vie parisienne recalled the Second Empire dancer Hérivaux, who was said to become lively and entertaining only in the company of men. She attended numerous dinner parties at Fontainbleau, the only woman in a crowd of men, the cream of the Jockey Club, and they enjoyed her "naturalistic" way of speaking.[83] Léonide Leblanc reportedly invited men to her country house and had them dress in actresses' nightgowns.[84] Observers praised theater women for participating in the revelry—although they knew that in reporting it, they were painting actresses as perverse.

The male culture of the Boulevard required theater women who were vulgar, and gossip constructed them as such. The celebrated literary circle that met at the Brébant Restaurant on the Boulevard reviewed the tawdry history of the Bernhardt clan or heard Aurélien Scholl brag about a star whom he had recently bedded.[85] Arsène Houssaye liked to tell about actresses who preferred men of bad intentions to those of good intentions, because the latter were so awkward and boring.[86] Edmond Got affirmed that, backstage, women were as free as men to act sexually and "almost always" initiated affairs. Language and gestures among the comrades of the wings were also said to be crude.[87] The café singer Suzanne Lagier told Maupassant (who told Goncourt) that she married her first husband because he was so good in bed and because she "was in ecstasy over the beauty of his penis [membre]."[88] Since theater women were uncouth and sexually charged, they were presumed to accept, or even enjoy, the physical mistreatment they received from men. One report on the banter between the prince of Wales and his "good friend" Jeanne Granier had her telling the prince that since her youth, theater directors had been molesting her by "putting her between their legs and kissing her" or pinching her buttocks. When the prince asked how she responded to the fondling, Granier was supposed to have replied, "The more they paw me, the more I enjoy it."[89] Maurice de Waleffe claimed that Count de Schonborn once thought he was seducing Sarah Bernhardt successfully until she stuck a hat pin in his back. Furious, the count dragged her by the hair to the floor and hit her, which made the star exclaim, "I adore you!" and give herself to him.[90] Actresses who did not meet expectations of sensuality were deprecated. Paul de Saint-Victor regaled diners at the table of Princess Mathilde Bonaparte about the faults of Amiée Desclée as a mistress. He reported that she was so lacking in playfulness that one lover left her apartment saying, "I am leaving my cold piece of veal."[91] It is not clear that any of these stories had a basis in fact, but their repeated tellings constructed theater women as pawns in the masculine mischief of the Boulevard.

Having filled their imagination and gossip with women who would be "agreeable animals," Boulevard men sometimes found the reality of keeping theater women difficult. At dinner with the usual assortment of *boulevardiers* (and Eugénie Doche), Gustave Flaubert declared that "to keep a theater woman one must be sentimental and take her seriously." The great novelist and his companions doubted that actresses were kept as much as people assumed, because of the obligation to take them seriously.[92] Theater women were different from other harlots, as numerous observers noted, because they were intelligent in addition to being beautiful.[93] Moreover, their careers limited the time and attention many could lavish on lovers. Even Edmond de Goncourt conceded that once rehearsals began, actresses ceased their sexual playfulness and became "artist-workers."[94] The Boulevard men who were not prepared to exercise patience, attention, and understanding with their mistresses had to endure a series of stormy liaisons.

Inventing an aristocratic debauchery supposedly mirroring elegant prerevolutionary practices and dedicated to enhancing the male's reputation in Le Monde made a good deal of sense in view of the competition for ascendancy between aristocrats and bourgeois. That is why the tradition had such a hold on the social imagination. Yet it was rarely relevant to lived experience. Only a few individuals could afford the grand gestures, and even those who could were often unprepared psychologically to abide by the dispassionate code of conduct. A considerable embourgeoisement of libertinism had occurred over the course of the century, but a bourgeois code would to have to encompass such contradictions that it would not have been coherent. Moreover, the couples brought so many conflicting desires to the relationships that libertinism had to play out on an ad hoc basis.

Erogenous Zones of the Boulevard

"What an admirable thing—the theater is a circle of debauchery! From the stage to the audience, from the wings to the stage. From the audience to the stage. Dancers' legs, actresses' smiles . . . It's like a night market in women."[95] The Goncourt brothers had an impeccable feel for the erotic lines of force in the theater. Advocates of the stage as a school for morality had an impossible battle against powerful myths, rituals, and memories that made the theater a "bath of love," to use the term of the actress Eve Lavallière.[96] Being near the stage evoked the possibilities, the missed opportunities, the promise of carnal love, even in—perhaps *especially* in—its most guarded corners. As always, the sense of the chic enhanced the theater's sexual charge.

Looking up performers' skirts was institutionalized behavior at productions with chorus lines. Directors rejected scripts that did not allow it or had costumes redesigned to permit the practice.[97] To paraphrase a comment frequently repeated by critics, women in the chorus lines wore costumes that were even more transparent than the dialogue.[98] The prominent director Victor Koning understood this as a particular appeal of musicals and worried about the state of the theater industry after the Franco-Prussian War because serious plays made a return and the musical stage declined (temporarily). He blamed the shift on actresses, who had the audacity to want to wear elegant street clothes in their roles and play in dramas, depriving men of the right to inspect their anatomy. In no way was Koning willing to define the change as an elevation of theatrical taste.[99] Despite the leggy chorus lines, the skin-colored tights, and the occasional bath scene, what explicitly happened on stage was not necessarily the most erotic aspect of a night at the theater. The theatrical establishment expected—hoped, even—that many things would be left to the libidinous imagination, and that male spectators would enjoy fantasies of the physical possession of an actress.

The Goncourts were correct to stress the amorous links reaching from the stage to the audience even as spectators became more silent and attentive during performances.[100] The effort that began in the early eighteenth century to isolate plays in their own reality by constructing an imaginary "fourth wall" in front of the stage and having actors perform as though the audience were not present, remained unachieved during the nineteenth century. Developing lighting sources that allowed the hall to go dark on command did not complete the work. Technological possibilities were passed up because the management and the audience did not want a completely dark hall.[101] The communication of erotic messages across the footlights was a prominent part of the theatrical experience for most of the nineteenth century.

The practice, so well established in the previous century, of wearing a lover's clothes and jewels as a message to the audience continued well into the nineteenth century, despite the shift to flowers as the most appropriate tribute to an actress. Mid-nineteenth-century spectators would no longer see posters advertising a star "in all her diamonds," as they did for Mademoiselle George under Napoleon.[102] Yet as late as 1876 audiences laughed derisively when an actress in an expensive dress and diamonds repeated her line, "I am no longer kept by the Prince." The claim seemed so improbable, given the magnificence of the costume.[103] Spectators were not simply isolated individual viewers in a darkened space; they remained collective witnesses to performers' sexual adventures.

Without exactly breaking out of character, theater women intentionally pierced the fourth wall by initiating or perpetuating amorous relationships with lovers in the audience. All experienced spectators knew to watch for the meaningful glances and gestures. Dancers at the Opéra were savvy about looking to the "infernal boxes," where members of the Jockey Club sat, the moment they stepped on stage.[104] Mademoiselle George used to select a young man in the audience at whom to direct her love lines; he would become something of a celebrity in the Latin Quarter for a time as a result of this favor.[105] In Edmond de Goncourt's *La Faustin,* the main character presumes that proclaiming her passion to a lover before an entire audience represents "the greatest pride and satisfaction an actress can give a man, the loving offer of her talent in the presence of and with disdain for the 2,000 people for whom she is acting and who are to her as if they do not exist." This was not just an extravagant fictional detail. Goncourt lifted it from life.[106]

Faustin's practice might have been modeled on Virginie Déjazet in the course of her love affair with Arthur Bertrand in the 1830s. Déjazet was a much-loved star of light musicals during the July Monarchy and Second Empire, while Bertrand was a fashionable man-about-town, twenty years her junior. Déjazet's letters to Bertrand demonstrate how important moments of their relationship took place while the actress was performing and her lover was seated in the audience. In an early, happy phase of the tortured affair, Déjazet wrote to the younger man, "If you only knew how I was filled with happiness, when, last evening, in the theater, separated by everyone [in the audience], my eye met yours and dove into your stare, which makes me desire all, forget all!"[107] Unfortunately for the star, Bertrand cared for her only in the way that a young man of the Boulevard might—with wandering eyes and undisciplined lust. She saw that clearly across the footlights one night: "Persuaded that yesterday, especially, you should have been at your most attentive, there I was [on stage], all spirit, all artist, my heart swelling, tears in my eyes, seeking in your [eyes] the recompense of my memories. But, alas, the glance [*regard*] that should have given me so much happiness was fixed completely on someone else!"[108]

In all likelihood, Déjazet did, indeed, share her perceptions of love and betrayal across the footlights with the other members of the audience. Because of her success as a cross-dress performer and her well-known penchant for younger men, the star had a reputation as a nymphomaniac.[109] Spectators "in the know" hoped to catch a glimpse of her sexual intrigues in progress. Moreover, few in the audience would have expected a man like Bertrand to be a faithful lover to an aging actress. Thus, part of the evening's entertainment entailed training one's opera glasses from time to time on Bertrand and seeing whom he was regarding. Dimming the house lights enough to make such observation impossible was a long time in coming. In 1891, the journal *La Vie parisienne* still reported that the audience was more fascinated with the love affairs in the house than with the play itself.[110]

Casting decisions also kept the fourth wall from enclosing the play in its own reality. Whereas Rousseau and Mercier, in the previous century, had fretted about the bad impression impure actresses would make when they recited noble lines, playwrights of the next century had something of the opposite concern. They wanted audiences to find a resonance between the impure actress and her role as a transgressing woman—and such characters were ubiquitous in the second half of the nineteenth century.[111] That is why Alexandre Dumas, Jr., chose Eugénie Doche (who had had affairs with Bertrand and Scholl, among others) to create the role of the first contemporary courtesan on the French stage, the part of Marguerite Gautier in *La Dame aux camélias*.[112] In Dumas's pseudonymous play *La Comtesse Romani* (1876), which contains a scalding look at marriage in the theater world, audiences inevitably applied the lines of a libertine character to the actress, herself. A review in *Le Figaro* claimed the attribution enhanced the impact of the play.[113] The same principle applied to the singer Anna Judic, who, though married, was reputed to have a colorful love life. Judic was notorious for raising the double entendre to an art form and for removing "the fig leaf from those unbecoming things one would not mention all too clearly." Her fans, according to one critic, were young men "who would rather have themselves chopped to bits than not to find an off-color remark in her most innocent phrases."[114]

Even intermissions could be sexually charged moments at the theater. Respectable ladies remained in their seats while men and a few daring or disreputable women converged on the lobbies. Whereas society columnists described the jewel-bedecked courtesans in their boxes as a glamorous presence, wives in the audience did not necessarily have the same response. The spouse of Auguste Sichels described how, at intermissions, her husband would visit with courtesans and actresses in their boxes and return to her with scorn in his eyes.[115] She was deeply humiliated. Asked to explain why intermissions in France seemed so interminable, one actress replied it was "so that gentlemen might have time to write [love] notes and receive replies."[116] Moreover, by not allowing the intermission to have a fixed duration, actresses added to the sexual mystery. They prolonged intermissions by remaining in their dressing room with their guests until the socializing came to its natural end.[117] As the breaks dragged on, audiences were left to speculate about what was transpiring in that dressing room, a space filled with erotic associations in any case.

It was no wonder that plays depicting backstage scandal rang true to "those who frequent that world" and the many who dreamed of doing so.[118] During intermissions and after the performance was over, the most fashionable men, those most likely to accompany an actress to her home for the night, went backstage, either to a dressing room, to the wings, or to the players' lounge. The wings had long been a focal point of the erotic imagination. Theater reformers of the eighteenth century had made provisions for purifying them a priority. Royal administrations had, from time to time, even tried to limit access to the wings so that gentlemen would have less opportunity to court potential mistresses. They proposed closing them to all but the parents of the performers.[119] Postrevolutionary governments assumed a hands-off approach, owing perhaps to pressure from powerful men who had no intention of relinquishing their right to socialize in such a fashionable arena. The habit of sexually charged mingling backstage, the prelude to midnight trysts, remained strong throughout the nineteenth century.

An actress's dressing room was very exclusive territory. Writers frequently described the chambers (there was no interest at all in those of actors), and they did so with a sense of awe—as if they were the most worldly and fashionable spaces imaginable. Admission to the dressing room of a star was a social coup of the first order, the mark of a genuine man-about-town. There was a presupposition that the room reflected the personality and the sex appeal of the artist. Thus, Louise Théo, having "sparkling eyes, luscious shoulders, [and] lascivious hair," naturally decorated her dressing room in reds and golds. Rooms that had touches of "Moorish baths" were common, especially in fictional accounts of theater life.[120] Cherubs on the ceiling, Turkish carpets, and portraits of celebrated eighteenth-century courtesans were other touches that accentuated the sensuality of the space.

Edmond de Goncourt likened actresses' dressing rooms to insane asylums, which had the air of normalcy but hid the suspension of the ordinary rules of life.[121] Descriptions of what transpired in dressing rooms usually elaborated on that perspective. One joke, retold often about this or that thespian, had her undressing when there was a knock on the door. Only when she realized that it was a male visitor did she reply, "Enter. I thought it was a woman knocking."[122] Disrobing in the presence of men was supposed to be normal, and descriptions usually added that the performer did it with such aplomb and naturalness that no one was embarrassed. Déjazet, wishing to demonstrate her modesty to an interviewer, did so by affirming that she never undressed with visitors in her room.[123]

Performers' lounges (called "green rooms" in the English-speaking world) were also Eldorados of the erotic imagination. Books described those at the Variétés and Vaudeville theaters as the "night markets" Goncourt had in mind.[124] The performers' lounge at the Comédie-française, however, was often extolled as "aristocratic," a veritable literary drawing room because the most celebrated writers gathered there. Nonetheless, plenty of sexualized socializing transpired there as well. One journal portrayed socializing in the elegant lounge in terms of "each actress surrounded by her little court in which flirtation exudes its adulating refinements."[125]

Far and away the most legendary performers' lounge belonged to the dancers—*rats*, as they were known—in the corps de ballet at the Opéra. Celebrated in the paintings of Edgar Degas, one writer called it "the promised land of all young imaginations"; another likened it to "a temple of sensuality."[126] So central was the dancers' lounge to the erotic imagination that commentators used it as a barometer of national morality. The perceived changes in the levels of wickedness indicated the rise or fall of bourgeois mores.[127] In fact, there was much more continuity in practice than the discourses would suggest. The Old Regime epithet for the corps de ballet, "the national harem," was still applicable on the eve of World War I.[128]

The objects of such attention, the *rats,* were the forty-eight girls who had graduated from the state-run Dance Academy into the performing corps at the Opéra. They had usually entered the school between the ages of seven and ten, and they could not be any older than sixteen. Successful students were paid 300 to 800 francs a year, tiny salaries that did not go far to support their families, who were often poor. Their poverty, as well as the need for protectors to advance their career, encouraged girls as young as twelve or thirteen to have liaisons with well-off men.[129] Some dancers reportedly resisted and went from the stage straight to the dressing room after a performance, but the culture and rituals of libertinism were well developed within the corps.[130]

The worldly periodical *La Vie parisienne* extolled the atmosphere in the dancers' lounge as "intimate and eminently aristocratic." Young dancers were the "cream of the demimonde," and to have one as a mistress was "the supreme test of epicurean habits." The columnist wanted to suggest that dancing was only one of the arts that these girls practiced. Tradition gave them the role of providing pleasure for the most fashionable men in the nation. "Born and raised in the harem, imbued with the traditions of the corps," the journal proclaimed, the girls were trained in "the art of pleasing" and understood their obligation to be attractive. The columnist also likened them to vestal virgins in a pagan temple. The gentlemen who were admitted to the lounge were their "lords and masters."[131]

The gentlemen of the dancers' lounge, engaged as they were in the most debonair behavior of the day, were subject to much commentary. Pierre Giffard claimed that deputies and senators were the most frequent keepers of young dancers. *La Vie parisienne* stressed membership in exclusive clubs, especially the Jockey Club. All observers were ready to draw psychological portraits in which two types of Monsieur were delineated. One was the "fox," who regarded the dancers as prey. He addressed them informally and gave them nicknames with sexual connotations. Foxes encouraged the dancers to take up vices—smoking, eating too much at late-night suppers, or addiction to luxuries. Writers elaborated more on the second type, the paternalist, especially under the Third Republic, because his sexual control was tempered by artistic ideals. One author described the type as "serious, exhibiting great but cold politeness." Paternalists addressed every dancer as "Mademoiselle." On holidays they sent fruit and pastries. Knowledgeable about ballet, they competently doled out praise and criticism of the performances. According to *La Vie parisienne,* paternalists did not forget that, whatever else dancers did, their art and career were important. One Monsieur, according to this journal, told his mistress right after intercourse, "Remember, you perform tonight!"[132]

The state knowingly permitted these arrangements and even promoted them, making them a form of state-sponsored prostitution. Only briefly, under the July Monarchy, when the Opéra was privatized, did the dancers' lounge escape state supervision. By 1840, the Opéra was back under government control.[133] Napoleon III removed the lounge from the supervision of the Fine Arts Ministry and placed it directly in his Household, to associate his regime with it. There was no meaningful break when the Third Republic replaced the Empire. The Republic may have repudiated the notorious frivolity associated with the previous regime, but it did nothing to change the way *rats* and gentlemen mixed backstage at the Opéra. It simply put the minister of the interior in charge of the libertinism.

The right to enter the dancers' lounge, technically known as "access to the connecting door" (*droit d'accès à la porte de communication*), was in the hands of the Opéra director, who consulted closely with the government. A decree of 1854 codified earlier understandings by giving access to men (only men) who rented a box for at least one day a week for the entire season. The minister had the right to confer the right on other men.[134] Enjoying the privilege by virtue of position were members of the diplomatic corps, cabinet ministers, the president of the Council of State, the prefect of the Seine, and the prefect of police. Access to the dancers came at a high price. In 1823, a full subscription for a box cost 2,400 to 4,000 francs a year. By 1880, the cost had risen to 6,000 to 8,000 francs, nothing less than a yearly middle-class income.[135] Not surprisingly, the lists of men who had the right to enter the lounge during the Second Empire read like catalogues of the social elite. Though the audience on a busy night might have numbered well over a thousand, very few could hope to enter the lounge. The number of gentlemen with the right of access averaged only twenty-three per performance during 1863.

The officials of the Third Republic carefully preserved the libertinism of the dancers' lounge. The minister of the interior required the Opéra director to send him weekly lists of the men with access for each performance. The privileged circle expanded a bit in size from the days of the Empire and was now usually above forty. For example, at the performance of Meyerbeer's L'Africaine, on October 3, 1887, fifty-seven men could enter the lounge, including Georges Clemenceau, Comte d'Adhémar, the marquis de Moderne, Charles Abbatucci, and Camille Saint-Saens. At no point did the Republic shrink from associating itself with mistress keeping that involved girls as young as twelve.[136] Even moments of public panic over the white-slave trade or syphilis epidemics at the turn of the century left the dancers' lounge unreformed.[137] The Republican officials probably thought that the link with debonair debauchery shed prestige on the state.

Another instance of state-sponsored prostitution involved the students at the Acting Conservatory. The students' liaisons were not quite so widely celebrated, though Auguste Renoir did immortalize them in his 1877 painting Leaving the Conservatory, and the subject came up occasionally in fiction. Moreover, government involvement was more ambiguous than in the case of the dancers' lounge. It was a matter of passively accepting the status quo and turning a blind eye toward it rather than supervising it.

Edgar Monteil, a writer who proposed pedagogical reform at the conservatory, devoted a substantial portion of his 1881 novel Cornebois to life at the school.[138] His description defended the libertine tradition by pointing out how impossible it was for female students to subsist without being kept. (Of course, he did not mention that male students were under the same economic constraints, even though the central character in this novel, Eugène Cornebois, was one of them.) He described some aspiring actresses arriving at the school in carriages and wearing elegant dresses. Their protectors would sit proudly in the audience on the day of the performance exercise (next to the girls' mothers) and use their influence to procure prizes. The mothers loom large in the novel. They accompany their daughters to the admission audition and to daily classes, whereas the male students arrive alone. However, the mothers' supervision is not honorable. They want to ensure that their daughters do not give themselves to impecunious students, and they push them into affairs with the rich men who wait outside the conservatory for classes to end. The mother of Hortense, the female protagonist in *Cornebois,* badgers her daughter with the example of a student who found a viscount and was able to take her mother on as a servant at a generous salary. Of course Hortense's mother forbids her to see Eugène, but the couple moves in together anyway. Economic pressures arise to destroy the couple's happiness. Hortense needs nice clothes and small luxuries. She does not even compete for a fellowship because she is not having an affair with a professor and does not have an influential protector. Eventually she meets a baron in a store; his face lights up when he learns she is a conservatory student. Soon he becomes her Monsieur, and Eugène grudgingly shares her. Monteil's point was not at all to stir up reforming zeal. He was interested in curriculum changes but had no urge to protect female students from predatory men. His novel was intent on explaining why morals in the theater were necessarily different from those of the outside world.

The French state had once been more careful with conservatory students than with the dancers and had offered the former limited supervision. Through the 1820s, the state ran a dormitory for female students and provided them with clothing in the express hope of maintaining good conduct. However, these protections were abandoned during the July Monarchy, mainly, it seems, to cut costs.[139] The regime of guardianship never returned, but there were calls for some active oversight of the students' morality from time to time. A reform proposal from 1871 focused on giving "moral guarantees" to female students and deplored the "current regime, which leaves them without any protection."[140] Nothing came of that project, but the government put the professors under pressure to maintain at least the appearance of propriety. Thus, the teachers forbade students to use sensual gestures that were standard practice on stage—for example, Tartuffe's putting his hand on Elmire's knee in performances of Molière's masterpiece.[141] There were some private initiatives for moral reform as well. The actress Jeanne Samary campaigned at the end of the century to create a separate school for female students and to expose them only to uplifting plays. The columnist Pierre Véron, however, reacted bitterly to the proposal because he perceived it as one more challenge to the libertine traditions of the stage. Véron wondered in print whether there were any virgins left to save at the conservatory. Perhaps a few, he conceded, "but they become rarer every day," and certain students, he claimed, displayed a "terrifying precocity." In any case, he did not give Samary's proposal any hope of success.[142] The public took the immorality of the female conservatory students as a given. According to Edmond de Goncourt, they drew suspicious looks on the street even when they wore simple black dresses.[143] To him, they appeared to be more advanced in their training as courtesans than as artists.

The French public of the first half of the nineteenth century was apt to find theater women revealing noble instincts, but because the performers were so much a part the erotic culture of the stage, they could not escape the status of outcasts. After 1848, the political and moral tide turned, and the place of theater women changed in the French social imagination. Even a limited acknowledgment of an actress's potential for goodness became rare. The Second Empire (1852 to 1870) was undoubtedly the golden age of the libertine culture of theatrical life because the political order supported it so completely. Jacques Offenbach's operettas satirized the unbridled pursuit of pleasure before an Imperial high society that was capable of laughing at its own excesses, though not capable of reigning them in.[144] In this new climate, actresses were vilified once again and viewed as a grave threat to the social order.

6

The Struggle against Pornocracy, 1848–1880

The conservative republican theater critic Jean-Jacques Weiss, looking back on French history at the hundredth anniversary of the Revolution, observed that the events of 1830 had inaugurated a reign of liberty and morality and that Louis-Napoleon Bonaparte's seizure of power in 1852 had ended it.[1] His periodization was based more on ideology than insight, but it nonetheless reflected a commonplace understanding of the national past. During what Weiss called a reign of liberty, theater women fared well in the French social imagination. The July Monarchy, with its high property qualifications for voting, its parliamentary life in the hands of the notables, and its myths of bourgeois rectitude, predisposed upper-class culture to presume that there was a self-disciplined male elite in control. The democratic republic of 1848 to 1852, followed by Louis-Napoleon's amalgam of personal dictatorship and democracy, did not do the same. Concerns about political and moral corruption caused representations of theater women to shift dramatically for the worse. Once capable of noble conduct, theater women after 1848 seemed committed to ruining men. Fear of pornocracy, the rule of harlots, prevailed for the next three decades. This demonization of stage women signified a crisis of confidence of femininity and anxiety about the place of upright, middle-class men in Imperial society.

Tales of Harlotry

Within a few weeks of the outbreak of the 1848 Revolution, Emile Augier had his new play, *L'Aventurière* ("The Adventuress") ready for production, and it was a decisive break from the line of fiction that had elevated the actress to the status of heroine.[2] George Sand praised the play as proper for a republic because of the severe morality it preached.[3] Perhaps to underscore a comparison with Hugo's *Angelo,* Augier also set his play in Renaissance Padua. Whereas Hugo's heroine, the actress La Tisbe, follows her womanly instinct for self-sacrifice to its tragic end, Clorinde, the actress in Augier's work, plots to undermine a bourgeois family. Disguised as a Spanish noblewoman fallen on hard times, Clorinde conspires with her brother Annibal to marry Mucarade, a retired merchant, and gain control of his fortune. Under her influence, Mucarade forgets the self-discipline that had made him a success and even dresses like a dandy. When Fabrice, the merchant's son, returns from a ten-year absence, he is appalled by his father's weakness and resolves to set things right. The plot is a test of wills between Clorinde, who has not yet met a man whom she could not master, and Fabrice, a paragon of male responsibility and capability.

When Fabrice deceives Clorinde into revealing her true identity, Mucarade is too much in love to be outraged. He even denounces the "evil prejudices" against actresses. Fabrice, however, upholds the stern morality of an upright man and scorns Clorinde as a creature that cannot be a true woman because she lacks modesty.[4] He saves the family honor by disguising himself as a foreign prince and tricking Clorinde into abandoning Mucarade for him. When Fabrice reveals himself, Clorinde realizes that her quest for wealth and respectability have collapsed. And Fabrice humbles this strong woman in another way, as well. Clorinde has fallen in love with Fabrice, the first man she could not dominate: "I feel the weaker and I am proud to be / Strange voluptuousness, to bow before a master."[5] Thus Fabrice has not only saved his family but has also reasserted the proper relation between the sexes.

L'Aventurière proved to be a template for the other fictional works about theater life during the Second Empire and the decade after its fall in 1871. The actress who was capable of noble action was decidedly out of favor. Almost without exception, fictional theater women were predatory, and morally weak men were their victims.[6] The works captured the diminished view of women's self-sacrificing qualities. Mid-nineteenth-century authors reexamined women's souls through their actress characters and found disturbing forces residing there: greed, independence, and assertiveness. Moreover, the men with the self-control necessary to contain unruly women no longer seemed to be firmly in control of the levers of power.[7]

Augier's play also offered an early example of a plot device that recurred often between 1848 and 1880 in fiction about the stage, the test of wills between an actress and a decent man who tries to foil her dastardly plans.[8] *Fanny Lear,* an 1867 play by Henri Meilhac and Ludovic Halévy, two of the most celebrated names of Second Empire theater, pits an actress against the one man capable of standing up to her.[9] Count de Frondeville is a virile and an upright man among weak men and corrupt women. He must look after a phlegmatic family friend, Jacques Birnheim, who had allowed his mistress, the English actress Fanny Lear, to dissipate his fortune and even beat him (which he enjoyed). This very Fanny is now Frondeville's neighbor, the new wife of the elderly Marquis de Noriolis. The actress plans to use her control over her husband to become a respectable lady and enter Le Monde, ruining the life of her stepgranddaughter in the process. Frondeville assumes the duty of thwarting her designs, assembles the men Fanny dominates, and appeals to their decency and self-dignity. Frondeville's strength proves tonic. Even the feeble marquis rallies. He rises from his sickbed to drag his wife home and force her into domestication.

Emile Augier returned in 1866 to his earlier theme in a new play, ominously entitled *La Contagion* ("The Contagion"). More clearly than *L'Aventurière,* this one dwells on tensions between aristocrats and bourgeois. Monsieur Tenacier, who identifies himself as a "solid bourgeois" and who honors the principles of 1789, deplores his son and daughter's weakness for aristocratic decadence.[10] The father's potential ally in the struggle against corruption is André Lagarde, his son's close friend. André is an engineer who is about to undertake a canal project that will add to French glory and prosperity. These two virtuous men contend with the actress Navarette and Baron D'Estrigaud, who pitilessly degrades respectable women and would even betray France for money. The two villains plot to corrupt Tenacier's children and sell André's project to the English. They almost succeed when, at a party Navarette arranges, André becomes infatuated with a beautiful actress and almost loses his moral compass. Needing cash to keep her, he agrees momentarily to sell his canal to D'Estrigaud and the English. However, Tenacier man-

ages to make the engineer see reason, and André refuses to be a victim of "the contagion—women, luxury, paradoxes."[11] He and Tenacier force the baron and the actress to flee the country in infamy.

Theater fiction of the mid-nineteenth century also treated a theme that had fascinated certain writers of the 1830s, the social consequences of marriage between a respectable man and a stage performer. Whereas pre-1848 literature had always celebrated the couple's passion in the face of oppressive social conformity, the later fiction uniformly portrays such marriages as disastrous for the men. Midcentury authors underscored the wisdom of strictures against such misalliances.

Among the most applauded plays about marriage to an actress was *La Fiammina,* written by Mario Uchard in 1857. Its opening gave the Comédie-française one of its modern dramatic successes and renewed hopes that the august institution could, indeed, remain viable in a culture that seemed to be turning its back on the classics.[12] The protagonist, Henri Lambert, resembles the heroic Fabrice of *L'Aventurière* in that he has to clean up the mess his father made when he became infatuated with an actress. Henri is so much the responsible bourgeois that even at the age of twenty, he is ready to forgo a period of youthful dissipation and marry wisely. He does not know that his mother is alive and that she is a famous Italian singer, La Fiammina. His father, Daniel, had married her in his youth, and she had abandoned her family for the glamour of the stage soon after giving birth to Henri. Now that Daniel must negotiate marriage arrangements for his son, he has to confess the truth. Daniel tells Henri, "The theater, my son, is a cruel enemy of familial felicity."[13]

Just as Daniel is making his revelation, La Fiammina is enjoying enormous success at the Théâtre-italien in Paris. She seems to have put her past behind her and is living with the dashing Lord Dudley as if his wife. Henri is so principled that he will even guard the honor of a mother who has abandoned him—and defending the honor of a stage woman is not easy. He thrashes his best friend for making a suggestive remark about the beautiful singer. Henri even finds that he must challenge Lord Dudley to a duel, though the act is tantamount to suicide. When La Fiammina discovers the virtue of the son she has deserted, she is finally filled with remorse. Henri's moral steadfastness recalls her to her motherly duties. She decides to separate from Dudley and retire to obscurity so that Henri can live his life in peace.

Alexandre Dumas, Jr., widely considered the most thoughtful play-wright of the day, also denounced marriage to actresses in his 1876 play *La Comtesse Romani*.[14] Count Romani of Italy proves himself the ulti-mate weak man by marrying the star Coecilia and forgetting his social obligations. His family disowns him, and he loses his fortune. Coecilia, in the meantime, becomes bored being a countess and talks her hus-band into allowing her to return to the stage. His disgrace is complete when she has an indiscreet affair. Coecilia is not the least bit repen-tant and tells him: "You know I am a bohemian, a girl of chance."[15] The count stabs himself in front of her but survives. Coecilia is momentarily moved, but she soon decides that her life is in the theater and leaves while the count's life is in shambles. The play provoked discussion in the press about marrying an actress. After citing exceptions, the columnists agreed that the unions usually ended badly.

Edmond and Jules de Goncourt did not let the theme of a fatal mar-riage with a theater woman get cold. In 1877, their novel *Charles Demailly* appeared, and it was a frightening tale of a weak man's destruc-tion at the hands of a strong actress.[16] Charles marries Marthe Mance, who seems to him the ingenue incarnate. Charles expects his wife to be pliant, instinctually adoring, and attentive to his emotional needs. To his great dismay, he finds that she has her own opinions; that she is capable of judging him; that she does what she wishes. Charles reluctantly con-cludes that his wife lacks a heart, the essence of womanhood.[17] His self-confidence deteriorates as he discovers his wife's independent nature, and he develops a case of nervous exhaustion, which only makes Marthe more aggressive. She eventually leaves him and plots with a journalist to undermine the success of Charles's new play. The humiliation Charles suffers drives him mad, and he spends time in the Charenton asylum. After being released, he attends a play, sees an actress who might be Marthe, and jumps to his death from his balcony seat.

Even more common than a test of wills or marriage as a plot device was following the fate of innocent men who become infatuated with stage women. Invariably the protagonist pays dearly for his weakness. The authors of these works were warning bourgeois men, in particular, that the theater wings were dangerous territory for them.[18] The first im-portant work of this sort was *Les Filles de marbre* ("Women of Marble"), a play by Théodore Barrière (with the collaboration of L. Thiboust).[19] It was one of the theatrical events of 1853, so successful that Napoleon III attended a performance and wept over the tragic ending.[20] Contemporaries understood the work as a response to one of the great love stories of the century, *La Dame aux camélias* by Alexandre Dumas, Jr., with its controversial theme of love redeeming courtesans. Barrière proclaimed himself a member of the literary "school of good sense" that opposed romantic flights of fancy about the redemptive power of love. The plot centers on Raphael, a young sculptor who lives quietly with an adoring mother. Hard work has enabled him to earn 10,000 francs, which he invests wisely. However, the life of this model bourgeois changes decisively when he meets the singer Marco. Raphael instantly looses his head over her and abandons any intention of romancing the pious and beautiful orphan Marie, who worships him.

The sculptor's obsession for Marco destroys his self-discipline and self-respect. He stops working and throws away his hard-earned fortune on the singer. The mother's entreaties and prayers are futile. Marco, fully aware of what she is doing, leads Raphael to destruction without the slightest sense of remorse. When the young man has exhausted his funds, Marco leaves him for a rich playboy. Raphael enters a state of delirium and dies.

Barrière takes pains to paint the theater woman as the enemy of bourgeois morality. What makes Marco especially despicable is that she purposefully sets out to destroy an upright man; catching aristocratic ne'er-do-wells in her web of deceit is not enough for her. Desgenais, the worldly-wise character in the play, explains that actresses who ruin rich aristocrats are only doing what courtesans *must* do. However, Marco crosses the line to strike at the bourgeoisie, the moral foundation of the social order. Women like her are therefore waging war against society, not just taking advantage of it.

Aurélien Scholl, one of the most familiar figures in the fashionable cafés on the Boulevard, added another dark tale of theater life in his 1862 novel, *Les Amours de théâtre* ("Love in the Theater"). Scholl sets Gaston Duthil, a talented poet of modest background, in the glittering, amoral entourage of Marthe, the glory of the Théâtre-italien. Marthe has many aristocratic lovers but retains Gaston as her "friend of the heart." Though he first rejoices in his charmed existence at Marthe's side, he eventually finds his life poisoned by jealousy and suspicion. Gaston had once lived by firm moral principles and had been repelled by the idle aristocracy and its influential courtesans. Ultimately, Gaston knows that his friend Robert is correct when he tells him, "A man is not strong unless he is true to himself. A mistress is nothing but a millstone."[21] Gaston struggles between being true to himself and enjoying Marthe's enticements. Finally he frees himself from Marthe by falling in love with Madeleine, Marthe's seventeen-year-old illegitimate daughter, whom Marthe has been mistreating. Gaston tries to poison Marthe, but Madeleine takes the potion instead and dies. The tale ends with the poet's life in ruins. Scholl announces in the introduction to the book that it is intended to be a serious study of Boulevard mores, but his deeper purpose seems to have been to warn bourgeois men to avoid the worldly life of the Boulevard.

By the time Emile Zola's *Nana* appeared in 1879, readers would have found its theme familiar. In fact, the novel climaxed and closed an era in which theater fiction dwelled on destructive harlots. Zola based Nana loosely on the courtesan and actress Blanche D'Antigny.[22] The opening scene at the Variétés theater, featuring the actress's sensuous body and golden hair driving the men in the audience wild with lust, would have rung true to a Louis-Sébastien Mercier. To sleep with her, men would submit to the most abject degradation. Count de Muffat, an officer of the Second Empire, abandons a lifetime of Catholic principles after just a few hours with Nana. The moral decay spreads to Muffat's family life— "a gust of gutter sex sweeping away . . . a hundred years of honor and Christian belief."[23] Nana subjects Muffat to one humiliation after another, and he watches his wife and children sink to his level.

Nana is morally indifferent rather than evil. Though Zola implies that she is taking revenge on the elite for the harm inflicted on the working class from which she sprang, it is in her nature to corrupt men. Once she has attracted a man, he is enslaved to her. She dreams of being a great lady but is so vulgar that only a society as corrupt as the Second Empire's could acclaim her. The sex she has with men is a matter of attaining power over them, while her sex with women affords pleasure. Finally, only a mortal disease can put an end to her depredations.

Nana was not only the last but also the paradigmatic novel of mid-nineteenth-century pornocracy. This is partly the result of Zola's single-minded and relentless depiction of moral corruption. He was bolder than any of the previous authors in evoking lewd detail and vulgar language. Moreover, Zola was explicit about the political consequences of harlots' rule. He connected the emasculation they wrought on honorable men first to the fall of a regime that had had a secure hold on power, and then to the national catastrophe of 1870, when Prussia violated France. The crowds' mindless cries of, "On to Berlin," ringing through the last pages of the novel, cap the destruction that the Nanas of the Second Empire had wrought.

The authors who denounced moral decay with such vehemence in their theatrical fiction were not usually pursuing a personal reform agenda.[24] With the exception of the republican Zola and of Dumas, Jr. (who had rejected the womanizing ways of his father to become an advocate of family purification), they were deeply enmeshed in Boulevard culture, which did not frown on mistress keeping.[25] Augier, himself, the ostensible scourge of courtesans, led a worldly life and kept Rachel's sister, the actress Sarah Félix, as a mistress.[26] It is telling that some of the very authors who denounced actresses in their own works attacked *Nana* for offering a lurid, unbalanced portrait of libertinism.[27] For all their hypocrisy, the Boulevard writers did know their audience and spoke to widespread anxiety about strong women. Even members of the theatrical establishment, which was generally a tolerant and worldly milieu, were convinced of the need to curb actresses' powers after 1848 for the sake of art and social order.

Neo-Rousseauist Revival

Actresses' portraits often graced the cover of the Boulevard weekly *L'Illustration,* and the typical article celebrated the glamour and artistic excellence of the stage. It was thus an odd journal to revive the attacks that Rousseau and his disciples had directed against theater women before 1789. Nonetheless, in the spring of 1854, *L'Illustration* published a long piece, signed by the journalist H. Mille-Noé, taking up once again Rousseau's argument that actresses' immorality was harmful to theater and dangerous to society.[28] Mille-Noé believed, as Rousseau had in his day, that plays featuring female characters were a recent innovation and marked a decline in artistic standards. Mille-Noé blamed actresses, themselves, for the change: "Today, our lady sovereigns despotically demand the central roles." Playwrights were powerless because they needed the actresses more than the stars needed the playwrights. Then, too, stage women extorted enormous salaries, making them "richer than ten German princes." Ever covetous, they diminished Parisian theater by touring the world and accumulating fortunes. The new breed of actress—for that is what the author believed her to be—demeaned even the classics by performing them "nearly nude." Mille-Noé concluded his exposé as a Rousseau or a Riccoboni would have, by expressing nostalgia for the unrecoverable days when women were banned from the stage.

L'Illustration was not in business to stir controversy or stimulate polemics, so running such an article presupposed that a deprecatory view of theater women, in abeyance since the Revolution of 1789, was self-evidently back in vogue. Indeed, a sober assessment of the state of theater from Auguste Muriel, the editor of a theatrical newspaper, also argued that there had been a sharp decline in artistic standards and identified actresses as the culprits. "There is an incredible penury of actresses devoted to their art," he proclaimed in his tract of 1855.[29] He was particularly irate about the prominence of "high celebrities of debauchery" on the stage, which he imagined to be an unprecedented phenomenon, at least on such a scale. The performers who attracted the most attention at the time, Muriel claimed, had no talent or inclination for the profession. They excelled only in physical appeal, and, unfortunately, their sensuality made them stars. Muriel's pessimistic conclusion was that "so long as theater remains the domain of debauchery and so long as gilded celebrities trump the talented [performers], there is no hope for regeneration."[30]

Muriel might have been able to cite some specific cases of kept women whose lovers put them before the footlights, but there was nothing at all new about the phenomenon. Nonetheless, the theme of harlots invading the stage was enough of a leitmotif for the Belgian writer and popular historian Frédéric de Reiffenberg to define the actress as a courtesan in his 1856 book, *Ce que c'est qu'une actrice* ("This Is What an Actress Is"). Reiffenberg denied actresses any of the qualities of womanhood. He called them "women of marble who would never have a heart for the man who is so foolish as to sacrifice his life for them." He maintained that they were more dangerous than the run-of-the-mill prostitute because they were often intelligent, which gave them the worst quality a woman could have, worldly ambition. Theater women sought not just a comfortable income but wealth. Hence, the gentlemen who kept them could expect nothing but ruin.[31] Writing a generation before Zola, Reiffenberg was just as apprehensive about theater women.

The Boulevard newspaper *Le Figaro* tapped into the disquiet about actreses' wiles in its distinctive way. Its columns had long entertained readers with occasional anecdotes about the outrageous behavior of female performers. However, these articles were never so frequent as in the 1860s and 1870s. The reader was treated to stories about "Mademoiselle X," who lived a lavish life on a salary of 150 francs a month and employed a handsome male servant who addressed her in a familiar tone even at elegant dinner parties in her home.[32] Subscribers might have also shaken their heads after reading about a married actress for whom a viscount had developed an uncontrollable passion. He went to see her perform every day. When the actress was on a summer tour, the lord could console himself only by meeting her husband in a café and singing her praises to him.[33] The gist of virtually every anecdote was that theater women were subverting the natural order of things, turning the world upside down. The explosion of these kinds of stories in *Le Figaro* in the 1860s cannot be explained in terms of a new columnist taking over the post. Jules Prévot remained the author throughout the mid-nineteenth century. Prévot must have sensed that subscribers during the 1860s and 1870s would welcome the perverse reports. They helped readers laugh at issues about which they had genuine anxiety—above all, theater women's subversion of morality and male reason.

Theatrical producers also exploited the widespread interest in the perversity of theater women. Though the floral tribute was too well established by now to be abandoned, producers dared once again to ask actresses to display their ill-gotten jewelry and to have audiences take in their corrupt splendor. Léonide Leblanc dazzled spectators of the 1860s with a neckless worth 500,000 francs and a ring given to her by the duke of Brunswick worth 30,000 francs.[34] Hortense Schneider was said to wear 800,000 francs worth of diamonds on her costumes for *La Périchole* (in the production of 1874). *Le Figaro* commented that "she must have discovered a diamond mine . . . and some miners."[35] Actresses' delicacy as women was put in question once again as they paraded their acclaimed bodies, decorated with tainted booty, before the public.

Just as the rising current of despair about actresses' powers in the eighteenth century had ended in attempts to remove them from positions of authority within the Comédie-française, so the revival of moral concern in the middle of the nineteenth century provoked new attempts to curb actresses' power.[36] The field of battle shifted to the composition of the reading committee, which reviewed scripts and selected the new plays that would be performed. Women troupe members were on the committee as the Second Empire began, and the attack on female authority focused on the dangers they posed as antipornocratic reform was once again the order of the day.

Prerevolutionary France had witnessed many attacks on the competence of the troupe to discern the best scripts. The reform proposals called for involving men of letters in the selection process so as to curb the players' control over what the public saw. No one had yet suggested the selection process would be better if women were not involved. Before 1789, all troupe members had the right to participate in the reading committee. Napoleon tried to make the committee more compact, but he betrayed his reputation for masculinist backlash by giving female and male thespians equal access. The relevant clause of the Moscow Decree of 1812, which reorganized the Comédie-française, established a reading committee composed of "nine people [*personnes*] chosen among the most senior troupe members."[37] The awkward wording left no ambiguity about the acceptability of actresses for this function. By the 1830s, all members of the troupe had regained their right to sit on the committee.[38] In that era of confidence in male reason and governance, actresses continued to exercise the same responsibilites as actors, without controversy.

In 1846, the Comédie-française was widely thought to have entered a grave financial and artistic crisis. Box-office receipts plummeted. Though the deep economic recession of the day was responsible for the drop in revenue, the government was concerned that the choice of plays had been poor, and it created a commission of experts, including Victor Hugo, Eugène Scribe, and Alphonse Lamartine, to examine the need for reform.[39] The commission did not so much as mention the removal of actresses as a desirable step. The only recommendation that emerged at this time was that the committee be made compact. The practice of allowing all the troupe members to participate who wished to seemed cumbersome to the experts. The commission recommended a committee composed of six troupe members. Like Napoleon, it treated men and women as equally suitable for the task.[40]

Up to the Revolution of 1848, then, opinion leaders had not connected the troubles of the Comédie with the presence of women in po-

This picture of the reading committee at the Comédie-française points to an entirely new organization of gender. It presents the image of male competence and control that the troupe wished to project after 1848.

sitions of authority. Although experts may have believed that female artists evaluated plays differently from male artists, they perceived the difference as complementary and beneficial. However, the acceptance of female influence did not survive much beyond the founding of the Second Empire. The attitudes of an Augier or a Barrière toward actresses began to weigh on the question, and in July of 1853, the minister of fine arts took the unprecedented step of excluding women from the reading committee. An official of the ministry explained the decision as a response to "complaints in the press and from the public." The fear was that "the presence of too many women and inexperienced troupe members does not provide sufficient guarantees of serious attention and enlightened evaluation." It was not just that actresses were deemed incompetent solely on the basis of their sex. The official made it clear that even if actresses showed great discernment, their presence on the reading committee could not be tolerated, because it "invited criticism." That is, theater women seemed to cast a disreputable aura over serious deliberations simply by being present.[41]

A campaign from within the Comédie also moved the government to reduce actreses' roles in decision making. Actors in the troupe complained repeatedly to the minister about their female colleagues' ignorance and lack of literary taste. The charge was really no different from what Mille-Noé, Muriel, and Reiffenberg would say in the next several years: theater women were basically harlots, not artists, and they could not be trusted with professional decisions because they were on stage to display their bodies. The actors submitted as proof one actress's report that characterized a script as a "belle ouvrage," showing she was too obtuse even to know grammar (*ouvrage* is a masculine word), let alone to exercise literary judgment.[42] The actors did not bother to make distinctions among individual actresses and had no desire to separate the capable from the ignorant. Instead, they used gender as an absolute marker of intellectual and aesthetic capacity. A renewed sensitivity to women's failings had suddenly overtaken actors, government officials, and the public. It had become unseemly to have actresses carry out so straightforward a task as reading scripts, which they had been doing for the past half-century without objection.

Making the reading committee all male did not stop criticism of its decisions; yet there was no rethinking of the gender issue until just before the First World War. In 1868, the government appointed a commission of experts to look into reforms, because the new plays at the Comédie were not well received. On the commission were distinguished writers (Augier; Dumas, Jr.; Ernest Legouvé), theater directors (Nestor Roqueplan and Adolphe Lemoine-Montigny), and an actor (Régnier). Unlike the previous commission of 1847, this one reconfirmed the desirability of an exclusively male membership. Its innovation was to allow playwrights the choice of submitting their scripts to all the male members of the company for a reading. In this era of intensified fear of female control over male domains, actors, ministers, and the public presumed the naturalness of removing actresses from any sort of decision making.[43] Excluding them was necessary to achieve proper authority and unimpaired reason—and to keep up appearances.

There can be no doubt that the railing at actresses' destablizing powers in the theater world resonated in society at large. Thinkers as varied as the radical social theorist Pierre-Joseph Proudhon and the conservative literary scholar Hippolyte Taine concluded during the 1860s that French women in general were too strong, too much like actresses. Proudhon probably coined the term *pornocracy* in his study of "women in modern times," published posthumously in 1875. He followed Rousseau in conceiving of actresses' strength as a symptom of a more general problem: French women's influence over men. He concluded that "the French people are feminized [*un peuple femme*]" as a result of the power of French women.[44] Like Rousseau, Proudhon viewed the theater as one of the chief sites from which harlots exercised their tyranny. He acknowledged the wisdom in the ancient Greek custom of allowing only men on stage, because having actresses amounted to "an official exhibition of women, an act that repels people of respectable opinion." Although he believed that the closing of theaters was impractical, Proudhon did solemnly warn that "every well-meaning family man is fostering prostitution if he takes his wife and daughter to the theater."[45]

The cautious and conservative Taine did not attack theater as such, but his *Notes on Paris* of 1866, a readable work that went through many editions, portrayed actresses as representing a particularly visible case of French women's insubordination.[46] He observed that the complementarity of the sexes was not working as it should in France. "In German countries," he asserted, "woman seems to be made from another stuff than man and serves as his complement. Here, nothing of the kind." He cited the example of an actress who forced a duke to kiss her slippers and another who berated her protector when he handed over a wallet stuffed with bank notes instead of buying her a house. Taine observed that French women used the same means as actresses (and prostitutes) to achieve ascendancy over men, giving them pleasure and exciting their senses. The two thinkers from opposite ends of the political spectrum attested to a loss of confidence in virtuous and nurturing womanhood. The pre-1848 magdalenes of the stage were not even objects of nostalgia; they were simply forgotten in favor of virulent representations.

The Politics of Gender Panic

That theater women and courtesans, once confined to the edges of society, had now taken over its center was a notion that seemed self-evident to a great many people during the Second Empire.[47] The selective memory of the July Monarchy of 1830 to 1848 did not include the fact that the cream of Le Monde was familiar at the home of the notorious courtesan Esther Guimont, that royal princes had cavorted with actresses, and that the son of Louis-Philippe's banker had married Marie Duplessis, the model for *La Dame aux camélias,* in 1846.[48] The fact that Victor Hugo and his son Charles shared the same mistress (the actress Alice Ozy) in 1847 was a real-life version of the decadence that Zola explored later in *Nana.*[49] Even though libertinism had flourished before 1848, fear of theater women's powers had been low, and sympathetic representations had abounded. The foundational political myths of the constitutional monarchies in the first half of the century created the perception of a male ruling class that was capable of exercising reason and resisting female treachery. The strife and radicalism of revolution in 1848 undermined that confidence, especially among the upper classes, who were frightened by the disorder of republican democracy. However, when Louis-Napoleon restored order and initiated an authoritarian government, he failed to revive confidence. It was not simply that courtesans may have displayed more outrageous levels of ostentation after 1851; the culture of the Second Empire was particularly attuned to the frivolities of the elite and the capacity of theater women to exploit powerful men.

The Second Empire afforded no reason to presume that France was once again governed by a responsible, self-disciplined elite like the bourgeoisie. The new regime was based on a unique fusion of personal authority, in the hands of Napoleon III, and democracy. This emperor never enjoyed the heroic stature of his uncle, nor did he provide the same guarantees of powerful, manly control. His style of governing, notorious for its secrecy and sudden shifts of direction in policies, contributed to a public sense of puzzlement. The notables of France were half-hearted in their support of Louis-Napoleon and conditioned their approval of him on order, prosperity, and preservation of their privileges.[50] His other base of support was the least educated segment of the electorate, the rural masses. In the presidential election of December 1848, the peasants had catapulted Louis-Napoleon, the outsider and the conspirator, into power because of the vague promises associated with his family name. They continued during the Second Empire to give him the electoral majorities he needed to validate his authority.[51] So important was the peasant vote to the emperor that he tried to remove them from the domination of the landed notables, whom he did not trust.[52]

Far from establishing a public sphere composed of reasonable (male) individuals, the Empire decisively curtailed the functioning of civil society (until the liberalization of the late 1860s.) The Second Empire's constitution reduced parliamentary activity to a relatively obscure corner of political life. There were heavy restrictions on free speech and on the press. The state seized control of institutions and voluntary associations (the university, the bar, the Freemasons, and so on) through which the public had formerly acted independently of officialdom.[53] The emperor was determined to exercise personal power and to make all political activities dependent on his will.[54]

While the Second Empire did not have a place in its political cosmology for a responsible and rational elite analogous to the enlightened bourgeoisie of the July Monarchy, it did require a highly visible ornamental elite. The Empire depended on public spectacle to dramatize the grandeur and prosperity that it promised the nation. Napoleon III believed that a dull court was as bad for the nation as a weak army, and he revived a glittering social life at the Tuileries palace and at Compiègne. He required his courtiers to put aside bourgeois dress for knee breeches, silk stockings, and fine frills.[55] The sweeping plans to rebuild Paris under the direction of Baron Haussmann were aimed at creating a monumental capital. The authorities expected *la vie élégante* to flourish on the broad, handsome thoroughfares they laid out to replace the city's twisted, medieval streets, and it most certainly did. Paris became the foremost playground for Europe's rich and fashionable. What was not anticipated was the invasion of the Boulevard by the urban masses, who witnessed and imitated, as best they could, the rituals of worldly leisure.[56]

Key figures in the Imperial administration and at court ostentatiously dedicated part of their life to the pursuit of pleasure. Count (later, Duke) de Morny, Duke de Rivoli, Prince Achille Murat, and Prince Napoleon were playboys, dandies, and ladies' men even before 1848.[57] Because their lives were more public than those of the sober members of the Second Empire's diverse Imperial elite, their conduct made a greater impression. Whether their comportment was truly more extravagant than that of Duke d'Aumale or Count Edouard de Perregoux during the July Monarchy is far from certain. However, the frivolities and womanizing of the Bonapartists were taken to be emblematic of the regime, because there was no cultural imperative to imagine an elite exercising self-control.[58]

Because these changes in political culture made the Second Empire seem indulgent and undisciplined, fears of actresses' illegitimate dominion were already well established when the powerful midcentury surge of economic modernization was just taking hold.[59] The most rapid growth of the century occurred during the 1850s. Frenchmen built a substantial railroad network, allowing capitalist markets to penetrate to new areas and encouraging more efficient methods of production. An unprecedented outburst of entrepreneurship produced investment banks, department stores, giant utility companies, and even chain grocery stores. The rapid accumulation of wealth, largely confined to the well-off half of society, spurred not only impressive feats of engineering but also unprecedented growth in the industries that made for public spectacle, such as fashion and commercialized leisure.[60] The rising consumption of goods and their public display provoked increased social tension and fed popular attacks on women as sowers of disorder.

Prosperity was one of the regime's proudest accomplishments, but it also produced severe social and psychological strains. The new wealth upset the many who did not accumulate much, as well as those who already had an established status. The resentment of parvenus and the anxiety that material desires and values were replacing nobler values were both widespread. The liberal nobleman and social observer Alexis de Tocqueville complained that the Second Empire encouraged "love of gain, a fondness for business careers, the desire to get rich at all costs, a craving for material comfort and easy living."[61] In 1857, the Goncourt brothers entered into their private journal a frightening vision of hierarchy being dissolved by money: "Never before has the lower depths of society reflected the upper reaches so much as nowadays. Business deals [*des affaires*] from top to bottom. The genius, the mood, the character of France completely transformed, turned toward prices, money, calculation . . . France has become an England, an America!"[62]

One of the chief ways of dealing with the tensions of rapid economic change was to project the undesirable behavior and influence onto women, especially the most public ones. Revealingly, the Goncourt brothers had personified the new, mercenary France as a type of harlot, the *lorette,* a "businessman-woman" whom, they claimed, had recently replaced the good-hearted whore, the *grisette.* The *lorette,* a label that could include kept theater women, was already a well-worn symbol of the economic free-for-all that many feared was taking place about them.[63] Women were associated with and responsible for the disorderly aspects of economic change for a number of reasons. The Imperial elite used wives and mistresses as objects of conspicuous consumption, to celebrate their wealth and to legitimize it. Augier spoke to a public made uneasy by the parade of expensively dressed women on Haussmann's boulevards and at the Bois de Boulogne when he denounced the contagion of "women, luxury, paradoxes." One of the most visible symbols of the intensified consumption was the appearance of the department store, and it was seen to be very much a female institution. Emile Zola's novel about the new enterprise, *Au bonheur des dames,* linked women and department stores by noting "the omnipresence of women, the scent of women," that dominated and corrupted the emporiums.[64] Kept women eager to display their conquests through dress, jewels, and carriages provided a powerful representation of the vulgarity of the new wealth. The recurrent image of theater women and courtesans usurping the centers of attention reflected the fear that money would remake the world and corrupt even the intimate corners of life that should be pure.[65]

The upper classes of the Second Empire were worried that "traditional" markers of distinction—birth, family, and rank—were losing their meaning. They feared that money, celebrity, and visibility at fashionable events were taking their place. Theater women did stand out at the races, in opera boxes, and on the Boulevard, as they always had. Because of the rapid transformations in the economic and social fabric and the decline in the faith that self-disciplined men were in charge, these visible women were targeted as dangerous enemies of order.

*   *   *

Theater women's presumed success at ensnaring the important men of the Imperial regime and distorting public morality made them pertinent to the political struggles within the Second Empire. Stage women became key figures in arguments about the proper relation between middle-class men and the prodigal Imperial aristocracy—an amalgam of recently titled families, friends of the Bonapartes, and politically opportunistic notables that qualified as an "aristocracy" only in the context of France's chaotic postrevolutionary history. The arguments were really much more about moral leadership than class identity or domination. Conservative and Catholic factions held actresses and their protectors responsible for their anxieties about disorder. Conservatives had rallied around Louis-Napoleon because they were tired of the July Monarchy's liberalism, disgusted by the bohemians' promise of liberation, and terrified by the radicalism and feminism thrown up by the Revolution of 1848. They wanted Napoleon III to reestablish clear social hierarchies and defend Catholic moral precepts.[66] The Imperial elite was a constant source of disappointment, as well as a danger, since conservatives saw that its corruption was contagious. The views of Count Horace de Viel-Castel illustrate how morally conservative supporters of the Empire blamed theater women for the destabilization of society. An officer of the Second Empire, a favorite of Empress Eugénie, and a regular at the table of Princess Mathilde, Viel-Castel wrote with the frustration of a man who saw the regime with which he identified rotting from within. He was acutely aware of the ostensible parallels between the twilight of the Old Regime and his own day. Fearing that history would repeat itself, he particularly wanted to defend the aristocracy, such as it was, against its enemy, the "vile bourgeoisie." It filled Viel-Castel with foreboding that the bourgeoisie—personified by the newspaper magnates Louis Véron and Emile de Girardin—was waiting in the wings to take advantage of the morally weak aristocracy. He believed that the bourgeois parvenus were just as corrupt, but they were more hypocritical about morality and better able to use their corruption to gain control. Viel-Castel's conspiratorial vision linked predatory women and ambitious bourgeois men in an unholy alliance against the Imperial establishment. Actresses and other harlots weakened the ruling class, family by family, by seducing their scions and appropriating their wealth. The count believed that courtesans used the bourgeoisie to extend the corruption. The hated Véron, for example, was under the actress Rachel's thumb, and he made his newspaper, *La Constitution*, a voice for the opposition because the government refused to reduce her obligatory performances at the Comédie below three a week. "This is how destiny plays out in France: because a minister did not want to give an actress more leisure," Viel-Castel lamented.[67] In his thinking, it was necessary to police gender boundaries to defend the elite against the vile bourgeoisie.

There was also a group of worldly and pragmatic supporters of the regime, including many Boulevard writers, who perceived the womanly threat from another perspective. Theirs was a conciliatory vision of class relations. They appreciated the elegance of the courtier's lifestyle and would not have wanted to see its withdrawal into austerity. They believed that the elite had a right to indulge itself, and that the privilege was harmless—so long as there was a self-disciplined and productive bourgeoisie to serve as social ballast. Their view of the classes was complementary: a feminine aristocracy and a masculine middle class cooperated to make the Imperial order both materially and culturally rich. What worried these worldly supporters of the Second Empire was the potential for the libertinism and materialism of the day to corrupt the social middle. When these defenders of the status quo wrote novels denouncing theater life as a threat to the bourgeoisie, it was not a call to sweep away depravity so much as a plea for each class to be true to itself. Whereas the lord's way of life called for courting actresses, the Raphaels and Andrés of France should stay clear of those dangerous women. For the worldly conservatives, too, policing gender boundaries was necessary for well-ordered class relations.[68]

Disquiet over the visibility of corrupt women was a particularly powerful mobilizing force for the antiimperial opposition. The mid-nineteenth century contained a "republican moment," when enemies of the Second Empire strove to reconstitute a civil society that could exert a salutary influence on the Bonapartist state. By the election of 1863, republicans were the leading force in Paris and other large cities. This resurgent republican sentiment was overwhelmingly "middle class" in tone.[69] It acted in the name of a dutiful, manly, and domestically virtuous bourgeoisie oppressed by a corrupting aristocratic establishment. Unruly women, principally actresses, were seen to be the allies of this frivolous elite that threatened to poison the worthy elements of society.

Republicans patronized plays denouncing actresses, because they addressed issues that seemed vital to the nation. Barrière's *Les Filles de marbre* was the most widely performed play in provincial France during the Second Empire.[70] Augier's *La Contagion* attracted such crowds that the Odéon theater had to suspend its usual schedule of classics on the weekends to accommodate the spectators.[71] Alexandre Dumas, Jr., became France's leading playwright with his works about the reform of family life.[72] The corruption of morals was one of the republicans' most pressing indictments against the Second Empire. They were distressed that wives' taste for luxury, encouraged by the regime's ostentation and by mistresses' outrageous displays, was undermining the quality of family life. Republicans proposed a program of companionate marriages, secular education for women, and more understanding from dutiful husbands in order to counter materialistic temptations and incline wives to rededicate themselves to family duties.[73] The menace of theater women awakened Frenchmen to the need to change the political regime, or at least subject it to the control of men who knew how to act responsibly in their private lives.

The audiences that cheered the plays of Barrière, Augier, and Dumas believed they were seeing not simple family dramas but politically engaged fare. Against his wishes, Emile Augier was fashioned into a republican advocate of moral reform. The stormy premier of *La Contagion* in 1866 mobilized the opposition-minded students of the Latin Quarter (the play opened at the neighborhood's Odéon theater), much to the author's disgust.[74] The spectators were quick to identify the fictional Baron D'Estrigaud with Duke de Morny (recently deceased), who had been closely associated with the regime's excesses. They jeered Navarette and D'Estrigaud and wildly cheered the "bourgeois" protagonists, Tenacier and André.[75]

Appearing when the political vulnerability and waning international prestige of the Second Empire was becoming ever more apparent, Augier's play galvanized discontent. The theater critic Francisque Sarcey praised *La Contagion* as "a very accurate, profound, and current study of mores."[76] At the opening of Augier's next play in 1868, *Paul Forestière,* the theme of which, according to one critic, was "the glorification of duty against the storm of illegitimate passions," *Le Monde illustré* endowed the playwright with a biography appropriate to a moral crusader. Rather than participating in the frivolity of the Boulevard, he was said to live a reclusive life, devoted to physical exercise, especially fencing. The playwright, according to the article, was known for his broad shoulders and "male vigor—in contrast to the dissipation of many writers."[77] Though Augier strenuously denied the political implications of his plays, his apotheosis of bourgeois virtue made him seem to republican audiences the implacable enemy of public women in Imperial society. The republicanizing middle classes took his outrage over female corruption as proof of his intense virility.

Unlike Augier, Dumas allied openly with republicans in the cause of family reform.[78] In his younger days, Dumas had written about the demimonde (a term that he coined) in permissive terms, but he became increasingly concerned about the plight of the bourgeois family and redirected his art to didactic works on the problem. He propagated the notion that harlots had taken over society's most visible spaces and were imposing their values on respectable women. This is what he had in mind when he ominously proclaimed in the 1867 edition of *La Dame aux camélias* that "we are heading toward universal prostitution!" Dumas was particularly alarmed by the incidence of adultery, which, he believed, had reached alarming proportions even outside of the aristocracy. Wishing to do all that was possible to promote the higher form of sex worthy of citizens, he was an early advocate of reducing male sexual prerogatives by sanctioning seducers with fines and allowing paternity suits, forbidden at that time by the civil code.[79]

Dumas's conversion from the romantic view of the "sovereignty of passion" to a social defense of the family was symptomatic of wider currents of opinion at midcentury. Republicans—and Catholics, too, no doubt—put so much pressure on the authorities that they had to address the anxieties about unruly women invading respectable society. For the first time, the government adopted a policy of screening Opéra subscriptions to ensure that women of ill repute did not hold prominent boxes.[80] How well enforced the policy actually was is unclear, but officials at least took a stand on a problem that was distressing the public. Furthermore, the attorney general in 1865 proposed to the Senate a sumptuary law aimed at curbing the extravagance of female fashion.[81] The operetta diva Hortense Schneider, who incarnated the spirit of the day to more than one observer, felt the sting of a public fed up with unruly women. Soon after a highly publicized auction of her jewels, the dialogue in a new play had the singer exclaim: "I count upon the public to offer me more diamonds." Rather than taking the statement in the expected spirit of worldly good humor, the audience reacted with anger, and the police insisted that the line be dropped.[82] Though widely admired, the café-con-cert singer Thérésa was so alarmed by the growing revulsion against ac-tresses by 1869 that she decided on an appeal to patriotism and added "La Marseillaise" to her performances.[83] It is not surprising, then, that Gustave Flaubert had planned a novel on the Second Empire with the announced theme of "The Degradation of Man by Woman."[84]

Moments of national crisis, such as the Franco-Prussian War and the Paris Commune in 1870–71, could transform the resentment about "those sorts of women" into rage against them for ruining not just the theater but also the moral fabric of France. The actress Blanche D'Antigny (the inspiration for Zola's *Nana*) had attracted notoriety as the companion of important men and used her reputation to make a ca-reer on stage, scoring a decisive success in Hervé's operetta *Chilpéric.* Having chosen to remain in Paris during the disastrous war and the Prussian siege of the capital, she became a symbol of Imperial debauch-ery to the distressed Parisians. Crowds taunted her on the street, and she felt so threatened that she asked for police protection. To improve her reputation, she ostentatiously spent time nursing wounded soldiers, but the underlying resentments festered as defeat produced the rising of the Communards in the capital.[85] D'Antigny fled Paris for the rela-tive safety of the suburbs without, apparently, realizing how incendiary her libertine conduct had become. In Saint-German-en-Laye, she, the equally notorious Anna Delions, and other courtesans held what the press referred to as an "orgy" at the elegant Pavillon Henry IV. The sound of the women singing triggered an angry response from a crowd outside. They broke windows with stones and screamed, "Down with them! To prison with them. Whip the bitches [*catins*]!" Police protection was again needed for the party to escape. According to the coverage in *Le Gaulois,* the women were specifically identified as the "sluts of the Folies Dramatique theater," where D'Antigny had recently performed. Thus, the crowd focused on the women's identity as actresses (even though not all of the courtesans were).[86] The anguish of defeat and popular revolt crystallized the inchoate resentment that had long made the public so uneasy with the Imperial aristocracy and its unruly female companions.

The writer Jules Lecomte, inspired by the true-to-life qualities he saw in Barrière's *Les Filles de marbre,* published a letter in several newspapers in the summer of 1853, just as the minister of fine arts was about to remove actresses from the reading committee of the Comédie. Lecomte denounced "those insupportable painted dolls, covered with diamonds (and little underwear!), with that brazen look in their eyes, and insolence on their faces." Such "creatures" got men to do unimaginable things for them through their "mysterious ways." They relegated honorable women to obscurity and stole the limelight even at the most "solemn occasions."[87] Heavy-handed though it was, the antipornocratic fiction of the mid-nineteenth century, from Augier's L'Aventurière to Zola's Nana, spoke to a crisis of femininity that the French public perceived to be acute. That is why a remarkable array of public officials, journalists, writers, and intellectuals, including Taine and Proudhon, thought it worth their while to warn the public about the dangers posed by women of the stage. The writers concluded that French society lacked moral ballast, that the corruption of theater women had infected the rest of society, that French women were now too ambitious to play the natural role assigned to their sex, and so men could not carry out their responsibilities. Catholics and republicans, though odd political bedfellows, could agree on these ills. The first group was reduced to pleading with the Imperial elite to behave better, whereas the latter could see a solution only in a change of regimes and the restoration of the virtuous middle classes to power.

After the disasters of 1870–71, the warnings seemed in retrospect not only fully justified but insufficiently urgent. Zola's Nana articulated a fundamental republican myth about France's fall from grace—which was itself a new rendition of lessons established by the Great Revolution.[88] Independent and corrupt women had feminized men and hastened France's moral collapse; furthermore, the nation had been rendered so out of touch with reality that it did not even realize the danger it was in. France could not begin to recover, let alone return to greatness, until the proper gender order was restored.

Powerful as the antipornocratic discourse was for thirty years, it quickly abated and left little memory once the Third Republic was firmly established. As in the years after 1789, the restoration of a political framework seeming to ensure the rule of male reason quieted the railing against harlots.

7

Imagining Republican Actresses, 1880–1914

At the height of the Paris Commune, Blanche D'Antigny became a victim of the righteous fury of a mob driven to despondency by national humiliation and the civil war. A mere decade later, the singer Marie Bière was lionized by the public, even after having created a scandal. Bière had gone to trial for attempting to murder her wealthy lover, Robert Gentien, who had impregnated and deserted her. Though there was no question that she had intentionally shot Gentien, the jury, the press, and the public treated her with sympathy, even sentimentality, as a victim and a mother who had resisted her lover's insistence that she have an abortion. By contrast, they saw Gentien as a cad whose code of libertinism was cold and outdated.[1] Whereas the notorious D'Antigny of 1871 had seemed to bring the nation to its knees, the defendant Bière of 1880 reassured now-republican France about the moral superiority of womanhood.

The public response to the Bière trial anticipated another shift in the representation of actresses. Even in the confident era of bourgeois patriarchy prior to 1848, actresses had been, at best, disgraced women who might atone for their mistakes though self-sacrifice. In the three ensuing decades, fear of pornocracy had run high. Could views of theater women transcend fears of sexual indulgence and seduction so that actresses might become honored citizens? Would they ever take their places as members of the second sex along with bourgeois wives and mothers? Improbable before 1880, these changes were realized under the Third Republic. Theater women were republicanized to fit the ideological needs of a regime based on equality and middle-class morality.

159

The Discourse of the Chastened Stage

By 1880, a series of elections had shown conclusively that the majority of French voters preferred a republic to a monarchy. The balloting demonstrated the political decay of the conservative notables and, to many observers, the rise to dominance of Léon Gambetta's middling social ranks.[2] France was now in the hands of genuine republicans who were intent on installing, defending, and perpetuating, a regime of "the people," socially conservative though it was. It was to be based on secularization, popular (male) sovereignty, and a reverence for bourgeois values. An intensification of associational life (clubs, business groups, professional societies, and the like) in provincial France empowered men by bringing them together in the public sphere. This was the basis of Third Republic democracy.[3]

The Republic triumphant permitted—even necessitated—the rehabilitation of theater women. This was partly because the class and ideological structures that had undergirded the representation of theater women as mistresses to elite men became irrelevant to national life under the Third Republic. By no means did the actual practices and social habits of elite men change so much. In fact, Le Monde continued to exist in the capital—as Marcel Proust knew so well—and may even have entered into an Indian summer of sociability. However, it was now only one little corner of the social order. The body politic did not depend on it, because the republican regime ensured that those aristocratic men-about-town were not the ruling class. Though by no means a classless society, the Third Republic rested on the broad, popular cross section of the population that participated in civic life. It was open to any man who adopted the values and self-discipline thought to be representative of the middle classes. Hence, the new regime made the moral instruction of "the people" its first priority and crowning achievement.[4]

The republic that took root in France was no longer so hostile to women in public. Republicanism out of power had retained much of its classically ascetic, civic-centered culture. Years spent struggling against monarchy and empire had promoted the notion of citizenship as a high calling, based on virility and virtue. Once the Third Republic became the established regime, its reigning myths and mechanisms of power had to defend the status quo and mobilize votes from the uncommitted.[5] The rallying of peasants and recent converts from monarchy meant that the regime had not only to accept existing social hierarchies but also to participate in their perpetuation. The Third Republic, as a regime of the status quo, quietly put aside the heroic model of virile citizenship that Jean-Jacques Rousseau had drawn from antiquity and accepted the task of governing through existing hierarchies. It reduced citizenship to periodic and limited consultations at elections. By the same token, a republicanism once suspicious of capitalism and large-scale market forces beyond the control of the citizen made the transition to a liberal, procapitalist culture. Material progress generated through free market choices became the preoccupation of the regime.[6]

Changes in the goals and mentality of republicanism meant that policing boundaries between bourgeois domesticity and aristocratic libertinism was no longer an ideologically significant task. In any case, domestic virtue was not among the arsenal of strengths the bourgeoisie brought to the Republic. Rather than consecrating the final triumph of domesticity and a transition to marriage based primarily on affection, the Third Republic witnessed a tidal wave of adultery.[7] The hypocrisies of sexual life under the Republic helped the regime's elite make its peace with the culture of the Boulevard. Georges Clemenceau and Edouard Lockroy, mainstays of the new regime, were as much denizens of the backstage and fashionable rendezvous as was the editor of the Bonapartist *Le Gaulois*, Arthur Meyer. The conservative writer Ernest Daudet even detected a republican tradition of libertinism—an inferior copy of the aristocratic one, to his mind. Daudet expressed disgust for the calm, domesticated liaison that one of his friends had with an actress. The writer could not fathom why the friend bothered to leave his legitimate *foyer* for one that was "still more bourgeois." The whole object of keeping an actress, according to Daudet, was to have a "wildly passionate affair," not to mimic bourgeois conformity.[8] The republican libertinism, in fact, had deep roots. As Alain Corbin has shown, new sensibilities among the masses transformed encounters with prostitutes from cash transactions to fantasies of seduction. Men at the middle and lower edge of society were trying to capture a bit of the glamour that elites had long enjoyed in keeping theater women.[9] Thus, the Third Republic brought a democratization—perhaps a banalization—of libertinism. Being against kept women no longer defined a republican or a bourgeois.

After having fought for the purification of women during the era of

Imperial moral excess, some of France's most ardent republicans went to Geneva in 1878 to commemorate the centenary of Jean-Jacques Rousseau's death.[10] Despite the reaffirmation of its roots in Rousseau, who had attacked theater women as a source of societal corruption, the Third Republic proved to be untrue to them. This was a polity conditioned by an expanding commercial culture of department stores and mass entertainment; as such, it depended on women as consumers.[11] Mass evasion of the ideal of domestic virtue was an open secret. The republican order could not even maintain the separation between public and private spheres. Instead, it created a burgeoning "social" sphere to protect the family.[12] The Third Republic became the sort of regime that eagerly admitted theater women to respectability and, eventually, to public honors.

Rather than accepting the erotic culture of the stage, public opinion under the Third Republic found the theater increasingly moralized. The prevailing political myths after 1880 admitted that while France had had an elitist ruling class, the theater had been a threat to domestic virtue; but now that the regime of the people was in power and the aristocracy was irrelevant, the theater world had lost its wickedness and become more or less chaste. There may have been little empirical evidence for the proposition—in fact, much evidence to the contrary—but the facts did not impinge on an imagined reality of a regime in which a licentious ruling class no longer mattered. Thus, the distinguished critic René Peter, writing just before World War I, proposed that the Third Republic had made "moral egalitarianism" the order of the day. Willing to acknowledge that there was a republican brand of libertinism, a restrained version of the aristocratic, he found that "under the influence of this ideal, actors and actresses, whose mores had once seemed so dissolute, have now become respectably aligned [aligné bourgeoisement], so to speak, with an orderly immoralism, with this state of modest [moyen] libertinism that defines good taste today." He ended his lengthy study of theater history on a nostalgic note, recalling "the actress of yesterday— who numbed our minds with fantasy and legends and who brought some poetry to our existence." Peter predicted that the new stars in the dawning age of cinema would have to be "drudges who do not even have time to fall in love," because of republican moral egalitarianism.[13] Whereas Peter accepted that domestic virtue was mainly a matter of ap-

This image of the ballerina, or *rat,* from just before World War I challenged Edgar Degas's familiar depiction of the dancers as sensual and preoccupied with finding rich gentlemen to be their lovers. Here, the dancers are serious, professional, and too tired for late-night trysts.

pearances, another prewar commentator, Octave Uzanne, attested to a moralization pure and simple. He began his study of women in Paris by asserting that "when one pronounces the word 'actress,' a fervor of desire electrifies the listener." However, Uzanne believed that the heyday of the erotic culture of the stage was well past. Theater life, he claimed, had become "more moral, more bourgeois." He found that "actresses and dancers are now very respectable." In fact, Uzanne did not think that there were any more *rats* at the Opéra. By his day, the "wild" dance students had been replaced by serious, career-minded ones.[14] The playwright Alfred Capus agreed with Uzanne that moral gains made for artistic losses. Capus expressed a nostalgia for the "old days" when actresses had come from the gutter. The "popular instincts" they brought to the stage had been effective. Capus believed that now most female performers came from respectable families, and their orderly lives made them too restrained on stage.[15]

Once again, the young dancers at the Opéra became a marker of the moral state of the theater and the regime. While gentlemen's backstage visits to the dancers' lounge continued in fact (and, as we have seen, were even sponsored by the republican government) commentators affirmed that the situation had changed. The quasi-pornographic illustrated journal *La Vie parisienne* insisted in 1895 that the libertinism in the dancers' lounge had reached a height of worldliness under the Second Empire and then collapsed during the Third Republic. It wondered if its readers even remembered that the lounge had once been "a well-heeled salon and a meeting place for the most elegant men."[16] The journal's coverage of the "good old days" under the Second Empire was informed by its Bonapartist political slant. When the late-nineteenth-century press acknowledged the presence of gentlemen in the *foyer de danse,* it portrayed the relationships in paternalistic terms.[17] Edgar Degas's paintings of the subject suggest to some critics an intention to depict a dying world of aristocratic libertinism.[18]

In 1886, *Le Monde illustré* expressed anxiety about a most unrepublican frenzy that the belly dancer Fatma was stirring in the capital. She seemed a return to the worst excesses of the Second Empire. The journal compared her performances to Cora Pearl's scandalous appearance as Cupid in Offenbach's *Orpheus in Hell* in 1867, which had shown France to be "a volcano just before the eruption."[19] The columnist worried that the Fatma phenomenon had the same implications. However, such anxieties grew rare as the Republic endured. The discourse of reformed morals prevailed. Even the wicked *La Vie parisienne,* with its cartoons of bare-chested women and couples engaged in passionate embraces, portrayed actresses as career women who might have discreet lovers but would no longer sacrifice careers to their lovers' needs. And furthermore, they did not need the money of a rich lover because they were earning so much on their own.[20] The celebrated cabaret singer Yvette Guilbert professed in 1896 that female performers had gone too far in making themselves into respectable women. She appealed to her sister performers to resist behaving "like the wives of notaries."[21]

Le Temps of 1895 seemed to go out of its way to challenge Alexandre Dumas, Jr., when he insisted once again on the inevitable immorality of theater women. The newspaper reprinted comments that the venerable playwright (now in the last year of his life) had made about actresses' inevitable lack of virtue: that "a theater woman will be independent, easy, and, to portray passions [on stage], will necessarily experience them." Appealing to a particular understanding of physiology, Dumas justified his assumptions with the argument that "feverous work, the quest for feigned emotions, the thirst for applause, the joys of triumph . . . raise their bodies to a temperature they must maintain in real life." Because of this heat, he concluded, "few actresses escape what I call the professional malady." While these ideas would have seemed self-evident during the middle third of the century, they were now unconvincing, and the editors took exception to them: "Haven't we seen the fantastic qualities of our actresses fade since the days when they have become good bourgeois women [and] excellent citizens?" countered the newspaper.[22] Indeed, the editors of *Le Temps* gave actresses a chance (finally) to respond, and they also disagreed with Dumas. Jane Hading and Blanche Pierson reminded the playwright that actresses portrayed virtue more often than vice on stage and turned Dumas's argument on its head. Berthe Cerny proposed that, with talent, a well-behaved actress could easily feign vice. In truth, *Le Temps* of 1895 did not even give Dumas's antipornocratic views a respectful hearing.[23]

The will to find actresses sufficiently chaste was so strong that one of the most eroticized spaces in the French social imagination, the theater woman's dressing room, could undergo an ostensible domestication. Louis Germont's detailed tour of the dressing rooms of the leading female performers of the late 1880s repeatedly made the point that he was dealing with domesticated women. Scoffing at the "legend" that actresses "walk on flowers, in the midst of crowds of admirers, with diamonds around their necks and an ironic smile on their lips," he argued that "today [they] have the same way of life off the stage as the bourgeoisie."[24] Germont did not suppress perversions entirely. He noted, for example, that the much admired singer Jeanne Granier, known for her cross-dress roles, reveled in "the male realm of exercise, dreamed of taking roles in which she fired pistols, dueled, and climbed ropes." Nor did Germont disregard the sexually suggestive lyrics that made Anna Judic such a popular singer.[25] Nonetheless, the dressing rooms he described were extensions of a proper home. Gone were the red satins and the oriental ornaments; the touches were now homey. He found the circle of visitors to be family friends. A recurring image in Germont's text was the reassuring one of the performer's children, waiting with their nurse in the dressing room for the return of their mother, who was eager to leave the stage to pamper her babies.

The Boulevard press fell into line with the new discourse on bourgeois actresses. For years, *Le Figaro* had served to its readers tantalizing anecdotes about one "Mademoiselle X" or another engaged in outlandish behavior. Not surprisingly, the scandalous tales were most frequent in its columns during the time when pornocracy was most feared, between the 1850s and 1870s. After the founding of the Third Republic, *Le Figaro's* gossip about unruly theater women became quite rare. Apparently the Boulevard newspapers no longer felt empowered to portray actresses as goddesses of sensual delight who lived beyond society's rules. Newspapers also dropped references to actresses' displays of precious jewels and other ill-gotten luxuries. Instead, theater women became models for female fashion.[26] Rather than appearing on stage as women who sold their bodies, they became women who sold elegant attire to society ladies.

A new mode for observing actresses emerged that departed from the erotic culture of the stage. It compartmentalized their lives into categories of "artist" and "woman," with the latter category assumed to be completely conventional. In his eulogy for Anna Judic in 1911, the powerful theater director Fernand Samuel treated the deceased star in precisely this way. Samuel praised the singer "as a woman" for her devoted motherhood and her work on behalf of "the most humble charities." Speaking of "the artist" allowed Samuel to extol her talent.[27] When

Suzanne Desprès talked of her "indifference" to the death of the actor Constant Coquelin in 1909, the director of *Le Figaro* took offense and claimed her remarks were "unwomanly" *("n'ont rien d'une femme")* and inappropriate for an artist, since Coquelin had contributed much to the profession.[28] The scandalous woman was no longer an appropriate reference.

The new discourse of the chastened stage entailed nothing less than a regendering of the theatrical experience. For so long, commentators had written about the theater as appealing to men because they could dream about sexual conquest. However, if actresses were now women whose virtue had to be respected, male interest in the stage would be much curtailed. The status of theater as a masculine domain was in question. Frenchmen in the decades after the Franco-Prussian War were anxious about their capacity as potent and productive men. The army's humiliating defeat and France's demographic and economic inferiority raised painful doubts about the ability of French men to fulfill their "natural" duties.[29] The crisis led to a search for new anchors for maleness, and the theater lost out as an appropriate arena for the expression of prowess. Rather than womanizing as a sign of male potency, the newer models were strongly influenced by the British ideal of the ascetic and athletic gentleman whose muscles and self-discipline expressed his masculinity. Once the Boer War began (in 1898), a preoccupation with warfare and international competitiveness further redefined the appropriate areas of male endeavor. Sports, warfare, and business became the ultimate terrain on which men competed by the end of the century.[30] There had always been a tendency in the ideological battles between aristocrat and bourgeois to feminize libertinism as a sign of weak character. Now this tendency was supported by major cultural shifts, and the theater became less plausible as a setting for real men to do what men do.

Gaston Jollivet, who followed the ways of fashionable men from the Second Empire through World War I from the perspective of the Boulevard, was sensitive to the shift in what was expected of a man-about-town. In his youth, he recalled, a man made his reputation in society by "protecting" a dancer at the Opéra; by the turn of the century, reputation came from keeping a stable of race horses, he claimed. Still clinging to the male culture of earlier days, he viewed the obsession with physical vigor as a perversion of the grand French sense of *savoir vivre*.[31] The photographically illustrated magazines that proliferated after 1890 showed in several ways that Jollivet was correct about a realignment of masculine associations. First, the magazines specialized along gender lines more than the older Boulevard press had. Men's magazines covered news and battles; women's covered fashion, art, and theater. Second, coverage of the new interest in sports and male musculature multiplied.[32] The Casino de Paris, for example, began to offer wrestling matches as entertainment and featured the visit of the American bodybuilder Maurice Sandow.[33] Two plays about boxers opened in 1912 alone.[34] The youthful Jollivet had seen a time when the theater was the premier rendezvous for worldly men, who had often attended nightly. In 1895, *La Vie parisienne* presented the theater as an excursion to which eager wives dragged indulgent husbands, who had better things to do with their time.[35]

As male erotic fantasies of the stage dissipated—or were supposed to—theatergoing became an increasingly feminized cultural event. Observers now took women to be the backbone of the audience.[36] The ties between women's fashion and the stage, never lacking, grew stronger than before. It was not accidental that theater columnists began to stress the ever escalating level of luxury in costumes after the founding of the Third Republic.[37] Productions were now expected to include scenes the only purpose of which was to show off beautiful dresses and excite the female spectators. A new explicitness in the way theater and fashion intertwined became apparent. Photographs in advertisements featured actresses in scenes from plays, and the captions named the performers, so there was no longer any guessing about the connection. The presumption that actresses were wearing the signature gifts of their protectors became a thing of the past. Famous clothing designers now attired them to advertise their creations.[38] Theater women under the Third Republic were finally performing for women and instructing them on good taste.

Stern republican morality à la Rousseau had long condemned the theater for feminizing males and teaching the wrong lessons to good women. The aristocratic Boulevard culture had long made the theater an arena for the display of male prowess and female transgression. Under the Third Republic, both cultures declined. Republicans were no longer unhappy with women as consumers or with women being fashionable in society. The aristocratic elite had to keep up appearances to retain some political influence. The theater had increasing relevance for women because it exposed them to art and fashion. Men in the audience were now problematical if they took the stage too seriously or pursued actresses too publicly.

Honoring Theater Women

The irreverent *La Vie parisienne* magazine of 1893 was not implying anything positive, from its point of view, when it printed a cartoon showing statues of actresses replacing those of canonical male heroes in the Panthéon.[39] However, the suggestion that theater women had become the paladins of French grandeur was already a commonplace around the turn of the century. Even observers who were pessimistic about France's place in the world had to admit that theater was one area in which French culture retained international preeminence. Touring French actresses were well known to whip foreign audiences into a frenzy of enthusiasm for Gallic culture.[40] The king of Norway decorated Sarah Bernhardt in 1883 for her artistic achievements.[41] Would her own country be willing to do the same? In a telling metaphor, the Goncourt brothers had equated official recognition to marriage for a fallen women (*"Le mariage, c'est leur croix d'honneur"*).[42] That was exactly the problem for those who argued in favor of giving actresses official honors. For the state to recognize the achievements of theater women would be to confer respectability on them, and a century after the French Revolution, there was still no consensus to do so. Earlier improvements in status had only feminized them as sinful women destined to remain on the margins of respectable society. With actresses so much in the limelight, so much the subject of fashionable patter, it was easy to lose sight of the unspoken taboos, the subterranean resentments they inspired. These hidden forces came to the fore when the state was challenged to recognize actresses' service to the nation. It would not prove easy for public officials to find the courage to do so.

Napoleon I created the Légion d'honneur in 1802 to give recognition to citizens who had served the state in a useful capacity. The ribbon (which a recipient wore after being admitted) quickly became one of the most coveted marks of distinction that a French person could attain.[43] There was a lively debate throughout the nineteenth century on whether the state should admit stage performers, first male ones and then female ones. Every commmentator recognized that the debate was a continuation of the one that had gone on for centuries over the outcast status of thespians in France. Until the very end of the nineteenth century, there was a rehashing of precisely the same issues raised centuries earlier by Catholic moralists. Advocates usually struck a tone of indignation that, decades after the National Assembly had decreed the honorable status of performers in 1789, the same motives for opposing recognition were still so potent.[44] For this reason, it was clear that a decision in favor of a male actor would be noteworthy; one decorating an actress would be an epoch-making event. It would lay to rest centuries of debate about the respectability of theater women and signify the final triumph of enlightenment over prejudice. It would confirm that a revolution in public attitudes had occurred. Admitting that this change had, indeed, occurred was frought with political difficulties, even at the turn of the century.

A number of near misses had raised hope for the recognition of male actors. The eighteenth-century campaign for a royal declaration rehabilitating performers, led by Mademoiselle Clairon in the 1760s, had forced Louis XV to think seriously about the proposal—only to decide that he could not act.[45] Napoleon I's comment that he would have decorated François Talma "if he had dared" was frequently quoted as an indication of the stakes entailed in the issue. The leftward shift of Napoleon III's political base after the initiation of his Italian policy in 1860 motivated some officials of his regime to consider the progressive gesture of admitting an actor to the Légion d'honneur. Attention was fixed on Joseph-Isidor Samson of the Comédie, and the emperor consulted widely on the subject. Prince Jérome was enthusiastic, but the playwright Emile Augier was characteristically timid and spoke of "complications." Louis-Napoleon chose caution, and his refusal to act stimulated a new round in the old debate.[46] A republican champion of admission, Maurice Dreyfus, found himself addressing the same objections that Bishop Jacques Bossuet had advanced in the seventeenth century and that Voltaire, among others, had tackled in the eighteenth. Was acting, itself, so degrading that it made an otherwise virtuous performer unworthy of honors? Dreyfus, as so many advocates of "reason" before him, argued emphatically not: "It is evident that any actor whose behavior is irreproachable has a right to consideration." Dreyfus, however, did not think that the principle of personal merit applied to women. He implicitly accepted the position, dear to Rousseau, that women debased themselves irretrievably by being on stage, whereas men did not. This line of reasoning disposed of still another argument against decorating male actors: that the decoration of female performers would inevitably follow.[47] These claims did not sweep aside all objections, but the Second Empire found a way to admit Samson anyway (in 1864), as a professor at the Conservatory, not as an actor.

Advocates of decoration for actors based their arguments on "reason" during the Second Empire and earlier, but once the Third Republic was on safe ground, a new emotional issue, the revolutionary tradition, gave weight to the cause. Admitting male actors to the Légion would complete the work begun by the National Assembly in 1789 when it made actors citizens. Republican political leaders believed that they had to take this action, just as they had to reinstate divorce.[48] In 1883, Louis Delauny of the Comédie-française became the first to be decorated as an actor. The importance of the revolutionary tradition in bringing about the event was underscored in 1889, the centennial of the French Revolution, when two more actors, Jean Mounet-Sully and Gustave Worms, received the ribbon in the same year.[49]

The revolutionary tradition did not offer the same approval to achieving women.[50] However, the republic of the 1890s was not the one of 1793. Political democratization had led to a certain democratization of social attitudes. Consumerism, mass culture, and the breakdown of the public-private dichotomy also contributed to a weakening of complementary thinking about the sexes. More than ever, a woman could have an individual destiny without exciting disdain. It had not been problematical to decorate women for contributing to art. The painter Rosa Bonheur had been the first woman admitted to the Légion d'honneur, in 1851. Nor was it controversial to reward women for extending their maternal instincts beyond the *foyer*. The actress Marie Laurent entered the Légion in 1888 as a reward for her charitable work. However, the decision to admit a stage woman as such would cross a line and mark a new epoch. It would establish that the state could honor a woman for being public. It would extend the notion of women's usefulness as citizens far beyond activities recalling self-sacrifice and nurturing. It would celebrate women who were presumed to be morally suspect in their private lives for excellence in worldly achievements and for professionalism. As was the case for women's suffrage during the Third Republic, the obstacles to crossing the threshold became more political than ideological.[51] Republican political leaders in the decade before the Dreyfus affair were looking for allies on the right and did not want to offend Catholics and social conservatives.

Another obstacle of a practical nature was the obvious candidacy of

Sarah Bernhardt. There would have been general agreement with Louis Germont's opinion that she was "the greatest artist of the century."[52] However, Bernhardt was a liability to the cause because she was too controversial. Her publicity seeking, legal tangles with the Comédie, sexual scandals, and outspokenness made her offensive to many politicians.

An emotional issue was necessary to move cautious republicans beyond the impasse. Militant anticlericalism had motivated them to take action in favor of women in the past (as, for example, in giving girls secular schooling), and it served the purpose once again. In the aftermath of the Dreyfus affair, the cabinet of premier Emile Combes was eager to punish Catholics for having opposed republican progress, and the decision to decorate an actress became an obvious choice.[53] The remaining question was which performer would be appropriate.

Thus, in 1904, that long-awaited or feared threshold was finally crossed. The state found the courage, thanks to post-Dreyfus republican euphoria, to admit a theater woman—in her capacity as performer—to the Légion d'honneur. That honor was given to Julia Bartet, long a leading light at the Comédie-française.[54] This was a calculated choice, and the government was sending a complex message through it. Bartet appealed to officials because she was unlike Bernhardt. She had been content with a limited career within the Comédie. Professional recognition had come to her without her seeking it. Personally, she was self-effacing—that is to say, womanly, as society understood it. She always insisted, while granting numerous interviews, on her disdain for publicity and her quest for personal privacy. There were few rumors of scandal. Politically, she was safe, too.[55] According to Réjane's son, Jacques Porel (who, admittedly, had a personal ax to grind), Bartet was the darling of cultural conservatives. This was because, in addition to all her other safe qualities, her acting was cold and correct. "With her, everything [on stage] happens as in an orderly salon," Porel claimed. "There is no performer who is more academic or reassuring." He called her the "schoolmarm for great French texts."[56] The noteworthy victory for reason and progress that accompanied admitting an actress to the Légion d'honneur was infused with a great deal of caution.

The breakthrough, achieved in this conservative manner, seemed to make recognition of performers a hostage to political calculations. Decisions would still turn, to a degree, on ancient prejudices and misogynistic associations. When the Ministry of the Fine Arts, pushed by

Aristide Briand, nominated Sarah Bernhardt for the Légion in 1906, the chancellery rejected the recommendation. Its grounds for doing so showed that it was still not possible to discount entirely the unruly influence theater women were supposed to have over important men. The officials countered Briand's recommendation with the objection that France "could not decorate all the dancers and music hall singers who are 'friends' of Messieurs, the ministers. We do not have enough awards for that!"[57] The fear that elite competition to please mistresses would besmirch the Légion d'honneur showed that an old taboo was still very much alive, though no longer a controlling force. The Third Republic had consecrated the idea of a republican actress—in part, to spite antirepublicans—but apprehension about actresses' domination of men still lingered.

Other sorts of recognition accompanied the collapse of the taboo against the state's acclamation of theater women. Paris, the world capital of theater at the time, had not named one street after an actress, but in July 1899 the municipal council finally voted to do so. It honored Rachel with a street named after her in the eighteenth arrondissement.[58] After 1890 the capital had a left-leaning council on which socialists and radical-socialists cooperated to pass progressive measures. The aldermen were eager to undertake even such endeavors as providing wage earners with rights in the workplace.[59] The Dreyfus affair and the will to defy the powerful nationalist movement in Paris encouraged the council to take symbolic steps to raise the ideological flag of the left. A flurry of proposals for politicized street naming followed. The aldermen voted more than once in 1899 to rename the boulevard d'Italie (thirteenth arrondissement) the boulevard Auguste Blanqui, after the working-class hero, only to have the national government annul the provision. The councilmen protested the interior minister's actions because his motivation, to avoid "wounding reactionary sensibilities," was just what they wished to accomplish in this era of republican militancy. Undaunted by the obstacles, Alderman Pierre Morel, speaking for the Republican-Socialist Committee, proposed naming a trio of streets after Liberty, Equality, and Fraternity. A few months later, the council passed the resolution in favor of the avenue Rachel, and the central government accepted the act.[60]

It must be said that the measure—still regarded as daring in many quarters—was aided by local interests and by pragmatic concerns. Alderman Adrien Veber pointed out that the merchants along the route preferred the new name to the lugubrious former one, rue du cimetière de nord (Northern Cemetery Street). Moreover, the councilmen were careful to rebaptize an out-of-the-way thoroughfare that would not draw much attention. Alderman Charles Vaudet joked that when the day came to name a street after Sarah Bernhardt, she would settle for nothing less the most central site in the city, the Place du Châtelet.[61]

Having named one street in the capital after an actress, the councilmen felt they had done enough and did not extend the honor to other performers. (Bernhardt did not get her street until 1936). The act apparently was too much of a provocation to repeat often. In any case, the city of Paris came under the control of conservatives in 1900, and the politics of honoring theater women in the capital faded out of fashion.[62]

Before the Third Republic, France did not have a single public monument honoring a stage performer. In connection with the effort to bring a male thespian into the Légion d'honneur in the 1880s, private individuals raised money for a statue of François Talma, intended for a site near the entrance to the Comédie-française. According to one newspaper, Talma was perfect to initiate the commemoration of performers because of his "proper behavior and elegant character." The journal admitted that a statue honoring an actress was out of the question, for the "difficulties of their private lives would raise resistance."[63] Demonstrating that shifting attitudes about theater women were not just confined to the capital, provincial France pushed ahead of Paris on this symbolic breakthrough. In 1895, the village of Saint-Saulve (Nord) was the first to defy the prejudice by erecting a statue to its native daughter, Mademoiselle Duchesnois, who had starred at the Comédie-française during the first years of the century. In 1896, the town of Condé (Nord) followed suit by inaugurating a statue to the great eighteenth-century performer Mademoiselle Clairon. Arriving at a consensus on honoring these stars was made easier by their being part of history (Duchesnois had died in 1835), so it was something of a political leap for Toulouse to erect a statue to Anaïs Fargueil the moment after her death in 1896.[64] Local pride and hopes of generating tourism played a part in these actions by municipal councils in the provinces. Yet the decisions also confirmed that political and ideological momentum was now decisively on the side of legitimizing actresses as women and women as achievers.

Not surprisingly, there was no controversy when actresses were finally restored (after a fifty-seven-year absence) to the reading committee of the Comédie-française in 1910. The administrator, Jules Claretie, proposed the reform to the fine arts minister on the grounds of equity, and both acted knowing that public opinion would accept the change.[65] For so long, the battle to give official recognition to theater women had sparked righteous outrage from both sides. The symbolic breakthroughs, when they came, inevitably entailed all sorts of ambiguities. The republican principle of being honor-bound to recognize women's accomplishments needed anticlericalism as a galvanizing force. Actresses continued to evoke contradictory and anxiety-producing responses even among the progressives who sought to do them justice. Nonetheless, with their enemies flailing about them, republicans did decide that celebrating female achievement and exonerating actresses from moral stain were principles on which they should act. They took an important step toward normalizing women who had the ambition to be in the public sphere.

Tales of Independent Women

Theatrical directors were reluctant to revive Emile Augier's antipornocratic classic, *L'Aventurière,* after 1880. When they did, they preferred to give it a new interpretation. The version that the Comédie-française mounted in 1910, with Cécile Sorel in the role of Clorinde, completely overturned the original thrust of the plot. Rather than featuring a predatory actress, the revival was about the moral redemption of the adventuress. New lines were added to support this interpretation.[66] In this way, the script came to fit into the corpus of fiction about theater life that was published under the Third Republic. Writers brought to their fiction the favorable attitudes of a society that was finally ready to admit that an actress might be a woman like any other.

Fiction about theater life exploded after 1880. There were at least forty-two novels and plays with actresses as protagonists written between then and the Great War. On a superficial level, the fiction was at odds with the discourse of the chastened stage that proliferated in the press and in descriptions of theater life under the Third Republic. Scenes of aristocratic libertinism still abounded (for the purpose of enticing readers, one must suppose). Nonetheless, writers took theatrical fiction in a direction consistent with the construction of republican actresses. The fear of harlotry disappeared entirely from novels.

There were simply no predatory actresses, even though the characters remained strong women. Moreover, sexual purity was no longer a necessary condition for theater women to be admirable.

Félicien Champsaur's novel *Dinah Samuel* of 1881 shows just how much of a sea change there had been, though it appeared only two years after Zola's *Nana*. Few readers would have had difficulty guessing that they were reading about the intimate life of the rising stage sensation Sarah Bernhardt. All of her notorious exploits (including her lesbian relationship with the painter Louise Abbéma) were recounted in great detail. Dinah, like the live Bernhardt, and like Nana, writes her own rules and does not pay much heed to social conventions. For all that, Dinah is by no means a threat to the social order. The male protagonist, Patrice Monclair, a dreamy young poet, pursues her and learns about life from her. The hard knocks he takes make him into a man. He gives up his impossible dreams and becomes a rich banker. Far from being destroyed by unruly women like Dinah, he ends up with the means to buy their love whenever he wishes.[67]

Champsaur's novel, in fact, explored one of the dominant themes in the fiction about theater life, the condition of the woman without a male master. Writers probed what would happen if women had the same freedom to pursue their interests and desires as men did. Although in earlier times this might have been a recipe for dire predictions about the social consequences, such was not the case in the theater fiction of the Third Republic. Society is now able to cope with independent women.[68]

Even the misogynistic Edmond de Goncourt was sensitive to the shifting cultural currents, and his 1882 novel *La Faustin* did not pose the kind of warning that *Charles Demailly* had only a few years earlier. In it, the great actress Faustin, modeled on Rachel and Fargueil, is not a predatory woman. She is a free woman who has devoted her life to the theater. She knows she should not marry and refuses the proposal of her lover, Lord Annandale. He dies suddenly, but she was not the cause. Faustin is simply true to her nature.[69]

The actress Marie Colombier contributed to the fiction on this theme with *La plus jolie femme de Paris* ("The Prettiest Woman in Paris") in 1887. The main character, Pauline, takes on a new identity as Lilli when she becomes an actress. Her life is a whirl of rich men and expensive gifts. However much she lives outside the boundaries of normal life, Lilli/Pauline is careful not to harm anyone. When the wife of her lover commits suicide because she has lost her husband's affection, Lilli realizes it is time to become Pauline again, for things have gone too far. Once the toast of Paris, Pauline retires to a life as the "happiest of countrywomen," demonstrating that even women without masters were guided by conscience and duty.[70]

Henry Bauer (probably the illegitimate son of Alexandre Dumas) put the theater world under a microscope in *Une comédienne: Scènes de la vie de théâtre* ("An Actress: Scenes from Theatrical Life") in 1889.[71] It is shown to be an amoral milieu in which promiscuity is rampant. The young actress Lucy is free to follow her ambitions and even her physical passions, but no one gets permanently hurt. The rich Lepic enjoys being Lucy's lover; when it comes to passing on his fortune, he is able to leave most of it to his family and presents his mistress with only a token of his affection. The young writer Paul Jourdan recovers from a stormy affair with Lucy and is ready to move on to deeper relationships. The protagonist, herself, marries a fellow actor, reins in her passions, and quietly pursues her career. Thus, after the orgy of debauchery, the characters settle into bourgeois conformity after all.

Paul Dollfus used the theme of the autonomous woman to comment on a situation that the neo-Rousseauists of midcentury had furiously denounced: harlots invading the stage. In his *Sociétaire: Moeurs de théâtre* ("Troupe Member: Theater Mores") of 1891, Lucinde Noirmond gets a trial appointment at the Comédie-française as a result of protection from powerful officials. Rather than portraying this as a matter of corruption and decline, the author treats Lucinde as a heroine who uses her wits to triumph over intrigue and become a permanent member of the troupe. The novel exposes the deplorable hypocrisy in the House of Molière, and the courtesan's arrival brings a breath of fresh air. Her original acting techniques raise the artistic level at the Comédie.[72] Forty years after the revival of neo-Roussseauist fears in the theater world, mistresses on stage no longer inspired anxiety.

In these and a few more novels, the authors gave women the autonomy men enjoyed. The result was often, but not always, libertinism. Yet independent women could find their way out of unruliness and live admirable lives. In any case, the disorder was contained. The novels made a case for tolerating ambitious and sexually liberated women.

The consequences of marriage to an actress was another theme to which writers often returned under the Third Republic, because it provided a particularly dramatic way to explore the tension between individual desire and social conformity. Prior to 1848, authors excoriated society for the prejudice against marrying an actress. Between 1848 and 1880, however, the prejudice was treated as a wise social convention, a bulwark against gold diggers who would invade respectable society.[73] The pendulum swung back again to the more tolerant attitude under the Third Republic. All the marriage novels presented the couples in a sympathetic light.[74]

Alfred Sirven's 1889 work *La Linda* had obvious parallels with the Dumas play (of 1876) *La Comtesse Romani,* in that both explore the trials of a nobleman who marries an actress but is not prepared to deal with the ramifications.[75] Sirven's work, however, does not treat the actress as the culpable party. When Laura Linda, a star at the Opéra, falls in love with the retiring Viscount Antonin de Bizeux, both have their worries. The singer struggles with her commitment to the stage; Antonin, with appearances. They are perfectly honest with each other and seek to make difficult compromises, but the marriage is tense and unsatisfying. After a crisis, however, Laura becomes pregnant and sincerely commits to *foyer* and motherhood.

Two other novels echoed the Goncourt brothers' *Charles Demailly* in recounting the difficulties of a husband whose wife had a life of her own; but in neither post-1880 fictional account did the man-slaying actress reappear. In Louis Vaultier's *Une etoile* ("A Star") of 1898, two performers marry but discover they cannot live happily. Luc soon becomes jealous of the success enjoyed by his wife, Rosette. While she remains a completely admirable figure, Luc's moroseness deepens into obsession, and he attempts to kill Rosette. She recovers and courageously goes on to start a new life. Vaultier reversed the Goncourts' formula and made the actress-wife the victim—and an innocent one, at that.[76] Paul Flat's *Le Roman de la comédienne* ("The Story of an Actress") even offers a happy ending. Jacques Bandol marries the beautiful and talented Jenny Servoz. She is an upright woman, filled with good sense. Reflecting on the temptations that endanger stage women, Jenny offers the view that "for those women who possess discernment and respect for themselves, the very frequency of the temptations and their vulgarity should be a call to order."[77] The two are able to live happily together for a while, but eventually Jacques is troubled by Jenny's success and by the fact that he is not the only focus of her existence. His crisis of confidence deepens, and eventually he flees to his native Provence. His taking stock and the advice of reasonable friends make him see that Jenny is his life. He returns to her, adapting to the situation. The novel seems to advocate the view that a decent man could have a wife who did not live only for him.

Thus, authors under the Third Republic returned to the support of the feminine actress and the unconventional marriage. Like writers of the first half of the century, they saw no reason why love should not conquer all. The bourgeois prejudice against theater women was once again portrayed as philistinism that had to be swept away. The writers assumed that the social order was not so fragile that it had to be on guard against adventuresses and women of marble.

Yet another theme in theatrical fiction of the Third Republic entailed measuring men's strength of character by the standards set by theater women. The cultural context was the fin-de-siècle crisis of masculine identity, when there was much anxiety about Frenchmen having sufficient courage and virility. However, female strength was not held responsible for instances of male weakness. Rather, stage women served as models for ways in which men ought to be strong.[78]

The title of Emile André's 1882 novel *Coulisses et salle d'armes* ("Theater Wings and Fencing Hall") refers to arenas in which one might expect to find, respectively, strong women and strong men.[79] Ludovic Espardenave, fencing master and decorated war hero—the quintessential manly man—falls in love with the actress Mademoiselle Mily. She is already living with the author Fayol and remains faithful to him. If Ludovic is out of place in the theater world, it is his own fault, for Mily never leads him astray. The fencing master has to admit that the actress is "more respectable than many society women, who often feign virtue."[80] Ultimately, Ludovic's manly qualities do not include control over his passions. His unrequited love for Mily gets him involved in a duel with Fayol, and he is bested. He leaves for the provinces a sadder but wiser man. The actress did not cause his failure; in fact, she might have served as a model of self-control and self-knowledge.

The 1899 novel *Le Fauvre: Moeurs de théâtre* ("The Wild Beast: Theatrical Mores"), by the prolific Joseph and Justin Boex, employed heavy-handed stereotypes to make its point.[81] Henriette Samy is a paragon as a woman and as an artist. She has great talent, grace, and beauty. She is still a virgin, having saved herself for the right man. Count Charles de Latorel would seem to be fully worthy of this prize. He is handsome, muscular and serious. His friends call him "the wild beast" because of his uncommon strength and spectacular physique. Charles has renounced the idle frivolity of his class to work at the profession of playwright, a decision that Samy respects. When the two fall in love, Charles has the virility to give Samy all the physical pleasure she could ever want. Having built up Charles's manly credentials, the authors proceed to show that he is not really virile enough to be worthy of Samy. Charles lacks the courage to stop his effeminate, class-conscious brother and shrewish mother from planning his marriage to an heiress (with tainted Jewish blood). Samy challenges him to choose between her and the family tradition, and Charles, not being up to the task, loses the most perfect of women.

In Jean Blaize's *Les Planches* ("The Stage") of 1892, Adrien Dul is haunted by his mother's fanatical Catholicism and royalism even as he strives to become an actor. An affair with the loving actress Hilda helps him grow. He comes to learn that the world is more complicated than the one in which his mother taught him to believe. Eventually he marries the charming actress Edmée and gets on with his life. Theater women help him transcend a feminizing piety and mother-worship to become an efficacious man.[82]

While the Third Republic claimed credit for conquering medieval prejudices and honoring actresses for their contribution to French culture, the fiction writers of the day took the matter a step further by presuming a widening consensus for women's individuality.[83] The authors portrayed actresses as autonomous, and their characters did not destroy themselves or society by living outside of masculine domination. Novelists had the courage to give actresses complexity and to break down negative stereotypes. The fictional theater women fell into degradation on their own but also rose above morally difficult circumstances. The writers made femininity compatible with achievement. In this way, they caught up with what many actresses were saying about themselves. Above all, the writers now defined actresses' strengths in terms of accomplishment and virtue, not in terms of the ability to ruin men.

The evidence for the invention of republican actresses flies in the face of the widespread understanding of late-nineteenth-century art and literature as misogynistic. According to many scholars, after the traumatic defeat of 1870, Frenchmen struggled against fears of decline on the international scene, biological and cultural pollution, and degeneration by redoubling efforts to dominate women. Art supposedly expressed a defensive reaction that had much invested in attacking any show of female independence.[84] However, the antifeminist reading of so much fin-de-siècle culture overlooks a rich vein of positive images of women. There had certainly been a noteworthy improvement since the Second Empire, when new money, conspicuous consumption, and social fluidity had all been represented by the kept woman.

Art accurately reflected the complicated but ultimately progressive path toward accepting an enlarged role for women at the turn of the century. Social attitudes, even among the upper classes, had democratized during the Third Republic. There was greater acceptance of personal expression and personal achievement for men, to be sure, but also for women. Women were less likely to be stigmatized for consuming, enjoying commercial leisure, and pursuing individual destinies. The idea of ambitious, achieving, and public women was no longer so frightening. To a notably greater degree than at any point since the Great Revolution, women were permitted to be autonomous individuals. However, the shift in attitudes took place more on a pragmatic level than on an ideological one. The acceptance of a certain degree of personal autonomy for women had to be accompanied by an affirmation of the primacy of domestic responsibilities and even by a denigration of the "New Woman," who embodied the liberties. Women's suffrage remained problematical, but more because of the politics of the issue than because women were perceived as hopelessly unworthy of full citizenship. Without the liberating changes in gender understandings, however, the Third Republic could never have conferred its official approval on actresses.[85] The fiction writers of the fin de siècle were thoroughly correct to presume that the public was ready for women who sought to develop their potential on their own terms. Actresses being held up as models to bourgeois women—once unthinkable—became a prosaic feature of life as the nineteenth century ended.

8

Performing a Self

The unstable representations of theater women that French society produced across the nineteenth century had a marked impact on the performers' personal identities. Actresses could not evade the power of prevailing stereotypes, but they could respond creatively as they developed strategies for giving meaning to their lives, claiming a sense of dignity, and relating to the men who mattered to them. The performers manipulated the public representations to their own purposes.[1] That is why their memoirs and private letters reveal a succession of trends in self-fashioning across the nineteenth century. Not surprisingly, during the first half of the century, actresses were particularly enthralled by the ideals of true womanhood and sought dignity by translating into their own idiom the code of honor laid down for chaste women. In the second half of the century, as the quest to be good women by conventional standards came to seem, at first, futile, then unnecessary, strategies for achieving self-worth increasingly focused on the quest for a place in the public sphere.

Magdalenes, Artists, and Vamps

"In Paris," proclaimed a columnist for *L'Illustration,* "one can be a woman without being a wife or daughter."[2] Whereas most women of the nineteenth century had to construct their identities around the men in their lives, actresses, "Parisian women" par excellence, had a much wider range of options. Yet, more often than not, actresses imagined their feminine natures in terms that mixed conventionality with defiance. Particularly in the first half of the nineteenth century, their lives featured a quest for authentic passion that led, in the end, to self-sacrifice, family obligations, and fidelity to a man. They even renounced opportunities for enrichment and independence in pursuit of their moral vision. Virginie Déjazet and her offspring well illustrate this mode of self-fashioning. This actress was one of the most beloved stars of the nineteenth century. Born in 1798, she began performing as a child and did not stop until she fell mortally ill in 1874. During that long span, critics rarely found her anything less than a delight. She had a celebrated voice, described as "crystalline" and "pure," and she brilliantly put over her comic songs. She was judged peerless in playing *travesti,* or cross-dress roles, in which she impersonated boys who were about to have their first romance, who sang silly songs (often with sexual innuendoes), and who got involved in preposterous situations. Her funeral in 1875 was the occasion for an enormous outpouring of devotion on the part of fans.[3] Henry James, as a newspaper correspondent in Paris, wrote that "150,000 people have followed her to the grave; she had the funeral of a crowned head."[4]

At the same time Déjazet was venerated as a performer, strange stories circulated about her sexual appetites. The star herself acknowledged having a reputation as a "madly passionate hysteric," in a remarkably frank interview given at the age of fifty, but rejected charges that she had had herself served to men on a silver platter at a banquet or that she had slept with some of the lovers with whom her name was linked.[5] The interviewer, for all his impudence, did not ask her directly about the ultimate basis of her reputation for sexual deviancy, a string of affairs with younger men.[6] It was easy for the public to connect her immodest sexuality to her skill at playing male roles and her tendency to dress occasionally as a man offstage.[7] The journalist Henri Rochefort referred to her affectionately as "the charming little hermaphrodite."[8]

While common opinion obsessed about theater women who preyed on men and their fortunes, Déjazet thought herself capable of a pure, selfless love that was too elevated for men to experience. It was a point of honor for her never to ask her lovers for money; in fact, they were often in debt to her. Even though she was often in financial difficulty due to her family's demands and unwise investments, she conceived of her liaisons as matters of passion.

At the height of her fame, in 1834, the actress began an affair with

Count Arthur Bertrand, the son of a deceased Napoleonic general. She was thirty-six years old, and he was just seventeen, one of those schoolboys who became infatuated with a stage star. Though charmed by his attentions, Déjazet did not take the relationship too seriously until Bertrand was in his twenties and had become very much the playboy. By this time, the actress desperately wanted all the attention he could shower on her—and more.

Déjazet's letters to Bertrand over a ten-year span show that she saw herself in three different roles, as mother, wife, and mistress (her term was *"maîtresse ordinaire"*). In the early days, Bertrand had worshipped her as his "second mother" while his biological one was dying. Déjazet claimed the mother had given her blessing to their liaison because the star offered her young admirer such good advice and kept him from an inclination toward "follies" inherited from his father. Déjazet maintained a fondness for the motherly role throughout the affair, and at moments of particular tension reminded Bertrand of his youthful devotion to her. "I keep you a child in my memory," she wrote to him. Her mothering may have been a point of contention between them, for in the face of her protests against his gambling and running up debts, he protested, "I am a man!"[9]

Despite her proclivity to be the mother, Déjazet yearned to be Bertrand's "wife," but she did not mean it literally, for she could not imagine that a woman "of her sort" could marry a man of Bertrand's social standing. Her notion of wife took its meaning from its opposition to "the common mistress." The latter, she wrote, "makes light of the past, accepts the present, and does not think about the future." Though she did not say it in so many words, being accepted as Bertrand's wife entailed devotion and fidelity on his part. It was a status that made the future seem "so beautiful, so sacred." When the two fought, she reminded him that he had called her his wife.[10]

The affair evolved over the ten-year period in grand emotional waves, offering Déjazet a great deal of elation and pain. She had trouble balancing her career and the affair. When Bertrand went to the provinces to visit his family, she was so distracted that she could not perform well. Yet, at a moment when Bertrand was being attentive to her, Déjazet decided that it was financially necessary to tour the provinces and leave him behind. Alone, often ill, faced with daily challenges on these tours, Déjazet tormented herself by imagining Bertrand's dalliances.[11]

Bertrand was young, handsome, and rich. He inherited the princely income of 100,000 francs but incurred the heavy expenditures of a play-boy and ran up gambling debts. The milieu in which he circulated did not encourage or even expect him to be faithful to a mistress. Young men like him wanted "agreeable animals." He pursued other women, Déjazet believed, as a matter of prestige, even though he continued to care for her. She claimed that Eugénie Doche and other actresses wanted Bertrand in order to humiliate her, attributing base motives to her rivals while believing that her own were pure.[12]

Déjazet went to great lengths to keep mercenary matters out of the affair. When the star had some financial reverses and creditors were on the verge of repossessing her home at Porte-Seine, she was disappointed that Bertrand did not offer to come to her aid, but she kept silent. She even lent him money to cover gambling debts and was never repaid. The model of the predatory mistress was abhorrent to Déjazet, and she fled from the stereotype.[13]

Weary of the tribulations of the affair, Déjazet finally broke with Bertrand in 1842. Within five years, the star was involved with another younger man, the actor Charles Fechter.[14] She was now fifty, and he was twenty-five and married. He was just at the beginning of his career (earning a mere thousand francs a month) and awed by his lover's fame. He referred to her as "the immortal Déjazet" and called her "the first actress of our day." Fechter's own career received a boost in 1852 when he created the male lead (Armand Duval) in *La Dame aux camélias*. The role gave him a certain cachet for a time, but he did not achieve the stellar status of his lover.

Déjazet was even more insecure about the relationship with Fechter than she had been with Bertrand. Though the actor's missives were uniformly warm and reassuring, she could not believe that he loved her nearly as much as she loved him. She was often painfully in doubt about his faithfulness. At times, she even resorted to dressing as a man ("Petit Paul" was the name she gave to this role) and walking on the Boulevard to see if she could find Fechter with another women. She would stand outside on icy nights to watch the silhouettes in the windows of Fechter's dressing room. She never caught him in the act, but that failed to comfort her.[15]

This was another affair in which the man did not bear any financial burden. She, as the partner with the greater earning power, lent money to Fechter. When he borrowed a thousand francs in 1854, he extolled the "masculine frankness [that] is growing between us." Though two lovers, they were also, he said, "two men of honor who esteem one another . . . hence, a service rendered by one translates into good fortune for the one who asked and happiness for the one who rendered it." Certainly, Fechter's gratitude was welcome, but the terms might well have made Déjazet worry that her independence reflected unfavorably on her femininity.

Since Fechter was married, Déjazet had to settle for the role of mistress. Both of the lovers expressed consummate respect for the convention of keeping up appearances. Fechter did not define the relationship as the kind of open secret that would raise his reputation among men of Le Monde. He described himself as a serious fellow who wanted nothing more than a life of tranquil domesticity with his wife and his lover. Déjazet, for her part, readily conceded to Charles's wife the respectability that she, as "the other woman," did not deserve. Even more than Fechter, Déjazet was willing to put his wife on a pedestal.[16] Her respect for appearances was undoubtedly sincere, but perhaps at the back of her mind was the hope to curb the actor's roving eyes by keeping him ensconced between his wife and his mistress.

A major bone of contention in the relationship was Déjazet's blindness to the faults of her son, Eugène. She was one of the many actresses who displayed exceptional devotion and indulgence for their children—who often had been born out of wedlock. (One source referred to actresses' ostentatious motherliness as a form of "expiation.")[17] Born in 1819 and never recognized by his father, Eugène was raised by Déjazet on her own. Perhaps because she spoiled him, he grew into a profligate young man who was financially dependent on her. He led a fashionable life on his mother's money. Fechter's letters were filled with sober advice about Eugène, but the indulgent mother was unable to heed it. The actor warned his mistress about investing in Eugène's ill-fated theatrical projects and tried to reduce the son's influence over his mother. In 1852, Eugène asked for money to carry on with a lover who had a reputation as a courtesan. He defended her as a woman who had been rehabilitated by her devotion to him. Fechter, though playing the character in *La Dame aux camélias* who makes exactly that claim about his lover, would have none of it. He urged the star to refuse to support the couple. Women like that, he wrote to Déjazet, "almost never have a heart capable of true love"; such "Manons" know only how to "deliver their senses to those who can pay." Fechter's declaration that he "held such people in horror" must have upset Déjazet, for, after all, she was striving to be exactly the sort of rehabilitated Manon whose existence Fechter denied. She must have been disappointed, indeed, that her own example did not inspire her lover to be more trusting. The tension between the lover and the family was one of the causes of the end of the affair.

Déjazet was in anguish much of the time, not only because of her problematical love affairs but also because of tense relationships with her progeny.[18] She was the matriarch of a family that was emotionally as well as financially demanding.[19] Eugène, his stepsister, Herminie, and three grandchildren were dependent on the star. Déjazet had managed to inculcate in her female offspring the ethic of sacrificing for the man who would not or could not marry them and of being the irreproachable "other woman" from the male point of view. Living this ethic brought many problems to the extended Déjazet family.

Herminie was the daughter (born in 1822) of Adolphe Charpentier, who sometimes inquired after her well-being but left her upbringing (and all the expenses) to Déjazet.[20] She attended the Conservatory of Music, and if she had a stage career, it was not noteworthy. Herminie became the mistress of César de Bazancourt and had three children by him. Though Bazancourt was a man of means—at one time, the expensive courtesan-actress Alice Ozy was his mistress—Herminie did not benefit materially from the relationship.[21] However, she gloried in the fact that he had died blessing her and asking his legitimate daughter to look after her (she did not). Herminie elevated her success as the other woman into the great achievement of her life.

After Bazancourt's death, Herminie seemed to suffer from depression and was unable to leave the house. Bazancourt's love loomed as the only good thing that had ever happened to her. In the meantime, she practiced emotional blackmail on her mother. Herminie wrote hysterically about her martyrdom, being left alone with her children and grandchildren, unable to work, scorned by the world. Her aging and tired mother, she claimed, was lucky because she could work and have friends. The mother had to support the daughter and her brood financially and emotionally.

Jeanne, Herminie's daughter (born in 1850), continued the family tradition of sacrificing for the men she loved. Jeanne was not the sort of woman who tolerated poverty easily; yet her high material expectations did not lead her to adopt the conduct of a gold-digging courtesan. The men she took as lovers were either not well off or unwilling to support her and the children she had with them. Thus, the third and fourth generations of Déjazet women became dependent on the star. When Virginie reproached Jeanne, Herminie defended her daughter, telling the singer, "She is only doing what you did."

Beset by the woes of her offspring and by creditors' demands, Déjazet turned to the church for consolation in her old age, a sign of the wounds from a life based on unceasing work and impulsive passions.[22] The case of the Déjazet clan gives coloring to the abstraction of women who were presumed to live outside accepted moral codes and to be enemies of bourgeois propriety. Whether or not Déjazet was directly inspired by the unconventional attitudes and behavior of George Sand (whom she knew), the performer had a similar vision for her own life.[23] Déjazet needed men for love, not for material support. She assumed the right to choose and discard lovers at will. Yet affairs of the heart were thorny, and Déjazet took on the obligation of being the self-sacrificing other woman, which was to have the burdens of true womanhood without being able to ask much of the male partner. Living up to the ideal was a test of personal dignity for the performer and also a severe limit on her freedom of action. In addition, she willingly accepted the responsibilities of a single mother. The prescriptions of patriarchal society weighed heavily on Déjazet, even though she did not have to recognize a male master.

The Déjazet clan was not at all the grand exception that proved the rule about actresses being adventuresses. The ideal of sacrificing for love had strong roots in the theatrical milieu, although it would be impossible to know if a majority practiced it. The celebrated eighteenth-century artist Hippolyte Clairon, who in 1799 penned the first autobiography of an actress, insisted that none of her notorious sexual affairs had been based on lucre.[24] The nature of aristocratic libertinism of the day might have allowed Clairon to reconcile her free choice of lovers with the accumulation of wealth. Actresses could have "friends of the heart" on the side while Monsieur paid the bills. The ideal of a consuming, exclusive love became more forceful among theater women and society in general about the time France became "bourgeois," around the Revolution of 1830.[25] The best known instances of theater women devoting themselves to their lover involved relationships with the writers of the Boulevard and of bohemia: Alfred de Vigny; Alfred de Musset; Victor Hugo; Alexandre Dumas, Sr.; Alphonse Karr; Jules Janin; Théophile Gautier; Paul de Saint-Victor; and many others.[26] The authors who so frequently represented actresses as capable of self-sacrifice drew on their own or their friends' experiences. The obligatory remorse and tragic ending for the fallen woman of fiction were required by the literary conventions of the day. Yet the tragedy also reflected, all too often, the actresses' painful lived experiences when they made sacrifices for the men they loved.

Marie Dorval, the star of the romantic stage in the mid-1830s, told Alexandre Dumas, Sr., that "there are men on whom you do not cheat" and that her lover, the poet Alfred de Vigny, was one of them.[27] She did, in fact, occasionally cheat on him, but she remained emotionally faithful, as her passionate letters to him while on tour demonstrate. Like Déjazet, Dorval was tormented by fears that her lover, whom she felt was so much her superior, would not be faithful. Vigny, for his part, once wrote of a "love more chaste than marriage," but his affair with Dorval was not quite so noble, in his mind.[28] The aristocratic Vigny brought to the affair the conventional prejudice that actresses were inevitably duplicitous. As a married man, and one who was aware of his social standing, Vigny wanted the relationship to be as discreet as possible, whereas Dorval had always been casual about her public reputation. She kept her husband, poorly raised children, and a former lover around her, even when Vigny visited. When the poet made up his mind to break with Dorval, he accused her of having become mannish—like her friend George Sand—from having had too many affairs. The poem he penned after the end of the liaison in 1838, "La Colère de Samson" ("Samson's Anger"), was the chief source of the legend of the lesbian love between Dorval and Sand.[29] A much shorter fling with Dumas, that turned into friendly affection, proved more rewarding for Dorval. The writer, not yet rich, sold his literary awards to pay for a gravesite for his friend, who had been terrified of being condemned to a paupers' ditch.[30]

Juliette Drouet initially experienced her fifty-year relationship with Victor Hugo (from 1833 to the poet's death in 1883) as nothing less than a redemption, though later in life she had to rethink its meaning. As a beautiful young actress just at the beginning of her career, Drouet became the lover of a fabulously wealthy Russian, Prince Anatole Demidoff. The gifts from this Monseiur allowed her to have "lovers of the heart," like the writer Alphonse Karr, and then Hugo.[31] Hugo, however, was not the sort to share the woman he loved with another man, not even one who paid the bills. The actress submitted to Hugo's reprimands about her "bohemian" lifestyle. She came to accuse herself of the basest behavior and looked to Hugo to lead her to a higher moral path.

The actress returned Demidoff's extravagant presents, gratefully accepted a modest pension from Hugo, and lived as the honest other woman. Hugo treated her as a fallen woman whom he had the duty to save.[32] Like the central character in Hugo's 1831 play *Marion Delorme,* who provoked audiences with her declaration that true (but illicit) love had returned her to virginity, Drouet believed that the writer's affection had restored her moral worth. Nonetheless, the restrictions under which Hugo had her live sometimes made her dream of a return to the stage, a step that Hugo strongly discouraged. Drouet could not imagine being unfaithful to the great writer, but he, struggling with a ferocious sensuality that came to the fore in his mature years, was not faithful to her.[33] Drouet refused to accept the evidence of his womanizing until it was too strong to deny. After sharing Hugo's long exile in Britain during the Second Empire, Drouet discovered Hugo's private records of his compulsive sexual adventures. She realized then that a part of their intense relationship had been a sham. Drouet had been Hugo's Tisbe, while he had been both her Angelo and her Adolfo.[34]

Up to 1848, actresses' pursuit of redemption and self-sacrifice was in step with the wider discourse about their potential for being true women. However, with the turn to antipornocratic anger against theater women, some actresses ceased judging their self-worth by patriarchal standards (were they cheating on men? exploiting men? sacrificing for men?)—standards that were now deemed unattainable for them, anyway. As the public came to regard actresses as courtesans who had little professional commitment, some stage women started to adopt a persona—to "perform a self"—centered exclusively on achieving artistic distinction. Through their example, they introduced the notion that being kept by men was not compatible with professional excellence. Theater women asked with growing urgency whether they might live for and through their art rather than being "condemned"—that was the term implied by the spirit of the debate—to living as kept women.

To many in the theater world, it was Aimée Desclée who dramatized the issue of whether an actress could live for her art. Born in 1836, the daughter of a lawyer with radical leanings, Desclée received an unusually good education, but financial setbacks made it necessary for her to work and even to support her ill parents.[35] Desclée chose acting, but her career did not go well. She soon combined stage work with living as a kept woman, and her friendly letters to the likes of Marie Colombier and Coraline Letessier suggest that she was far more successful at being a courtesan than an artist.[36] At one point, she even took to working in a "girly show," in which her job was to display her legs.

Desclée became despondent about her gilded existence. She explained to her sister courtesans that this was not the life for her, that her dream was to make a living from her profession as a performer.[37] It was not that Desclée had conventional moral ideas or religious beliefs that made her abhor her circumstances. Desclée was frank about her sexual needs and did not feign respectability for the sake of appearances. When Alexandre Dumas, Jr., referred to her as a "loose woman" (*"vagabonde"*), she countered that "even in an irregular position a woman can be honorable and not loose. Virtue is a convention, a rationalized thing, but honor is instinctive. Women who are not meant to marry need not be virgins."[38]

Rather than shame in a conventional sense, a quest for dignity motivated Desclée to leave the life of a courtesan. She judged such a life, with its petty obligations and dependencies, demeaning to an intelligent woman. Moreover, she sensed she had as yet undiscovered potential to achieve greatness in her career. Desclée pined to be not a good woman by the ideals of the day, but an impressive artist.[39] Desclée left her lovers in the mid-1860s and devoted herself to her artistic development. She toured Italy and won so much praise that word returned to Paris about her surprising effectiveness on stage. Dumas, Jr., the leading playwright of the day, went to see her perform in Brussels and was so impressed that he talked the director of the Gymnase theater into casting her in the lead of a new Meilhac-Halévy play, *Froufou*. It turned out to be one of the big hits of the 1860s, and Desclée's performance was acclaimed. Dumas gave her the lead role in his next several plays, and she received stunning notices. Desclée had made herself into a universally admired performer.

Supporters did not know of or did not openly discuss a second crisis that occurred in the actress's life just as she was transforming herself from courtesan to artist. She met a man for whom she had deep feelings. An army officer from a wealthy family, he is known to posterity only as Fanfan. At first Desclée welcomed the relationship, but she soon discovered that her renewed career was so demanding that she did not have time for both him and it. Although the choice was painful, Desclée began to discourage his visits. He offered to marry her, but she would not agree to it, telling him that her nature would not allow her "to belong to a man."[40]

Intense work became the central fact in the rest of Desclée's life. With the cancer that would kill her already spreading, she left for an engagement in London and another tour of Europe. She returned to Paris in 1874 and died at the age of thirty-eight. Dumas gave the moving eulogy at the funeral. He initiated the legend that she had died from the overwork that true artistry demanded. The playwright portrayed her as a martyr to a "harsh trade" that actresses have to disguise behind a smile.[41] With so many neo-Rousseauists lamenting that courtesans were invading the stage, Desclée's life was a hopeful sign that they could raise themselves to high levels of professional distinction.

Escape from the mistress's gilded cage was a frequent theme in autobiographies written by actresses just before and after World War I. The idea that there was a conflict between being kept and being an acclaimed performer had not appeared in earlier autobiographies, but in the late nineteenth century the two statuses came to seem incompatible. Aimée Tessandier, who published her memoirs in 1912, might well have modeled the narrative she gave to her life on Desclée's. Her autobiography relates her struggle to rise above being a courtesan and excel as a performer.[42]

Tessandier ran away from her working-class home before the age of fifteen, in the 1860s. While she was living on the streets, a rich man noticed her beauty (and youth) and took her as his mistress. She quickly became one of the celebrated *demi-mondaines* of Bordeaux. Tessandier claims that, despite the luxurious surroundings in which she found herself, she hated her situation. Having been exposed to the theater as a kept woman, she found the applause and adulation that actresses received inviting. The director of the major theater in Bordeaux was happy to put her in a production because he believed her notoriety as a leading courtesan would be sure to draw an audience. However, the fashionable men of the town resented her striving for independence, and she believed that they ruined her debut. Still only a teenager, she left the gilded life behind her and began touring the provinces. Exalting in her modest success, Tessandier recalled thinking after a well-received performance in Brussels, "I am free! Free! Free! I am fully responsible for living my dream."[43]

Dumas saw her perform in the provinces and took her under his wing. He convinced her that her successes up to that point had mainly been the result of her beauty and that she was not yet respected for her talent. Her subsequent career in Paris would be a quest to achieve such respect, although the path to artistic achievement would not be easy. She decried the absence of professional guidance. The actress found that being self-taught had left distressing holes in her education. In an engagement at the Comédie-française, she was completely out of her element because she knew nothing about the classics. When the actor Mounet-Sully realized that Racine was hardly more than a name to his new colleague, he patronizingly grabbed her by the arm, led her to the library, and made her read the dramatic masterpieces. Always insecure at the Comédie, Tessandier left that troupe and worked tranquilly at the Odéon theater for a while, but had to depart when she quarreled with the director. Her memoir ends with her quest for artistic distinction only partly achieved.

Eve Lavallière came closer to accomplishing Tessandier's dream of artistic distinction but did not have the psychological makeup to enjoy it.[44] She suffered from a traumatic childhood and was depressed and even suicidal throughout her life. Her working-class parents had neglected her, and when she was eighteen, her absent father had returned home and killed her mother during a fight. She had fled her hometown of Perpignon with traveling performers. Taking the name Eve Lavallière, with its doubly sinful association (Lavallière was one of Louis XIV's mistresses), she wound up on the streets of Paris in the 1880s. She was soon seen at elegant nightspots with rich, older men. Following the example of another courtesan, Emilienne d'Alençon, Lavallière joined the chorus line at the Variétés theater so that she would be on display for playboys. Although she had no theatrical experience, the manager took one look at her legs and hired her.

Entering that theater changed the direction of Lavallière's life. She had a serious relationship with the director of the theater, Fernand Samuel, and stopped living as a courtesan. He inspired her to excel in his troupe, considered the best in Paris at the end of the century. The public took a liking to her waiflike figure, huge eyes, and short-cropped hair, which anticipated the postwar look of the *garçonne*.[45]

Ultimately, Lavallière aspired to a state of redemption that artistic success would not fulfill. Even in her most degraded moments, she had retained a childlike piety, defined by her own lights. In 1910, after a serious illness, she took the first steps toward withdrawing from the world for the contemplative life. She was at the height of her celebrity at the time and in a relationship with a German diplomat who was serious about marrying her, and few observers took her religious vocation seriously. Yet Lavallière was no longer measuring her life by the standards of worldly success, and she eventually retired to a life of solitude under the spiritual guidance of priests.

These examples of the pursuit of self-worth through professional success inspired emulation by other theater women, but also a current of pessimism about the enterprise.[46] Marie Colombier identified with the goal of fleeing the gilded cage of male "protection" in her three-volume autobiography, published in 1900, but did not offer much hope of success. Colombier used the untimely death of her friend Desclée to justify her own failure to escape. Colombier took up Dumas's theme of Desclée's martyrdom and applied it to the cause of actresses who strove to achieve personal dignity. The implication was that the price was so high that the goal was usually unrealistic.[47] Mandy Berry did not find much grounds for optimism, either. With all the talk of moral improvement and reform in the theater after 1880, Berry's perception as a young performer just before 1914 was that nothing had changed. "Directors and authors insist on hiring elegant performers, and that meant young actresses need men to keep them." She praised thoughtful directors for placing novices at stage front so that they could attract the attention of rich men and have careers. "Women *must* [her emphasis] sell themselves to be on stage" was her firm conclusion.[48]

Whether out of discouragement or indifference, some actresses of the late nineteenth century would not fashion themselves exclusively in terms of a quest for independence and professional distinction. In fact, as the public after 1880 became more comfortable with, even insistent on, the representation of the actress as moral, some theater women were prepared to move in the opposite direction and take to heart Yvette Guilbert's lament (of 1896) that her sister performers had become too much like "notaries' wives."[49] They began to reassert the image of the temptress—not because it was naughty but because it was powerful. Furthermore, they sensed that they could now escape recrimination as strong women.

A dispute between Aimée Tessandier and Cécile Sorel, then a novice at the Odéon theater, expressed the difference in spirit between the theater women who sought professional dignity and those who celebrated the tradition of the femme fatale. Sorel dressed for the role of a peasant girl as seductively as possible, and Tessandier advised her young colleague to strive for greater realism. Sorel exploded that she had "an innate passion to be pretty, beautiful and adulated," regardless of the role.[50] As she matured and became more famous, Sorel did not pursue artistry single-mindedly, though she became an admired performer. She constructed her identity around the model of the liberated aristocratic woman of the eighteenth century, whom she conceived as a salon mistress, daring lover, confidante to the powerful men of the day, and paragon of refined elegance. Supported by the stage and by lovers, Sorel purchased the townhouse of the duchess de Mazarin, whom she called "that delectable eighteenth-century woman," and installed what she claimed to have been Madame Dubarry's bed, which she shared with many prominent republican politicians of the prewar era.[51] A Déjazet or a Drouet could not have imagined flaunting such conduct.

An unplanned incident brought national attention to Sorel's performance as a femme fatale. She was the mistress of the president of the turn-of-the-century republic, Félix Faure, who supposedly died in her arms in a back room of the Elysée Palace on February 16, 1899. Sorel exploited the potential scandal by daring to show up at the funeral. (In her memoirs, published years later, she claimed that an official car was sent for her.) Faure's death occurred at the height of the Dreyfus affair, and the politicians who opposed the effort to clear Dreyfus's name had counted on Faure's inaction. The anti-Dreyfusards were furious at Sorel for causing the president's heart attack, and they spread rumors that she had worn a red dress to the funeral, had shown no remorse, and had immediately moved on to other lovers.[52] Sorel was probably delighted with the publicity.

The "exotic" singer and dancer Caroline Otéro (known professionally as the Beautiful Otéro), would also have welcomed such piquant publicity. Pursuing scandal and seeking high-profile love affairs was how this Spaniard advanced her career after her Parisian debut in 1889. Rich protectors allowed her to buy a splendid mansion just off the Champs-Elysées and to gamble with abandon at Monte Carlo. Her solo act involved flirting with the men in the audience; she presumed that not one of them could resist her charms.[53] Her most famous song contained the lines, "I roll both at a time / Men and a cigarette / Between my pretty fingers."[54]

The café-concert singer Polaire was another performer who had no hesitations about engaging in scandal because of the power it gave her. While she was trying, in the years just before the Great War, to make the transition to an acting career, she met and became the mistress of "Willy," Henri Gauthier-Villars, the husband of Colette and a literary showman. (He was known as the Barnum of Letters.) Willy launched his wife and mistress in a publicity stunt in which he had them dress as twins and show up with him in all the most visible places. He dared the public to consider them a ménage à trois.[55] Polaire was also drawn into another scandal when the son of a judge, recently married, abandoned his wife for the singer, showered her with expensive gifts, and ran up huge debts. The family tried to keep Polaire away but finally had to have the man declared mentally incompetent and locked up in an asylum.[56]

Marie Colombier's memoirs, which appeared in 1900, capitalized on the public's indulgence for republican actresses by titillating the reader with stories of sexual disorder while at the same time making a case for the author's excellent intentions. Colombier admitted to many affairs, which she often described in some detail, but she always gave them a favorable interpretation: she had never exploited her lovers for all they were worth; the men had been in charge; she had curbed their excesses; and, finally, the affairs had all been based on affection, with gifts given as an afterthought. As the memoirs were being published, Colombier was involved in an opprobrious lawsuit, and she used the autobiography to tell her side of the story. One of Colombier's lovers had been the important industrialist Petrus Richarme, owner of the glassworks at Rives-de-Gier. Richarme's business partners were suspicious of the liaison. They accused him of building a depot in Paris and spending so much time there only to be near his mistress. Worse still, they insinuated that Richarme was spending company funds on Colombier. Richarme's health deteriorated, and he vowed to leave Colombier a "proof of his tender feelings in the will." Having a fortune of 10 million francs, Richarme wanted to endow his lover with a yearly income of 60,000 francs. A lawyer suggested that they marry to simplify the inheritance, but Colombier would not hear of it, she said, because that would be self-serving and disrespectful, even though Richarme had told her

many times that she was his wife in spirit. Colombier admitted to help-
ing Richarme write the will, but claimed she did so in a disinterested
manner. Understandably, the other heirs saw Colombier as an adventuress pure and simple and contested the will. Colombier's ultimate defense was that if she had been more of a vamp she would be Madame
Richarme, beyond the reach of lawsuits and certain of her rights to in-
herit.[57]

A Déjazet, a Desclée, and a Colombier each created and performed a
self by responding in a complicated, often dialectical way to the prevailing representation of theater women. While Déjazet incorporated as
much of the conventional standards for womanliness that she could into
her deviant life, Desclée made artistry her highest standard when, after
1848, it became difficult to imagine actresses being "good" by patriarchal standards. Colombier and others took advantage of the loosening
surveillance of actresses' sexual conduct after 1880 by reclaiming the
powers of a femme fatale. What was constant was the refusal to live, as
was expected of nineteenth-century women, in the shadows of the men
in their lives. Actresses were inevitably cynosures. Far from fearing to
draw still more attention to themselves, many actresses turned their visibility to a higher purpose. Whether they thought of themselves as magdalenes, artists, or even seducers, they often sought to be useful citizens.
Theater women found French public opinion increasingly receptive to
their quest to be of service to the nation in the final two decades of the
century.

Reentering the Public Sphere

The writer, director, and socialite Arsène Houssaye was quite correct in
claiming that "though actors confine themselves pretty much within
their own precincts, actresses stray nearly everywhere—into the world
of sports, into the diplomatic world, into the literary world."[58] The lucky
few who won a name for themselves on the stage mapped out other areas
in which they might be women who counted.

They did, indeed, "stray" into politics and diplomacy, but the first
arena of achievement beyond the stage was Parisian social and literary
life. As soon as they had a bit of fame, actresses inevitably situated themselves in relation to Le Monde. Claiming to be integral participants in
high society would have been controversial, but theater women assumed

they might influence it in important ways. Genuine society ladies, born to prominent families, were either competitors, role models, or both. Actresses defined themselves as society ladies *manquées,* if they wished to acknowledge their exclusion from respectable life; or they defined themselves as the successors to the highborn women of yesteryear, because contemporary ladies had become domesticated and no longer enlivened Le Monde. Whereas men in the theatrical establishment usually linked actresses with the notorious courtesan-performers of the past, actresses, themselves, were more likely to identify with another historical figure, the liberated, aristocratic salon woman of the prerevolutionary era. Actresses took her to be a model of elegance and a contributor to French civilization.[59]

Jenny Thénard, who was at the Comédie-française at the turn of the century and whose ancestors had been there since the mid-eighteenth century, scorned actresses like Aimée Desclée for isolating themselves in their career. She admired those theater women who "conscientiously exercise their craft and know how to take part, at the same time, in relations with high society [*relations mondaines*]." Thénard made it her business to push herself into "distinguished circles that had closed their doors to actresses but might open them to a lady." She used fashionable charitable work, private theater, and readings at balls as her entrée. It is not surprising that Thénard was given to habitual name dropping in her autobiography of 1909, because she was determined to present herself as close to, if not exactly, a society lady.[60] The diva Louise Fusil had done that, too, in memoirs published half a century earlier. Though Fusil's husband had been a militant republican during the Revolution, she recalled the prerevolutionary Monde fondly and found the model of the eighteenth-century society lady conducive. As she remembered it, "An instinct for coquetry quite different from what we have today characterized women of high society; things were less serious, the century was more frivolous; pleasure was the preoccupation."[61]

By "pleasure," Fusil had in mind charming sociability entailing refined conversation. Gentlemen of the Boulevard were just as nostalgic for this "lost" elegance, and they tried to reproduce it, often calling on actresses for assistance. Providing the pleasures of sociability was serious work, and theater women earnestly undertook being salon mistresses and dinner hosts as society once again permitted them these roles.[62] The men who kept mistresses often expected them to be the center of their worldly existence, because they had not or would not marry women who could undertake such fashionable entertaining. Actresses were well positioned to recruit guests for their salons. They were in touch with the writers of the Boulevard and could draw in the cream of theater audiences, who sought them out backstage.

Augustine Brohan, who was at the Comédie from the 1840s through the 1860s, was a prominent salon mistress who had a more active style of engagement in cultural life. She did not strive to be Thénard's "lady" or to take up the "frivolity" that charmed Fusil. Brohan was an intellectual who happened to be a woman. A journalist for *Le Figaro* called her "brilliant" and noted that she had a mind "that caresses and wounds at the same time." She lacked, he claimed, modesty and tenderness. Instead, she knew "how to defend herself and how to attack." The journalist was probably referring to her celebrated wit, which was mordant, when he mentioned her lack of tenderness. A frequently cited example of Brohan's repartee entailed a conversation with an actress of questionable morality. The actress performed cross-dress roles and worried that "half of Paris will think I am a man," to which Brohan replied, "Not to worry; the other half *knows* you are not."[63]

The novelty-loving Monde of the Second Empire included some men who appreciated Brohan, at least as a curiosity. Arsène Houssaye made her a fixture at his parties, which were known for their decadence. The director of *Le Figaro*, Hippolyte de Villemessant, chose her to take over his column on Parisian cultural events in 1857. A woman had not written the column before. Brohan assumed the freedom to express her own, strong opinions. In one of her very first columns, she attacked Victor Hugo for having been unfair to the poet Alphonse Lamartine. Hugo's friends were outraged, especially because their idol was in exile and could not defend himself. Alexandre Dumas, Sr., was so irate that he would not allow the actress to perform in any of his plays.[64] Brohan had to give up the column in face of the outcry, and Villemessant returned to a male columnist. Beyond a narrow circle of iconoclastic Boulevard men, Brohan's lack of femininity was unacceptable.

Indeed, most theater columnists were so unenthusiastic about Augustine Brohan's intellectual persona that they tried to hide it. The easiest way was to assimilate her into the more conventional image of salon mistress as womanly, charming, and sensitive. In their reports, she was gracious and self-effacing. The journalists were also careful to distinguish Brohan from the despised bluestocking; she had "too much heart and too much true sensitivity," claimed one reporter. Besides, she was too pretty. Her wit and her effort to be intellectually substantial repulsed Count Horace de Viel-Castel, who chronicled the mores of Imperial high society as omens of impending moral collapse. Brohan personified for him "the sickness of that world: the fabrication of words." Her reputation under the Third Republic would sink to that of a remnant of Imperial decadence.[65]

Theater women did not stop at seeking to serve high society; they wished to serve the nation. Mademoiselle X of the Comédie-française, probably a composite figure, took the title of Madame Prime Minister in her alleged autobiography. As mistress to the premier (identified only as "Alexandre") at the end of the nineteenth century, she claimed to speak freely at cabinet meetings held in her home and to lead the politicians toward wise decisions.[66] Cécile Sorel took credit for nothing less than the victory of 1918 by giving her American lover, Warren Whitney, almost single-handed responsibility for bringing the United States into the war—and he had done it for her![67] These claims exaggerated a creditable phenomenon: theater women were carving out ways for women to contribute to national life beyond motherhood and domesticity. Though actresses rarely, if ever, denied that men and women had distinctive ways of participating as citizens, they were engaged in broadening the possibilities for women to be useful citizens. Through their actions and the attendant publicity, stage women were reclaiming a place in the public sphere.

Taking a stand on a controversial public issue was not easy for an actress. She could expect criticism from betrayed fans. Moreover, the belief that women had no place in serious political debate was strong. Mademoiselle George had affirmed soon after the Bourbon monarchy returned in 1815 that "I, a woman and actress, am never so silly as to have an opinion." However, she inherited an oppositional political position because she had been one of Napoleon's mistresses and was known as "the Corsican's widow."[68] Actresses served themselves best by steering clear of politics, as Léonide Leblanc did. She had both the Radical Georges Clemenceau and the royalist Duke d'Aumale (the youngest son of former king Louis-Philippe) as regular guests at her salon and even as lovers.[69] Theater women realized that they would pay a price when they took ideological stands. Despite the dangers, however, performers who used their visibility to promote their beliefs were not rare. In this way, nineteenth-century actresses (particularly, those in the last third of the century) renewed Clairon's tradition as women actively engaged in the public sphere.

Rachel demonstrated how actresses could lend their prestige to new and precariously established regimes. Just a few weeks after the Revolution of 1848 made France a republic, Rachel electrified audiences at the Comédie-française with her rendition of "La Marseillaise." The officials of the Second Republic were so inspired that they sent the star on a provincial tour that stirred the country. Rachel stepped out on the national political stage again ten months after Louis-Napoleon's coup d'état created the authoritarian republic. When she read the poem "L'Empire,

Efforts to keep theater women out of the public sphere did not always succeed, because actresses were famous and admired. In this image, Rachel confers her prestige on President Louis-Napoleon Bonaparte's political ambitions by reciting "The Empire Means Peace."

C'est la Paix" ("The Empire Means Peace") to the prince-president and the audience of the Comédie on October 22, 1952, she became the muse of the Second Empire. Louis-Napoleon took the tumultuous applause as one more sign that France wished him to complete his work by founding an empire.[70]

The republican Rachel of 1848 was probably an inspiration to the activist Mademoiselle Agar, who personified Marianne, the female incarnation of the French Republic, during the Paris Commune of 1871.[71] She had come to Paris as a young girl without any familiarity with the theater. On a whim, she took work as a singer in a café-concert (she had previously sung for family gatherings), but she became entranced by the idea of being a tragic actress. Despite Agar's commitment to radical republicanism, patronage from the highest levels of the Second Empire helped her to realize her impossible dream. The actress managed to procure an audience with Princess Mathilde Bonaparte, during which she read a poem that so moved the emperor's cousin that Agar was rewarded with an offer from the Odéon theater. Mathilde saw talent in her protégée, so she worked to promote Agar's career. She arranged for Agar to perform at the Tuileries Palace, and the emperor stated aloud that it would please him to see her on the stage of the Comédie-française. Inevitably, an offer soon arrived. Imperial patronage did not, however, make Agar grateful to the regime. During the intensified republican agitation in the capital in 1868, she appeared at Masonic rallies with a blue-white-and-red sash. On the night that war against Prussia was declared (July 18, 1870), the audience demanded the recitation of "La Marseillaise," and Agar spontaneously stepped forward to declaim it; she had to do it every night for the next several months.[72] Although later forced to deny her actions, Agar probably did perform the anthem at public meetings during the Commune.[73] These appearances were the basis for her lasting reputation as a "queen of the barricades." Her conservative colleagues at the Comédie regarded her as a shrew and an unsavory enemy after the Commune was crushed, and the new director, perhaps with encouragement from the government, found reasons to dismiss her. She suffered again for her political stance several years later, when a spectator insulted her and injured her by throwing a bottle as she read a patriotic poem.[74] By the time Agar penned her memoirs (she died in 1891), she wanted to eradicate her reputation for radicalism. She ended her autobiography by stating that she had "*never* been a political woman but simply a good *French woman* [her emphasis]." Her denials were an attempt to rewrite an unhappy past.

Eugénie Buffet's political mobilization brought her to the extreme right.[75] Born in Oran (Algeria) in 1866, Buffet worked as a singer in café-concerts, mostly in Marseilles, until a wealthy count became infatuated with her. He took her to Paris and taught her how to be a fashionable mistress. She mixed with the playboys of the Boulevard and put herself on display by working in the chorus at the Variétés theater. She spent freely and ran up debts. Despite the superficial gaiety of her life, she wanted a serious career in the theater. Increasingly desperate about her empty existence, she went to the female journalist Séverine for advice, who gave it to her in one word, "Work."[76]

Buffet coupled the quest for a meaningful career with politics. Just as she began to withdraw from being a kept woman, she was also caught up in the Boulangist agitation of 1889. She attended one of the founding rallies of the League of Patriots and sang "La Marseillaise" for the nationalists. Buffet may well have met the actress and future feminist newspaper editor Marguerite Durand in the Boulangist movement, but Buffet followed the mixed political currents in the opposite direction and wound up on the chauvinistic right during the 1890s. She was the darling of anti-Dreyfusards like Paul Déroulède and Henri Galli. She celebrated the life of the patriotic common people in her songs, borrowing from the populist poems that entertainers like Aristide Bruart had made familiar. She performed daily at the Parisian Exposition of 1900 and opened up a café of her own in the Pigalle neighborhood, but the police closed it just before the 1902 election because it was a meetingplace for right-wing enemies of the regime.[77]

As the nationalist movement in Paris faded and merged with mainstream conservatism, Buffet remained a populist entertainer. She developed the persona of "the Call Girl" and sang songs meant to evoke "the sinister laments, tubercular poetry, and black, sad tales of these beings." She strove for a reputation as "queen of the slums" by staging performances in the streets and even in coal mines. However, her evocation of lower-class life did not prevent her from getting work at fashionable café-concerts, making international tours, or even performing for the royal court in Brussels.

The Dreyfus affair so polarized opinion that anyone taking a pronounced stand inevitably made enemies. Most politicians tried to be as

uncommitted as possible for as long as possible. Yet two of the most re-
nowned actresses of the day, Bernhardt and Réjane, dared to make their
position known. Réjane was such an engaged Dreyfusard that she broke
with close friends over the controversy. To publicize her support for the
captain, she ostentatiously attended the second court-martial in Rennes
in 1899. The right-wing press reacted with predictable hostility.[78]

Bernhardt was also a staunch Dreyfusard (so much so that she quarreled bitterly with her beloved son), and the public associated her with
the cause. Spectators came to take lines in her plays as political references and applauded or hissed depending on their own politics. There
were demonstrations in front of Bernhardt's theater, the Renaissance.
A contemporary biographer, Louis Verneuil, claims that the star told
him that she had a crucial role in convincing Emile Zola to publish
"J'accuse," his sensational exposé that opened a new phase of acrimony
in the affair. Bernhardt later wrote to Zola that she had contemplated
taking a more open stance herself on the issue, but had decided it would
only inflame the right and prove counterproductive. Her critics would
not have suspected her capable of such restraint.[79]

A far surer path to admiration in the public sphere for actresses was to
personify the nation. The Third Republic was increasingly accustomed
to seeking reflected glory in its stage women. Originating in an anxiety
over national decline, the growing will to identify France with actresses
pointed to a rethinking of how women might serve the public. France's
diminished place in the diplomatic stratosphere and a sense of intensified danger from abroad created a climate in which people were grateful
to those who could project French prestige. Performers' international
tours began to serve this function around the turn of the century in a
way that Rachel's tour of the Americas a half-century earlier had not.
That tour, like Bernhardt's first American visit in 1880, had been treated
more as an imposition on Parisian patience and even a manifestation of
Jewish avarice.[80] However, an increasingly insecure French public was
happy to see the citizens of New York or Chicago embrace French performers with adulation. Newspaper columnists who had once lamented
the absence of the stars from the Parisian stage turned to reporting
proudly on the enthusiasm of the foreign crowds. Bernhardt told reporters that her American tour had extinguished any interest in studying the
German language; French culture reigned supreme in the New World after her visit.[81] Jane Hading, Jeanne Granier, and Polaire appealed to patriotic sentiment by featuring the tricolor at their departure festivities.[82]

The inevitable mixing of theatrical tours, patriotism, and national prestige was ripe for parody by the turn of the century. *L'Illustration* in 1902 published a satirical account of Sarah Bernhardt's return from a continental tour. In the story, the National Guard was at the train station to meet her, and the band played "La Marseillaise." Crowds threw flowers at her feet for the next two hours. In the meantime, she spoke to reporters, bragging of having made the German people love the French through her performances. She then complained about the silence of the French press regarding her achievements; each newspaper allocated only a column a day to them! Identifying with her gender, Bernhardt described herself as "suffering, as women do, from betrayal." Finally, she announced a meeting for the next day to discuss Franco-German relations with the foreign minister.[83] The situation on which the parody commented was a matter of current debate. Pressure on the state to honor theater women for their contribution to national grandeur, long dreaded and resisted, was becoming overwhelming.

Julia Bartet managed brilliantly to symbolize France by staying home. Foreign Minister Théophile Delcassé had chosen her to read a poem welcoming the czar to France during a visit in 1899 designed to cement the crucial Franco-Russian alliance. Bartet did not wear the classical garb of a Marianne this time but rather a costume that evoked the eighteenth century, perhaps meant to suggest a continuity between royalist and republican France that would please the czar.[84] During the second Moroccan crisis of 1911, when the threat of war with Germany loomed large, Bartet scored a public relations coup of major proportions. Emperor William II had invited her to perform in Berlin, and she ostentatiously turned down the invitation, to the adulation of French patriots everywhere. The press treated her refusal as a stunning display of the resolve all French people needed to show in the face of German aggression. Even after the Great War, one army officer still recalled, in a personal letter to Bartet, how that display of patriotism had stirred his soul.[85] The acclaim for Bartet unleashed a wave of refusals to play in Berlin—some, no doubt, declared by actresses who had not actually been invited.

Actresses' contacts with diplomats, ministers, and international financiers gave them additional opportunities to bridge the public and private spheres as they served France. Marie Colombier took credit for facilitating the Franco-Russian entente of 1891, the cornerstone of her country's foreign policy. The Russian ambassador had explained to her sometime earlier that the Russian people resented French coldness toward them, which they especially felt during the Russo-Turkish War. He suggested that some show of sympathy, however unofficial, would be helpful in furthering diplomatic talks between his country and hers. The actress consulted with the newspaper editor Villemessant, and they decided that the best plan would be for Colombier to organize a fund-raiser to aid the Russian war victims. Colombier did this, and the ambassador assured her that she had vastly improved the chances that an entente would be reached.[86]

Women who so readily headed for the limelight, who eagerly sought public accomplishments, and who often had a strong sense of self-importance inevitably had fruitful engagements with feminism, even when they were not openly advocates. Marguerite Durand, the founder (in 1896) of the first feminist newspaper published by women, had had a prior career as an actress, which explains much about her brand of feminism.[87] Durand struggled to show women that they could be powerful and independent even as they were objects of male pleasure. She set about to reconcile feminism with bourgeois conventionality and also with femininity. The actress-turned-editor strove to convince the public that women could be beautiful, desirable, wifely, and capable of achievements outside the home.[88] Her efforts exemplified a type of mainstreaming that marked the progress of feminism during the Belle Epoque. Theater women could readily be party to this.

Feminists of the Belle Epoque seriously debated how independent women could be, whether marriage and children were necessary for their happiness, how individualistic they were by nature, and so on.[89] Actresses' own lives were examples of the answers that radical feminists might have given. Theater women were almost spontaneously New Women of the day by virtue of their lifestyles and their performances. The singer Jeanne Bloch, in a 1902 interview, claimed to have "preached feminism at the café-concert." Performing in a military jacket and pants, she made it a point to "play women with the gestures of men, with a male tone of voice, and with male attitudes" to signify that "women can do everything that men do."[90] Yet, despite isolated examples, it would be misleading to presume a feminist consciousness for most theater women just because they lived as exceptions to the conventional expectations for women. Their liminal situation did not, in the end, provide many of them with a privileged position from which to pierce routine thinking

on gender and see it as artificially imposed. In fact, the same mystificat-
ions that prevented the vast majority of French women from challenging the constructions of gender identity operated effectively on stage
women, making them followers rather than leaders on feminist issues.[91]

Julia Bartet is a good test case of feminist consciousness for actresses,
because she pursued the image of a serious, independent woman who
lived for and through her career.[92] One might have thought her well
placed to question the fundamentals on which the domestic imperative for women rested, but she did not. In a personal letter written to
an unidentified "feminist" during the 1890s, Bartet claimed that she
understood why so few French women took an interest in expanding
women's rights. This was because they had the "instinct of being, not the
inferiors of men, but unequal [*inégales*] to men." Until this instinct
changed, women could take "consolation" in "relying on men who take
care of them." The star returned to the idea that women could earn
men's trust mainly through subservience and self-effacement. She allowed that women could have "confidence" in the advice they submitted
to their men "without it having any obligatory status."[93] The considerable press coverage portraying Bartet as the achieving artist who lived
quietly and contentedly on her own could easily be appropriated by feminists for their purposes, but she was not one of them.

Even Bernhardt, for all the extraordinary conquests in her life, may
have retained surprisingly masculinist views about personal achievement. In 1896, Bernhardt wrote to her lover at the time, the actor Pierre
Berton, that "women are not good for many things . . . It is a truth upon
which the veritably wise have never been at variance. Woman's mission
is simply to have children and to be as beautiful and charming as she
can. To these all things may be added but they are two of the things
which constitute her fortune. When she goes beyond this and puts her
foot into other things, she invariably makes an ass of herself."[94] Assuming that the star was not simply being outrageous, she found the role
of woman insufficiently capacious for her life. Perhaps she had even in-
ternalized the Boulevard writers' representation of her as a person of intermediate gender. Bernhardt formally denied intending to expose the
artificiality of gender constructions by playing cross-dress roles. She defended acting as Hamlet, the duke de Reichstadt (Napoleon's sole legitimate son, who died young), or Lorenzaccio (a whimsical character in a
play by Alfred de Musset) on the grounds that these were boys who were

devoid of virility. She never played the role of a mature, powerfully masculine man. "It is not male [dramatic] parts but male brains that I prefer," she declared.[95]

Ironically, the implication that the achieving individual was exclusively male was becoming reactionary, partly under Bernhardt's influence. The status quo that most actresses accepted was mildly progressive on women's rights. Theater women on the eve of World War I had lived to see their colleagues honored by the state, identified with national grandeur, and equated with respectable women. In any case, actresses' personal commitments mattered less than the example they set and the appropriation of those examples by the media. Whatever a Bartet or a Bernhardt thought about the category of "woman," the stars were typical of a new sort of celebrity at the end of the century, models of personal achievement and success for citizens of both sexes. As women at the center of attention, actresses could hardly have failed to nudge gender identities in a more fluid direction.

9

From Notorious Women to Intimate Strangers

Félicien Champsaur noted what he thought was a new wrinkle in stage culture in his 1881 novel based on the life of Sarah Bernhardt, *Dinah Samuel*. The press, he said, was making actresses into "public women" by freely revealing the details of their private lives. The consequence was that "every reader sees, through the eyes of a journalist, into actresses' homes as one sees into a house of glass. He [the reader] thereby attends the awakening and the retirement because, after applauding the actresses at the theater, he always has the curiosity to size them up again when they are dressed transparently in a nightgown."[1] The novelist could not possibly have been correct about this sort of curiosity being new. He described, after all, the already dated erotic culture of the stage. Attached to the old ways, Champsaur was hiding from himself or his readers the innovative ways in which theater women were able to relate to their fans, particularly their female ones, by the end of the century.

Under the Male Gaze

The concept of celebrity is understood as differentiated from "fame." Persons who become famous for particular achievements gain attention for their own sake; according to a widely cited definition, a celebrity is "a person whose name, once made by the news, now makes the news."[2] A public seeks to know more about the people who capture attention, particularly, details of their lives that are unrelated to their achievements. The quest for revelations about celebrities leads to the illusion of a narrowing gulf between the famous and the spectator. Celebrities become "intimate strangers" for those who follow the media coverage.[3] The current scholarship on celebrity presumes that it is a phenomenon of mass society and that the well-off theater patrons and newspaper readers in a more class-bound society would never have allowed themselves to become fascinated by the private lives of entertainers. However, these assumptions are not only arbitrary, but also serve to deprive celebrity of a history.[4] Upper-class interest in celebrity, often intense, evolved and eventually merged into the mass phenomenon.

Celebrity came into existence through a public sphere—a collectivity of private individuals who speak for the public—and its handmaiden, print culture. A public sphere emerged in France by the mid-eighteenth century. The new public conferred its attention on people who stood out as a result of their achievements or distinguished status. The growing number of arenas where opinion could be expressed—newspapers, books, salons, masonic lodges, academies, and reading clubs among them—broke what before had been largely the monopoly of the crown, to designate those worthy of renown.[5] Given the importance of print culture to the public sphere, it is hardly surprising that the earliest celebrities were writers and performers. The much-admired ballet dancer Gaetan Vestris claimed that the three most famous people in the world in his time were Frederick the Great, Voltaire, and himself.[6]

Public figures of this sort provoked interest beyond their positions or achievements. Though the eighteenth-century public was small and elitist by the standards of mass society, it still had a lively curiosity about those it deemed famous. Commentary in newspapers and especially conversation within salons and literary circles support this point beyond question.[7] The exclusive and largely male public of prerevolutionary France was very much inclined to confer celebrity status on female stage performers. Their artistry was the subject of discussion, as were what they wore, what they said on topics unrelated to their profession, and with whom they had frequent contact. Two questions, in particular, dominated interest in theater women: how beautiful they were and with whom they were sleeping.

Prerevolutionary French people could read about the offstage life of actresses in scandal sheets, usually smuggled into the country after publication abroad, but otherwise there was not much printed material on them. The theater public was small enough at first that face-to-face communication went far toward satisfying curiosity about stage idols of the time. That public was presumably not much larger than the exclusive, aristocratic circle designated as Le Monde. About the time that the first autobiography of an actress, that of Mademoiselle Clairon, appeared in 1799, so did a new sort of publication that provided readers with personal information about performers. This was the biographical dictionary of theater personnel, a type of reference that contained sketches of the lives and professional activities of all those listed. One or two such publications appeared before the Revolution, but it became a distinctive genre around 1800.[8] During the first half of the nineteenth century, new dictionaries were written and old ones were reissued at a steady pace.[9] The proliferation of personal detail indicates that the theater public had widened well beyond Le Monde. The demand for information about theater people had created a new market. The dictionaries were one of the means by which early notions of celebrity were constructed.

The availability of theatrical guides came at a time of growth in the entertainment industry after Napoleonic restrictions on theater licensing were relaxed. One purpose of the collective biographies was to keep readers up to date on the expanding number of people involved, whom they wanted to know as individuals. The dictionaries presented entries not only on performers but also on directors and theatrical columnists. One guide, published in 1821, even offered "silhouettes" of stagehands at the principle theaters.[10] However, the purpose of the dictionaries was never simply to catalogue the personnel of a growing and increasingly complicated entertainment industry. Even the most mundane guide promised privileged revelations about the performers and tantalizing insights into offstage life. The title of one of the earliest dictionaries led the reader to expect "intimate truths." Later ones promoted themselves by offering "1,001 secret truths" or even "1,223 secret truths." A collection of biographical sketches appearing in 1826 claimed to describe performers "in their boudoirs as well as on stage and in society."[11] The marketing formula was to turn an uninformed public into cognoscenti. For the price of the book, the readers could share privileged information about celebrated persons.

Despite the editorial promise of comprehensiveness, theater women received disproportionate coverage and distinctive treatment in the guides. Authors of the sketches treated male performers primarily in terms of their professional competence. Readers could expect to learn the type of roles the actors played and read some critical assessment of their skills. Entries on actresses, however, made short shrift of their professional activities and were mainly about physical appearance or, more to the point, sensual appeal. Women who were aging or unattractive were the subject of scorn, while youth and beauty were lyrically celebrated, with enthusiastic descriptions of the body parts that drew attention. A number of dictionaries included performers' home addresses, which held out the promise of a personal encounter.

The biographical dictionaries were candid, if playful, about actresses' sexual escapades. About Madame Dugazon, *L'Espion des coulisses* ("The Backstage Spy") noted, "In the annals of libertines, Dugazon holds as distinguished a place as in annals of the theater."[12] The *Nouvelle biographie théâtrale* ("New Theatrical Biography") of 1826 warned readers that viewing the eyes and breasts of Mademoiselle Dupont (of the Comédie-française) would drive them wild with desire. Mademoiselle Florentine, a dancer at the Porte Saint-Martin Theater, received praise for "bringing distinction to her name by refraining from ruining eligible young men."[13]

The preface to one of the guides claimed that theater women, in particular, dreaded having their biographical sketches published. "The actresses become pale," the preface claimed, "when they read the words 'theatrical biography,'" indicating that they did not wish to have their private lives revealed.[14] In truth, actresses did not have much to worry about. There were general allegations of debauchery, to be sure, but not the revelation of salacious details that the titles promised. The privacy of actresses was stripped away only to the extent that their age and a few points about family background were mentioned. Otherwise the references to their conduct were vague. The overriding purpose of the guides was to praise the physical attributes of the artists. Theater women were treated as goddesses who would ignite the (male) reader's senses.

Starting in the mid-1840s, theatrical dictionaries were largely replaced by collections of biographical sketches devoted exclusively to actresses. The new titles were "The Pretty Actresses of Paris," "The Pretty Women of Paris," "Our Queens of the Footlights," "Our Adored Actresses," and the like.[15] There were no corresponding publications for male performers. As the considerable sympathy for actresses apparent before 1848 gave way to darker, more explicitly sexualized images, theater women came to monopolize attention from the compilers of theatrical biographies. The publishers renounced the pretense of providing information on the theater industry as a whole and concentrated on assuring the reader that the book was about seductive women. Although the term "the pretty women of Paris" was a synonym for actresses, certain guides did include famous courtesans, thereby confirming a link that seemed to many all too close. The biographical sketches of the 1850s through the 1880s focused intently on the actresses' most alluring body parts and made playfully vague allusions to debauchery.

Even more important for the construction of celebrity in the first half of the nineteenth century than the biographical dictionaries were the society columns in newspapers. These began to appear irregularly during the Bourbon Restoration. One of the prototypes for such columns, "Parisian Letters" in Emile de Girardin's *La Presse*, started in 1836.[16] This innovative journal had taken a step toward the mass-circulation daily by cutting its subscription price to 40 francs, half of the standard rate up to that point. Its readers were propertied but not necessarily affluent. They, in particular, might have been expected to seek a vicarious familiarity with the worldly by reading about them through the society column. The innovation in *La Presse* was such a success that other cut-rate newspapers, like *Le Siècle*, quickly added the new feature to their pages.[17]

Emile de Girardin entrusted the *La Presse* society column to his wife, Delphine, a talented writer who was much admired by the leading authors of the day. She avidly nurtured the concept of celebrity and was one of the first in France to use the term regularly. Madame de Girardin gave it a most favorable connotation, as a synonym for "people of talent." For example, she advised her readers on a new type of social event, the "celebrity ball." At one of them, she found the opera singer Madame Damoreau among the likes of Victor Hugo, François Guizot, and Honoré de Balzac.[18]

Girardin's construction of celebrity was guided by her liberal republican notions of merit and her strong political commitment to the ascendancy of the achieving bourgeoisie over the idle aristocracy. She appeared to despise ladies of high birth ("society ladies") who lacked other distinctions. So much was this the case that she had no regrets when she found "young gentlemen" at the races accompanied by courtesans rather than by women of their own caste.[19] The emerging visibility of celebrities represented in Girardin's eyes the triumph of talent over birth. Writing under the male pseudonym Viscount de Launay, she nonetheless championed women's achievements, which she touted often in her reporting. She openly affirmed that French women (though not women of all nationalities) were intellectually superior to French men. The superiority explained to her why French women had what she took to be an astonishing amount of influence over public and private decisions and why French men were so keen to exclude women from official positions of authority. She managed to reconcile her protofeminist stance with an acceptance of the status quo by portraying women as too savvy to want to jeopardize their behind-the-scenes influence by seeking public recognition.[20]

It is in this ideological context that we must interpret Girardin's controversial assumption that women of the theater had come to surpass society ladies in prestige.[21] The author of this early society column was pleased to place actresses at the center of attention. At a theater opening in 1837, she described the gaze of the audience turning first to the members of the royal family and then, immediately thereafter, to the actresses who were in attendance ("After the royal princesses, the princesses of the theater").[22] Provincial visitors to the capital, she claimed, would want to be able to return home with the report that they had laid eyes on Mademoiselle George.[23] She elevated the star of the Comédie-française, Mademoiselle Mars, to the level of one of the principle sights of Paris. According to Girardin, when Rachel entered the Chamber of Deputies to hear a debate, as fashionable people had a habit of doing, all eyes, including those of the deputies, were fixed on the actress.

Reflecting at length on why it was that Rachel captured the attention of all, Girardin betrayed some of her ideological preoccupations. In her view, Rachel stood out because of her extraordinary achievement in her field, what the columnist called her "individual rank." Other actresses, she claimed, had talent but were not nearly so visible because their artistic achievement was not as great. In this curiously labored column, which showed Girardin struggling to find the language appropriate for celebrity, she ended by defining it as a reward for exceptional merit.[24]

Other society columnists of the day, such as Pierre Durand of Le Siècle, Eugène Briffault of Le Temps, and the various authors under the "Courrier de Paris" rubric in L'Illustration, constructed celebrity in a different manner. They did not presume a significant female readership, as Girardin did, or at least they kept actresses steadily under a male gaze. No less ideological than Girardin, but in a different way, they were committed to the Boulevard notions of fashionable elegance and persisted in seeing the theater as a mixing of art and eroticism. The other columnists did not take the position that merit was the core of celebrity.

How did the dancer Fanny Essler "take Paris"? asked the society columnist of *L'Illustration*. "She smiled with her siren's lips and her white teeth; she moved her arms, her legs, her head, all her body with the grace of a true daughter of Eve. Her waist, filled with damnation, issued a dare."[25] Columnists other than Girardin described the thrill that the performer communicated to the viewer in sensuous, forbidden terms. Because they would not break the link between actresses' personal lives and scandal, they could not admit actresses to the center of high society. Respectful of Le Monde, as Girardin was not, they had to keep the performers corralled in the theater, either on stage (as artists) or in the erotic backstage zones. One columnist felt it necessary to apologize for following a description of a ball at the Tuileries Palace with an account of happenings at the Opéra and Comédie. "To jumble together . . . the [social] distance that separates the Tuileries and the Opéra; to jump from the official and diplomatic world to the world of performers and dancers, isn't this exceedingly bold?" he asked.[26] Not even respect for the deceased weakened the connection between scandal and actresses' private lives for most society columnists. The obituary for Mademoiselle Mars in *L'Illustration* did not hesitate to mention millionaire lovers as part of the star's glorious legacy (though it did note that "the gossip that regularly surrounds celebrated actresses was less troubling in her case than in others"). When Rachel died in 1857, the columnist warned women against appearing too eager to purchase the "trophies of libertinism" at the auction of her effects.[27] Whereas Girardin found the celebrity of actresses an inspiration for achieving women, other columnists continued to see grave moral danger in allowing respectable women to be caught in the spell of actresses' renown.[28]

Thus, an intense interest in celebrity did not await the rise of mass society. The notables of nineteenth-century France were hardly immune to the allure of celebrity. During the 1820s, the much embattled minister Count de Villèle wished that his unpopular bills had come before the Chamber of Deputies at precisely the time that the *pays légal* (the male elite with voting rights) was abuzz with gossip about the sensational end to the nine-year affair between Mademoiselle Mars and Antoine de Brach. "I would have passed [the legislation] in obscurity," Villèle declared.[29] Actresses certainly embodied the definition of celebrity as people whose names made the "news" of the day. The media constructed them as celebrities mainly to the extent that they stirred men's desires. The society columnists and compilers of theatrical dictionaries did not grapple with the way celebrities expressed a growing public intoxication with glamour or success, but others would.

Picturing Glamour and Personal Freedom

When the writer Sophie Gay was invited to the salon run by the actress Louise Contat in the 1790s, she was especially thrilled at the prospect of meeting a famous actress face-to-face for the first time. Gay found the experience slightly disturbing, because this extraordinary figure was suddenly reduced to flesh and blood, and the metamorphosis was disillusioning.[30] Gay's daughter, the innovative society columnist Delphine de Girardin, was surely familiar with the larger-than-life qualities of actresses, with the *frisson* they evoked even among distinguished people (such as her mother). Yet Girardin tended to intellectualize celebrity rather than penetrate its mystique. Other society columnists of her day and beyond were no better able to capture the excitement that Gay identified. They could not grasp or, more likely, chose to ignore the popular appeal of celebrity status.

Nonetheless, this appeal was noticed and exploited by very different types of people, who almost surely did not think of themselves as agents of celebrity. These were the merchants on the busy commercial thoroughfares of the capital. They gave actresses' faces much exposure by placing their photographs in the shop windows, where thousands of passersby had the opportunity to see them. Encouraging window shopping by adding theater women's pictures to displays was an inexpensive means of luring shoppers into the stores. After the establishment of commercial photography in the 1850s, shopkeepers took advantage of the technical and aesthetic advances, giving some two hundred new firms in the capital more than 6 million francs of business by the end of the decade.[31]

Images of actresses were widely available at photography shops by the 1850s.[32] Shopkeepers who wished to decorate their windows could also write to an actress for a free picture; a performer would be happy to supply one to publicize her current play or keep her face before the public. Merchants would probably also request a hand-written endorsement on the margin of the photograph so that customers could read the actress's personal testimony on the merchandise.[33] The symbiotic relationship between merchants and theater women kept the arrangement informal and cheap—and widespread, as well. Henry James, as a reporter for the *New York Tribune* in Paris, described the pictures as being "in every second window" in the 1870s.[34] His surprise at the profusion of images suggests that strollers in New York or London would not have found the same abundance. In the eyes of many old-fashioned habitués of the Boulevard, the popular decorations had gotten completely out of hand. One stroller, during the Exposition of 1867, complained to the press that a recent outing had exposed him to no fewer than seventy-three pictures of the opera singer Adélina Patti.[35] A columnist for *L'Illustration* in 1880 presumed that all the readers would have been able to identify the performers who attended a recent festival celebrating Offenbach because "their photographs fill all the windows of Paris, familiarizing [*popularisant*] everyone with their images." The journalist even opined that "schoolboys know [the actresses'] faces better than those of their girlfriends."[36] Thus, the photographs in Boulevard windows were already generating the anxiety that celebrity culture was crowding out more authentic relationships.

There are very few descriptions of the images themselves. Most were probably head shots or pictures of actresses in costume, though there were some revealing ones.[37] The comments of the stroller who was overwhelmed by the images of Patti suggest that merchants had learned to concentrate on a limited number of artists who seemed to have a special hold on the crowds. The selection had a self-reinforcing quality, producing a hierarchy of stars, and it is no coincidence that the proliferation of Boulevard photographs accompanied the growing prominence of the "star system" in theatrical productions.[38] Male actors received far less attention. Merchants chose actresses to personify the essence of Boulevard life. Commonly referred to as "the beautiful women of Paris" or "Parisian women," actresses presided over the leisure, people-watching, shopping, and fantasizing about urban pleasures that Parisian crowds performed with such intensity. These faces were possibly the first celebrity icons.

It was also not a coincidence that the elevation of actresses into goddesses of Boulevard life accompanied the rising anger against these women in the middle third of the nineteenth century. To reformers and republicans, aghast over the decadence of Imperial high society, theater women, their faces peering from shop windows, seemed to be inviting the public to engage in leisure, consumption, and idleness, all morally suspect. These activities emasculated citizens and corrupted women. Little wonder that Zola thought to include in his novel *Nana* the detail that as "queen of the first-class tarts . . . [Nana's] photo was on display in every shop window and her name featured in every newspaper."[39]

Since actresses' photographs were widely available and their price rapidly dropped below a franc, they soon found their way into consumers' homes as well. The columnist Jules Lecomte instructed Parisians in 1860 that such images were being used for a parlor game in the most fashionable homes. The game entailed collecting pictures of famous people and having guests identify the faces. Eager to impress the reader with the pedigree of those who had adopted this pastime, he directed them to deluxe shops on the rue de la Paix or the passage de l'Opéra to procure the pictures—"whether of royalty or of actresses at the Bouffes theater." Lecomte also recommended playing the game by pairing the photographs in stark oppositions: the Pope and Garibaldi, General Turr and Madame Ulgalde, Cardinal Antoinelli and Madeleine Brohan, the shah of Persia and a *rat* at the Opéra. The columnist claimed that such "diversity" would create "happy, irresistible, and salutary entertainment."[40] His oppositions seemed to be pointing to—without naming—the difference between fame as traditionally conferred by title and status and the new sort of celebrity that actresses personified in his mind. Lecomte's pairings were clearly intended to sustain hierarchies: high/low; dignified/unruly; established/bohemian. Perhaps he insisted on the hierarchies to ensure that celebrity worship did not dissolve them.

Certainly the photographs disseminated well beyond those fashionable homes so dear to Lecomte. In Edmond de Goncourt's mind, the ubiquitous outlets hawking cheap pictures of actresses symbolized the decline of the once-elegant Boulevard by 1888.[41] The photographs even spread deep into the provinces. The director of the Comédie-française, Emile Perrin, found that his featured performer, Suzanne Reichemberg, had made a mark in the mountains of Savoy. A trip to bucolic Aix-les-Bains in 1877 showed him that "here, as in Paris, in Chambéry, as on the Boulevard, there are Nadar photographs of Mademoiselle Reichemberg [in her role as Suzel in *L'Ami Fritz*]."[42] Perrin would not have doubted that Savoyard peasants were becoming Frenchmen in part by participating in the celebrity culture radiating from the heart of the capital.

Photographs became a new venue in which actresses performed—and had to perform—celebrity. Though they might lament the intrusion of the press in their lives, actresses could not afford to pass up an opportunity to get a photograph of themselves out before the public. Whenever a newspaper, even a minor one, invited them to a photo session, the artists responded with alacrity.[43] The more actresses put their portraits before the public, the more critics bemoaned the actress-obsessed culture. Yet consumerism and performers' celebrity would continue to burgeon together.

Sarah Bernhardt came of age as actresses' photographs proliferated on the Boulevard. This may have helped her intuit that the public might be fascinated by theater women for reasons beyond their bodies and fashionable sexual liaisons. She began to attract attention at the moment that early mass culture was born. The central feature of this culture was the representation of everyday life as the basis for commercial entertainment.[44] Bernhardt offered up her eventful life for public consumption. Her frenzied daily activities—acting, directing, sculpting, painting—were public knowledge. Her slender figure became a symbol of the nervousness of modern life. Many ordinary Parisians were likely to know her eccentricities, that she slept in a coffin and kept a menagerie of wild animals in her home. Embarking on foreign tours gave Bernhardt opportunities to receive publicity on her herculean preparatory efforts, her potential for making millions, and the veneration she received from crowds abroad. She claimed to be an unofficial ambassador of French cultural grandeur. Bernhardt piqued the interest of the public but also challenged the established notion of celebrity. This star would not remain in the shadows of stylish notoriety, where the theatrical elite wanted to keep actresses. Though there was plenty of material for scandal in her life, she lived through a series of glamorous and lucrative adventures, and many people were fascinated. Bernhardt became the embodiment of possibility for the individual, male or female, in an open, success-orientated society. This was probably what the novelist Champsaur sensed was new about the publicity surrounding Bernhardt, but he failed to conceptualize it in this way—or did not care to mention it.

Journalists within the theatrical establishment took Bernhardt as a challenge. Her status as an "intimate stranger" to the public was not compatible with the convention of casting actresses as goddesses of male desire. By and large, the journalists were oblivious or hostile to celebrity as a manifestation of glamour and freedom in an individualistic society.[45] Most members of the establishment tried to tame Bernhardt as best they could. Acting more on the values of the Boulevard than of the press, they admonished her for her aggressive quest for publicity. The theater critic and playwright Charles Monselet thought her public relations strategy so threatening that he took the unusual step in 1887 of turning his review column into a commentary on Bernhardt's career. Monselet began by acknowledging that Bernhardt was a great artist, but he recognized that talent did not explain the spell she cast over the audience. The critic found the key to her success in publicity and the hold she gained over the public's imagination. News about her assailed newspaper readers on a daily basis. "Each morning," Monselet claimed, "Parisians awake to read what she did and said the night before." Her stage appearances were almost beside the point, because the public wanted to know about her private activities—and not just with whom she slept. It was excited by her balloon flights and by the bizarre features of her home. In London, during her tour with the Comédie in 1879, shops sold her sculptures and paintings and even charged two shillings for people to look at them. Monselet noted that Bernhardt opened up much of her personal life to reporters; some journalists even snooped about to find details that the actress had not made accessible.[46]

Monselet, like most of his sort, would have been happier with the kind of celebrity constructed in the biographical dictionaries. Bernhardt's emergence as the personification of freedom, glamour, and achievement threatened to redefine the theatrical experience away from art (because the public was not much interested) and away from libertinism (because debauchery had to be treated with oblique references, at best) and toward an infatuation with celebrity. In truth, Monselet seemed confused about whom to blame for the innovation. He chided the public for its interest in knowing Bernhardt so completely. He also blasted reporters for their indiscretion. Above all, he blamed Bernhardt for creating the undesirable situation by sharing herself with abandon.

Laments such as Monselet's were not new by 1887. Several years earlier, his colleague Pierre Véron had deplored Bernhardt's violation of Chateaubriand's dictum, "One must not occupy too much of a place in one's century." The star's name, Véron claimed, had been ubiquitous for the past four years. He assumed—or at least hoped—that the readers were becoming sated: "A daily report on [her] projects, her melancholies, joys, new moods, discouragements . . . this has truly become too much for one and the same public."[47] Journalists like Véron and Monselet wished to contain Bernhardt (along with the democratizing attitudes that made her type of celebrity possible). They urged her to stop touring, to stop her ceaseless activity, for her own sake and for the sake of Parisian theater. The critics called for her to return to the Comédie-française and concentrate on her career within it. Such a step would consecrate Bernhardt as France's supreme performer and allow her to attain the artistry of which she was capable; it would also be a symbolic sort of domestication, in the House of Molière. Bernhardt would cease being "the lithe figure with muscles of steel" (Monselet's words) and become a settled woman. Of course, members of the theatrical establishment would have been happy if she had also settled into the routine of a kept woman with one of France's remaining grandees. Then the old order would truly have been restored.

A scandal involving the star at the end of 1883 compelled journalists to confront their prejudices about the kind of celebrity Bernhardt represented and crystallize their thinking about publicity. The so-called Sarah Barnum affair took its name from an offensive fictional autobiography, *Les Mémoires de Sarah Barnum,* that the actress Marie Colombier published in December.[48] Bernhardt had invited Colombier, who was a friend, to take part in her 1880 American tour at the last minute, when Sarah's sister, Jeanne, became too ill to perform. Colombier, in debt and out of work, took the offer but received deplorable treatment. All the while, she sent back reports to France for publication in *L'Evénement.* Although sharp-tongued and satirical, the reports did not reach the level of indecency that the *Mémoires* would three years later.

The outrageous disclosures may have been an act of revenge by Colombier for her poor treatment while on tour, but she was probably not the book's sole author. According to informed speculation, the idea for an exposé of Bernhardt was the collective work of Colombier and a few well-known writers—Arsène Houssaye, Albéric Second, and Paul Bonnetain (who wrote the preface)—though the actress was the only one to put her name on the title page.[49] The *Mémoires* were really a revival of the eighteenth-century genre of the tale of scandal (the *libelle*). Obscene behavior was described relentlessly and in detail. A strong current of anti-Semitism gave it a contemporary tone.[50] Bernhardt was portrayed as obsessed with sex, money, and, above all, the need for self-promotion. With her fictional name, the authors were identifying the actress with the acknowledged master of vulgar showmanship and sensationalism.

The publication of the vicious book did not create the affair. In fact, the press simply ignored the book as long as it could. The revelations were just too unpleasant to mention, and journalists fell back on their tradition of discretion in the face of actresses' debauchery. What did generate the affair was sensationalistic action on the part of the Bernhardt family. Several weeks after the *Mémoires* appeared, Bernhardt's hothead son, Maurice, burst into Colombier's home, threatened her, and demanded that she name a defender so that he could fight a duel over his mother's honor. Later, the star herself, armed with a horse whip and dagger, stormed into the house. She was accompanied by the playwright Jean Richepin, who threatened a visitor with a table knife after Colombier, herself, fled in terror. Not long afterward, Octave Mirbeau, one of the few theater critics to come to Bernhardt's defense, fought a duel with the coauthor Bonnetain. The press could not ignore the clamor, and the events received extensive international coverage.[51] The enraged behavior also made the *Mémoires* a commercial success. The 10,000 copies quickly sold out, even though the price of the biography rose from five to fifteen francs.[52] Colombier was convicted of publishing an obscene book and sentenced to three months in prison and a 2,000-franc fine.[53]

The Sarah Barnum affair proved to be an important moment of reckoning for celebrity culture so far as the French press was concerned. Up to then, Bernhardt had had a free hand in managing her publicity, and the press had responded passively and in an ad hoc manner. With the scandal exploding, journalists took stock of the demands to report on the private lives of the famous and denounced publicity à la Bernhardt. Although no one seriously entertained Colombier's claim that the book was purely a work of fiction, most journalists implicitly defended her by blaming Bernhardt for the embarrassing affair. The commentators saw the scandal as a natural outcome of Bernhardt's performance of celebrity.

"This woman who exists only through self-promotion [*la réclame*] is going to succumb through self-promotion," argued a writer for *La Presse*.[54] Charles Gérard of *L'Opinion* asserted that Bernhardt had forfeited any right to a "private life" through her quest for publicity. "I would like to know," Gérard asked, "if Madame Sarah Bernhardt has not rendered her life outrageously public by opening her salon, her workshop, her bathroom, even her [sleeping] alcove to full view." Her "mania for ruckus" made her an accomplice to the affair, the journalist concluded. There was even a strong suspicion that Bernhardt had plotted the affair from the start to generate more publicity. The delay of several weeks between the publication of the *Mémoires* and the attacks seemed odd. Accusers also noted that Bernhardt was then starring in a lackluster play by one of her supporters, Richepin, and that it was languishing at the box office.[55]

Bernhardt eventually became more conventional in her publicity. Her salon, workshop, and alcove became less visible, and she was more likely to stage public events centered on her theatrical career. In December 1896, she and her friends orchestrated a successful promotional event, Sarah Bernhardt Day. The event began with a banquet luncheon at the Grand Hotel for more than six hundred, including the social and artistic elite of the capital. Then a caravan of carriages carried the guests from the hotel down the Boulevard to the Renaissance theater. There, Bernhardt performed scenes from *Phèdre* and other plays. When the curtain rose at the end, the guest of honor was seated under a golden canopy on a flower-strewn stage. Young actresses in classical robes and crowns of roses waited on the star as friends and writers came to the stage to read tributes. Crowds (of unspecified size) observed the coming and going of the celebrants at the hotel and theater.[56] The event received front-page treatment in many newspapers.

Le Figaro characterized the day as "the most glorious and enviable triumph of her career." In specifying that it "took place in an irreproachable harmony and an atmosphere filled with cordiality and admiration," the Boulevard newspaper might well have been signaling its approval of this kind of publicity over Bernhardt's former antics.[57] It was a celebration of her artistry, not her eccentricity. This was the kind of distinguished, decorous ceremony that the press devoured, but it only capped the mark Bernhardt had already made on celebrity history.

The journalists' objections to Bernhardt's more controversial innovations had the air of sincerity. The pressmen, after all, were committed to

Boulevard values. They considered the erotic culture of the stage an integral aspect of theatrical life, of fashionable life. Moreover, the writers relished taking the moral high road as besieged defenders of the right to privacy. With conviction, they stigmatized celebrity reporting as a lowly form of journalism that only unspecified others would practice. However, the journalists' struggle with new attitudes toward celebrity was superficial. The press would inevitably be hypocritical, having it both ways: putting out stories on intimate strangers and denouncing such stories.[58] One newspaper, after having presented a column, with pictures, on Yvette Guilbert's home, sympathized with the famous singer as the "prey of reporters, interviewers, and photographers."[59] Ultimately, the journalistic response emerging from the Sarah Barnum affair was to be more active in managing celebrity stories.

Bernhardt, as the larger-than-life personality in a society that was coming to value personal freedom, had been so in tune with cultural forces of the day that she effectively normalized celebrity status. At the very same time pressmen decried celebrity reporting, they were seeking to identify the *next* Bernhardt and pounce on her power to galvanize public interest. Thus, Yvette Guilbert, Réjane, Caroline Otéro, and the exotic dancer Loie Fuller received an extraordinary amount of attention. Their private lives and exceptional exploits were treated in a high-profile manner. These stars could summon interviewers at will, but journalists did insist on doing more than they had with Bernhardt to shape stories about performers' opinions and offstage lives.

Defenders of the erotic culture of the stage (stressing the need to be discreet about performers' private lives) found themselves in a weak position as the nineteenth century came to an end. The moralizing discourse about theater women marginalized them. Furthermore, the respect for privacy that they advocated was professionally problematical. In an era when the performers, themselves, took charge of their publicity, discretion on the part of journalists meant loss of control over their columns. One journalist rebuked the seductive Otéro for gathering reporters to talk about the value of her jewels and scolded the reporters for showing up.[60] The columnist conveniently forgot that the value of actresses' diamonds had long been a regular news item in coverage of stage stars. Not surprisingly, many journalists (possibly of a younger generation than defenders of libertinism) eventually made their peace with celebrity reporting. They were eager to initiate stories that presented stars as intimate strangers rather than accept what the stars planted. However, the journalists did not have to work only with the model that Bernhardt had offered, the paragon of success, freedom, and glamour. The feminizing of the theatrical experience, the improved moral status of actresses, and the growing respect for female achievement permitted other configurations of celebrity. Recognizing the possibilities, pressmen constructed a new representation of theater women, one that allowed actresses to connect with their female fans, but in a more decorous and domesticated manner than Bernhardt had.

Under the Female Gaze

The society columnist for *L'Illustration* in 1879 found the public addicted to an unfortunate "tendency of our age," being concerned with the private lives of performers. He claimed that such a focus compromised enjoyment of a performance and made audiences insensitive to genuine talent. Especially worrisome, the columnist thought, was that women in the audience were "on the same slippery slope." Asked for their thoughts on a play, female spectators offered a "description of the furniture [on stage] or of the jewels the actress wore."[61] Published the same year that *Nana* appeared, the column was still another airing of widely shared anxieties about the corrupting influence actresses could have on respectable women. However, such lamentations would not continue much longer. It was not just that the republican discourse of the chastened stage soon took root. What had been unthinkable since the days of Rousseau had come to pass: actresses were accepted as models for bourgeois women. As such, celebrity in the fin de siècle took a distinctly novel direction.

Typical of the new direction was a two-page article that appeared in *Fémina* in 1903, "A Day with Madame Réjane." Mainly an excuse to display photographs of the admired actress at home, the report did not revolve around any news-making event at all. Instead, it depicted the bourgeois comforts and domestic bliss of the performer's private life. She began her day with gymnastics, followed by breakfast with her beloved children, "an intimate and tranquil hour which she savors with joy." The reporter's visit offered the opportunity to solicit Réjane's opinion on fashion, home decoration, and her favorite actresses (Bernhardt and Eleanor Duse).[62] Readers probably finished the article knowing more about how Réjane spent her day than they knew about how their neighbors did. In addition, readers came away with the impression that Réjane's private life was characterized by restrained elegance and propriety. This was the image of the theater woman as celebrity at the turn of the century.

A 1911 article pursued the same effect. Entitled "Madame Is Served: Our Actresses at Meals," the piece was basically a photo essay showing performers dining. They were alone or with domestic pets (a dog or a cat—no more wild animals à la Bernhardt). The meals were models of good sense and good taste. The decor was "charming," the linens were "adorable," the flowers were "fresh." The cuisine could not have been further from the decadent delicacies consumed at the gastronomical palaces on the Boulevard of old. These actresses ate only fruit with tea or water, for "they are constrained to gastronomical privation by love of their art." The article ended by reminding the reader that "everyone" was dieting at the time.[63]

The coverage was now about the *ordinariness* of actresses' lives. The mass-circulation dailies that emerged after 1880 developed some of the basic facets of this approach but were not on the cutting edge of the trend. Their pages did dispense with salacious stories about unruly women and, instead, gave front-page coverage to theater women when events that could happen to anyone happened to them—grave accidents, crimes, serious illnesses, and the like.[64] Stories like the page-one report in *Le Matin* surveying actresses' opinions on whether men should have facial hair was still an exception in the Big Four mass dailies.[65] However, this sort of article was becoming familiar in a still newer sort of publication, the monthly (or bimonthly) photographic magazine. These started to appear just as the nineteenth century ended.[66] The magazines presented another facet of ordinariness, everyday situations with which *female* readers could identify: Yvette Guilbert recovering from an operation, Bernhardt playing with grandchildren, and so on.[67] The magazines established the personal links between theater women and female subscribers. In doing so, the eccentricities that had made Bernhardt's name were put aside; so were the old prejudices about actresses' inherent vulgarity (a sign of their impurity), as their taste now became a model of correctness.

Magazine editors took advantage of the technology that freed photography from the studio and brought readers into actresses' homes. The *foyer* became the favored space in which to make theater women visible. Actresses had become mistresses of well-ordered homes rather than creatures of the backstage. Taking a house tour was de rigueur, and reporters inevitably found the rooms to display not strong personalities or exotic luxuries but rather solid bourgeois values. When the *Revue illustrée* invited readers to spend "An Hour with Madame Jane Hading" in 1893, they learned that she lived in "a quite simple, quite bourgeois house" on the Boulevard des Batignolles. Finding the door to Hading's bedroom open and asking permission to enter, the reporter discovered the "austere" retreat of a "hard-working woman."[68] The promise of that 1826 dictionary to shed light on the secrets of actresses' bedrooms had finally been fulfilled, but there was no longer a den of illicit pleasures to reveal.

Second in frequency to the home as a locale in which to situate theater women was the vacation retreat. The vacation was a part of everyday life, yet one that was tinged with luxury and playfulness. Paid vacations were just coming to be a regular benefit for the best-situated employees.[69] The masses could now aspire to experience them and identify with them while they still remained a symbol of the rich. According to the magazine articles, actresses took their vacations far from the corrupt pleasure of the Boulevard. They put their time to healthful use, relaxing with family, reading, fishing, or hiking.

For most women of the nineteenth century, of course, family and marriage were the bedrock of ordinary existence. The magazine articles were reassuring about actresses' commitments to family, too. Pictures of theater women striking maternal poses with their children were ubiquitous. Mother, children, nurse, and husband (when there was one) were dressed immaculately though informally, as if they had been caught by surprise in their daily routine. The text of the articles extolled actresses' capacity for marriage and railed against the "prejudice" that they destroy their husbands or violate social taboos in wedding. A piece in *Fémina* in 1912 found that all the "theoretical" reasons why marriage to an artist could not work failed the test of experience. The writer asserted that actresses have "an extraordinary instinct for marriage, and experiences have generally been happy." Moreover the reputed libertine behavior was a false image. In reality, he wrote, theater women are "hard-working, down-to-earth [*pot au feu*] kind of people" who return home immediately after the play is over. They value their "calm domestic life."[70] The magazines often sent photographers to cover actresses' weddings (the church ceremonies, never the civil ones); sometimes they omitted to identify who the husband was.

It was not that the journalists denied that actresses were career women, but they presumed that readers wanted a glimpse into their lives offstage. Moreover, the articles assumed, or sought explicitly to illustrate, that there were no conflicts at all between careers and wifely duties. The convention was to portray the actress spending her day being a caring mother, racing off to the theater without inconveniencing her kin, and returning home at once after having thrilled the audience with her artistry. Far from finding the most meaningful part of her life before the footlights, actresses derived their deepest satisfaction—as real women should—from the correct fulfillment of family duties.[71]

Magazine publishers assumed that actresses who were dutiful wives and mothers would not capture men's imagination. The journalists took it as axiomatic that female readers would identify with the domesticated artists (and gave no encouragement to women who might have identified with their unruly sisters). Actresses in this turn-of-the-century coverage distinguished themselves through their seriousness, serenity, and good taste, not their sexual appeal, and new titles on "the beautiful women of Paris" became rare. In their place, the Flammarion publishing house began a new series, "Parisian Women at Home." This was the coup de grâce for the republican discourse on the chastened stage. The magazines that were preoccupied with actresses (and royalty) sent men away to read about sports, war, and business in other publications and turned to writing for women.

Once theater women had reached the milestone of being models for respectable women, there was no reason they could not also be saints. It was perhaps inevitable that zealous fans would canonize them. This happened to Anna Judic, despite her saucy performances, which some critics thought more appropriate for the barracks than for an audience that included women. A sixteen-year-old girl from a poor family idolized Judic and even made a shrine for her worship. The girl had one photograph of her idol, which she surrounded with candles and flowers. It happened that this fan had to undergo brain surgery. During her uncertain and painful recovery, the girl begged her mother to write to the singer and ask her to come see her daughter. Judic complied. According to an article in *L'Eclair*, the performer brought her maternal love to the girl, and there was a "miraculous" improvement in her condition after the visit.[72] In the mid-nineteenth century, *Le Figaro* had entertained readers with sensational anecdotes about disorderly actresses, but now newspapers could inspire readers with reports of actresses' good deeds.

Although the photographic magazines happily reported on theater women's domesticity, they did not dismiss their careers or worldly achievements. Indeed, the magazines were strongly supportive of women's endeavors outside the home. *Fémina* set itself up as a cheerleader for female accomplishment in the arts and elsewhere. Published by the Pierre Lafitte Company and headquartered in a large townhouse, with a theater, on the Champs-Elysées, the magazine sponsored plays by female playwrights and concerts by female musicians. The editors campaigned for women's admission to the Académie française and even held a contest for designing the uniform that académiciennes would wear.[73] The magazine covered approvingly women who had entered a "man's" world: for example, a female philosophy teacher at a boys' lycée and a countess who flew airplanes. One of its reporters interviewed Pope Pius X in 1906 and claimed to have extracted from His Holiness approval for women to enter the liberal professions.[74] Articles even described positively women who ran (illegally) for public office.[75] There was often a pro-Catholic, royalty-friendly tone to the magazines. Yet their enthusiasm for women's achievements outside the home was strong.

Ultimately, *Fémina* and other photo monthlies practiced the same sort of mainstreaming of feminism as the leftist editor of *La Fronde,* Marguerite Durand.[76] The strategy was to celebrate and normalize the most advanced aspects of the status quo. Women in tiny numbers had been attending universities in France and entering the professions since the 1880s.[77] The magazines attempted to portray these exceptional cases as fully compatible with conventional notions of femininity. Without becoming too polemical, the articles rejected the image of career women as mannish and unnaturally self-absorbed. Working women, they implied, could be fully feminine and unthreatening to their husbands. Here, the magazines touched on an unacknowledged contradiction at the heart of French family life. French men demanded devoted and unthreatening wives but also craved the fashionable, elegant, and worldly woman— whose strength was threatening. The magazines "resolved" the contradiction by assuring their readers that women could be both worldly and devoted. The domesticated actresses were models in precisely this way.

So intent were the editors on inspiring female readers with new models of behavior that they did not hesitate to omit unpleasant details that countered the positive image of the actress-wife. While ostensibly reporting on the "real life" of actresses through visits to their homes, every detail mentioned in the articles was selected and staged. When facts inconveniently got in the way, they were buried. Actresses' lives were made to appear serene because the writers covered up the messy details behind their divorces, desertions, out-of-wedlock births, and other disorderly events. The coverage offered an illusion of everyday life just as it offered an illusion of intimacy.

Boulevard journalists of earlier times had treated scandal discreetly—revealing just enough to stir the imagination. The magazine writers who promoted the "intimate stranger" were actually far more ruthless in erasing scandal. They judged any hint of it to be detrimental to their rehabilitative purposes and avoided it. The darlings of the photo magazines, Julia Bartet, Yvette Guilbert, Réjane, Cécile Sorel, and Jane Hading, were not up to the task of serving as models of propriety without significant embellishment. Guilbert presented herself as an upright woman but admitted that her songs got audiences "all worked up and erotically excited."[78] Réjane had an affair with an Italian actor and divorced her husband while the press worked on giving her the image of the perfect mother. Sorel had to promote a desired image as a "priestess of love" in her autobiography, because the magazines refused to report on her sensuality.[79] How Bartet had become the mother of two children without being married was a question that her numerous interviewers refused to explore.[80] The magazine editors, rejecting the lead of the boldest novelists of the prewar era, clung to the convention of female purity as an all-or-nothing quality.

The public that craved even a whiff of scandal was left to its own devices. The readers of the 1893 interview with Jane Hading in *La Revue illustrée* would never have guessed from the text that this actress, portrayed as austere and reclusive, had been the subject of nasty rumors for the previous several years. In 1887 she had embarked on a notorious tour of America with the actor Benoit-Constant Coquelin, against the wishes of her husband, the prominent producer Victor Koning. According to noted theater figure Albert Carré, "For [the next] three years there was nothing but discussion of Koning's divorce proceedings in Paris and the scandals unleashed by Coquelin, the echoes of which crossed the Atlantic." So tainted was Hading as an adulteress that, when she returned, she had to renege on the contract to star in the revival of Dumas's *La Comtesse Romani*, a play about an actress's unfaithfulness.[81] Yet the scandal circulated entirely as a matter of gossip; the press did not touch the issue. When columnists did mention the divorce, they explained it in terms of feuds over Hading's career or even an interfering mother-in-law.

The magazines apparently judged a story for its ability to support the chastened view of actresses, not for its drama. *Fémina* in 1908 deemed the return of Marthe Brandès to the stage after an eighteen-month absence a worthy subject. She had been mourning the loss of her mother, or so the article claimed, and had been enticed back, she said, by the opportunity to play "the role of a *woman* [her emphasis], a true woman, with all her foibles but also her qualities, heart, and spirit." Brandès posed as a quiet scholar and protested that "my life will not interest anyone. I am sensible [*sage*]."[82] The magazine was obviously expecting that the nonstory of Brandès's ordinary life would be of interest to women. The journalists certainly were aware that there were more dramatic facts to relate about the actress. In fact, she had not always been sensible. Brandès had recently been involved in a tumultuous affair with the actor-director Lucien Guitry. She even left a flourishing career at the Comédie-française for him and suffered dreadfully when he gave her unsuitable roles and took up with another woman. At her death in 1930, journalists made this tragedy the central story of her life, but those of the fin de siècle found it worthy only of suppression.[83] Their cover-ups were a measure of their seriousness about promoting actresses as respectable New Women.

Celebrity makers of the prewar years were trying, in some ways, to put square pegs into round holes. They were on a mission to construct theater women as models of propriety. Actresses and royalty (who graced the magazine covers in about equal numbers) drew attention, so that was the material with which they had to work. The journalists had to sanitize their lives to make them models of propriety. The public, even politicians, were now ready and willing to countenance moralized actresses. Profeminist journalists were pleased to have the chance to advance their own agenda of normalizing achieving women. They seemed to believe that the goal justified protecting their readers from a more sordid truth. In addition to ideological goals, the magazine publishers were guided by economic self-interest, for advertising gave them a reason to promote actresses as proper bourgeoises.

In the closing two decades of the nineteenth century, advertisers ea-

This advertisement (c. 1895) presents a personal letter from Sarah Bernhardt endorsing La Perle beauty products. The success of the ad depended on the bond of trust and affection between Bernhardt and her female fans.

gerly sought actresses' endorsements for their products. The level of public interest Bernhardt attracted was unique, so advertisers wanted to associate their product with her, despite her equivocal reputation. Yet there were problems on precisely those grounds. Ads for La Diaphane hair powder and perfume that featured an image of Sarah Bernhardt ran in *La Vie parisienne* as early as 1880, just as the Bernhardt frenzy was building. It was not an accident that this was a journal that respectable ladies could not acknowledge reading in public because of the nudity in the drawings. Moreover, resentment of the star could rub off on a product. *Le Courrier français* of 1886 coldly mocked Bernhardt's endorsement of an inexpensive, mass-produced candy, claiming that the star would never eat such vulgar treats, herself.[84] The satire left the reader to believe—after the Sarah Barnum affair—that only Bernhardt's legendary greed would motivate her to deceive her fans.

Building brand loyalty called for great care in choosing the person who would represent a product to the public. An irreproachable moral reputation presented the fewest problems and most reassurances to cautious advertisers. Moreover, the commercial world wanted the glamour that actresses signified to be defined primarily as a purchasable commodity, not as sexual adventure (though the two were compatible). Above all, the image of the actress as a true woman would minimize the visibility of the cash nexus behind the endorsement. Thus, the actress's status as an upright bourgeoise became a marketable commodity. Being an intimate stranger of this sort took on a worth it had never had before.

Developments in early advertising paralleled closely the logic of the articles that constructed theater women as intimate strangers. Just as magazines soon ran out of new angles from which to discuss the ordinariness of the biggest stars (Bernhardt, Sorel, Guilbert, Réjane) and turned to pieces on "rising stars" (many of whom quickly dimmed), so advertising quickly came to mobilize a host of fresh faces. They often had to be identified in a legend, because their faces were not known to the public. Advertising took to the strategy of domesticating actresses. Around 1910, ads began to present pictures of performers at home using the product, rather than having their faces peer out from an indeterminate space. The increased emphasis on homeliness no doubt reinforced the aura of authenticity.

Fashion was another area in which it was increasingly important to establish a basic identity between the actress and the consumer. Theater women's considerable influence over fashion was a constant. What had not been constant was the openness with which the links were acknowledged. Before the Revolution, even the queen recognized stage women as inspirations for attire. Under the July Monarchy, a textile manufacturer from Lyons had convinced Mademoiselle Mars to make a costume of his yellow fabric, and he soon could not keep up with the orders.[85] Many such examples attest to the ability of actresses to establish women's fashion, and there might be many more examples if it had always been socially correct to acknowledge that influence. Particularly during the middle third of the nineteenth century, when antipornocratic sentiment was so strong, the styles that actresses set had to be decried for the sake of propriety. Touted as "the most beautiful women of Paris" and able to employ the most prominent designers, theater women then were well positioned to set fashion, but strictures against mentioning the link were particularly strong. Thus, a Charles Worth dress that Sylvie Arnould-Plessy wore on stage in 1867 had been copied by department stores so many times that the actress needed a new gown for the revival two years later. Yet the inspiration for the ready-made dress had to remain a secret, if an open one.[86] As the columnist who wrote for L'Illustration in 1879 had noted, admiring actresses' fashions put women on the "slippery slope" that threatened to contaminate respectable society with the harlot's values. It was what made Alexandre Dumas, Jr., think that France of the 1860s was heading for universal prostitution.

Rather than according theater women legitimacy in promoting fashion, opinion makers for most of the nineteenth century found it more correct to warn women away from imitating them. The argument was that, as harlots, adventuresses, and corrupt women, they could have only poor taste; their feeble efforts at correctness would be obvious to the discerning eye. It was necessary to denounce the excess and vulgarity even though stage costumes during the Second Empire were not so costly and elaborate as they would become later (when, ironically, actresses' influence was more open).[87] Statements to this effect abounded, particularly in the 1860s, to police the boundary between respectable society and the demimonde.[88]

Powerful and ambitious courts also discouraged openness about stage influences on style. Under the July Monarchy this was not a problem, because the royal court was so unassuming.[89] It became so when the Second Empire returned to a glittering court life and sought to make it the arbiter of taste. To cite the stage as a source of fashion was an impertinence to the empress and her circle. The inevitable competition between society ladies and theater women over trend setting, visibility, and lovers became a tense matter when courtiers demanded precedence. Making comparisons between the two sets of women inevitably turned into a statement about the moral state of the times.

The obstacles to legitimizing the influence of the stage on fashion weakened dramatically once the Third Republic was established. There was no more court to demand its due, and the ideals of republican motherhood even dissolved the category of "society lady." Moreover, the discourse of the moralized actress made her an acceptable model for married women. The media were no longer under pressure to vilify actresses' taste. The magazines that constructed actresses as intimate strangers took the lead in publicizing and legitimizing the links between stage and fashion. They were never so explicit.

An article in *Fémina* acknowledged the problems of the past: "There was a time when a society lady would hesitate to copy the dress of an actress. The latter passed for being an odd creature back then. There was a style for the stage and one for the city."[90] The magazine found no reason to hide the connections or lament them by the time the article appeared in 1906. The leading dress designers, it claimed, launched their creations from the stage. It noted—without hand-wringing this time—that the gowns were a major reason why women went to the theater. The author was even comfortable with the possibility that ticket sales to women interested in fashion kept mediocre plays afloat. The society columnist who wrote about the slippery slope for women in 1879 would never have understood this complacency.

Fémina started a column on fashions from the theater, entrusting it to Madame Catulle Mendès. The column was enthusiastic about actresses' influence on fashion. "Certainly," declared Mendès, "it is in the theater that one deploys the most genius in dressing. What imagination! What attention to detail! What lavishness!" She cited Bernhardt, Bartet, and Sorel as the outstanding influences on fashion of the day, and the direction they imparted was always beneficent, to her mind.[91] This and other magazines frequently interviewed theater women on their ideas about taste. The vague and anodyne responses were unlikely to offend. Asked what constituted chic in 1910, Marcelle Lender, Mistinguett, and Polaire defended "classical style" and the right of each woman to wear what was best for herself.[92] No one could charge these actresses with advocating vulgar excess.

The fashion industry came to formalize the ties between the stage and its product. Advertising used images of actresses on stage, in costume, rather than anonymous models. The identity of the elegantly attired women was specified in a legend, so that there was no doubt that the gaze was upon an actress. The "naturalness" of finding fashion on the stage was so well established by 1911 that the great dressmakers began to install theaters in their showrooms. Called *salons des lumières*, they were raised platforms with footlights. Clients inspected the new styles by seeing them on models who were situated on the stage, frozen in place, as if a photograph had caught them in a scene from a play.[93] The theatrical idiom of fashion had triumphed.

Theater women had lent their names and faces to not just one but several types of celebrity by the time the mass media emerged. The Boulevard press remained faithful to the erotic culture of the stage as long as it could. Identifying actresses' renown with their bodies reflected a social order that could not easily admit a legitimate connection between stage women and proper women. But merchants pushed aside such moral niceties and chose actresses as icons of consumption and leisure on the democratizing Boulevard of the second half of the century. With Sarah Bernhardt, celebrity became a model for the self that the individual would want to create for personal success. When the mass daily newspaper *Le petit parisien* surveyed its vast readership in 1906 on "the ten most illustrious French people who lived during the nineteenth century," the results of a reported 15 million votes placed Bernhardt sixth, behind the likes of Louis Pasteur, Victor Hugo, and Napoleon I.[94] That a woman was able to personify the supreme achiever reveals the extent of the breakthrough in understandings of gender—and also the lingering ambiguities about celebrating individual success. Magazines intended for an upper-class (even Catholic) female readership developed the representation of actresses as distinguished women whose fame rendered fascinating what they shared with ordinary women. This model was more respectful of gender orthodoxies than Bernhardt's. Yet it was progressive, too, in normalizing women's achievements outside the home. Aided by advertising, the feminine, achieving theater woman was the most prominent image of the French actress on the eve of World War I.

Conclusion

The people who had been pleased when an actress was finally awarded the Légion d'honneur ribbon in 1904 must have been even more delighted in 1921, when Sarah Bernhardt and Jeanne Granier were both decorated. Their postwar honors were a further step toward the normalization of actresses' status. This time, the recognition came without the moral caution and political calculation of the first. Neither Bernhardt nor Granier had been paragons of womanly virtue. Their flaws were there for all to see. The performers were decorated, as men were, for scaling the heights of their profession and for being celebrated. The subversive meanings theater women had carried for so long, wielding illegitimate power over men and having the capacity to unleash disorder, were receding. Instead, actresses signified women's achievement and success. An incipient celebrity culture was maturing.[1]

For a good two centuries, the French lived with the embarrassing, vexing paradox that theater women were exceptionally prominent and, at the same time, peculiarly proscribed. Calls for moral reform were aimed at reducing actresses' visibility, but reformers never attained their goal because the women were too central to elite and masculine identities. Advocates of "reason" pushed for eliminating barriers to actresses' acceptance but did not command respect because they could not explain how to protect the public against the pornocracy that stage women were seen to promote. In the meantime, levels of insecurity regarding actresses shifted sharply with each change of political regime and ideology. Arguments from morality or logic could not resolve the issue. The debate was really over preserving male authority and admitting women to the public sphere. It could be settled only in these terms.

With the slow collapse of absolutism and the rise of a public sphere in eighteenth-century French political culture, theater women became worrisome figures because they distorted men's powers of reason. They also reminded reformers how far France was from having a virtuous civil society. The Revolution pursued the ideal of a masculine public sphere and a private sphere purified by women's special qualities. Once revolutionaries transferred sovereignty from the king to male citizens, they found that they could safely tolerate strong, worldly women on the margins. In effect, actresses were able to continue with their previous style of living because women in general were excluded from power. Even republicans pursued the "lower" form of sexual conduct that had once condemned the aristocracy in their eyes.

Early in the nineteenth century, the language of class began to explain and naturalize the place of women in the social order. The bourgeoisie based its claim to the status of a ruling class on its morally responsible behavior. In moments of idealism, it found the germ of true womanhood even in actresses, but it also stigmatized them for being antagonistic to the legitimate order of things. The many who were disappointed by the Revolution of 1830 seized on stage women as rich symbols of the hypocrisy and oppression inherent in bourgeois liberalism. Yet, when the Revolution of 1848 led to authoritarian government, the pendulum quickly swung against theater women. With crinoline occupying too much public space, the Second Empire elite seemed helpless in the hands of actress-harlots. Once again, a republican voice rang out to demand the reform of women.

The cycles of sympathy and suspicion surrounding theater women subsided under the Third Republic. Eager to establish the moral and political capacity of the people, republicans wanted to believe again in the womanliness of actresses and the self-discipline of men. Ancient taboos proscribing actresses collapsed. Once infamous, stage women emerged as a source of French national identity. Fame now conferred on actresses the power and even the responsibility to instruct bourgeois women. Sarah Bernhardt became the Marianne to a nation of consumers and strivers. Women's achievement and femininity ceased to be inevitable opposites and became compatible to a significant degree. Representations of actresses show that the culture was ready to think about achieving women in positive ways, not just as omens of disaster. The rhetoric about moral actresses helped reconcile women as individuals in the public sphere with their roles as wives and mothers, thereby opening a pathway into the public sphere for all women.

This sequence of representations is so at odds with the conventional understanding of the late-nineteenth-century French crisis of masculinity as a defensive reaction against women's progress that a rethinking of the paradigm is necessary. Far from ending a long era of male self-confidence, the crisis had several predecessors that traced back to the prerevolutionary decades, taking the form of the public's lack of faith in the self-mastery of the men who governed. A distinctive feature of the post-1870 crisis was that it arose almost exclusively from France's defeat at the hands of Prussia and from the chronic international insecurities that ensued, not from Frenchmen's doubts about being able to control their wives, daughters, and mistresses. Accordingly, a backlash against all signs of women's emancipation was not the outstanding consequence of the crisis. In fact, the Third Republic even consecrated the feminist position on the New Woman by bestowing official honors on actresses. In fin-de-siècle France, perceptions of women's strength no longer implied men's weakness and vice versa, probably because men had found new measures for their masculinity in war, sports, and business.[2] Since the crisis of masculinity (and the backlash it caused) has served as a touchstone for much of modern French gender history, this reinterpretation invites a new vision of women's exclusion from and reintegration into the public sphere.

The standard interpretation of French gender history leads us to expect deepening intolerance for actresses, and all other "exceptional women," as society shifted from being organized around privilege (when everyone was "exceptional") to being organized around equality and the "rights of man."[3] Yet the case of theater women shows a more complicated trajectory. The degree to which women's exceptionalism was openly recognized varied with the state of civil society; tacitly accepting deviations from the domestic ideal by denying their salience was an option that French culture exercised when politically useful. Furthermore, postrevolutionary France did not have a uniform and stable approach to women who achieved in the public sphere. The regimes that required men to be self-controlled and reasonable allowed an opening for women's individuality. The Rousseauist formula on the sexual balance of power, that for men to be strong, women must be weak, has insinuated itself into gender history, but scholars would do well to apply it selectively. Men's and women's strengths were not inevitably opposed but rather were contingent on the prevailing configuration of political life.

Thinking about theater women (and, by implication, other identity-shaping categories), far from occurring away from "politics" in an intimate recess of private life, engaged the very principles on which public life was organized.[4] The narrative that had theater women becoming well behaved under the Third Republic was not at all the final result of the steady assault of reason on prejudice. Rather, its acceptance as empirical reality demonstrates the primacy of current political ideologies in producing key social perceptions.[5] As such, the constructions of perception were (and are) inevitably plays of power, deployed in the fields of class and gender. The nation's assumption of sovereignty in 1789 imposed the necessity of imagining the middling sort of man to have a strong character so as to act rationally in the public sphere. At the same time, France's decadent aristocracies did not inspire confidence, and when regimes dispensed with an active civil society, the belief that women were out of control resurfaced. The tension produced powerful cultural pressures in favor of parliamentary government.

Discourses on actresses' unruliness supported patriarchy by attempting to regulate women's desires. Two strategies emerged: either to denounce stage women as enemies of society or to mitigate their deviancy by willfully assimilating them into a universal model of self-effacing womanhood. These attempts at managing women may not have been particularly effective in the end because they were diluted by other goals. Even when disapproval of theater women was at its strongest, men subverted the sanctions by covering the women with the prestige of being desired. The alternative, finding women who had not actually surrendered their independence to be "good bourgeoises" and holding them up as models for all women, might actually have sent a liberating message. Since the strategies had to serve conflicting aims (including asserting a sexualized masculinity, upholding the separate spheres, and sentimentalizing women), more efficacious ones may have been unattainable.

Actresses were revealing as barometers of the acceptance of women in the public sphere. More than that, theater women eventually became agents of reintegration. Since the rise of the modern gender order, actresses were among the most visible transgressors of proper womanly roles, but their ability to subvert orthodoxies on gender had long been limited. Theater women were mainly models of unruliness or, when feminized, of contrition. On more than one occasion, women in general lost rights partly because of the anxiety stage women inspired in men. Once again, the Third Republic marked a decisive break. By refusing to inquire any longer into the actresses' sexual conduct, the regime paved the way for them to personify the New Woman. Then, in turn, the Republic had to catch up when feminists—and also advertisers— eagerly presented actresses as perfectly suitable models for decent wives. The editors of fin-de-siècle photographic magazines knew exactly what they were doing when they called on performers to inspire upper-class women to raise their sights and seek accomplishments outside the home. The celebrity and worldliness of theater women made them particularly convincing paragons of success.

Just because theater women served as a site for constructing male and female identities and for projecting dominant political ideologies, the naturalness of women performing on stage was learned, dismissed, and relearned as one regime succeeded another. Men's comfort with the desire actresses excited in them also had to be learned and relearned. Representing theater women's powers brought out prevaricating habits of mind. Fear and resentment, not reason, periodically came to the fore. Hence, the astounding resiliency of ancient prejudices. Men applied the classic collective techniques of evading responsibility: stereotyping, demonizing, and projecting guilt. When they felt in control, they sentimentalized. The reference point was always the political myths about the adequacies or inadequacies of men to exercise reason. Fortunately, theater women themselves could manipulate the identities ascribed to them so as to claim their dignity. In moments of tolerance, they could even subvert the stereotypes and, by virtue of their prominence, demonstrate how to combine femininity and achievement.

NOTES

Introduction

1. This claim may well prove premature, for scholarly investigation allowing for cross-cultural comparisons is very little advanced. For a start, see Faye E. Dudden, *Women in the American Theatre: Actresses and Audiences 1790–1870* (New Haven, 1994); Laura Levine, *Men in Women's Clothing: Anti-Theatricality and Effeminization 1579–1642* (Cambridge, 1994); Katrina Straub, *Sexual Suspects: Eighteenth-Century Players and Sexual Ideology* (Princeton, 1992); Sandra Richards, *The Rise of the English Actress* (New York, 1993).

2. Albéric Deville, *Arnoldiana, ou Sophie Arnould et ses contemporaines* (Paris, 1813), p. 242.

3. Stendhal [pseud. Marie-Henri Beyle], *Journal intime* (Paris, 1969), pp. 106, 157.

4. Edmond and Jules de Goncourt, *Journal: Mémoires de la vie littéraire*, ed. Robert Ricatte, 4 vols. (Paris, 1956), 3: 1, 154.

5. Michelle Perrot, "Women, Power, and History: The Case of Nineteenth-Century France," in *Women, State, and Revolution: Essays on Power and Gender in Europe since 1789*, ed. Sian Reynolds (New York, 1986), p. 44.

6. *Le Journal amusant*, no. 125 (February 18, 1854): 1.

7. Goncourt, *Journal*, 1: 102.

8. Cited in Anthony R. H. Copley, *Sexual Moralities in France, 1780–1980: New Ideas on the Family, Divorce, and Homosexuality* (London, 1992), p. 207.

9. Angus McLaren, *Twentieth-Century Sexuality: A History* (Oxford, 1999), p. 6.

10. Victoria Thompson, *The Virtuous Marketplace: Women and Men, Money and Politics in Paris, 1830–1870* (Baltimore, 2000); Gay Gullickson, *Unruly Women of Paris: Images of the Commune* (Ithaca, N.Y., 1996); Edward Berenson, *The Trial of Madame Caillaux* (Berkeley, 1992); Karen Offen, "Depopulation, Nationalism, and Feminism in Fin-de-Siècle France," *American Historical Review* 89 (June 1984): 648–676.

11. On the notion of civil society, see John A. Hall, ed., *Civil Society: Theory, History, and Comparison* (Cambridge, 1995), and John Ehrenberg, *Civil Society: The Critical History of an Idea* (New York, 1999).

12. On the construction and reconstruction of civil society, see Philip Nord, *The Republican Moment: Struggles for Democracy in Nineteenth-Century France* (Cambridge, Mass., 1995).

13. Joan Scott, "The Evidence of Experience," *Critical Inquiry* 17 (Summer 1991): 773–797. See Roger Chartier, *On the Edge of the Cliff: History, Language, and Practices,* trans. Lydia G. Cochrane (Baltimore, 1997), for the debate between experience and social construction.

14. A few moments of transition between one regime and the next (February to June 1848, and the Monarchist Republic between 1877 and 1879) do not fit my chronology as tightly as I would wish, but even then the evidence is ambiguous. Victoria Thompson reports a parallel evolution in representations of homosexuals before and after the Revolution of 1848 in "Creating Boundaries: Homosexuality and the Changing Social Order in France, 1830–1870," in *Homosexuality in Modern France,* ed. Bryan Ragan and Jeffrey Merrick (New York, 1996), pp. 102–127.

15. Models for my approach to the links between political and cultural change are Thomas Laqueur, *Making Sex: Gender and the Body from the Greeks to Freud* (Cambridge, Mass., 1990); Carole Pateman, *The Sexual Contract* (Stanford, Calif., 1988); Michel Foucault, *The History of Sexuality: An Introduction,* vol. 1 (New York, 1978); Leora Auslander, *Taste and Power: Furnishing Modern France* (Berkeley, 1996); Pavla Miller, *The Transformation of Patriarchy in the West, 1500–1900* (Bloomington, Ind., 1998).

16. A respected study of reading practices that uses a similar approach to texts is Peter Fritzsche, *Reading Berlin 1900* (Cambridge, Mass., 1996), especially pp. 47–49.

17. Bonnie G. Smith, *Ladies of the Leisure Class: The Bourgeoises of Northern France in the Nineteenth Century* (Princeton, 1981).

18. Defending actresses' behavior was controversial among feminists. See Laure Adler, *A l'aube du féminisme: Les premières journalistes* (Paris, 1979), p. 95.

19. On men's monopoly over urban observation and women as objects of the male gaze, see Janet Wolff, "The Invisible Flâneuse: Women and the Literature of Modernity," in *Feminine Sentences: Essays on Women and Culture,* ed. Janet Wolff (Berkeley, 1998), pp. 34–50. Sharon Marcus, *Apartment Stories: City and Home in Nineteenth-Century Paris and London* (Berkeley, 1999), confirms my findings of an enlarged female gaze.

20. Geneviève Fraisse, *Reason's Muse: Sexual Difference and the Birth of Democracy,* trans. Jane Marie Todd (Chicago, 1994); Joan Landes, *Women and the*

Public Sphere in the Age of the French Revolution (Ithaca, N.Y., 1988); Joan Wallach Scott, *Only Paradoxes to Offer: French Feminists and the Rights of Man* (Cambridge, Mass., 1996).

21. Lynn Hunt, *The Family Romance of the French Revolution* (Berkeley, 1992); Paul Andrew Friedland, "Representation and Revolution: The Theatricality of Politics and the Politics of Theater in France, 1789–1794," Ph.D. diss., University of California, Berkeley, 1995; Olwen Hufton, *Women and the Limits of Citizenship in the French Revolution* (Toronto, 1992).

22. Robert Nye, *Masculinity and Male Codes of Honor in Modern France* (New York, 1993); Berenson, *Madame Caillaux.*

1. Setting the Scene

1. Robert Isherwood, *Farce and Fantasy: Popular Entertainment in Eighteenth-Century Paris* (Oxford and New York, 1986), chap. 7; Martine de Rougemont, *La Vie théâtrale en France au XVIIIe siècle* (Paris, 1988), pp. 213–278.

2. Henry James, *Parisian Sketches: Letters to the* New York Tribune *1875–1876* (New York, 1957), p. 44.

3. Henri Lagrave, *Le Théâtre et le public à Paris de 1715 à 1750* (Paris, 1972), pp. 189–191.

4. Rougemont, *La Vie théâtrale,* pp. 222–224.

5. *L'Illustration,* no. 1,311 (April 11, 1868), p. 234.

6. Pierre Giffard, *Nos moeurs: La vie au théâtre* (Paris, 1888), pp. 2–3.

7. Jean Duvignaud, *L'Acteur: Esquisse d'une sociologie du comédien* (Paris, 1965), p. 40.

8. James H. Johnson, *Listening in Paris: A Cultural History* (Berkeley, 1995), chap. 3.

9. Jeffrey S. Ravel, *The Contested Parterre: Public Theater and French Political Culture 1680–1791* (Ithaca, N.Y., 1999), chap. 1.

10. Emile Campardon, *Les Spectacles de la foire: Documents inédits et recueillis aux Archives nationales,* 2 vols. (Geneva, 1970).

11. F. W. J. Hemmings, *Theatre and State in France, 1760–1905* (Cambridge, 1994), chap. 2. Some commercial theaters also opened at the Palais Royal.

12. Pierre Gascard, *Le Boulevard du crime* (Paris, 1980).

13. Michele Root-Bernstein, *Boulevard Theater and Revolution in Eighteenth-Century Paris* (Ann Arbor, Mich., 1984), chaps. 1–2.

14. Philip Mansel describes the escape from the formality of court dress in "Monarchy, Uniform, and the Rise of the Frac, 1760–1830," *Past and Present,* no. 96 (August 1982): 103–132.

15. Jacques Héressay, *Le Monde des théâtres pendant la Révolution, 1789–1800* (Paris, 1922); André Tissier, *Les Spectacles à Paris pendant la Révolution: Répertoire, analytique, chronologique, et bibliographique* (Geneva, 1992), pp. 25–49.

16. Maurice Albert, *Les Théâtres des boulevards (1789–1848)* (Paris, 1902), pp. 209–216; L.-Henry Lecomte, *Napoléon et le monde dramatique* (Paris, 1912).

17. Frank Rahill, *The World of the Melodrama* (Univeristy Park, Pa., 1967); Peter Brooks, *The Melodramatic Imagination: Balzac, Henry James, and the Mode of Excess* (New Haven, 1976), pp. 1–108; Marvin Carlson, *The French Stage in the Nineteenth Century* (Metuchen, N.J., 1972), chaps. 1–3.

18. Donald Olsen, *The City as a Work of Art: London, Paris, Vienna* (New Haven, 1986), pp. 137–151, describes the growing social segregation in Parisian neighborhoods.

19. Patrice de Moncan, *Les grands boulevards de Paris: De la Bastille à la Madeleine* (Paris, 1997), pp. 24–27, 33–37, 164–175. My necessarily succinct account leaves out the Palais Royal, which was another space for fashionable socializing that declined in the 1830s.

20. Ibid., pp. 87–98.

21. Arnold Mortier, *Les Soirées parisiennes par un monsieur de l'orchestre,* 11 vols. (Paris, 1875–1885), 1: 415–420.

22. F. W. J. Hemmings, *The Theatre Industry in Nineteenth-Century France* (Cambridge, 1993), pp. 62–64.

23. Archives nationales (Paris), F21 1130, Director to Minister, March 25, 1860. (Hereinafter, Archives nationales cited as AN.)

24. Gascar, *Le Boulevard du crime,* pp. 9–60.

25. Bibliothèque de l'Arsenal (Paris), fol. NF 11079. (Hereinafter, Bibliothèque de l'Arsenal cited as BA.) Arnold Mortier, a columnist for *Le Figaro,* claimed that an evening at the theater might cost a family as much as 100 francs, half the monthy pay of many office clerks. See *Les Soirées parisiennes,* 10: 203.

26. Cited by Pierre Boussel in "Cafés," *Dictionnaire de Paris* (Paris, 1964), p. 80.

27. Paul D'Ariste, *La Vie et le monde du boulevard (1830–1870) (Un dandy: Nestor Roqueplan)* (Paris, 1930); Gustave Claudin, *Mes souvenirs: Les boulevards de 1840–1870* (Paris, 1884); Georges Montorgeuil, *La Vie des boulevards* (Paris, 1896); Roger Boutet de Monvel, *Les Anglais à Paris, 1800–1850* (Paris, 1911), pp. 230–250.

28. Vanessa R. Schwartz, *Spectacular Realities: Early Mass Culture in Fin-de-Siècle Paris* (Berkeley, 1998), pp. 13–26; Moncan, *Les grands boulevards,* pp. 66–86, 164–175.

29. Moncan, *Les grands boulevards,* pp. 78–82.

30. Dean de Le Mott and Jeannene Przyblyski, eds., *Making the News: Modernity and the Mass Press in Nineteenth-Century France* (Amherst, Mass., 1999), pp. 1–12. Scholars are now referring to such journals as *La Presse* as "the early mass press."

31. Marcel Rouff and Thérèse Casevitz, *La Vie de fête sous le Second Empire: Hortense Schneider* (Paris, 1931), pp. 62–74; Siegfried Kracauer provides a survey of the Boulevard elite in *Orpheus in Paris: Offenbach and the Paris of His Time* (New York, 1938), chap. 8.

32. *Le Monde illustré*, no. 2,140 (April 2, 1898), p. 268.

33. Arthur Meyer, *Ce que je peux dire* (Paris, 1912), pp. 18–25; D'Astide, *La Vie du boulevard*, pp. 1–35, 71–95, 107–136.

34. Claudin, *Mes souvenirs*, p. 8.

35. A case in point would be Nestor Roqueplan, who was director of the Variétés theater and of the Opéra. He was also said by some to have invented the "girly show." See D'Astide, *La Vie du boulevard*, pp. 1–35, 71–95, 107–136. Another example was Arsène Houssaye, a prominent novelist whom the actress Rachel chose to run the Comédie-française.

36. Edmond Got, *Journal d'Edmond Got, sociétaire de la Comédie-française 1822–1901*, 2 vols. (Paris, 1910), 1: 175.

37. Mortier, *Les Soirées parisiennes*, 1: 83.

38. Claudin, *Mes souvenirs*, p. 293. See Hippolyte de Villemessant, *Mémoires d'un journaliste*, 6 vols. (Paris, 1867–1878).

39. See the observations of the American J. Brander Matthews, *The Theatres of Paris* (New York, 1880), p. 201.

40. Claudin, *Mes souvenirs*, pp. 240–241. The antichamber to Schneider's dressing room was known as the "princes' passage." See Auriant [pseud.], *Les Lionnes du Second Empire* (Paris, 1935), p. 70.

41. *L'Illustration*, no. 1,284 (October 3, 1867), p. 211.

42. *Annuaire statistique de la ville de Paris* (Paris, 1880–1900). The figures concern revenue at legitimate theaters only.

43. *Le Temps*, no. 13,825 (November 12, 1900), p. 3.

44. Lenard R. Berlanstein, *The Working People of Paris, 1871–1914* (Baltimore, 1984), chap. 2.

45. Schwartz, *Spectacular Realities*, chaps. 1, 4.

46. Jean Dubois, *La Crise théâtrale* (Paris, 1895).

47. Concetta Condemi, *Les Cafés-concerts: Histoire d'un divertissement (1849–1914)* (Paris, 1992), pp. 67–158.

48. The *Annuaire statistique de la ville de Paris* provides figures on box office revenues by theater. In 1905, for example, the Opéra took in 3.5 million francs; the Comédie-française, 2.0 million francs; and the most successful privately run theater for that year, the Variétés, earned 1.25 million.

49. Marc Martin, *Médias et journalistes de la République* (Paris, 1997), chap. 4.

50. Edmond and Jules de Goncourt, *Journal: Mémoires de la vie littéraire*, ed. Robert Ricatte, 4 vols. (Paris, 1956), 2: 1,043.

51. Camillo Antona-Traversi, *Réjane* (Paris, 1931), p. 205.

52. Schwartz, *Spectacular Realities*, chaps. 2–4.

53. *L'Illustration*, no. 2,674 (May 26, 1894), p. 438; ibid., no. 2,699 (November 17, 1894), p. 398; Arthur Meyer, *Ce que mes yeux ont vu* (Paris, 1911), p. 183.

54. Louis Lacour, *Les Premières actrices françaises* (Paris, 1921), pp. 5–48.

55. BA, Rt 6385, fol. 5 (unidentified newspaper clipping.)

56. AN, F21 1286.

57. AN, AJ13 453, "Examen de la danse."

58. See below, chap. 8.

59. AN, AJ13 453, Baronne de Valézieux to Director, October 22, 1856.

60. AN, AJ37 352–397.

61. BA, Archives de la Bastille, no. 10237, fols. 387–388.

62. Ibid., no. 10237, fols. 205–209.

63. Andrée Mégard-Gémier, *Et l'on revient toujours . . . Souvenirs d'une co-médienne* (Paris, 1932), pp. 8–48.

64. AN, AJ13 322.

65. Mistinguett, *Toute ma vie* (Paris, 1959), p. 20.

66. AN, F21 1086.

67. Arsène Houssaye, *Behind the Scenes at the Comédie-française and Other Rec-ollections*, trans. Albert D. Vandam (London, 1889), p. 73.

68. Hemmings, *Theatre and State*, chap. 11; L.-Henry Lecomte, *La Montansier: Ses aventures, ses entreprises* (Paris, 1904).

69. On the increasingly "closed shop" for playwrights, see Hemmings, *Theatre Industry*, chap. 16.

70. The Duke de Richelieu was a case in point. See Casimir Carrère, *Les Amours "scandaleuses" du maréchal-duc de Richelieu 1696–1788* (Paris, 1980).

71. BA, no. 13031, Lavallière to Gauthier, undated.

72. Jules Huret, *Sarah Bernhardt* (Paris, 1899), p. 23.

73. BA, Rt 7459, fol. 5 (undated clipping by Sarcey).

74. Bibliothèque de la Comédie-française, Bartet file, Bartet to "Mon cher," May 14, 1897.

75. BA, Rt 7459, fol. 5.

76. Louis Marcerou, *La Comédie-française: L'association des comédiens français* (Paris, 1925). In the nineteenth century, an actor at the Comédie was supposed to receive a regular review of his or her competence every ten years.

77. Théophile Gautier (*Souvenirs de théâtre, d'art, et de critique* [Paris, 1883],

p. 184) observed that exposure to the intrigues of the wings would provide the perfect training for future diplomats.

78. According to Arthur Pourgin, (*Dictionnaire historique et pittoresque du théâtre et des arts qui s'y rattachent* [Paris, 1885], p. 756), "The star is a modern product of the performer's vanity and dates only from the last thirty or forty years."

79. BA, Henri Bachimont Collection, Chaumont file.

80. Victor Hugo, "Angelo, Tyran de Padua," *Oeuvres complètes de Victor Hugo: Théâtre* (Paris, 1904), 3: 254.

81. BA, Rondel Collection, Théâtre de Vaudeville file, Director to Raymond Deslandres, undated; Aimée Tessandier, *Souvenirs, recueillis et rédigés par Henri Fescourt* (Paris, 1912).

82. On the turmoil Rachel unleashed at the theater, see Houssaye, *Behind the Scenes,* pp. 6–14, 22–28.

83. AN, AJ13 1.

84. AN, F21 1052.

85. Francisque Sarcey, *Journal de jeunesse,* ed. Adolphe Brisson (Paris, 1903), p. 362.

86. See the contracts and manuscripts providing salary figures in BA, Henri Bachimont Collection.

87. AN, F21 1087. Her pay consisted of a special subsidy of 42,000 francs plus a share in profits and a bonus.

88. Huret, *Bernhardt,* p. 58.

89. On the trials and rewards of a tour, see Marie Dorval, *Lettres à Alfred de Vigny,* ed. Charles Gaudier (Paris, 1942), pp. 49–57, 90–95, 139, 155, 173–178; BA, Virginie Déjazet Collection, Déjazet to Monsieur Hubert, 1870; to Monsieur Forest, n.d.

90. Huret, *Bernhardt,* p. 79.

91. Auguste Germain, *Les Dessous du théâtre: Les agences dramatiques et lyriques* (Paris, 1891).

92. See Judith Coffin, *The Politics of Women's Work: The Paris Garment Trades, 1750–1915* (Princeton, 1996); Joan W. Scott and Louise Tilly, *Women, Work, and Family* (New York, 1978).

2. Theater Women and Aristocratic Libertinism

1. Michel Feher, ed., *The Libertine Reader: Eroticism and Enlightenment in Eighteenth-Century France* (New York, 1997), pp. 10–20.

2. Peter Brooks, *The Novel of Worldliness: Crébillon, Marivaux, Laclos, Stendhal* (Princeton, 1969); Raymond Trousson, "Preface," in *Romans libertins du XVIIIe siècle,* ed. Raymond Trousson (Paris, 1993), pp. i–lxviii.

3. Colette Cazenobe, *Le Système du libertinage de Crébillon à Laclos* (Oxford, 1991), pp. 11–61, 432–444; Philip Stewart, *Le Masque et la parole: Le langage de l'amour au XVIIIe siècle* (Paris, 1973), chaps. 1, 3; Brooks, *Novel of Worldliness*, pp. 184–210.

4. Trousson, *Romans libertins*, pp. xliii–xlviii; Stewart, *Le Masque*, pp. 28–38.

5. Brooks, *Novel of Worldliness*, p. 213.

6. Péter Nagy, *Libertinage et révolution* (Paris, 1975), pp. 151–154; Trousson, *Romans libertins*, pp. lix–lxi.

7. On the status of these novels as descriptions of the society producing them, see Stewart, *Le Masque*, pp. 9–11.

8. Jules Cousin, ed., *Le Comte de Clermont, sa cour et ses maîtresses: Lettres et documents inédits,* 2 vols. (Paris, 1867), 1: 110–147.

9. BA, Archives de la Bastille, no. 10237, fols. 5–9; Cousin, *Clermont*, pp. 84–88.

10. Archives de l'Opéra, dossiers d'artistes, Mademoiselle Leduc. After facing financial setbacks, Clermont made his peace with God and married Leduc in what turned out to be the last year of his life.

11. Jacques Castelnau, *Le Maréchal de Saxe: Amours et batailles* (Paris, 1937), chaps. 3–5.

12. Adrienne Lecouvreur, "Lettres à Maurice de Saxe," *Revue des deux mondes* 36 (1926): 804–42; 37 (1927): 104–128, 349–371.

13. Jean-François Marmontel, *Mémoires*, ed. John Renwick, 2 vols. (Clermont-Ferrand, 1972), 1: 96.

14. Ibid., pp. 96–97. On Beauménard, see Paul Ginisty, *Une Comédienne au XVIIIe siècle: Mademoiselle Gogo, Mademoiselle Beauménard de la Comédie-française (1730–1799)* (Paris, 1913).

15. Castelnau, *Le Maréchal de Saxe*, chap. 5; Jean-Pierre Bois, *Maurice de Saxe* (Paris, 1992), pp. 436–442.

16. Ellery Schalk, *From Valor to Pedigree: Ideas of Nobility in France in the Sixteenth and Seventeenth Centuries* (Princeton, 1986), chap. 6; Mark Motley, *Becoming a French Aristocrat: The Education of the Court Nobility 1580–1715* (Princeton, 1990).

17. Jean-Michel Pelous, *Amour précieux, amour galant (1654–1675): Essai sur la représentation de l'amour dans la littérature et la société mondaines* (Paris, 1980), p. 476.

18. Ibid., pp. 134–155, 245–273, 402–463. Seventeenth-century libertinism also involved couples of the same sex. See Guy Richard, *Histoire de l'amour en France* (Paris, 1985), pp. 105–156. The perception of libertinism became more exclusively "heterosexual" in the eighteenth century.

19. Jean Hervez, *Les Femmes et la galanterie au XVIIe siècle* (Paris, 1907), pp. 86–93.

20. Thomas Laqueur, *Making Sex: Body and Gender from the Greeks to Freud* (Cambridge, Mass., 1990), chaps. 1, 6.

21. Pelous, *Amour précieux*, p. 250.

22. Léopold Lacour, *Les Premières actrices françaises* (Paris, 1921), pp. 5, 28, 34.

23. Georges Mongrédien, *Daily Life in the French Theatre at the Time of Molière*, trans. Claire Elaine Angel (London, 1969).

24. Jean Hervez, *La Régence galante d'après les mémoires, les rapports de police, les libelles, les pamphlets, les satires, les chansons du temps* (Paris, 1909), pp. 103–121; Charles Kunstler, *La Vie quotidienne sous la Régence* (Paris, 1960), pp. 38–59, 78–87, 95–99, 203–204.

25. Liz Dalby, *Geisha* (Berkeley, 1983), p. viii.

26. Pelous, *Amour précieux*, pp. 249–251.

27. Roger Duchêne, *Ninon de Lenclos: La courtisane du grand siècle* (Paris, 1984), chaps. 9–12.

28. Ibid., p. 90.

29. Guillaume Imbert de Boudeaux [pseud. Alexandre Grimod de la Reynière], *La Chronique scandaleuse, ou mémoire pour servir à l'histoire de la génération présente (1788–1791)* (Paris, 1912), p. 298.

30. Gaston Campon and Robert Yve-Plessis, *Fille d'Opéra, vendeuse d'amour: Histoire de Mademoiselle Deschamps* (Paris, 1906), pp. 57–59.

31. Stewart, *La Masque*, pp. 17–18.

32. Jonathan Dewald, *Aristocratic Experience and the Origins of Modern Culture: France, 1570–1715* (Berkeley, 1993). Also, James Farr, *Authority and Sexuality in Early Modern Burgundy (1550–1730)* (New York, 1995); Norbert Elias, *The Civilizing Process*, trans. Edmund Jephcott (New York, 1982).

33. Niklas Luhman, *Love as Passion: The Codification of Intimacy*, trans. Jeremy Gaines and Doris L. Jones (Oxford, 1986), chap. 5.

34. Sarah Maza, *Private Lives and Public Affairs: The Causes Célèbres in Prerevolutionary France* (Berkeley, 1993); Richard Rand, *Intimate Encounters: Love and Domesticity in Eighteenth-Century France* (Princeton, 1997).

35. BA, Archives de la Bastille, 10235, fol. 362; 10237, fols. 489–492.

36. Ibid., registers 10235–10237.

37. François Bluche, *Les Magistrats du Parlement de Paris au XVIIIe siècle* (Paris, 1960); Yves Durand, *Les Fermiers généraux au XVIIIe siècle* (Paris, 1971).

38. BA, Archives de la Bastille, no. 10235, fols. 71–107.

39. Ibid., no. 10236, fols. 3–48.

40. Capon and Yve-Plessis, *Deschamps*, pp. 138–140.

41. Camille Piton, ed., *Paris sous Louis XV: Rapports des inspecteurs de police au roi*, 3 vols. (Paris, 1909), 1: 29–33; Gaston Capon and Robert Yve-Plessis,

Paris galant au dix-huitième siècle: La vie privée du Prince de Conty (Paris, 1907), pp. 202–299.

42. BA, Archives de la Bastille, no. 10237, report of October 30, 1753.
43. Ibid., no. 10235, report of December 5, 1753.
44. Piton, *Paris*, 1: 341.
45. Cousin, *Clermont*, 1: 159–160.
46. Piton, *Paris*, 1: 329–330.
47. BA, Archives de la Bastille, no. 10236, fols. 457–485.
48. Ibid., no. 10235, report of October 23, 1753.
49. Piton, *Paris*, 1: 341.
50. BA, Archives de la Bastille, no. 10237, report of February 3, 1751.
51. Ibid., no. 10235, report of June 10, 1755.
52. Ibid., no. 10235, Dallière, report of April 24, 1750, and Beauchamps, report of December 24, 1756.
53. Ibid., no. 10237, Romainville, report of July 18, 1756.
54. Piton, *Paris*, 3: 9–10.
55. BA, Archives de la Bastille, no. 10235, Clairon, report of August 22, 1752; Courat, report of June 14, 1748; Caroline, report of December 11, 1755; ibid., no. 10236, Deschamps, report of October 31, 1755; Granier, report of May 22, 1750.
56. Ibid., no. 10237, Le Marquis, report of October 22, 1753.
57. Ibid., no. 10236, report of June 18, 1754.
58. Ibid., no. 10235, fols. 24–32.
59. Ibid., no. 10237, fols. 176–191.
60. Ibid., no. 10235, report of June 14, 1748.
61. Ibid., no. 10237, report of April 20, 1753.
62. Ibid., no. 10235, report of August 7, 1749.
63. Ibid., fols. 395–461.
64. Lynn Hunt, *The Family Romance of the French Revolution* (Berkeley, 1992), chaps. 1–2; Roger Chartier, *The Cultural Origins of the French Revolution*, trans. Lynda G. Cochrane (Durham, N.C., 1991), chaps. 5–6; Maza, *Private Lives*, pp. 43–44, 73–76, 99–101, 152–154; Roddy Reid, *Families in Jeopardy: Regulating the Body Social in France, 1750–1910* (Stanford, Calif., 1993), chaps. 2–4; Anne Vincent-Bouffault, *The History of Tears: Sensibility and Sentimentality* (London, 1991), chaps. 1–5; James H. Johnson, *Listening in Paris: A Cultural History* (Berkeley, 1995), chap. 3.
65. I base these observations on police reports in BA, Archives de la Bastille, no. 10235–10237; Piton, *Paris*; and Lorédon Larchy, ed., *Documents inédits sur le règne de Louis XV, ou anecdotes galantes sur les actrices, demoiselles entretenues, grisettes, etc. formant le journal des inspecteurs de Monsieur le lieutenant de police de Sartine* (Paris, 1863).

66. BA, Archives de la Bastille, no. 10237, report of February 3, 1751.

67. [Anon.], *La Vie publique et privée des françaises à la ville, à la cour, et dans les provinces depuis la mort de Louis XV jusqu'au commencement du règne de Charles X,* 2 vols. (Paris, 1826), 2: 99.

68. BA, Archives de la Bastille, no. 10237, August 21, 1755.

69. On the integration of financiers into Le Monde, see Yves Durand, *Finances et mécénat: Les fermiers généraux au XVIIIe siècle* (Paris, 1976), pp. 526–547.

70. Marmontel, *Mémoires,* 1: 98; François-Antoine Chevrier, *Le Colporteur: Histoire morale et critique* (London, n.d.), p. 175.

71. BA, Archives de la Bastille, no. 10237, Lekain, report of November 12, 1753.

72. Ibid., no. 10236, Dallière, report of October 3, 1755.

73. Chevrier, *Le Colporteur,* p. 63.

74. Alexandre de Tilly, *Mémoires du comte Alexandre de Tilly pour servir à l'histoire des moeurs à la fin du XVIIIe siècle,* ed. Christien Melchoir-Bonnet (Paris, 1986), p. 217.

75. Charles Collé, *Journal et mémoires sur les hommes de lettres, les ouvrages dramatiques, et les évenéments les plus mémorables du règne de Louis XV,* 3 vols. (Geneva, 1967), 3: 6–7.

76. François-Marie Mayeur de Saint-Paul, *Le Désoeuvré, ou l'espion du boulevard du Temple* (Paris, 1907), p. 131, and see his *Le Vol plus haut, ou l'espion des principaux théâtres de la capitale contenant une histoire abrégée des acteurs et actrices de ces mêmes théâtres* (Paris, 1784).

77. Chevrier, *Le Colporteur,* p. 9.

78. Jean-Marie Goulemont, *Forbidden Texts: Erotic Literature and its Readers in Eighteenth-Century France,* trans. James Simpson (Philadelphia, 1994), p. 85.

79. Pierre Gaillard de la Bataille, *Histoire de Mademoiselle Cronel, dite Frétillon, actrice de la Comédie de Rouen écrite par elle-même,* ed. Jean Hervez (Paris, 1911).

80. De Sainte-Croix, *La Comédienne, fille et femme de qualité, ou mémoires de la marquise de XXX* (Brussels, 1756). Isabelle de Charrière's *Caliste, ou lettres écrites de Lausanne,* originally published in 1788, has an actress character in the background.

81. Bernadette Fort and Jeremy Popkin, "Introduction: Secret Intelligence/ Public Knowledge," in *The* Mémoires secrets *and the Culture of Publicity in Eighteenth-Century France,* ed. Jeremy Popkin and Bernadette Fort (Oxford, 1998), pp. 1–8.

82. Pamela Cheek, "The *Mémoires secrets* and the Actress: Tribadism, Performance, and Property," in *Culture of Publicity,* ed. Popkin and Fort,

pp. 107–128; Jeffrey Merrick, "The Marquis de Villette and Mademoiselle de Raucourt: Representing Male and Female Sexual Deviance in the Late Eighteenth Century," in *Homosexuality in Modern France,* ed. Bryan Ragan and Jeffrey Merrick (New York, 1995), pp. 30–53.

83. Jennifer M. Jones, "The Taste for Fashion and Frivolity: Gender, Clothing and the Commercial Culture of the Old Regime," Ph.D. diss., Princeton University, 1991; Daniel Roche, *The Culture of Clothing: Dress and Fashion in the "Ancien Régime,"* trans. Jean Birrell (New York, 1994), pp. 220, 509.

84. Edmond de Goncourt, *La Guimard d'après les registres des menus-plaisirs, de la bibliothèque de l'Opéra, etc.* (Paris, 1893), p. 147.

85. Edmond de Goncourt, *La Saint-Huberty d'après sa correspondance et ses papiers de famille* (Geneva, 1973), p. 228.

86. Cited in Jones, "Taste for Fashion," pp. 238–239.

87. Marmontel, *Mémoires,* 1: 136.

88. Thomas E. Kaiser, "Madame de Pompadour and the Theaters of Power," *French Historical Studies* 19 (Fall 1996): 1,025–1,044.

89. Jean-Baptiste Fleury, *Mémoires de Fleury de la Comédie-française de 1757 à 1820,* 6 vols. (Brussels and Leipzig, 1835–38), 2: 16–19, 51–52. Hector Fleishmann, *Le Cénacle de Mademoiselle Raucourt de la Comédie-française* (Paris, 1912), pp. 78–80, 141; Piton, *Paris,* 1: 46, 60.

90. Hector Fleishmann, *Les Pamphlets libertins contre Marie-Antoinette* (Geneva, 1976), pp. 50–52.

91. Cited in Emile Lenglande, *Rose Bertin: The Creator of Fashion at the Court of Marie-Antoinette* (New York, 1913), p. 58.

92. The term came into use between the late 1830s and early 1840s. See Prosper Poitevin, *Nouveau dictionnaire universel de la langue française,* 4 vols. (Paris, 1856–1860), 1: 416. On actresses as celebrities, see below, chap. 9.

93. Tilly, *Mémoires,* p. 497. On libertinism as it was actually practiced in England, see Randolph Trumbach, *Sex and the Gender Revolution* (Chicago, 1998), chap. 3.

94. John McManners, *Abbés and Actresses: The Church and the Theatrical Profession in Eighteenth-Century France* (Oxford, 1986).

3. Defining the Modern Gender Order

1. See James Collins, *The State in Early Modern France* (Cambridge, 1995), chap. 5, on the emergence of a "new France" between 1720 and 1750.

2. Louis Riccoboni, *De la réformation du théâtre* (Paris, 1743), chap. 4. On the author, see Xavier de Courville, *Un apôtre de l'art du théâtre au XVIIIe siècle* (Paris, 1943–1945).

3. Louis Riccoboni, *Histoire du théâtre-italien* (Paris, 1727), pp. 266–275.

4. Riccoboni, *De la réformation,* pp. 99–115. The citation is from p. 115.

5. Gaston Maugras, *Les Comédiens hors la loi* (Paris, 1877); Moses Barras, *The Stage Controversy in France from Corneille to Rousseau* (New York, 1933); John McManners, *Abbés and Actresses: The Church and the Theatrical Profession in Eighteenth-Century France* (Oxford, 1986).

6. See Abigail Solomon-Godeau, *Male Trouble: A Crisis in Representation* (New York, 1997), on the proliferation of women's bodies as spectacle.

7. Liselotte Steinbrügge, *The Moral Sex: Women's Nature in the French Enlightenment,* trans. Pamela Selwyn (New York, 1995), pp. 4–26, 36–42.

8. Thomas Laqueur, *Making Sex: Gender and the Body from the Greeks to Freud* (Cambridge, Mass., 1990), chaps. 5–6.

9. Steinbrügge, *Moral Sex,* pp. 105–108 and *passim.*

10. Lindsay Wilson, *Women and Medicine in the French Enlightenment: The Debate over Maladies des Femmes* (Baltimore, 1993), p. 165.

11. The most obvious sign of the growing cultural weight of individualism was the emphasis on personal volition in eighteenth-century thought. See Peter Gay, *The Enlightenment,* vol. 2: *The Science of Freedom* (New York, 1969). On the growing importance of personal autonomy in private life, see Roger Chartier, ed., *Passions of the Renaissance,* vol. 3 of *A History of Private Life,* ed. Philippe Ariès and Georges Duby, trans. Arthur Goldhammer (Cambridge, Mass., 1987–1991).

12. Laqueur, *Making Sex,* pp. 194–207.

13. Sarah Maza, *Private Lives and Public Affairs: The Causes Célèbres in Prerevolutionary France* (Berkeley, 1993), p. 322.

14. Albert Hirschmann, *The Passions and the Interests* (Princeton, 1977); Elizabeth Fox-Genovese, *Origins of Physiocracy: Economic Revolution and Social Order in Eighteenth-Century France* (Ithaca, N.Y., 1976).

15. Dena Goodman, "Public Sphere and Private Life: Toward a Synthesis of Current Historiographical Approaches to the Old Regime," *History and Theory* 31 (February 1992): 1–20; Keith Michael Baker, "Defining the Public Sphere in Eighteenth-Century France: Variations on a Theme by Habermas," in *Habermas and the Public Sphere,* ed. Craig Calhoun (Cambridge, Mass., 1992), pp. 181–209; Maza, *Private Lives.* Joan Landes brings in gender in *Women and the Public Sphere in the Age of the French Revolution* (Ithaca, N.Y., 1988).

16. Roger Chartier, *The Cultural Origins of the French Revolution,* trans. Lydia G. Cochrane (Durham, N.C., 1991), p. 109.

17. Ibid., p. 196.

18. Isabel Hull, *Sexuality, State, and Civil Society in Germany, 1700–1815* (Ithaca, N.Y., 1996), pp. 297–298; Robert Nye, ed., *Sexuality* (New York, 1999), pp. 67–83. Antoine de Baecque, *The Body Politic: Corporeal Meta-*

phor in Revolutionary France, 1770–1800, trans. Charlotte Mandell (Stanford, Calif., 1997) describes the revolutionaries' disdain for aristocrats' dissolute bodies.

19. Victor Wexler, "Made for Man's Delight: Rousseau as Antifeminist," *American Historical Review* 81 (April 1976): 266–291.

20. Jean-Jacques Rousseau, *Lettre à Monsieur D'Alembert sur les spectacles,* ed. Max Fuchs (Lille and Geneva, 1948), pp. 63–65, 102, 111–115, 121, 133–144. Citations on pp. 63, 136.

21. Ibid., pp. 121–135. Citation on p. 123.

22. Scott Bryson, *The Chastened Stage: Bourgeois Drama and the Exercise of Power* (Saratoga, Calif., 1991).

23. On the contradiction, see Nina Gelbart, *Feminine and Opposition Journalism in Old Regime France* (Berkeley, 1987), pp. 212–213.

24. Louis-Sébastien Mercier, *Nouvel essai sur l'art théâtral* (Amsterdam, 1773), pp. 347–372. Citations on pp. 357, 361.

25. Mark Poster, "The Concepts of Sexual Identity and Life Cycle in Restif's Utopian Thought," *Studies on Voltaire and the Eighteenth Century* 73 (1970): 241–271; Pierre Testaud, *Rétif de la Bretonne et la création littéraire* (Geneva, 1977), pp. 313–365.

26. Nicolas-Edme Rétif de la Bretonne, *La Mimographe* (Amsterdam, 1770), pp. 17–44, 175–232.

27. Ibid., pp. 448–466. Citation on p. 465.

28. Madelyn Gutwirth, *The Twilight of the Goddesses: Women and Representation in the French Revolutionary Era* (New Brunswick, N.J., 1992); Landes, *Women and the Public Sphere,* chaps. 1–2.

29. Jean-François Marmontel, "Apologie du théâtre," in his *Contes moraux,* 2 vols. (Paris, 1767), 2: 162–271.

30. Jean D'Alembert, *Lettre de Monsieur D'Alembert à Monsieur Jean-Jacques Rousseau sur l'article* Genève *tiré du septième volume de l'Encyclopédie* (Amsterdam, 1759).

31. L. H. Dancourt, *L. H. Dancourt, arlequin de Berlin, à Monsieur Jean-Jacques Rousseau, citoyen de Genève* (Amsterdam, 1759). Citations on pp. 172–173.

32. Jules Bonnassies, *La Comédie-française: Histoire administrative 1658–1757* (Paris, 1874), p. 140; Emile Campardon, *Les Comédiens du roi de la troupe italienne pendant les deux derniers siècles,* 2 vols. (Paris, 1880), 2: 330–332.

33. William H. Sewell, Jr., "Social and Cultural Perspectives on Women's Work: Comments on Loats, Hafter, and De Groat," *French Historical Studies* 20 (Winter 1997): 52.

34. Sarah Hanley, "Engendering the State: Family Formation and State Building in Early Modern France," *French Historical Studies* 16 (Spring 1989): 4–27, and Hanley, "Family and State in Early Modern France: The Mar-

riage Pact," in *Connecting Spheres: Women in the Western World, 1500 to the Present,* ed. Marilyn J. Boxer and Jean B. Quataert (New York, 1987), pp. 53–63.

35. Landes, *Women and the Public Sphere,* chap. 2.

36. Georges Mongredien, *Daily Life in the French Theatre at the Time of Molière,* trans. Claire Elaine Angel (London, 1969), p. 28.

37. Jean-Marie Apostolidès, *Le Prince sacrifié: Théâtre et politique au temps de Louis XIV* (Paris, 1985), pp. 178–181.

38. It was the custom at the Comédie-française for men in the audience to remove their hats out of respect for the king, represented by his seat in the royal box. The king was always present. Noëlle Guilbert and Jacqueline Razzannikoff, *Le Journal de la Comédie-française, 1787–1799: La Comédie aux trois couleurs* (Paris, 1989), p. 106.

39. Denis Papillon de la Ferté, *L'Administration des menus: Journal (1756–1780),* ed. Ernest Boysse (Paris, 1887), p. 109.

40. Bonnaissies, *La Comédie,* p. 140; Lenard R. Berlanstein, "Women and Power in Eighteenth-Century France: Actresses at the Comédie-française," *Feminist Studies* 20 (Fall 1994): 481–486.

41. Papillon de la Ferté, *L'Administration,* pp. 99, 118, 143, 152, 232, 245, 251, 320. Citation on p. 232.

42. Jeffrey Ravel, "Actress to Activist: Mademoiselle Clairon in the Public Sphere of the 1760s," *Theatre Survey* 35 (May 1994): 73–86.

43. On the Dubois affair, see Friedrich-Melchoir Grimm, *Correspondance littéraire, philosophique, et critique par Grimm, Diderot, Raynal, Meister, etc.,* ed. Maurice Tourneux, 16 vols. (Paris, 1882), 5: 447–448; 4: 256–259, 281; Ferté, *L'Administration,* pp. 159–183; Maugras, *Les Comédiens,* pp. 283–293.

44. Ferté, *L'Administration,* pp. 164–190, 197, 205.

45. A medallion bearing Clairon's face was being sold to the public in 1765. See Charles Collé, *Journal et mémoires sur les hommes de lettres, les ouvrages dramatiques, et les événements les plus mémorables du règne de Louis XV,* 3 vols. (Geneva, 1967), 3: 6–7.

46. Jacques Boncompain, *Auteurs et comédiens au XVIIIe siècle* (Paris, 1976); Jacques Bonnassies, *Les Auteurs dramatiques et la Comédie-française au XVIIe et XVIIIe siècles* (Paris, 1874), pp. 57–99; Gregory Brown, "A Field of Honor: The Cultural Politics of Playwrighting in Eighteenth-Century France," Ph.D. diss., Columbia University, 1997.

47. Jean-François Marmontel, *Mémoires,* ed. John Renwick, 2 vols. (Clermont-Ferrand, 1972), 1: 70.

48. Nina Rattner Gelbart, "'Frondeur' Journalism in the 1770s: Theater Criticism and Radical Politics in the Pre-Revolutionary French Press," *Eigh-*

teenth-Century Studies 17 (Summer 1984): 493–514, and her *Feminine and Opposition Journalism.*

49. *Les Comédiens, ou le foyer: Comédie en un acte et en prose* (London, 1777).

50. Ibid., p. 28.

51. Rétif's ideal reading committee would be composed of the four most senior playwrights and eight of the "most able" actor- or actress-citizens. See *La Mimographe,* p. 71.

52. Charles Palissot de Montenoy, *Les Courtisanes, ou l'école des moeurs* (Paris, 1775). Brown revises Palissot's reputation in "Field of Honor," pp. 254–261.

53. Jean-Baptiste Lafitte, ed., *Mémoires de Fleury de la Comédie-française de 1757 à 1820,* 6 vols. (Brussels and Leipzig, 1835–1838), 2: 242–246, 64; Brown, "Field of Honor," chap. 4.

54. Nicolas François de Neufchâteau, *Mémoire à consulter pour le sieur Palissot de Montenoy contre la troupe des comédiens françois* (Paris, 1775), p. 7.

55. Alexandre du Coudray, *Lettre à Monsieur Palissot sur le refus de ses Courtisanes* (Paris, n.d.), pp. 21–22.

56. Bonnassies, *Les Auteurs dramatiques,* pp. 71–74. The royal administration created an all-male committee to supervise the decisions of the gender-mixed assembly at the Italian Theater in 1774. See Campardon, *Les Comédiens du roi,* 2: 327–329.

57. See Dena Goodman's *The Republic of Letters: A Cultural History of the French Enlightenment* (Ithaca, N.Y., 1994), chap. 6, for the attack on female authority in salons.

58. *Cahier des doléances, remonstrances, et instructions de l'assemblée de tous les ordres des théâtres royaux de Paris* (n.p., n.d. [April 10, 1789]).

59. Lynn Hunt, *Politics, Culture, and Class in the French Revolution* (Berkeley, 1984).

60. *Cahiers, plaintes, et doléances de messieurs les comédiens français* (Paris, 1789), p. 1. I am well aware that the authenticity of this document is in dispute. Even if it is not a fully reliable account of the deliberations, the important point for my purposes is that the need to exclude actresses was being discussed in 1789.

61. Ibid., p. 7.

62. Ibid., pp. 7–8.

63. There were fourteen or fifteen men present. Eight voted for exclusion.

64. Paul Andrew Friedland finds that pamphlets after 1789 held actresses responsible for the immorality of the theater and exonerated actors. See "Representation and Revolution: The Theatricality of Politics and the Politics of Theater in France, 1789–1794," Ph.D diss., University of California, Berkeley, 1995, pp. 280–281, 288–289.

65. *Cahiers, plaintes,* p. 13; Hector Fleischmann, *Les Pamphlets libertins contre Marie-Antoinette* (Geneva, 1976), p. 60.

66. *Cahiers, plaintes,* pp. 14–15.

67. Bibliothèque de la Comédie-française, Louise Contat file (copy of the deliberations of the general assembly of March 30, 1782).

68. Landes, in *Women in the Public Sphere,* argues for the masculinist interpretation. For the other side, see Dominique Godineau, *Les Citoyennes tricoleuses: Les femmes du peuple à Paris pendant la Révolution française* (Aix-en-Provence, 1988).

69. Cited in Guilbert and Razzonnikoff, *Le Journal,* p. 63.

70. On the *Charles IX* affair, see ibid., pp. 99–132.

71. *Les Révolutions de France and de Brabant,* no. 45 (October 4, 1790), p. 253.

72. Ibid., no. 40 (August 30, 1790), pp. 42–48.

73. *Révolutions de Paris, dédiées à la nation et au district des Petits-Augustins,* no. 70 (November 6–13, 1790), pp. 246–248.

74. Ibid., no. 75 (December 11–18, 1790), p. 527.

75. Patrice Higonnet, *Class, Ideology, and the Rights of Nobles during the French Revolution* (Oxford, 1981), p. 55; James H. Johnson, "Revolutionary Audiences and the Impossible Imperative of Fraternity," in *Re-Creating Authority in Revolutionary France,* ed. Bryan T. Ragan and Elizabeth A. Williams (New Brunswick, N.J., 1993), pp. 57–78; Friedland, "Representation and Revolution," pp. 406–423.

76. Arthur Pougin, *L'Opéra-comique pendant la Révolution de 1788 à 1801* (Paris, 1891), pp. 99, 103, 105, 113–114.

77. Louise Fusil, *Souvenirs d'une actrice,* 2 vols. (Paris, 1841), 1: 278–280.

78. On libertinism during the Terror, see L.-Henry Lecomte, *La Montasier: Ses aventures, ses entreprises* (Paris, 1904), pp. 124–129; Henri D'Almeras, *Emilie de Sainte-Amaranthe: Le demi-monde sous la Terreur* (Paris, 1904), 86–88, 170; Ernest Lebègue, *Boursault-Malherbe: Comédien, conventionel, spéculateur, 1752–1842* (Paris, 1935).

79. Jacques Vincent, *La belle Mademoiselle Lange* (Paris, 1932), pp. 39, 89–139; Béatrix Dussane, *La Célimène de Thermidor: Louise Contat (1760–1813)* (Paris, 1929), pp. 152–227.

80. Jean-Pierre Garnier, *Barras, le roi du Directoire* (Paris, 1970), pp. 152–178; Jacques Vivent, *Barras, le "roi" de la république, 1755–1829* (Paris, 1938), chap. 12.

81. Dussane, *La Célimène de Thermidor,* pp. 181–227; Vincent, *La belle Mademoiselle Lange,* pp. 95–148; Charles Kunstler, *La Vie privée de l'Impératrice Joséphine* (Paris, 1939), pp. 103–135; Frédéric Masson, *La Société pendant le Consulat* (Paris, n.d.), pp. 66, 87–108.

82. Marguerite Joséphine George, *Memoirs of Mademoiselle George, a Favor-*

ite of Napoleon, ed. Paul Cherany (New York, 1909), p. 158; Roselyne Laplace, *Mademoiselle George, ou un demi-siècle du théâtre* (Paris, 1987), p. 80.

83. Micheline Baudet, *Mademoiselle Mars, l'inimitable* (Paris, 1987), p. 183.

84. Nestor Roqueplan, *La Vie parisienne* (Paris, 1858), pp. 79–81; Jules Vernière, "Les Coulisses de l'Opéra," *Revue de Paris* (1836), pp. 309–311.

85. Jean Savant, *Les Amours de Napoléon* (Paris, 1956), pp. 98–115; Arthur Pougin, *Une cantatrice "amie" de Napoléon: Guiseppina Grassini, 1773–1850* (Paris, 1920).

86. George, *Memoirs,* pp. 114–180.

87. Kunstler, *La Vie privée,* p. 147.

88. Jacques Godechot, *Les Institutions de la France sous la Révolution et l'Empire* (Paris, 1951), pp. 691–696.

89. Lynn Hunt, *The Family Romance of the French Revolution* (Berkeley, 1992), chap. 3.

4. Magdalenes of Postaristocratic France

1. Jean Savant, *Les Amours de Napoléon* (Paris, 1956), p. 117.

2. Barbara Corrado Pope, "Women and Retreat: Upper-Class French Women after 1789," in *Women, War and Revolution,* ed. Carol Berkin and Clara Lovett (New York, 1979), pp. 215–236; Margaret Darrow, "French Noblewomen and the New Domesticity," *Feminist Studies* 5 (1979): 41–64.

3. *Notice sur l'enterrement de Mademoiselle Raucourt* (Paris, 1821).

4. Robert Nye, *Masculinity and Male Codes of Honor in Modern France* (New York, 1993), p. 46.

5. Sophie Gay, *Salons célèbres* (Paris, 1837), p. 69.

6. Ibid., pp. 69–145. Citation on p. 84.

7. J. Rousseau described the fashionable, mostly male circle that frequented Mars's home in *Code théâtral: Physiologie des théâtres* (Paris, 1828), pp. 245–252.

8. Sarah Maza, "Luxury, Morality, and Social Change: Why There Was No Middle-Class Consciousness in Prerevolutionary France," *Journal of Modern History* 69 (June 1997): 199–229.

9. This interpretation owes much to Sarah Maza, who is currently working on the "myth of the bourgeoisie" in France from 1750 to 1830. In anticipation of Maza's book, there is the suggestive analysis in Dror Wahrman, *Imagining the Middle Class: The Political Representation of Class in Britain, 1780–1840* (Cambridge, 1995), chap. 8.

10. Jean-André Tudesq, *Les grands notables en France (1840–49): Etude historique d'une psychologie sociale* (Paris, 1964); Christophe Charle, *Social History of France in the Nineteenth Century,* trans. Miriam Kochan (Provi-

dence, R.I., 1994), chaps. 1–2; A. Jardin and A. J. Tudesq, *La France des notables: La vie de la nation 1815–1848* (Paris, 1973).

11. David Garrioch, *The Formation of the Parisian Bourgeoisie 1690–1830* (Cambridge, Mass., 1996), pp. 265–266.

12. Wahrman, *Imagining*, pp. 276–284.

13. On the "social" aspects of the Revolution of 1830, see Roger Magraw, *France 1815–1914: The Bourgeois Century* (New York, 1984), chap. 2.

14. H. C. A. Collingham, *The July Monarchy: A Political History of France, 1830–1848* (New York, 1988), chaps. 2, 5, 9, 21, 24, 25.

15. Philippe Perrot, *Fashioning the Bourgeoisie: A History of Clothing in the Nineteenth Century,* trans. Richard Bienvenu (Princeton, 1994), chap. 2.

16. Francette Pacteau, *The Symptom of Beauty* (Cambridge, Mass., 1994), p. 147.

17. See above, chap. 2.

18. Adeline Daumard, *Les Bourgeois et la bourgeoisie en France depuis 1815* (Paris, 1987); Eric Mension-Rigau, *Aristocrates et grands bourgeois: Education, traditions, valeurs* (Paris, 1994).

19. *Le Monde illustré,* no. 583 (June 13, 1868), p. 370.

20. Ibid., no. 768 (December 30, 1871), pp. 410–411.

21. *La Revue illustrée,* 11 (December 1890–June 1891), p. 137.

22. *Le Figaro,* no. 234 (September 6, 1874), p. 3.

23. Jules Mayret [pseud. Félix Pyat], *Les Filles d'actrices* (Paris, 1832). Citations on p. 138.

24. Collingham, *July Monarchy,* chaps. 4, 10, 11, 13; Claire Goldberg Moses, *French Feminism in the Nineteenth Century* (Albany, N.Y., 1984), chaps. 1–2.

25. Sarah Maza's pathbreaking work in progress on "the myth of the bourgeoisie" leads to questioning whether one can usefully speak of bourgeois values being the dominant ones in this era.

26. Domna C. Stanton, *The Aristocrat as Art: Study of the* Honnête Homme *and the Dandy in Seventeenth- and Nineteenth-Century French Literature* (New York, 1980), pp. 2–7, 85–98.

27. Anne Martin-Fugier, "La Cour et la ville sous la Monarchie de Juillet d'après les feuilletons mondaines," *Revue historique,* no. 563 (1987): 133.

28. Anne Martin-Fugier, *La Vie élégante, ou la formation du Tout-Paris, 1815–1848* (Paris, 1990), pp. 376–391.

29. On the development of Boulevard culture, see above, chap. 1.

30. According to Jerrold Siegel (*Bohemian Paris: Culture, Politics, and the Boundaries of Bourgeois Life 1830–1930* [New York, 1986], p. 100), "Dandyism reconstructed aristocracy so that it could become a vehicle for the modern exaltation of the individual self."

31. Gerda Grothe, *Le Duc de Morny* (Paris, 1966), pp. 25–38; A. Augustin-

Thierry, *Son Elégance, le duc de Morny* (Paris, 1951), pp. 244–259; Gustave Claudin, *Mes Souvenirs: Les Boulevards de 1840 à 1870* (Paris, 1884), p. 173.

32. *L'Illustration*, no. 111 (April 12, 1845), pp. 103–107.

33. César Graña, *Bohemian versus Bourgeois: French Society and French Men of Letters in the Nineteenth Century* (New York, 1969), chap. 11.

34. Martin-Fugier, "La Cour et la ville," pp. 107–133. There were opportunities for enrichment for the few lucky writers who published novels in serial form in the burgeoning press. See Graña, *Bohemian*, p. 34.

35. Willem Van der Gun, *La Courtisane romantique et son rôle dans la Comédie humaine de Balzac* (Leiden, 1963), pp. 38–68.

36. Alexandre Dumas, Sr., had to defend his great stage success, *Antony,* against charges of portraying adultery in a positive light. He asserted that "in Molière's day, it was called cuckoldry, and one laughed at it. In our day, it is called adultery, and one rages against it." See Dumas, *Mes mémoires 1830–1833* (Paris, 1989), p. 475.

37. William H. Sewell, *Work and Revolution in France: The Language of Labor from the Old Regime to 1848* (Cambridge, 1980), chaps. 7–9.

38. Charle, *Social History,* pp. 32–35.

39. William M. Reddy, *The Invisible Code: Honor and Sentiment in Post-revolutionary France, 1814–1848* (Berkeley, 1997), chaps. 4–6; Jo Burr Margadant, "Gender, Vice, and the Political Imaginary in Nineteenth-Century France: Reinterpreting the Failure of the July Monarchy, 1830–1848," *American Historical Review* 104 (December 1999): 1,461–1,497.

40. Pierre-Joseph Proudhon, *La Pornocratie, ou les femmes dans le temps moderne* (Paris, 1875), pp. 72, 236.

41. Mona Ozouf, *Women's Words: Essay on French Singularity,* trans. Jane Marie Todd (Chicago, 1997), pp. 64–87; Geneviève Fraisse, *Reason's Muse: Sexual Difference and the Birth of Democracy,* trans. Jane Marie Todd (Chicago, 1994), pp. 124–128.

42. Michelle Perrot, "Women, Power, and History: The Case of Nineteenth-Century France," in *Women, State, and Revolution: Essays on Power and Gender since 1789,* ed. Sian Reynolds (London, 1986), p. 55; Abigail Solomon-Godeau, *Male Trouble: A Crisis of Representation* (New York, 1997).

43. The fictional work that comes closest to being an exception is Charles Baudelaire's 1847 novel, *Fanfarlo.* Baudelaire does not sentimentalize the eponymous dancer, but the plot involves a society lady who prevails over her and takes back her husband. Even in this work, the actress's wiles are contained.

44. François Andrieux, *La Comédienne: Comédie en trois actes en vers* (Paris, 1916), citations from act 1, scene 6 (p. 16).

45. Casimir Delavigne, *Les Comédiens: Comédie en cinq actes et en vers* (Paris, 1820).

46. BA, Rf 24174 (press clipping dated October 21, 1821).

47. Eugène Guerin, *Une Actrice,* 2 vols. (Paris, 1833). Guerin wrote another theatrical novel, *La Dame de l'Opéra* (1838), but I have not been able to obtain a copy of this work. Another novel on the theme of marrying an actress is Madame R. R. de Thellusson's *Lucile, ou la cantatrice* ("Lucile, the Diva") of 1833. It has a happier ending than Guerin's work.

48. Guerin, *Actrice,* 1: 52, 239.

49. Georges Touchard-Lafosse, *La Pudeur et l'Opéra,* 2 vols. (Paris, 1834).

50. Honoré de Balzac created the character of the Jewish beauty Esther in *Splendeurs et misères de la courtisane,* published in serial form between 1839 and 1847. Esther "loved Lucien [de Beaupré] for years with the love of an actress and courtesan who, having wallowed in mud and impurity, thirsts after the nobility, the devotion of real love in all its exclusiveness." Balzac, *A Harlot High and Low,* trans. Rayner Hippenstall (New York, 1970), p. 129.

51. Victor Hugo, "Angelo, tyran de Padua," in *Oeuvres complètes de Victor Hugo,* vol. 3: *Théâtre* (Paris, 1904), pp. 136–262. Citations from act 1, scene 1; act 2, scene 5.

52. Jules Guex, *Le Théâtre et la société française de 1815 à 1848* (Paris, 1900), pp. 137–141; Neil Cole Arvin, *Eugène Scribe and the French Theatre 1815–1860* (New York, 1924).

53. Augustin-Eugène Scribe and Ernest Legouvé, *Adrienne Lecouvreur* (Paris, 1849). There are a few fictional works that were intrinsically part of the romantic era but were published after 1848. George Sand wrote a play, *Molière,* in 1851 that reevaluated Armande Béjart, the actress and wife of the great playwright, in a favorable manner. Her 1861 novel *Pierre qui roule* featured an impossibly chaste actress as its heroine. A particularly interesting novel about a theater woman is Arsène Houssaye's *Les Filles d'Eve* ("Daughters of Eve") of 1852. The central character, Béatrix, is the victim of a society lady's plots and sacrifices her happiness to the welfare of others.

54. Gérard de Nerval, *Sylvie* (Montreal, 1946), p. 9. Nerval wrote several novels about theater women prior to 1848, but they were published later because of the author's mental breakdown: *Sylvie* (1853), *Les Filles de feu* (1854), and *Aurélie* (1855). Though the central characters fit comfortably into the pattern discerned in my analysis, the works do not easily lend themselves to comparisons with the rest of the novels. Nerval did not intend to examine moral and social issues of the day. The female characters in his fiction are archetypal figures suffused with personal meaning.

Memories of the actress Jenny Colon, for whom Nerval had an intense but distant devotion, figure heavily in his fiction. See Benn Sowerby, *The Disinherited: The Life of Gérard de Nerval, 1808–1855* (London, 1973), and Jean Richer, *Nerval: Expérience et création* (Paris, 1970).

55. Corvée Flore, *Mémoires de Mademoiselle Flore, artiste du théâtre des Variétés,* 3 vols. (Paris, 1845), 2: 73–88. This actress mentions receiving money and jewels, but not flowers.

56. Charles de Boigne, *Petits mémoires de l'Opéra* (Paris, 1857), p. 41; Anon. ["Un vieil abonné"], *Ces demoiselles de l'Opéra* (Paris, 1887), p. 135.

57. *Le Monde illustré,* no. 368 (April 30, 1864), pp. 274–275.

58. Ibid., no. 994 (April 29, 1876), p. 307.

59. Claudin, *Mes souvenirs,* p. 26.

60. Edmond and Jules de Goncourt, *Journal: Mémoires de la vie littéraire,* ed. Robert Ricatte, 4 vols. (Paris, 1956), 4: 335.

61. See above, chap. 3.

62. *Les Mystères galants des théâtres de Paris (Actrices galantes)* (Paris, 1844), p. 53; AN, F21 1046, report of January 26, 1838.

63. Herbert Lottman, *Flaubert: A Biography* (Boston, 1989), p. 31; Stendhal, *Journal intime* (Paris, 1969), pp. 106–127; Alphonse Lemonnier, *Les petits mystères de la vie théâtrale: Souvenirs d'un homme de théâtre* (Paris, 1895), pp. 43–49; Chateaubriand, *Mémoires d'autre-tombe,* 6 vols. (Paris, n.d.), 1: 149–153, 161–162; Robert de Flers, *Le Théâtre et la ville: Essai de critique* (Paris, n.d.), p. 169; Maxime Du Camp, *Souvenirs d'un demi-siècle,* 2 vols. (Paris, 1949), 1: 179.

64. Paul Smith [pseud. Désiré Monnais], *Portefeuille de deux cantatrices* (Paris, n.d.), p. 115.

65. Gaston Jollivet, *Souvenirs de la vie de plaisir sous le Second Empire* (Paris, 1927), p. 243.

66. Nestor Roqueplan, *La Vie parisienne* (Paris, 1857), pp. 68–74.

67. Aimée Tessandier, *Souvenirs, recueillis et redigés par Henri Fescourt* (Paris, 1912), pp. 43–44; *Le Monde illustré,* no. 100 (March 12, 1859), p. 163.

68. BA, Rt 8576, fol. 13 (undated clipping).

69. *Le Monde illustré,* no. 100 (March 12, 1859), p. 163.

70. Justin O'Brien, *The Novel of Adolescence in France: The Study of a Literary Theme* (New York, 1937), pp. 4–20.

71. Jollivet, *Souvenirs,* p. 249.

72. BA, Rt 7444 (unidentified clipping entitled "Mademoiselle Fargueil" by "Philoxene").

73. Goncourt, *Journal,* 3: 145.

74. BA, Rt 7995 (clipping from *L'Entre'acte,* March 12, 1883).

5. The Erotic Culture of the Stage

1. *Le Monde illustré*, no. 557 (December 14, 1867), p. 362.
2. Cited in Paul Arbelet, *Premier voyage de Stendhal au pays des comédiennes* (Paris, 1928), p. 10.
3. Denise Davidson explores women's attendance at theaters in "Constructing Order in Post-Revolutionary France: Women's Identities and Cultural Practices, 1800–1830," Ph.D. diss., University of Pennsylvania, 1997, chap. 2. Women were most noticed in the audiences of moralizing melodramas.
4. Arnold Mortier, *Les Soirées parisiennes par un monsieur de l'orchestre*, 11 vols. (Paris, 1875–1885), 1: 18.
5. Francisque Sarcey, *La Comédie-française à Londres: Voyage de 1879* (Paris, 1880), pp. 72–97, 103–108. Citation on pp. 103–104.
6. *Le Journal amusant*, no. 1,154 (March 3, 1878), p. 2.
7. Montjoyeux [pseud. Jules Poignard], *Les Femmes de Paris* (Paris, 1889), pp. 17–18.
8. Ibid., p. 20.
9. Octave Uzanne, *The Modern Parisienne* (New York, 1912), p. 147.
10. Nestor Roqueplan, *La Vie parisienne* (Paris, 1857), pp. 68, 71–72.
11. Pierre Giffard, *Nos moeurs: La vie au théâtre* (Paris, 1888), pp. 254–255; Louis Couailhac, *Physiologie du théâtre à Paris et en province* (Paris, 1842), pp. 117–120.
12. Alphonse Lemonnier, *Les petits mystères de la vie théâtrale: Souvenirs d'un homme de théâtre* (Paris, 1895), pp. 100–101.
13. Edmond Benjamin and Henry Buguet, *Les Coulisses de Bourse et de théâtre* (Paris, 1882), p. 254.
14. *Le Figaro* advised worldly young men that it was the height of chic to fall madly in love with Mesdemoiselles Théo and Judic (no. 164 [June 14, 1874], p. 3): "A young men who has self-respect and lives in a certain milieu can hardly do otherwise," asserted the columnist.
15. See, for example, AN, F21 953 for theatrical reforms aimed at raising the moral standards of the public.
16. Tracy Davis, *Actresses as Working Women: Their Social Identity in Victorian Culture* (London, 1991); Sandra Richards, *The Rise of the English Actress* (New York, 1993); Gail Marshall, *Actresses on the Victorian Stage: Feminine Performance and the Galatea Myth* (Cambridge, 1998).
17. *L'Illustration*, no. 2,812 (January 16, 1897), p. 340. See also Ernest Daudet, *Les Coulisses de la société parisienne* (Paris, 1895), p. 116; Jacques Duflot, *Les Secrets des coulisses des théâtres de Paris*, p. 56.

18. *Le Figaro,* no. 322 (November 17, 1876), p. 3.

19. *Le Journal amusant,* no. 1,056 (November 25, 1876), p. 2.

20. Giffard, *Nos moeurs,* p. 231.

21. Louis Germont, *Loges d'artistes* (Paris, 1889), p. 341.

22. On the case of Anna Judic and her husband, see Charles Bernheimer, *Figures of Ill Repute: Prostitution in Nineteenth-Century France* (Cambridge, Mass., 1989), p. 233. Emile Zola based the corrupt character of Mignon in his novel *Nana* on Monsieur Judic.

23. Alphonse Daudet, *Entre les frises et la rampe* (Paris, 1894), pp. 176–177.

24. Cited in Georges Duval, *Artistes et cabotins* (Paris, 1878), p. 24.

25. René Peter, *Le Théâtre et la vie sous la Troisième République,* 2 vols. (Paris, 1945), 1: 171–172.

26. Arsène Houssaye, *Behind the Scenes at the Comédie-française and Other Recollections,* trans. Albert D. Vandam (London, 1889), p. 91.

27. Edmond de Goncourt, *La Faustin,* trans. G. F. Monkshood and Ernest Tristan (New York, 1976). Citation on p. 94.

28. Houssaye, *Behind the Scenes,* pp. 191, 193. He argued that male actors "prided themselves on their morality."

29. Cited in Charles Maurice, *Histoire anecdotique du théâtre, de la littérature, et des diverses impressions contemporaines,* 2 vols. (Paris, 1856), 2: 213.

30. Lemonnier, *Les petits mystères,* p. 72.

31. *Le Monde illustré,* no. 1,270 (July 30, 1881), p. 66.

32. Ibid.

33. Vanessa R. Schwartz, "Up-Close and Personal: A Genealogy of the Celebrity Interview," paper presented at the Western Society of French History meeting, Las Vegas, 1995. In 1891, Alphonse Daudet referred to the "interview" (using the English term) as "a very new means, without much effort, of intellectual propaganda." Goncourt, *Journal,* 4: 8.

34. Jacques le Souffleur, *Petit dictionnaire des coulisses* (Paris, 1835), pp. 17–18.

35. *Le Monde illustré,* no. 1,351 (February 17, 1883), p. 98; no. 1,394 (December 15, 1883), p. 370.

36. See below, chapter 9.

37. *L'Illustration,* no. 2,812 (January 16 1897), p. 34.

38. On Lenclos and the courtesan's tradition see above, chap. 2.

39. Yvette Guilbert, *The Song of My Life: My Memoirs,* trans. Béatrice de Holthier (London, 1929), p. 256.

40. L.-Henry Lecomte, ed., *Un Amour de Déjazet: Histoire et correspondance inédite, 1834–1844* (Paris, 1907), p. 134.

41. For example, Arsène Houssaye, *Princesses de comédie et déesses de l'Opéra*

(Paris, 1860); Emile Gaboreau, *Les Comédiennes adorées* (Paris, 1891); Gaston Capon and Robert Yve-Plessis, *Paris galant au dix-huitième siècle* (Paris, 1907); Ludovic Celler, *La Galanterie au théâtre* (Paris, 1875); Adolphe Jullien, *La Comédie et la galanterie au XVIIIe siècle* (Paris, 1874); Lorédan Larchy, ed., *Documents inédits sur le règne de Louis XV, ou anecdotes galantes sur les actrices, demoiselles entretenues, grisettes, etc. . .* (Paris, 1863). Many more works could be cited.

42. Roqueplan, *La Vie parisienne*. p. 73.

43. Goncourt, *Journal*, 3: 639. The book was was first published in the 1860s, and a successful new edition appeared in 1887.

44. Marie Dorval and George Sand, *Correspondance inédite*, ed. Simone André-Maurois (Paris, 1953), p. 54.

45. *La Vie illustrée*, January 19, 1899, pp. 180–181.

46. Sarah Bernhardt, *Love Letters to Pierre Berton*, trans. Sylvestre Dorian (Gerard, Kans., 1924), p. 29.

47. Goncourt, *Journal*, 4: 483. On the eighteenth-century female artist as man-woman, see Mary Sheriff, *The Exceptional Woman: Elizabeth Vigée-Lebrun and the Cultural Politics of Art* (Chicago, 1996), chap. 6.

48. Houssaye, *Behind the Scenes*, p. 51.

49. Vernon Rosario II, "Pointy Penises, Fashion Crimes, and Hysterical Mollies: The Pederasts' Inversion," in *Homosexuality in Modern France*, ed. Bryan T. Ragan and Jeffrey Merrick (New York, 1996), pp. 146–176.

50. George Chauncey, *Gay New York: Gender, Urban Culture, and the Making of the Gay Male World, 1890–1940* (New York, 1994), pp. 21–66. On sexuality replacing gender as the organizing principle, see Arnold Davidson, "Sex and the Emergence of Sexuality," *Critical Inquiry* 14 (Autumn 1987): 16–48; Robert Nye, ed., *Sexuality* (Oxford, 1999), pp. 115–204.

51. Edmond de Goncourt, Alexandre Dumas, Jr., and other writers discussed Sarah Bernhardt at one gathering, commenting on the tireless energy of "this creature." Alphonse Daudet asserted that all other women appeared to be "hysterics" compared to her. Goncourt, *Journal*, 3: 961.

52. Pierre Véron, *Les Coulisses artistiques* (Paris, 1876), chap. 13.

53. *Le Monde illustré*, no. 1,514 (April 3, 1886), p. 211.

54. Anne McClintock, *Imperial Leather: Race, Gender, and Sexuality in the Colonial Conquest* (New York, 1995), chap. 1; Sander L. Gilman, *Difference and Pathology: Stereotypes of Sexuality, Race, and Madness* (Ithaca, N.Y., 1985).

55. *Le Monde illustré*, no. 431 (July 15, 1865), p. 35.

56. Ibid., no. 1,321 (July 22, 1892), p. 51.

57. Ibid., no. 914 (October 17, 1874), p. 251.

58. BA, Rt 10020, fols. 19–22 (undated press clippings).

59. Félicien Champsaur, *L'Amant des danseuses* (Paris, 1888), p. 3.
60. Fritz, "Le Mariage d'une comédienne," *La Vie parisienne*, February 26, 1887, pp. 115–118.
61. The prince told Aphonso XIII of Spain that he had to know Jeanne Granier and Réjane to know Paris. BA, Rt 7996, fols. 12–14 (clippings from *Le Plaisir,* January 3, 1906).
62. *L'Illustration*, no. 1,375 (July 3, 1869), p. 11.
63. Alexandre Dumas, *La Dame aux camélias,* trans. David Coward (New York, 1986), p. 89.
64. On the eighteenth-century code of libertinism, see above, chap. 2.
65. Domna Stanton, *The Aristocrat as Art: A Study of the* Honnête Homme *and the Dandy in Seventeenth- and Nineteenth-Century French Literature* (New York, 1980).
66. William M. Reddy, *The Invisible Code: Honor and Sentiment in Postrevolutionary France, 1814–1848* (Berkeley, 1997).
67. Gaston Jollivet, *Souvenirs de la vie de plaisir sous le Second Empire* (Paris, 1927), pp. 171–172.
68. Ibid., p. 174.
69. Roqueplan, *La Vie parisienne,* pp. 74–75.
70. Uzanne, *Moderne Parisienne,* pp. 214–215.
71. Henry Gauthier-Villars, "Les Amours d'un prince naïf," *La nouvelle revue* 5 (August 15, 1900): 515–553. On the life of the actress, see E. de Crouzat, *Une petite actrice du théâtre des Variétés: Mademoiselle Esther de Bongars* (Lille, 1912).
72. *La Vie parisienne,* July 20, 1895, p. 412.
73. Giffard, *Nos moeurs,* p. 183.
74. Goncourt, *Journal,* 4: 576.
75. Dumas, *La Dame,* p. 94.
76. Edmond and Jules de Goncourt, *The Goncourt Journals,* trans. and ed. Louis Galantière (New York, 1937), p. 47.
77. Edmond Got, *Journal d'Edmond Got, sociétaire de la Comédie-française,* 2 vols. (Paris, 1910), 1: 294.
78. Jacques Porel, *Fils de Réjane: Souvenirs,* 2 vols. (Paris, 1951), 1: 164. It is true that Porel was going through a divorce at the time.
79. Robert Wheaton, "Introduction," in *Family and Sexuality in French History,* ed. Robert Wheaton and Tamara K. Hareven (Philadelphia, 1980), pp. 3–26.
80. Goncourt, *Journal,* 2: 1,189.
81. Paul Ginisty, *Souvenirs de journalisme et de théâtre* (Paris, 1930), p. 62. On Maupassant's erotic life, see Jacques-Louis Douchin, *La Vie érotique de Guy de Maupassant* (Paris, 1986).

82. Marie Colombier, *Mémoires: Fin d'Empire* (Paris, 1900), p. 187. Such toys had been available in Paris since the beginning of the nineteenth century. See Laure Adler, *Secrets d'alcôve: Histoire du couple de 1830 à 1930* (Paris, 1983), p. 145.

83. *La Vie parisienne,* November 7, 1891, pp. 624–625.

84. Goncourt, *Journal,* 4: 603.

85. Ibid., 1: 239; 2: 1,102.

86. Houssaye, *Behind the Scenes,* p. 510.

87. Got, *Journal,* 1: 200; Adolphe Laferrière, *Souvenirs d'un jeune premier* (Paris, 1884), pp. 72–73.

88. Goncourt, *Journal,* 4: 224.

89. BA, Rt 7995, fol. 79 (clipping dated July 1, 1935).

90. Maurice de Waleffe, *Quand Paris était un paradis* (Paris, 1947), p. 38.

91. Goncourt, *Journal,* 2: 1,075.

92. Ibid., 1: 668. Flaubert and his companions also noted actresses' "unbelievable influence" over their lovers.

93. Adler, *Secrets,* p. 158.

94. Goncourt, *Journal,* 2: 215.

95. Ibid., 1: 1,025.

96. BA, Rt 8579, fol. 13.

97. Victor Koning, *Les Coulisses parisiennes* (Paris, 1864), p. 104.

98. *Le Monde illustré,* no. 432 (July 22, 1868), p. 50.

99. Koning, *Les Coulisses,* pp. 104–106.

100. Adolphe Jullien, *Les Spectateurs sur la scène: Etablissement et suppression des bancs sur les scènes de la Comédie-française et l'Opéra* (Paris, 1875); James H. Johnson, *Listening in Paris: A Cultural History* (Berkeley, 1995), chap. 3; Jeffrey Ravel, "Seating the Public: Spheres and Loathing in the Paris Theater, 1777–1788," *French Historical Studies* 18 (Spring 1993): 173–210; William Weber, "Did People Listen in the Eighteenth Century?" *Early Music* (November 1997): 678–691.

101. According to the thespian Jenny Thénard, writing in 1909, the Comédie-française had only recently started darkening the house during performances. See *Ma Vie au théâtre: Choses vues, choses vécues* (Paris, 1909), p. 49.

102. BA, Rt 7874, fol. 45 (undated clipping by Ernest Blum).

103. *Le Figaro,* no. 322 (November 17, 1876), p. 3.

104. Jules Lan, ed., *Mémoires d'un chef de claque: Souvenirs de théâtre* (Paris, 1883), p. 106.

105. BA, Rt 7874, fol. 41.

106. Goncourt, *La Faustin,* p. 180. On the author's inspiration for the character, see Goncourt, *Journal,* 3: 131, 148, 712–713.

107. Lecomte, *Un Amour de Déjazet,* p. 17.
108. Ibid., p. 23.
109. Lemonnier, *Les petits mystères,* pp. 155–156.
110. *La Vie parisienne,* February 28, 1891, p. 117.
111. See Clifford Bissell, *Les Conventions du théâtre bourgeois contemporain en France, 1887–1914* (Paris, 1930), on the place of adultery and family scandal in the theater of the day.
112. Jollivet, *Souvenirs,* p. 179.
113. *Le Figaro,* no. 322 (November 17, 1876), p. 3.
114. BA, Rt 8288, fols. 6–15 (unidentified clippings).
115. Goncourt, *Journal,* 3: 1,174–5; Giffard, *Nos moeurs,* p. 118.
116. Quoted in F. W. J. Hemmings, *The Theatre Industry in Nineteenth-Century France* (Cambridge, 1993), p. 57.
117. Félix Galipaux, *Les Souvenirs de Galipaux* (Paris, 1937), p. 184.
118. *Le Figaro,* no. 322 (November 17, 1876), p. 3.
119. Gaston Capon and Robert Yve-Plessis, *Fille de l'Opéra, vendeuse d'amour: Histoire de Mademoiselle Deschamps* (Paris, 1906), p. 33.
120. BA, Rt 11000, fol. 20 (clipping dated December 16, 1899).
121. Goncourt, *Journal,* 1: 688.
122. Maurice, *Histoire anecdotique,* 1: 138.
123. Lemonnier, *Les petits mystères,* p. 156.
124. Jacques Arago, *Physiologie des foyers de tous les théâtres de Paris* (Paris, 1841), and *Les Mystères galants des théâtres de Paris (Actrices galantes)* (Paris, n.d.).
125. *Le Monde illustré,* no. 1,713 (January 25, 1890), p. 50. Houssaye, *Behind the Scenes,* p. 191.
126. Michel-Morin [pseud. Jules Chabot de Bouin and Auguste Dubois], *Le Gil Blas du théâtre,* 2 vols. (Paris, 1833), 2: 69; Nérée-Desarbres, *Sept ans à l'Opéra: Souvenirs anecdotiques d'un secrétaire particulier* (Paris, 1864), p. 69; Couailhac, *Physiologie du théâtre,* p. 5.
127. During the July Monarchy, writers stressed the improved moral climate at the Opéra. See Roqueplan, *La Vie parisienne,* p. 86; Jules Vernier, "Les Coulisses de l'Opéra," *Revue de Paris* (1836), pp. 320–321. Honoré de Balzac wrote that keeping a dancer as a mistress was unfashionable in his day; see *A Harlot High and Low,* trans. Ragner Heppenstall (New York, 1970), p. 27.
128. Capon and Yve-Plessis, *Fille de l'Opéra,* p. 26.
129. AN, AJ13 197, "Règlements du corps de ballet."
130. Even in the 1990s, the young mistresses of rich old men in France were still called "little dancers." See Richard Bernstein, *Fragile Glory: A Portrait of France and the French* (New York, 1990), p. 172.
131. *La Vie parisienne,* September 19, 1891, pp. 528–529.

132. Ibid.
133. AN, F21 1046, report of April 14, 1840.
134. AN, AJ13 798. Renting a box did not guarantee access. The director's permission had to be requested and obtained.
135. AN, AJ13 113.
136. AN, AJ13 798. For the complete collection of lists, see AJ13, 644, 787–798, 855–858, 1,011–1,015.
137. Alain Corbin, *Filles de noces: Misère sexuelle et prostitution aux 19e et 20e siècles* (Paris, 1978), pp. 385–452.
138. Edgar Monteil, *Cornebois* (Paris, 1882). For his reform project, see AN, F21 1284, "Lettre sur le Conservatoire."
139. AN, F21 1281.
140. AN, F21 1283, "Projet de réorganisation du Conservatoire."
141. AN, F21 1284, Monteil, "Lettre," p. 14.
142. *Le Monde illustré,* no. 2,031 (February 29, 1896), p. 158.
143. Goncourt, *Journal,* 4: 413.
144. Siegfried Kracauer, *Orpheus in Paris: Offenbach and the Paris of His Time* (New York, 1938).

6. The Struggle against Pornocracy

1. Jean-Jacques Weiss, *Le Théâtre et les moeurs* (Paris, 1889), pp. x–xx.
2. Emile Augier, *L'Aventurière: Drame en cinq actes* (Paris, 1851).
3. Gay Manifold, *George Sand's Theatre Career* (Ann Arbor, Mich., 1985), p. 37.
4. Augier, *L'Aventurière,* act 2, scene 7; act 4, scene 5. When Clorinde protests Fabrice's insults to her, a woman, he replies: "You, a woman? Is a coward a man? A woman without modesty deserves the same scorn as a man without courage."
5. Ibid., act 5, scene 1.
6. I know of only one fictional work of the period in which an actress is a heroine, Théodore de Banville's 1854 play, *La Vie d'une comédienne* ("The Life of an Actress"). The very next year, however, de Banville published a short novel with the same title (subtitled *Minette*), that portrayed the theater in lurid terms with grotesque, violent characters.
7. The popular playwright Victorien Sardou even wrote a play in 1860 called *Les Femmes fortes* ("Strong Women"), a scathing satire about emancipated women. On unruly women in the literature of the time, see Sidney D. Braun, *The "Courtisane" in French Theatre from Hugo to Becque (1831–1885)* (Baltimore, 1947).
8. Two works based on this theme that I am not going to summarize below

are Léonide Leblanc's *Les petits comédies de l'amour* (1865) and Edouard Cadoul's 1874 novel, *Rose: Splendeurs et misères de la vie théâtrale.*

9. Henri Meilhac and Ludovic Halévy, *Fanny Lear: Comédie en cinq actes* (Paris, 1889).

10. Emile Augier, *La Contagion,* in *Théâtre complet d'Emile Augier,* 6 vols. (Paris, 1890–1892), 5: 284–452. The citation is from act 5, scene 3.

11. Ibid., act 5, scene 5.

12. Mario Uchard, *La Fiammina: Comédie en quatre actes, en prose* (Paris, 1857); see BA, Rf 48.585 on the play's reception.

13. Uchard, *La Fiammina,* act 1, scene 8 (p. 36).

14. Dumas wrote it in collaboration with Eugène Fould, and they used the pseudonym Gustave de Jalin. *La Comtesse Romani: Comédie en trois actes* (Paris, 1877).

15. Ibid., p. 66.

16. Edmond and Jules de Goncourt, *Charles Demailly* (Paris, 1877).

17. Ibid., p. 298.

18. The midcentury works on this theme that I do not treat below are Raymond Deslandres and Louis Lurine, *Les Comédiennes: Comédie en quatre actes* (Paris, 1857); Adrien Robert, *Le nouveau roman comique* (Paris, 1861); Pierre Véron, *Les Gens du théâtre* (Paris, 1862); and Alphonse Lemonnier, *Les Femmes du théâtre* (Paris, 1865).

19. Théodore Barrière and L. Thiboust, *Les Filles de marbre: Drame en cinq actes* (Paris, 1853).

20. BA, Rondel Manuscript Collection, Letters of Charles Fechter to Virginie Déjazet, undated; Edmond and Jules de Goncourt noted the exceptional success of the play in *Journal: Mémoires de la vie littéraire,* ed. Robert Ricatte, 4 vols. (Paris, 1956), 1: 233.

21. Aurélien Scholl, *Les Amours de théâtre* (Paris, 1862), p. 103.

22. Bernice Chitnis, *Reflecting on Nana* (London, 1991).

23. Emile Zola, *Nana,* trans. Douglas Parmée (New York, 1992), p. 353.

24. One more theater novel that did not fit into the thematic categories used above is Victor Perceval, *La Pupille du comédien* (Paris, 1869), a Cinderella story with an actress as the villainous stepsister.

25. Carlos Noël, *Les Idées sociales dans le théâtre d'A. Dumas fils* (Paris, 1912), pp. 32–72.

26. Goncourt, *Journal,* 3: 1,102; Henry Gaillard de Champris, *Emile Augier et la comédie sociale* (Paris, 1973), pp. 66–68.

27. Auriant [pseud.], *La véritable histoire de "Nana"* (Paris, 1942), pp. 17, 23–29, 43–91, 99–105.

28. *L'Illustration,* no. 582 (April 22, 1854), p. 254–255. Mille-Noé is an ob-

scure figure today. Aside from having edited *La Revue libérale* in the 1860s, he has not left his mark.

29. Auguste Muriel, *Le Théâtre aujourd'hui* (Paris, 1855), p. 59.

30. Ibid., pp. 63–64, 69, 74–76. Muriel even pitied actors for having to put up with actresses.

31. Frédéric de Reiffenberg, Jr., *Ce que c'est q'une actrice* (Paris, 1856). Citation on p. 6.

32. *Le Figaro*, no. 182 (July 1, 1874), p. 3.

33. Ibid., no. 178 (June 27, 1874), p. 3.

34. BA, Rt 8602, fol. 19 (undated clipping from *Le Figaro*).

35. *Le Figaro*, no. 120 (April 30, 1874), p. 3.

36. See below, chap. 3.

37. Hippolyte Buffenoir and Maurice Hoquette, eds., *Le Décret de Moscou et la Comédie-française: Historique et texte intégral* (Paris, 1902), p. 35.

38. AN, F21 4648, report of April 22, 1869.

39. Edmond Got, *Journal d'Edmond Got, sociétaire de la Comédie-française, 1822–1901*, 2 vols. (Paris, 1910), 1: 211.

40. AN, F21 4648, "Commission chargée de réviser l'organisation du comité de lecture."

41. Ibid., "Note pour Monsieur le Ministre" (June 26, 1853).

42. Adrien Bernheim, *Autour de la Comédie-française: Trente ans de théâtre* (Paris, 1913), p. 140.

43. AN, F21 4648, "Note pour le Ministre" (December 14, 1868). On male control of the reading committee at the Odéon theater, see AN, F21 4654, "Comité de lecture."

44. Pierre-Joseph Proudhon, *La Pornocratie, ou les femmes dans le temps moderne* (Paris, 1875), p. 233.

45. Ibid., pp. 85–86.

46. Hippolyte Taine, *Notes sur Paris: Vie et opinions de Monsieur Frédéric-Thomas Graindorge* (Paris, 1867), pp. 58–69. Despite the subtitle, the work is accepted as Taine's own. See André Cresson, *Hippolyte Taine: Sa vie, son oeuvre* (Paris, 1951), p. 10.

47. T. J. Clark shows how frequently the complaint was articulated, in *The Painting of Modern Life: Paris in the Art of Manet and His Followers* (New York, 1985), pp. 103–139. Alain Corbin notes that anxiety over kept women accompanied a heightened concern about prostitutes during the Second Empire and after the Commune, in *Les Filles de noces: Misère sexuelle et prostitution aux 19e et 20e siècles* (Paris, 1978), pp. 42–45.

48. Joanna Richardson, *The Courtesans: The Demi-Monde in Nineteenth-Century France* (New York, 1967), chaps. 2, 10.

49. Graham Robb, *Victor Hugo: A Biography* (New York, 1997), p. 260.
50. Alain Plessis, *The Rise and Fall of the Second Empire, 1852–1871,* trans. Jonathan Mandelbaum (Cambridge, 1985), chaps. 1, 2, 4, 5.
51. André-Jean Tudesq, *L'Election présidentielle de Louis-Napoléon Bonaparte, 10 décembre 1848* (Paris, 1965).
52. Theodore Zeldin, *The Political System of Napoleon III* (London, 1958), pp. 160–163.
53. Philip Nord, *The Republican Moment: Struggles for Democracy in Nineteenth-Century France* (Cambridge, Mass., 1995), chap. 1.
54. Plessis, *Rise and Fall,* p. 11.
55. Matthew Truesdell, *Spectacular Politics: Louis-Napoleon Bonaparte and the Fête Impériale, 1849–1870* (New York, 1997), pp. 68–72, 100.
56. Donald Olsen, *The City as a Work of Art: London, Paris, Vienna* (New Haven, 1986), pp. 219–224.
57. Frédéric Loliée, *Le Duc de Morny,* trans. Bryan O'Donnell (London, 1910), pp. 206–234; A. Augustin-Thierry, *Son Elégance, le duc de Morny* (Paris, 1951), pp. 174–260; Edgar Holt, *Plon-Plon: The Life of Prince Napoleon, 1822–1891* (London, 1973), pp. 45–125. On the sexual adventures of the emperor, see Hector Fleischmann, *Napoléon III et les femmes* (Paris, 1923).
58. In the annals of Second Empire libertinism, the same names tended to reappear. There apparently was a limited circle of celebrated men-about-town. See Siegfried Kracauer, *Orpheus in Paris: Offenbach and the Paris of His Time* (New York, 1938), chap. 8.
59. Plessis, *Rise and Fall,* chap. 3.
60. On the growing cultural importance of bourgeois leisure, see Robert Herbert, *Impressionism: Art, Leisure, and Parisian Society* (New Haven, 1988).
61. Alexis de Tocqueville, *The Old Regime and the French Revolution,* trans. Stuart Gilbert (New York, 1955), p. xii.
62. Goncourt, *Journal,* 1: 312.
63. Victoria Thompson traces the image of the *lorette* and her association with the unbridled pursuit of self-interest back to the 1840s, in "Gender, Class and the Marketplace: Women's Work and the Transformation of the Public Sphere in Paris, 1825–1870," Ph.D. diss., University of Pennsylvania, 1993, pp. 200–225.
64. Cited in Philippe Perrot, *Fashioning the Bourgeoisie: A History of Clothing in the Nineteenth Century,* trans. Richard Bienvenu (Princeton, 1994), p. 63. Also on the anxieties created by women consumers, see Lisa Tiersten, "Sisterhood of Shoppers: Bourgeois Women and Consumer Culture in Late Nineteenth-Century Paris," Ph.D. diss., Yale University, 1991, chaps. 1–3.
65. Clark, *Painting of Modern Life,* p. 108.

66. Robert W. Reichert, "Anti-Bonapartist Elections to the Académie Française during the Second Empire," *Journal of Modern History* 35 (March 1963): 33–45.

67. Horace de Viel-Castel, *Mémoires du comte Horace de Viel-Castel sur le règne de Napoléon III (1851–1864)*, 6 vols. (Paris, 1883), 1: 74, 107, 155; 2: 29, 195, 240; 3: 11, 17, 65–66, 138, 173, 179, 246, 258; 4: 33, 70, 101. Citation from 1: 124–125.

68. Marcel Morter, *Aurélian Scholl et son temps* (Paris, n.d.), pp. 216–273; Gaillard de Champris, *Augier,* pp. 67–68, 177, 350, 357; Maxime Du Camp, *Souvenirs littéraires,* ed. Daniel Oster (Paris, 1994), chaps. 22–26.

69. Nord, *Republican Moment,* chap. 9.

70. Edwin Colby Byam, *Théodore Barrière, Dramatist of the Second Empire* (Baltimore, 1938), p. 31.

71. Mademoiselle Agar, "Mémoires d'une tragédienne," *La Revue littéraire et critique,* no. 5–15 (March–October 1893), no pagination.

72. Noël, *Les Idées sociales,* pp. 62–74.

73. Jules Michelet, *La Femme* (Paris, 1860), pp. i–iii, xiv; Eugène Pelletan, *La Famille: La mère* (Paris, 1865) and Pelletan's *Nouvelle Babylon: Lettre d'un provincial en tournée à Paris* (Paris, 1862); Nord, *Republican Moment,* pp. 220–232; Judith Stone, "The Republican Brotherhood: Gender and Ideology," in *Gender and the Politics of Social Reform in France 1870–1914,* ed. Elinor Accampo, Rachel Fuchs, and Mary Lynn Stewart (Baltimore, 1995), pp. 42–45.

74. Just a few months earlier, there had been a noisy demonstration at the Comédie-française over the Goncourt brothers' play *Henriette Maréchal,* because it was known that Princess Mathilde had a hand in getting the work produced. On student politics and theatrical protest, see Jean-Claude Caron, *Générations romantiques: Les Etudiants de Paris et le quartier latin* (Paris, 1991), pp. 146–151.

75. BA, Rf 37.410, fols. 13–15 (clipping from *Le Temps,* October 4, 1913).

76. BA, Rf 37.410, fol. 8 (undated clipping from *L'Opinion nationale*).

77. *Le Monde illustré,* no. 564 (February 1, 1868), p. 67.

78. On the playwright's subtle opposition to the Second Empire, see Viel-Castel, *Mémoires,* 3: 141, 176; 4: 21, 177.

79. O. Gheorghiu, *Le Théâtre de Dumas fils et la société contemporaine* (Nancy, 1931), pp. 41, 69–74, 214–260, 443–486; Alexandre Dumas, Jr., *L'Homme-Femme: Réponse à Monsieur D'Ideville* (Paris, 1872), pp. 1–2, 8, 57–60, 97–99. The 1867 preface is cited in Noël, *Les Idées sociales,* pp. 67–68.

80. Steven Huebner, "Opera Audiences in Paris, 1830–1870," *Music and Letters* 70 (May 1989): 216.

81. Ernest Feydeau, *Du Luxe, des femmes, des moeurs, de la littérature, et de la vertu* (Paris, 1866), p. 202.
82. Jules Claretie, *La Vie moderne au théâtre,* 2 vols. (Paris, 1869–1875), 2: 249.
83. Auriant [pseud.], *Les Lionnes du Second Empire* (Paris, 1935), p. 75.
84. Charles Bernheimer, *Figures of Ill Repute: Representing Prostitution in Nineteenth-Century France* (Cambridge, Mass., 1989), p. 228.
85. Guy Vauzat, *Blanche D'Antigny: Actrice et demi-mondaine* (Paris, 1933), pp. 23–54.
86. BA, Rt 5610, fol. 9 (undated clipping entitled "Le Scandal de Saint-Germain" from *Le Gaulois*). The journal did not identify the men at the "orgy."
87. *L'Illustration,* no. 536 (June 4, 1853), p. 356.
88. *Nana* was first serialized in the republican newspaper *Le Voltaire* before being published as a book.

7. Imagining Republican Actresses

1. Anne-Louise Shapiro, *Breaking the Codes: Female Criminality in Fin-de-Siècle Paris* (Stanford, Calif., 1996), pp. 37–39.
2. See Herman Lebovics, *The Alliance of Iron and Wheat in the Third French Republic, 1860–1914: Origins of the New Conservatism* (Baton Rouge, La., 1988), pp. 26–96, on the weakness of conservative notables. Also, Christophe Charle, *A Social History of France in the Nineteenth Century,* trans. Miriam Kochan (Providence, 1994), pp. 179–211.
3. Patricia Regina Turner, "Class, Community and Culture in Nineteenth Century France: The Growth of Voluntary Associations in Roanne, 1860–1914," Ph.D. diss., University of Michigan, 1994.
4. Barry H. Bergen, "Molding Citizens: Ideology, Class, and Primary Education in France, 1870–1914," unpublished manuscript; Phyllis Stock-Morton, *Moral Education for a Secular Society: The Development of Moral Laïque in Nineteenth-Century France* (Albany, N.Y., 1988); Yves Déloyé, *Ecole et citoyen: L'individualisme républicain de Jules Ferry à Vichy* (Paris, 1994).
5. Claude Nicolet, *L'Idée républicaine en France, 1789–1924: Essai d'histoire critique* (Paris, 1982). Francis Ronsin, *Les Divorciaires: Affrontements publiques et conceptions du mariage dans la France du XIXe siècle* (Paris, 1992), p. 353.
6. Jacques Capdevielle, *Fétichisme du patrimoine: Essai sur un fondement de la classe moyenne* (Paris, 1986). Sudhir Hazareesingh argues that these changes in republican ideology were already visible under the Second Em-

pire. See his *From Subject to Citizen: The Second Empire and the Emergence of Modern French Democracy* (Princeton, 1998), chap. 4.

7. Anne-Marie Sohn, "The Golden Age of Male Adultery: The Third Republic," *Journal of Social History* 28 (Spring 1995): 469–491, and also Sohn's "Les Rôles féminins dans la vie privée à l'époque de la Troisième République," doctorat d'état, Université de Paris I, 1993, chap. 13.

8. Ernest Daudet, *Les Coulisses de la société parisienne* (Paris, 1885), pp. 118–121.

9. Alain Corbin, *Les Filles de noce: Misère sexuelle et prostitution aux 19e et 20e siècles* (Paris, 1978), pp. 171–314.

10. Judith Stone, "The Republican Brotherhood: Gender and Ideology," in *Gender and the Politics of Social Reform in France, 1870–1914*, ed. Elinor Accampo, Rachel Fuchs, and Mary Lynn Stewart (Baltimore, 1995), p. 30.

11. Lisa Tiersten, "Sisterhood of Shoppers: Bourgeois Women and Consumer Culture in Late Nineteenth-Century Paris," Ph.D. diss., Yale University, 1991, chap. 5. On the partial "feminization" of republican political culture, see Whitney Walton, *Eve's Proud Descendants: Four Women Writers and Republican Politics in Nineteenth-Century France* (Stanford, Calif., 2000), chaps. 5–6.

12. Jacques Donzelot, *The Policing of Families*, trans. Robert Hurley (New York, 1979); Elinor A. Accampo, Rachel Fuchs, and Mary Lynn Stewart, eds., *Gender and the Politics of Social Reform in France, 1870–1914* (Baltimore, 1995).

13. René Peter, *Le Théâtre et la vie sous la Troisième République*, 2 vols. (Paris, 1945–1947), 2: 304–307.

14. Octave Uzanne, *The Modern Parisienne* (New York, 1912), pp. 144, 147, 153.

15. Alfred Capus, *Les Moeurs du temps* (Paris, 1891), pp. 528–529.

16. *La Vie parisienne* (September 19, 1891), pp. 528–529. See also Capus, *Les Moeurs*, pp. 95–100; Francisque Sarcey, *Le Théâtre* (Paris, 1893), pp. 41–42.

17. Albert Flament, "Les Abonnés de l'Opéra," *Fémina*, May 15, 1909, pp. 261–264; Jeanne Broussan-Goubert, "Une Leçon de danse à l'Opéra," *Fémina*, July 1, 1912, p. 401.

18. Eunice Lipton, *Looking into Degas: Uneasy Images of Women and Modern Life* (Berkeley, 1986), p. 115.

19. *Le Monde illustré*, no. 1,529 (July 17, 1886), p. 34.

20. *La Vie parisienne*, July 20, 1895, p. 412.

21. Yvette Guilbert, "Prologue," in Ferdinand Bac, *Femmes de théâtre: Album inédit en couleur* (Paris, 1896), no pagination.

22. *Le Temps,* no. 12,352 (March 24, 1895), p. 3.

23. Ibid., no. 12,356 (March 28, 1895), p. 3.

24. Louis Germont, *Loges d'artistes* (Paris, 1889), p. 27. See also "Les Loges de nos jolies comédiennes," *Je sais tout,* June 15, 1906, pp. 627–631.

25. Ibid., pp. 130, 149.

26. See below, chap. 9.

27. BA, Rt 8288, fols. 39–40.

28. BA, Rt 7058, fol. 61 (clipping dated February 2, 1909).

29. Robert Nye, *Masculinity and Male Codes of Honor in Modern France* (New York, 1993); Edward Berenson, *The Trial of Madame Caillaux* (Berkeley, 1992), chap. 5; Annelise Mauge, *L'Identité masculine en crise au tournant du siècle* (Paris, 1987).

30. Angus McLaren, *The Trials of Masculinity: Policing Sexual Boundaries 1870–1930* (Chicago, 1997), pp. 13–38; Christopher S. Thompson, "The Third Republic on Wheels: A Social, Cultural, and Political History of Bicycling in France from the Nineteenth Century to World War II," Ph.D. diss., New York University, 1997.

31. Gaston Jollivet, *Souvenirs de la vie de plaisir sous le Second Empire* (Paris, 1927), p. 29.

32. The photographic periodical *La Vie illustrée* provides a good example of these trends. The magazine first appeared in 1898 and was aimed at both male and female readers. By 1902 it was much more exclusively aimed at male readers. It developed a sports column with frequent photographs and covered international news extensively. At the same time, less and less space was devoted to actresses and fashion.

33. *La Vie illustrée,* December 1, 1899, pp. 135, 144; September 28, 1899, p. 40.

34. *Le Journal amusant,* no. 689 (Sept. 7, 1912), p. 11.

35. *La Vie parisienne,* January 5, 1895, p. 10.

36. Jules Simon and Gustave Simon, *La Femme du vingtième siècle* (Paris, 1892), p. 36.

37. See above, chap. 5.

38. Designers often dressed well-known actresses at their own expense for the sake of the publicity. See Mademoiselle X, comédienne française, *Ce que mes jolies yeux ont vu* (Paris, 1913), p. 100–101.

39. *La Vie parisienne,* July 15, 1893, pp. 388–389.

40. See *L'Illustration,* no. 2,412 (May 18, 1889), p. 420, which claimed that the applause for a touring French troupe was applause "for France."

41. *Le Monde illustré,* no. 1,369 (June 23, 1883), p. 402.

42. Cited in Jules Claretie, *La Vie moderne au théâtre,* 2 vols. (Paris, 1869–1875), 2: 28.

43. R. Anchel and Pierre-François Caillé, *Histoire des décorations françaises contemporaines* (Paris, 1933).

44. BA, Rt 11331 (press clippings on the issue). Ernest Legouvé, *La Croix d'honneur et les comédiens* (Paris, 1863).

45. See below, chap. 3.

46. BA, Rt 11331 (clipping from *Le Gaulois,* October 14, 1905).

47. Marcus Nothing [pseud. Maurice Dreyfus], *Les Comédiens et la Légion d'honneur* (Paris, 1863), pp. 8, 11, 14–15.

48. On the politics of divorce, see Theresa McBride, "Divorce and the Republican Family," in *Gender and the Politics of Social Reform,* ed. Accampo, Fuchs, and Stewart, pp. 59–81, and McBride's "Public Authority and Private Lives: Divorce after the French Revolution," *French Historical Studies* 17 (Spring 1992): 747–768.

49. For a survey of thespians who were admitted to the Légion up to 1894, see *Le Temps,* no. 12,230 (November 21, 1894), p. 3.

50. On the ambiguous status of women as individuals in liberal political ideology, see Joan Wallach Scott, *Only Paradoxes to Offer: French Feminists and the Rights of Man* (Cambridge, Mass., 1996).

51. Steven C. Hause, *Women's Suffrage and Social Politics in the French Third Republic* (Princeton, 1984), p. 16.

52. Germont, *Loges,* p. 351; see *Le Temps,* no. 12,976 (December 10, 1896), p. 3, for Bernhardt's supporters.

53. On the political dynamics of the era, see Jean-Marie Mayeur, *La Vie politique sous la Troisième République* (Paris, 1984), chaps. 2, 3, 5, 6.

54. On Bartet's career, see the admiring biography by Albert Dubeux, *Julia Bartet* (Paris, 1938).

55. Joseph Gaultier, "Les Grandes artistes modernes: Bartet," *Je sais tout,* April 15, 1910, pp. 370–372. On Bartet's dismissal of feminist ideas, see below, chapter 8.

56. Jacques Porel, *Fils de Réjane: Souvenirs,* 2 vols. (Paris, 1951), 1: 168.

57. BA, Rt 11331 (clipping dated 1906).

58. Bernard Stéphane, *Dictionnaire des noms des rues de Paris* (Paris, 1989), p. 571.

59. Lenard R. Berlanstein, *Big Business and Industrial Conflict in Nineteenth-Century France: A Social History of the Parisian Gas Company* (Berkeley, 1991), chaps. 2, 6, 8.

60. Conseil municipal de Paris, *Procès-verbaux: Année 1899,* 2 vols. (Paris, 1899), 1: 1,309, 1,683.

61. Ibid., 2: 179–180.

62. Philip Nord, *Paris Shopkeepers and the Politics of Resentment* (Princeton, 1986), chaps. 9–10.

63. *Le Monde illustré,* no. 1,434 (September 21, 1884), p. 179.

64. *Le Temps,* no. 12,788 (June 4, 1896), p. 2.

65. F. W. J. Hemmings, "Playwrights and Play-actors: the Controversy over the *comités de lecture* in France, 1757–1910," *French Studies* 43 (October 1988): 416–420.

66. BA, Rf 37,300. See especially fols. 3, 5–10, 27 (various press clippings on the play).

67. Félicien Champsaur, *Dinah Samuel* (Paris, 1881), pp. 73, 79–80, 129, 321–326.

68. The fictional works in this category that I will not be able to cite in the text are: Arsène Houssaye, *La Comédienne* (Paris, 1884); A. Reney–Le Bas, *Confessions d'une cantatrice* (Paris, 1885); and Emilie Lerou [pseud. Pierre Nakor], *Sous le masque: Une vie au théâtre* (Paris, 1908).

69. Edmond de Goncourt, *La Faustin,* trans. G. F. Monkshood and Ernest Tristan (New York, 1976).

70. Marie Colombier, *La plus jolie femme de Paris* (Paris, 1887), p. 388.

71. Henry Bauer, *Une comédienne: Scènes de la vie de théâtre* (Paris, 1889). On the author's background, see Léon Daudet, *Souvenirs et polémiques,* ed. Bernard Oudin (Paris, 1992), pp. 87–91.

72. Paul Dollfus, *Sociétaire: Moeurs de théâtre* (Paris, 1891).

73. See above, chaps. 4 and 6.

74. Two novels of the period blamed society's prejudices for undermining marriages that contained much potential to bring happiness to the couple: Jean Lorrain, *Le Tréteau: Roman des moeurs théâtrals et littéraires* (Paris, 1906), and Pierre Huguenin, *Célinie Jacobin de la Comédie-française* (Paris, 1907). Another work of fiction in this category is Sarah Bernhardt's play *Adrienne Lecouvreur: Drame en six actes* (Paris, 1907).

75. Alfred Sirven, *La Linda: Roman parisien* (Paris, 1889).

76. Louis Vaultier, *Une étoile: Moeurs de théâtre* (Paris, 1898).

77. Paul Flat, *Le Roman de la comédienne: Roman* (Paris, 1906).

78. Two more novels address this theme: Yvette Guilbert, *La Vedette* (Paris, 1902), and Charles-Henry Hirsh, *La Demoiselle de la comédie* (Paris, 1904). In addition, Victorian Sardou's play *La Tosca,* which was the basis for the Giacomo Puccini opera, belongs in this category as much as any other, since the eponymous singer behaves heroically under adversity; Tosca also has elements of the pre-1848 actress-heroine, because she sacrifices her life for her love. The play premiered in 1887.

79. Emile André, *Coulisse et salle d'armes: Roman d'actualité* (Paris, 1882). On the importance of dueling as a symbol of masculintiy, see Nye, *Masculinity,* chap. 8.

80. André, *Coulisse et salle d'armes*, p. 87.
81. J.-H. Rosny [pseud. Joseph Boex and Justin Boex], *Le Fauvre: Moeurs de théâtre* (Paris, 1899).
82. Jean Blaise, *Les Planches: Roman moderne* (Paris, 1892).
83. A good number of fictional works of the time are not easily categorized around a common theme. They are either character studies with slight plots, or they involve a series of loosely related incidents. All, however, portray theater women sympathetically. Edgar Monteil, *Cornebois* (Paris, 1881); Jules Guillemot, *Florimond, grand premier rôle* (Paris, 1891); Charles d'Héricault, *Une reine de théâtre* (Paris, 1891); Jean Richepin, *La Miseloque: Chose et gens de théâtre* (Paris, 1893); Jules Claretie, *Brichanteau, comédien* (Paris, 1896); Charles Foley, *Drames de coulisses* (Paris, 1902); Gaston Derys, *Contes de coulisses* (Paris, 1910); Georges Beaume, *Cyprien Galissart: Lauréat du Conservatoire: Roman* (Paris, 1912); Louis Verneuil, *Régine Armand: Pièce en quatre actes* (Paris, 1922); Paul Ginisty, *Francine: Actrice de drame: Roman de la vie théâtrale* (Paris, 1909); E. Coquelin and M. Lupin, *Sur les planches: Moeurs théâtrales* (Paris, 1913); Félicien Champsaur, *L'Amant des danseuses* (Paris, 1888); and Catulle Mendès, *La Femme-enfant* (Paris, 1891).
84. Bram Dykstra, *Idols of Perversity: Fantasies of Female Evil in Fin-de-Siècle Culture* (New York, 1986); Hollis Clayton, *Painted Love: Prostitution in French Art of the Impressionist Era* (New Haven, 1991); Shapiro, *Breaking the Codes* (connecting fears of women to the ills of modern urban life); Elaine Showalter, *Sexual Anarchy: Gender and Culture at the Fin-de-Siècle* (New York, 1990); Naomi Schor, *Breaking the Chain: Women, Theory, and French Realist Fiction* (New York, 1985); George Ross Ridge, *The Hero in French Decadent Literature* (Athens, Ga., 1961); Jennifer Waelti-Walters, *Feminist Novelists of the Belle Epoque* (Bloomington, Ind., 1990). For Great Britain, see Judith R. Walkowitz, *City of Dreadful Delight: Narratives of Sexual Danger in Late-Victorian London* (Chicago, 1992).
85. For another sphere opened to women, see Leora Auslander, "The Gendering of Consumer Practices in Nineteenth-Century France," in *The Sex of Things: Gender and Consumption in Historical Perspective*, ed. Victoria de Grazia, with Ellen Furlough (Berkeley, 1996), pp. 79–112.

8. Performing a Self

1. This chapter adopts a "new biography" approach to individual lives that presumes that identities are unstable and constructed around personal needs and the cultural imperatives of the day. See Jo Burr Margadant, "In-

troduction: Constructing Selves in Historical Perspective," in *The New Biography: Performing Femininity in Nineteenth-Century France,* ed. Jo Burr Margadant (Berkeley, 2000), pp. 10–34.

2. *L'Illustration,* no. 1,375 (July 3, 1869), p. 11.

3. See the obituary in *L'Illustration,* no. 1,710 (December 4, 1875), pp. 361–362.

4. Henry James, *Parisian Sketches: Letters to the* New York Tribune *1875–1876,* ed. Leon Adel and Ilse Dusoir Lind (New York, 1957), p. 22.

5. Alphonse Lemonnier, *Les petits mystères de la vie théâtrale: Souvenirs d'un homme de théâtre* (Paris, 1895), pp. 150–180.

6. Ibid., p. 176; Edmond and Jules de Goncourt, *Journal: Mémoires de la vie littéraire,* ed. Robert Ricatte, 4 vols. (Paris, 1956), 3: 879.

7. Lenard R. Berlanstein, "Breeches and Breaches: Cross-Dress Theater and the Culture of Gender Ambiguity in Modern France," *Comparative Studies in Society and History* 38 (April 1996): 343–345, 363–365.

8. BA, Rondel Manuscript Collection, Henri Rochefort to Virginie Déjazet, n.d.

9. L.-Henry Lecomte, *Un amour de Déjazet: Histoire et correspondance inédite, 1834–1844* (Paris, 1907), pp. 11, 24, 35, 39, 40, 42, 63, 125.

10. Ibid., pp. 25, 35, 38–39, 44.

11. Ibid., pp. 29, 34, 45, 84, 89.

12. Ibid., pp. 53–57, 72, 84.

13. Ibid., pp. 29, 34, 45, 72.

14. Most of my account of this affair is based on the correspondence in BA, Rondel Manuscript Collection, letters of Charles Fechter to Virginie Déjazet. Since the letters are undated and have not been catalogued, I will not cite them individually.

15. L.-Henry Lecomte, *Une comédienne au XIXe siècle: Virginie Déjazet: Etude biographique et critique d'après des documents inédits* (Paris, 1892), pp. 326–345.

16. Ibid., pp. 328–330, 347–348.

17. BA, Rt 9555. The citation is from an obituary for Céline Montaland published in 1891.

18. My account of the life of the family is based on the letters in BA, Rondel Manuscript Collection, Déjazet cartons. Once again, because few of the letters are dated, I will not cite them individually.

19. On Déjazet as an affectionate grandmother who refused to discipline her grandchildren, see Louise France, *Les Ephémères m'as-tu-vu: Souvenirs de théâtre* (Paris, n.d.), p. 92.

20. Déjazet even had to take in a penniless Charpentier in his (and her) old age. See Lecomte, *Une comédienne,* p. 372.

21. BA, Henri Bachimont Collection, Alice Ozy to Cézar de Bazancourt, n.d. On the actress-courtesan, see Louis Loviot, *Alice Ozy* (Paris, 1910).

22. Lecomte, *Une comédienne*, chap. 10.

23. On Sand's celebrated plea for women's right to pleasure and fulfillment, as expressed in her 1833 novel *Lélia*, see Mona Ozouf, *The Words of Women: Essay on French Singularity*, trans. Jane Marie Todd (Chicago, 1997), pp. 111–131; Pierre Vermeylen, *Les Idées politiques et sociales de George Sand* (Brussels, 1984).

24. Claire-Joséphe Hippolyte Clairon, *Memoirs of Hippolyte Clairon, the Celebrated French Actress* (London, 1800).

25. On the history of love in France, Richard Guy, *Histoire de l'amour en France: Moyen Age à Belle Epoque* (Paris, 1985); Laure Adler, *Secrets d'alcôve: Histoire du couple de 1830 à 1930* (Paris, 1983).

26. The best single source on the private lives of writers is Goncourt, *Journal*. Alexandre Dumas, Sr., had at least twenty-four mistresses, of whom more than half were actresses. See Dumas, *Mes mémoires, 1830–1833* (Paris, 1989), pp. 1,290–1,313.

27. Dumas, *Mes mémoires*, p. 307.

28. The essential source on the affair is Marie Dorval, *Lettres à Alfred de Vigny*, ed. Charles Gaudier (Paris, 1942). The best secondary account is Simone André-Maurois, "Introduction," in Marie Dorval and George Sand, *Correspondance inédite*, ed. Simone André-Maurois (Paris, 1953), pp. 1–222. Vigny is quoted on p. 33.

29. André-Maurois marshals extensive evidence against a physical relationship between Dorval and Sand, in Dorval and Sand, *Correspondance*, pp. 197–199.

30. See Dumas's moving account of her death in his *La dernière année de Marie Dorval* (Paris, 1855).

31. The basic source is Juliette Drouet, *Lettres à Victor Hugo 1833–1882*, ed. Evelyn Blewer (Paris, 1985). Insightful accounts of Drouet's life and of the affair include: Henri Troyat, *Juliette Drouet* (Paris, 1997); Arlette Blum-Mandérieux, *Juliette Drouet et Victor Hugo* (Paris, 1960); Paul Souchon, *La Servitude amoureuse de Juliette Drouet à Victor Hugo* (Paris, 1943), and Souchon's *Juliette Drouet, inspiratrice de Victor Hugo* (Paris, 1942).

32. Jeanne Huas, *Juliette Drouet: Le bel amour de Victor Hugo* (Paris, 1985), pp. 82–84, 130.

33. On Hugo's sexual life, see Henri Guillemin, *Hugo et la sexualité* (Paris, 1954).

34. Drouet believed that she had inspired the character of Tisbe and had hoped to create the role, but Mademoiselle Mars received the part. See Troyat, *Drouet*, pp. 126–129.

35. On Desclée's life, see Emile de Molènes, *Desclée: Biographie et souvenirs* (Paris, 1874), and Pierre Berton, "Desclée: Scènes de la vie de théâtre," unpublished study, Bibliothèque de l'Arsenal, 1973.

36. See the letters between Desclée and the actress-courtesan Marie Colombier, sharing "secrets of the trade," BA, Henri Bachimont Collection, Aimée Desclée file.

37. Marie Colombier, *Mémoires: Fin d'Empire* (Paris, 1900), pp. 220–235.

38. BA, Rt 7019, fol. 55 (letter to Dumas published in an unspecified issue of *La nouvelle revue*).

39. Colombier, *Fin d'Empire*, pp. 220–238.

40. Aimée Desclée, *Lettres d'Aimée Desclée à Fanfan*, ed. Paul Duplan (Paris, 1895), p. 82.

41. Berton, "Desclée," pp. 29–34.

42. Aimée Tessandier, *Souvenirs, recueillis et redigés par Henri Fescourt* (Paris, 1912).

43. Ibid., p. 64.

44. Eve Lavallière, *Ma conversion* (Paris, 1930); Jacqueline Lenoir, *Eve Lavallière* (Paris, 1966); Omer Englebert, *Du moins je sais aimer: Vie et conversion d'Eve Lavallière* (Paris, 1963); BA, Rt 8579 (press clippings on Lavallière).

45. Mary Louise Roberts, *Civilization without Sexes: Reconstructing Gender in Postwar France, 1917–1927* (Chicago, 1994), chap. 2.

46. Another example of a theater woman who strove to live by her art, or so she claimed in her autobiography, was the café singer Mistinguett. See *Toute ma vie* (Paris, 1954), pp. 97–101.

47. Marie Colombier, *Mémoires: Fin de siècle* (Paris, 1900), pp. 26, 61–63, 69.

48. Mandy Berry, *Cinquante ans sur les planches: Mémoires d'une servante* (Paris, 1962). Citations on pp. 50–51.

49. Yvette Guilbert, "Prologue" in Ferdinand Bac, *Femmes de théâtre: Album inédit en couleurs* (Paris, 1896), no pagination.

50. Cécile Sorel, *Les belles heures de ma vie* (Monaco, 1946), p. 25.

51. Ibid., pp. 126–129. See also the image she gives herself in a second memoir, *La Confession de Célimène* (Paris, 1948).

52. Sorel, *Les belles heures*, pp. 33–38.

53. Caroline Otéro, *My Story: La Belle Otéro* (London, 1927), pp. 129, 264.

54. Cited in *L'Illustration*, no. 2,725 (May 18, 1896), p. 418.

55. Polaire, *Polaire par elle-même* (Paris, 1933), pp. 117–120, 128–142.

56. Ibid., pp. 146–151.

57. Marie Colombier, *Mémoires: Fin du tout* (Paris, 1900), pp. 34–51, 233–260, and *passim*. The outcome of the lawsuit is unknown.

58. Arsène Houssaye, *Behind the Scenes at the Comédie-française and Other Recollections*, trans. Albert D. Vandam (London, 1889), p. 83.

59. On this model, see Ozouf, *Women's Words*, pp. 1–20.

60. Jenny Thénard, *Ma vie au théâtre: Choses vues, chose vécues* (Paris, 1909), pp. 192–201.

61. Louise Fusil, *Souvenirs d'une actrice*, 2 vols. (Paris, 1841), 1: 111.

62. Laure Rièse, *Les Salons littéraires parisiens du Second Empire à nos jours* (Toulouse, 1962), pp. 29, 39, 46, 77, 87–88, 126–127. Rièse claims that the dressing rooms of Sarah Bernhardt, Réjane, and Eve Lavallière were virtually literary salons.

63. BA, Rt 6236. Citation from undated press clippings; Paul Gaulot, *Les trois Brohan* (Paris, 1930), p. 76.

64. Gaulot, *Brohan*, p. 55.

65. BA, Rt 6236. Citations from undated press clippings; Horace de Viel-Castel, *Mémoires du comte Horace de Viel-Castel sur le règne de Napoléon III*, 6 vols. (Paris, 1883), 4: 101.

66. Mademoiselle X, comédienne française, *Ce que mes jolies yeux ont vu* (Paris, 1913), pp. 245–246.

67. Sorel, *Les belles heures*, pp. 53–55.

68. Roselyne Laplace, *Mademoiselle George, ou un demi-siècle de théâtre* (Paris, 1987), pp. 136–139.

69. BA, Rt 8062–8063 (various undated press clippings).

70. Rachel M. Brownstein, *Tragic Muse: Rachel of the Comédie-française* (New York, 1993), pp. 183–197. For another example, see George Sand, *Lettres inédites de George Sand et de Pauline Viardot (1839–1849)*, ed. Thérèse Marix-Spire (Paris, 1959), pp. 71–72.

71. My account of Agar's career is based on her file at the Archives de la Préfecture de Police (hereinafter cited as APP), B/a 927, and on her memoir, "Souvenirs d'une tragédienne," *La Revue littéraire et critique*, nos. 5–15 (March–October 1893), no pagination.

72. Georges D'Heylli [pseud. Edmond Poinsot], *Journal intime de la Comédie-française (1852–1870)* (Paris, 1879), p. 540.

73. APP, B/a 927, Agar file, presents evidence for her appearance at the Tuileries on May 6, 1871, and Agar's own denial, years later.

74. France, *Les Ephémères*, p. 225. According to France, Agar cried over the incident until her death.

75. My account of her career is based on her memoirs, *Ma vie, mes amours, mes aventures* (Paris, 1930), and on her file in APP, B/a 1644.

76. On this journalist, see Evelyne Le Garrec, *Séverine (1855–1929)* (Paris, 1982).

77. APP, B/a 1644, reports of 1902.

78. Jacques Porel, *Fils de Réjane: Souvenirs*, 2 vols. (Paris, 1951), 1: 82.

79. Arthur Gold and Robert Fitzdale, *The Divine Sarah: The Life of Sarah Bernhardt* (New York, 1994), pp. 274–278. Alain Pagès, *Emile Zola: Un intellectuel dans l'Affaire Dreyfus* (Paris, 1991), pp. 100–103, 132.

80. See, for example, *L'Illustration*, no. 646 (July 14, 1855), p. 19.

81. Jules Huret, *Sarah Bernhardt* (Paris, 1899), p. 90.

82. Jane Hading, "Les Coulisses des tournées théâtrales," *Je sais tout*, August 15, 1907, pp. 42–45.

83. *L'Illustration*, no. 3,117 (November 22, 1902), p. 402.

84. Albert Dubeuf, *Julia Bartet* (Paris, 1938), p. 219.

85. Bibliothèque de la Comédie-française, Bartet file, General Debenet to Bartet, January 19, 1920.

86. Colombier, *Fin de siècle*, p. 216; see also *L'Illustration*, no. 2,475 (August 2, 1890), p. 92, on Suzanne Reichemberg, another actress who took credit for improving relations with Russia.

87. Mary Louise Roberts, "Acting Up: The Feminist Theatrics of Marguerite Durand," *French Historical Studies* 19 (Fall 1996): 1,103–1,138.

88. Roberts argues that Durand advanced the idea of female beauty as a "political act." See ibid., p. 1,119.

89. Laurence Klejman and Florence Rochefert, *L'Egalité en marche: Le féminisme sous la Troisième République* (Paris, 1989), pp. 66–78.

90. J. Hermissains, "L'Idéal au café-concert," *La Vie illustrée*, December 29, 1902, pp. 184–185.

91. Marcelle Yrven, who claimed to be a feminist actress, was disappointed by the small number of performers who shared her views. See her *La Comédienne et le féminisme* (Paris, 1914).

92. Joseph Galtier, "Les grandes artistes modernes: Bartet," *Je sais tout* (April 15, 1910), 371–378.

93. Bibliothèque de la Comédie-française, Bartet file, undated letter to "Madame."

94. Sarah Bernhardt, *Love Letters to Pierre Berton*, trans. Sylvestre Dorian, ed. E. Halderman-Julius (Girard, Kans., 1924), p. 10.

95. Sarah Bernhardt, *The Art of Theatre*, trans. H. J. Stenning (London, 1924), p. 137. To place Bernhardt's cross-dress roles in context, see Berlanstein, "Breeches and Breaches," pp. 351–363.

9. From Notorious Women to Intimate Strangers

1. Félicien Champsaur, *Dinah Samuel* (Paris, 1881), pp. 135–136.

2. Irving Rein, Philip Kottler, and Martin Stoller, *High Visibility* (New York, 1987), p. 15.

3. Richard Schickel, *Intimate Strangers: The Culture of Celebrity* (New York, 1985).

4. Leo Braudy, *The Frenzy of Renown: Fame and Its History* (New York, 1986); Joshua Gamson, *Claims to Fame: Celebrity in Contemporary America* (Berkeley, 1994). Rhonde K. Garelick, *Rising Star: Dandyism, Gender, and Performance in the Fin-de-Siècle* (Princeton, 1998), examines the French roots of the media cult personality.

5. Daniel Roche, *France in the Enlightenment,* trans. Arthur Goldhammer (Cambridge, Mass., 1998), pp. 485–547, 608–674; Roger Chartier, *The Cultural Origins of the French Revolution,* trans. Lydia G. Cochrane (Durham, N.C., 1991), chap. 2.

6. Gaston Capon, *Les Vestris: Le "diou" de la danse et sa famille (1730–1808)* (Paris, 1908), p. 125.

7. Historians are well informed about salon conversation, thanks to newsletters that were eventually published: Friedrich-Melchoir Grimm, *Correspondance littéraire, philosophique, et critique par Grimm, Diderot, Raynal, Meister, etc.,* ed. Maurice Tourneux, 16 vols. (Paris, 1882); Louis Petit de Bachaumont, *Mémoires secrets pour servir à l'histoire de la république des lettres en France depuis 1762 jusqu'au nos jours,* 36 vols. (London, 1777–1789). On the early theatrical press, see Maurice Descotes, *Histoire de la critique dramatique en France* (Paris, 1980), chaps. 1–3.

8. The very earliest dictionary I have found is Antoine de Léris, *Dictionnaire portatif, historique, et littéraire des théâtres* (Paris, 1763). Thereafter, there were: *Petites vérités au grand jour sur les acteurs, les actrices, les peintres, les journalistes, l'Institut, le Portique républicain, etc., etc.* (Paris, 1800); *L'Espion des coulisses: Nouvelle critique sur les acteurs des principaux théâtres de Paris* (Paris, 1800); *Les Acteurs et actrices du jour par l'ombre de Collé* (Paris, 1803); *Nouveau jugement porté sur les acteurs, actrices, auteurs ... par Ch. C——* (Paris, 1803); Théophile Du Mersan, *Le Coup de fouet, ou nouvelle revue de tous les théâtres de Paris, des journalistes, des coteries littéraires, et de plus de cinq cents acteurs, auteurs, et compositeurs de musique très connus* (Paris, 1803); Alexandre Grimod de la Reynière and Fabien Pillet, *Revue des comédiens, ou critique raisonnée de tous les acteurs, danseurs, et mimes de la capitale* (Paris, 1808); Saint-Saveur, *Galerie dramatique, ou acteurs et actrices célèbres qui se sont illustrés sur les trois grands théâtres de Paris* (Paris, 1808).

9. Charles Severling, *Le Rideau levé, ou petite revue des grands théâtres* (Paris, 1818); Amiable Villain de Saint-Hilaire, *Petite biographie dramatique, ou silhouettes des acteurs, actrices, directeurs, directrices, régisseurs, souffleurs, danseurs, danseuses, figurants, figurantes, peintres, et machinistes des*

théâtres de la capitale (Paris, 1821); Soyé, *Ces Messieurs et ces dames, ou les acteurs de la capitale: Tableaux mêlés de couplets* (Paris, 1823); [Maurice Alhoy] *Grande biographie dramatique, ou silhouettes des acteurs, actrices, chanteurs,* . . . *de Paris et des départements* (Paris, 1824); *Grande biographie dramatique par l'hermite du Luxembourg, ou silhouettes des acteurs, actrices de Paris et des départements* (Paris, 1824); *Dictionnaire théâtral, ou douze cent trente-trois vérités secrètes sur les directeurs, régisseurs, acteurs, actrices* . . . *de Paris* (Paris, 1824); *Petite biographie dramatique faite avec adresse par un mouchard de chandelles* (Paris, 1826); *Nouveau dictionnaire théâtral, ou mille et une vérités sur les acteurs, actrices, chanteurs, cantatrices, danseurs, danseuses de Paris* (Paris, 1827); *Biographie théâtrale pour l'année 1829, contenant les adresses des acteurs et actrices de Paris* (Paris, 1829); *Petite biographie des acteurs et actrices des théâtres de Paris avec l'âge de ces dames* (Paris, 1831–1832); *Nouvelle grande biographie dramatique* (Paris, 1831); Charles Monselet, *Physionomies parisiennes: Acteurs, actrices, etc., avec dessins par E. Lorsey* (Paris, 1837); Léonard Géreon, *La rampe et les coulisses, esquisses biographiques des directeurs, acteurs, et actrices de tous les théâtres* (Paris, 1832); Emile Abraham, *Les Acteurs et les actrices de Paris: Biographie complète* (Paris, 1861).

10. Saint-Hilaire, *Petite biographie dramatique, ou silhouettes des acteurs, actrices*.

11. *Nouvelle biographie théâtrale, ou les acteurs, actrices* . . . (Paris, 1826). This dictionary is attributed to Maurice Alhoy.

12. *L'Espion des coulisses*, pp. 81–82.

13. Ibid., pp. 48, 60–62, 76.

14. Saint-Hilaire *Petite biographie dramatique*, p. iii.

15. *Actrices célèbres contemporaines* (Paris, 1843); Edouard Lodreau, *Les jolies actrices de Paris en l'an de grâce 1843* (Paris, 1843); *Silhouettes d'actrices* (Paris, 1846); Raymond Deslandre, *Les jolies actrices de Paris* (Paris, 1849); Edouard Texier and Maurice Alhoy, *Paris-Actrice, par les auteurs des Mémoires de Bibloquet* (Paris, 1854); Paul Mahalin, *Ces petites dames du théâtre* (Paris, 1862); L. de Monchamp and Charles Mosant, *Les Reines de la rampe* (Paris, 1863); Félix Savard, *Les Actrices de Paris* (Paris, 1867); Paul Mahalin, *Les jolies actrices de Paris* (Paris, 1868); Charles Diguet, *Jolies femmes de Paris* (Paris, 1870); Eugène Hulurt et Christien de Trogoff, *Les Actrices de Paris* (Paris, 1872); Emile Gaboreau, *Les Comédiennes adorées* (Paris, 1878); Pierre Desgenais, *Les Parisiennes* (Paris, 1882); Paul Mahalin, *Au bout de la lorgnette* (Paris, 1883); Eugène Billard, *Nos étoiles: Sonnets, portraits des jolies actrices de Paris* (Paris, 1886).

16. For a brief but insightful history of early society columns, see Anne Mar-

tin-Fugier, "La Cour et la ville sous la Monarchie de Juillet d'après les feuilletons mondains," *Revue historique,* no. 563 (1987): 108, n. 2.

17. Delphine de Girardin, *Lettres parisiennes du vicomte de Launay,* ed. Anne Martin-Fugier, 2 vols. (Paris, 1986), 1: v–viii.

18. Ibid., 2: 45–49.

19. Ibid. 2: 89.

20. Ibid., 2: 204–215. For a more nuanced discussion of Girardin's feminism, see Whitney Walton, *Eve's Proud Descendants: Four Women Writers and Republican Politics in Nineteenth-Century France* (Stanford, Calif., 2000), pp. 82–89, 96–124, 163–171, 185–188.

21. Girardin, *Lettres parisiennes,* 1: 629.

22. Ibid., 1: 311–313.

23. Ibid., 1: 313.

24. Ibid., 1: 637–646.

25. *L'Illustration,* no. 95 (December 21, 1844), p. 247.

26. Ibid., no. 152 (January 24, 1846), p. 322.

27. Ibid., no. 753 (August 1, 1857), p. 74.

28. In one of the earliest studies of celebrity culture in France, Louis Tourdan and Taxtile Delord claimed that only men could be celebrities, because women who enjoyed "glory" were inevitably the subject of rumors about their passions and sexual adventures and, thus, not judged on their talent. See *Les Célébrités du jour, 1860–61* (Paris, 1860), pp. 305–306.

29. Cited in Micheline Baudet, *Mademoiselle Mars, l'inimitable* (Paris, 1987), pp. 252–258. Mars, who was much older than Brach, had proposed marriage, and Brach humiliated the actress by backing out at a celebration dinner.

30. Sophie Gay, *Salons célèbres* (Paris, 1837), p. 82.

31. Elizabeth Anne McCauly, *Industrial Madness: Commercial Photography in Paris, 1848–1871* (New Haven, 1994), chap. 2, and McCauly's *A.A.E. Disdéri and the Carte de Visite Portrait Photography* (New Haven, 1985), p. 53.

32. McCauly, *Disdéri,* p. 111.

33. "Le Type idéal de la jeune fille française," *Fémina,* no. 169 (February 1, 1908), p. 60.

34. Henry James, *Parisian Sketches: Letters to the New York Tribune, 1875–1876,* ed. Leon Edel and Ilse Dusoir Lind (New York, 1951), p. 46.

35. *Le Monde illustré,* no. 524 (April 27, 1867), p. 251.

36. *L'Illustration,* no. 1,969 (November 20, 1880), p. 330.

37. A picture of Alexandre Dumas with a scantily clad Adah Menkin (an American actress known for her Lady Godiva act) sitting on his lap found

its way into shop windows. Dumas sued the photographer. See Alexandre Dumas, *Mes mémoires, 1830–1833* (Paris, 1989), pp. 1, 311. McCauly, *Disdéri*, chap. 4, provides a brief survey of early celebrity photographs.

38. On the star system, see below, chap. 1.

39. Emile Zola, *Nana*, trans. Douglas Parmée (New York, 1992), p. 274.

40. *Le Monde illustré*, no. 186 (November 3, 1860), pp. 290–291.

41. Edmond and Jules de Goncourt, *Journal: Mémoires de la vie littéraire*, ed. Robert Ricatte, 4 vols. (Paris, 1956), 3: 754. On the "decline" of the boulevard, see above, chap. 1.

42. Arsène Alexandre, *Suzanne Reichemberg: Les ingénues au théâtre* (Paris, 1898), p. 64.

43. BA, MSS 13031–13032. These cartons contain performers' replies to a writer at the *Revue théâtrale* who solicited photographs for an article.

44. Vanessa R. Schwartz, *Spectacular Realities: Early Mass Culture in Fin-de-Siècle Paris* (Berkeley, 1998).

45. For the democratic implications of celebrity, see Lawrence M. Friedman, *The Horizontal Society* (New Haven, 1999).

46. *Le Monde illustré*, no. 1,580 (July 9, 1887), p. 26.

47. Ibid., no. 1,351 (February 17, 1883), p. 98.

48. Marie Colombier, *Les Mémoires de Sarah Barnum* (Paris, 1883).

49. For Colombier's account of the scandal, see her *Mémoires: Fin de siècle* (Paris, 1900), chap. 11, and *Mémoires: Fin du tout* (Paris, 1900), pp. 60–126.

50. Carol Ockman, "When Is a Jewish Star Just a Star? Interpretating Images of Sarah Bernhardt," in *The Jew in the Text*, ed. Linda Nochlin and Tamar Garb (London, 1995), pp. 121–139.

51. Cornelia Otis Skinner, *Madame Sarah* (New York, 1988), chap. 10.

52. In 1900, the 170th edition of an expurgated edition was published.

53. Colombier, *Fin du tout*, p. 85. Colombier's punishment was eventually commuted to fifteen days in an asylum.

54. BA, Rt 5930 (undated clipping).

55. *Affaire Marie Colombier–Sarah Bernhardt: Pièces à conviction* (Paris, 1884), pp. 56–62. This work reprints several editorials on the affair.

56. Ibid; Skinner, *Madame Sarah*, pp. 255–258.

57. *Le Figaro*, no. 345 (December 10, 1896), p. 1. Also, *Le Temps*, no. 12,976 (December 10, 1896), p. 3.

58. On the ambiguity of French elites toward mass culture, see Marjorie Beale, *The Modernist Enterprise: French Elites and the Threat of Modernity, 1900–1940* (Stanford, Calif., 1999).

59. *L'Illustration*, no. 3,021 (January 19, 1901), p. 43.

60. Ibid., no. 3,074 (January 25, 1902), p. 50.

61. Ibid., no. 1,914 (November, 1 1879), p. 274.

62. Romain Coulis, "Une Journée de Madame Réjane," *Fémina,* December 1, 1903, pp. 743–44.

63. "Madame est servie: Nos actrices à table," *Fémina,* January 1, 1911, pp. 12–13.

64. I have examined systematically two of the "Big Four" mass dailies, *Le petit journal* (for 1900, 1905, 1907, and 1910) and *Le Matin* (for 1906, 1910, and 1912).

65. "Le Rasoir ou la barbe: Que préférez-vous, mesdames?" *Le Matin,* March 5, 1912, p. 1.

66. On the technological and entrepreneurial developments making their appearance possible, see Anne-Claude Amboise-Rendu, "Du dessin de presse à la photographie (1878–1914): Histoire d'une mutation technique et culturelle," *Revue d'histoire moderne et contemporaine* 39 (1992): 6–28.

67. See, for example, "Madame Bernhardt," *Je sais tout,* February–July 1905, pp. 304–305; "Chez Madame Guilbert," ibid., December 15, 1907, pp. 597–601; "La Rentrée d'Yvette Guilbert," *La Vie illustrée,* January 18, 1901, pp. 253–255.

68. C. de Nérode, "Une heure chez Madame Jane Hading," *La Revue illustrée,* May 1, 1893, pp. 347–353.

69. Lenard R. Berlanstein, *Big Business and Industrial Conflict in Nineteenth-Century France: A Social History of the Parisian Gas Company* (Berkeley, 1991), pp. 97, 218.

70. René Blum, "Ménages d'artistes," *Fémina,* May 1, 1912, p. 245.

71. See, for example, Jane Catulle Mendès, "Réjane," *Je sais tout,* March 15, 1909, pp. 447–454; Adolphe Brisson, "Céline Montaland," *La Revue illustrée,* June 1, 1891, pp. 133–141; Henri Barbousse, "Une ménage d'artistes: Jacques Richepin et Madame Richepin-Laparcerie," *Fémina,* November 1, 1903, pp. 737–738.

72. BA, Rt 8288, "La petite opérée de la Charité et Madame Judic," *L'Eclair,* January 12, 1895.

73. Simone d'Ax, "La Marche de l'Académie," *Fémina,* January 1, 1909, pp. 12–16; Patrice de Latour, "Les Femmes et l'Académie," ibid., p. 18; Hélène Avryl, "Projet de costume pour les académiciennes," ibid., January 1, 1911, pp. 9–11.

74. *Fémina,* June 1, 1906, p. 241.

75. Paul Escudier, "La première candidate," ibid., June 1, 1908, p. 264; Hélène Avryl, "Aux urnes, citoyennes," ibid., April 1, 1910, pp. 200–211.

76. Mary Louise Roberts, "Acting Up: The Feminist Theatrics of Marguerite Durand," *French Historical Studies* 19 (Fall 1996): 1,103–1,138.

77. Michelle Perrot, "The New Eve and the Old Adam: Changes in French

Women's Conditions at the Turn of the Century," in *Behind the Lines,* ed. Margaret Higonnet (New Haven, 1987), pp. 51–60.

78. Yvette Guilbert, *The Song of my Life: My Memories,* trans. Beatrice de Holthoir (London, 1929), p. 171.

79. Cécile Sorel, *La Confession de Célimème* (Paris, 1949), p. 279. See the description of the lust that she felt on seeing the naked torsos of Warren Whitney and the boxer Georges Carpentier, pp. 33–34, 285–286.

80. The reporter André Belesert recounts how he was astonished to have Bartet introduce him to her son. BA, MSS 13457, clipping from the *Journal des débats,* August 14, 1938.

81. Albert Carré, *Souvenirs de théâtre* (Paris, 1976), p. 145.

82. Robert Dieudonné, "La Rentrée de Mademoiselle Brandès," *Fémina,* February 1, 1908, pp. 79–82.

83. BA, Rt 6175 (various press clippings and obituaries).

84. *Le Courrier français,* February 7, 1886, p. 1.

85. *Le Figaro,* no. 201 (August 4, 1874), p. 3.

86. Bibliothèque de la Comédie-française, Arnould-Plessy file, Arnould-Plessy to Edouard Thierry, n.d.

87. BA, Rt 6446, fols. 23–24; Rt 8287, fol. 12 (undated clippings).

88. See, for example, Loydreau, *Les jolies actrices,* p. 105; BA, Rt 4144, fol. 25 (undated clipping from *Le Figaro*). The courtesan Cora Pearl claimed that one of the influences that women of her sort had on fashion was to add masculine detail (collars, cravats, walking sticks) to women's attire. The appropriation of masculine authority was, naturally, implicated. See Cora Pearl, *Grand Horizontal: The Erotic Memoirs of a Passionate Lady,* ed. William Blatchford (New York, 1983), p. 95.

89. Philip Mansel, *The Court of France, 1789–1830* (Cambridge, 1988).

90. "La Mode au théâtre," *Fémina,* November 15, 1906, pp. xvii–xviii. The first time *L'Illustration* openly approved of fashion being set by performers was in 1890. See no. 2,490 (November 15, 1890), p. 423.

91. Madame Catulle Mendès, "Robes de théâtre," *Fémina,* October 15, 1908, pp. 474–76.

92. R. Irébor, "Qu'est-ce que c'est le chic?" ibid., November 1, 1910, pp. 576–7.

93. "Le Théâtre du grand couturier," ibid., December 15, 1911, p. 697. Charles Worth had been known for presenting his creations under lighting conditions that resembled that of a society ball.

94. Micheline Dupuy, *Le petit parisien: "Le plus fort tirage des journaux du monde entier"* (Paris, 1989), p. 83. The results were published in the issue of December 22, 1906.

Conclusion

1. For a thoughtful analysis of celebrity culture, see Lawrence M. Friedman, *The Horizontal Society* (New Haven, 1999), pp. 27–43.
2. The same changes in political culture that reduced the threat of actresses may have increased the threat of Jews and homosexuals.
3. Geneviève Fraisse, *Reason's Muse: Sexual Difference and the Birth of Democracy*, trans. Jane Marie Todd (Chicago, 1994); Joan Landes, *Women and the Public Sphere in the Age of the French Revolution* (Ithaca, N.Y., 1988); Janis Berman-Carton, *The Woman of Ideas in French Art, 1830–1848* (New Haven, 1995); Gay Gullickson, *Unruly Women of Paris: Images of the Commune* (Ithaca, N.Y., 1996); Ann-Louise Shapiro, *Breaking the Codes: Female Criminality in Fin-de-Siècle Paris* (Stanford, Calif., 1996).
4. For a parallel argument about the concept of sexuality, see David Halperin, "Is There a History of Sexuality?" *History and Theory* 28, no. 3 (1989): 257–274.
5. Foucault describes sexuality as "a dense transfer point for relations of power," in *The History of Sexuality*, vol. 1: *An Introduction* (New York, 1978), p. 103. For suggestions about the ways in which socially constructed perceptions became lived experience, see Dror Wahrman, *Imagining the Middle Class: The Political Representation of Class in Britain, c. 1780–1840* (Cambridge, 1995); Michael Sonenscher, *Work and Wages: Natural Law, Politics, and the Eighteenth-Century French Trades* (Cambridge, 1989); Donald Reid, *Paris Sewers and Sewermen: Realities and Representations* (Cambridge, Mass., 1991); Judith G. Coffin, *The Politics of Women's Work: The Paris Garment Trades, 1750–1914* (Princeton, 1996); Ian Hacking, *Rewriting the Soul: Multiple Personality and the Sciences of Memory* (Princeton, 1995).

INDEX

Absolutism, 57–58, 59, 67, 69. *See also* Civil society

Actors (male), 24, 59–60, 63, 68, 110, 128, 169–171, 211, 266n; attacking actresses, 73, 75–76, 145, 147

Adultery, 43–44, 127, 156, 161, 230, 262n. *See also* Libertinism

Advertising, 216–219, 231–233, 236, 241

Agar, Mademoiselle (actress), 202–203

Alexandre, prince of Württemburg, 120

André, Emile, 179

Andrieux, François, 96

Antona-Traversi, Camillo, 21

Aristocrats, 7, 11; affairs of, 33, 35, 37–38, 103, 105; lifestyle of, 13, 16, 21, 42, 119; politics of, 80, 85–88, 91–92, 153–154. *See also* Libertinism

Arnould, Sophie, 1, 114–115

Arnould-Plessy, Sylvie, 234

Astrodi, Rosalie, 43–44

Audiences, at theaters, 21–22, 29, 46, 105–106, 125, 128; size of, 6–7, 18–19. *See also* Gendering

Augier, Emile, 135–138, 142, 152–153, 155–156, 170

Aumale, Duke d', 151, 200

L'Aventurière, 135–136, 175

Balzac, Honoré de, 15, 213, 263n

Barrière, Théodore, 139–140, 147, 154, 157

Bartet, Julia, 28, 172, 205, 207, 230, 235

Bauer, Henry, 177

Beauchamps, Mademoiselle (dancer), 48

Beauménard, Mademoiselle (actress), 36

Bernhardt, Sarah: career of, 27, 30–31, 106, 169, 171–172, 237–238; publicity about, 204–205, 207–209, 219–224, 226, 232–233, 235–236, 267n; sexuality of, 115–116, 123

Berry, Mandy, 194

Bertrand, Arthur, 100, 126–127, 184–185

Bière, Marie, 157

Blaize, Jean, 180

Bloch, Jeanne, 206

Boex, Joseph and Justin, 179

Bohemia. *See* Writers

Bonaparte, Louis-Napoleon. *See* Napoleon III

Bonaparte, Princess Mathilde, 123, 153, 202, 275n

Bongars, Esther de, 120

Bonheur, Rosa, 171

Bonnetain, Paul, 221

Bouillon, duchess of, 35–36, 98

Boulevard, 6, 20; culture of, 108, 120–124, 150–151, 154–155, 161, 217–218, 220, 224, 236; development of, 18, 150–151; fashionableness of, 21, 91–92, 117, 214; theaters on, 14–16, 27

Boulevard du Temple, 13, 15, 54

Bourbon Restoration, 84–87, 95, 200, 213

Bourgeoisie, 7, 135, 238; formation of, 85–95, 124, 149–151, 154, 261n; moral vision of, 103, 105–106, 118–119, 129, 137, 140–141, 153–156, 240

Brandès, Marthe, 231

Briffault, Eugène, 214

British theater, 26, 106, 108

Brohan, Augustine, 115, 199–200

Brohan, Madeleine, 101, 218

Bruart, Aristide, 203

Buffet, Eugénie, 203

Café-concerts, 14, 19–20, 196, 203, 206

Camargo, Mademoiselle (dancer), 35

Careers, of actresses, 22–32, 109–110, 124, 130, 165

Casting couch, 26–27

Catholic Church, and actresses, 23, 44, 58, 60, 65–66, 70, 85, 153, 158, 170, 172, 229
Celebrity, 9, 27, 57, 91, 112, 152, 208–236, 237
Cerny, Berthe, 165
Champsaur, Félicien, 22, 176, 209, 219
Charles IX affair, 78–80
Charles Demailly, 139, 176, 178
Chateaubriand, 101, 221
Chaumont, Céline, 30
Chevrier, François, 54
Civil society, 4–5, 59, 62, 66, 83, 150–151, 160, 238
Clairon, Mademoiselle (actress), 2, 47, 114–115, 174; autobiography of, 54, 188, 211; protest by, 70–71, 170, 201, 257n
Claretie, Jules, 175
Clemenceau, Georges, 132, 161, 200
Clermont, count of, 35–36, 46–47, 52–53, 250n
Colette, 196
Collé, Charles, 54
Colombe, Adeline, 53
Colombier, Marie, 176, 191, 194, 196–197, 205–206, 221–222
Comédie-française, 11, 20, 25, 46, 221, 257n; administration of, 69–70, 74–76, 202; attacks on, 71–72, 78–80; performers at, 28–30, 121, 129, 172; reading committee at, 6, 72–73, 144–149, 158, 174–175, 258n
Comédie-italienne, 11–12, 59–60, 68, 258n
Commune revolt, 157, 159, 202
Complementarity, of sexes, 3, 5, 61–62, 148–149, 158, 181, 207–208, 238, 240
La Comtesse Romani, 108–109, 127, 139, 178, 231
Conservatory of Dramatic Arts, 7, 14, 22, 23–25, 132–134, 171
Consumerism, attitudes toward, 150, 152, 162, 168, 171, 181, 236
La Contagion, 137–138, 155–156
Contat, Louise, 76, 78–80, 82, 86, 114, 216
Conti, prince of, 43, 46
Costumes, theatrical, 13, 43, 46, 111, 125–126
Coudray, Alexandre du, 73
Coupée, Mademoiselle (dancer), 50, 53
Courtesans, 2, 39–40, 93, 106, 149, 152, 213; and actresses, 5, 57, 93, 140, 177,

190, 192; in theater, 106, 127–128, 143, 157–158
Critics, theatrical, 14, 20, 27, 105, 111–112
Cross-dress roles, 21, 183, 206–208
Cruvelli, Sophie, 30–31

D'Alembert, Jean, 62, 66–67
Dallière, Mademoiselle (singer), 45
La Dame aux camélias, 106, 118, 121, 140, 149, 156, 185
Dancers, of Opéra, 121, 126, 129–132, 164, 167, 270n
Dancourt, L. H., 67
Dandies, 91–92, 261n
Dangeville, Madame (actress), 69
D'Antigny, Blanche, 157, 159
Daudet, Ernest, 101, 161
Degas, Edgar, 129, 164
Déjazet, Virginie, 31, 113, 126–127, 129, 183–186; family of, 186–188
Delauny, Louis, 171
Delavigne, Casimir, 96
Delions, Anna, 157
De Metz, Mademoiselle (singer), 48, 50–51
Demidoff, Anatole and Paul, 17, 189
Democratization, of social attitudes, 9, 21, 161, 171, 216, 224
Desclée, Aimée, 123, 190–191, 197, 198
Desmoulin, Camille, 78–79
Desprès, Suzanne, 167
Diderot, Denis, 64, 109
Diplomacy, and actresses, 200, 205–206
Directors, 23, 27, 65, 125; actresses as, 26, 30
Doche, Eugénie, 127, 185
Doligny, Mademoiselle (actress), 76
Domesticity, 42, 62, 90; of actresses, 110, 161–162, 225–227; as standard, 5–6, 51, 74, 81, 88–89
Dorval, Marie, 31, 189
Drama, 64–65
Dressing rooms, of actresses, 128–129, 165
Dreyfus, Maurice, 170
Dreyfus affair, 171–173, 195, 203–204
Drouet, Juliette, 189–190
Dubois affair, 70–71
Du Camp, Maxime, 101
Duchesnois, Joséphine, 82, 174
Dugazon (actor), 75–76

Dugazon, Madame (actress), 212
Dumas, Jr., Alexandre, 20, 142, 148, 155–156, 165, 191–192; works by, 108–109, 118, 121, 139–140
Dumas, Sr., Alexandre, 177, 189, 199, 262n, 283n, 289n
Duplessis, Marie, 149
Dupont, Mademoiselle (actress), 212
Durand, Marguerite, 203, 206, 229, 286n
Durand, Pierre, 214

Essler, Fanny, 215

Fargueil, Anaïs, 102, 174
Fashion, and actresses, 55–56, 104, 111–112, 152, 156, 233–236
Fatma (dancer), 164
Faure, Félix, 195
La Faustin, 103, 110, 126
Favart, Marie, 28
Fechter, Charles, 185–186
Félix, Sarah, 142
Female gaze, 7, 225–226
Fémina, 225, 227, 229, 231, 235
Femininity, 2, 4, 7, 9, 22–23, 99–100, 182–183; changes in, 180, 206, 241; crisis of, 8, 135–136, 148–149, 158
Feminism, 8, 91, 115, 206–208, 214, 229–230, 239, 241
Le Figaro, 6, 17–18, 144, 166–167, 199
First Gentlemen of the Bedchamber, 11, 26, 46, 69–71, 76
Flat, Paul, 178
Flaubert, Gustave, 101, 124, 157, 269n
Flore, Corvée, 100
Florentine, Mademoiselle (dancer), 212
Flowers, as tribute, 99–100
François de Neufchâteau, Nicolas, 73
Fuller, Loïe, 224
Fusil, Louise, 198

Gaillard de la Bataille, Pierre, 54
Gaussin, Madame (actress), 52, 71
Gauthier-Villars, Henri, 196
Gautier, Théophile, 21, 110, 189
Gay, Sophie, 86, 216
Gendering, of theater, 105–106, 167–168, 246n
Geneva, theater in, 62–64, 67, 73
Geoffroy, Julien, 111

George, Mademoiselle (actress), 82, 84, 126, 200, 214
Giffard, Pierre, 10, 107, 109, 121, 130
Girardin, Delphine de, 213–216
Girardin, Emile de, 16–17, 153, 213
Goncourt, Edmond (and Jules) de, 2, 115; observations of, 121–122, 124, 129, 134, 139, 151–152, 169, 218; works by, 103, 110, 114, 139, 176
Got, Edmond, 17, 20, 122–123
Gramont-Caderousse, Duke Ludovic de, 16–17
Granier, Jeanne, 3, 117, 123, 165, 237, 268n
Grassini, Guiseppina, 82
Grisi, Carlotta, 30–31
Guerin, Eugène, 96
Guilbert, Yvette, 113, 165, 194, 224, 226, 230
Guimard, Marie, 56–57, 80
Guimont, Esther, 149
Guitry, Lucien, 231

Hading, Jane, 165, 204
Halévy, Ludovic, 137, 191
Hérivaux (dancer), 122–123
Honor, codes of, 34, 45, 48, 51–52, 119–120
Houssaye, Arsène, 17, 26, 110, 123, 197, 199, 221, 247n
Hugo, Victor, 97, 115, 136, 145, 149, 189–190, 199, 213
Humbert, Alphonse, 121

Identities, of actresses, 113–118
L'Illustration, 18–19, 92, 142–143, 214–215
Images, of actresses, 2–6, 8–9, 112, 123, 182; anxieties over, 22–24, 53–55, 59–60, 62–64, 66, 74, 89–90, 134; improving, 80, 82–85, 95, 98–99, 110, 169, 175–176, 180; rehabilitation of, 70, 92, 162–167, 169, 237; scandalous, 22–24, 53–55, 74, 103–104, 135–136, 142–143, 209
Intermissions, 128

Jacobins, 8, 80–81, 119
James, Henry, 10, 217
Janin, Jules, 189
Jewels, as tribute, 46, 50, 99–100, 125–126, 156, 224, 225
Jockey Club, 123, 126, 130
Jollivet, Gaston, 101–102, 119, 167–168

Journalism. *See* Newspapers
Judic, Anna, 117, 127, 166, 228, 266n
July Monarchy. *See* Orléanist regime

Karr, Alphonse, 189
Koning, Victor, 125, 230

La Chanterie, Mademoiselle (dancer), 47
Lagier, Suzanne, 123
Lainez (singer), 79
Lamartine, Alphonse de, 145, 199
Lange, Mademoiselle (actress), 82
Laurent, Marie, 171
Lavallière, Eve, 27, 193–194
Leblanc, Léonide, 116, 123, 144, 200
Lecomte, Jules, 157, 218
Lecouvreur, Adrienne, 36, 98
Leduc, Mademoiselle (dancer), 36, 46–47, 52
Légion d'honneur, 169–174, 237
Legouvé, Ernest, 98, 148
Lekain (actress), 52
Lemonnier, Alphonse, 101, 107–108
Lenclos, Ninon de, 40–41, 113–114
Lender, Marcelle, 235
Le Riche de la Popelinière, Alexandre, 48, 52–53
Lesbianism, 53, 115–116, 176, 189
Libertinism, 33–42, 89, 108, 161, 220; after 1789, 118–124, 132–134, 150–151, 161–164, 175; during Revolution, 76, 80–83; under Old Regime, 45–52, 62
Lighting, theatrical, 125, 269n
Louis XIII, 68, 71
Louis XIV, 11, 37, 39, 42, 69–70
Louis XV, 11, 37
Louis XVI, 56, 71
Love, 38, 40–41, 49–51, 60, 188; of schoolboys, 101–103

Male gaze, 7, 105–106, 209
Marat, Jean-Paul, 79, 81
Marianne, actresses as, 157, 201–203, 205, 238
Marie Atoinette, 56–57, 75, 80
Marmontel, Jean-François, 36, 48, 66
Marriage, of actresses, 108–109, 138–140, 177–179, 184, 196, 228
Mars, Mademoiselle (actress), 29, 82, 86, 214–215, 234, 289n

Masculinity, 9, 43, 106; crisis of, 3, 8, 167–168, 179–181, 239; norms of, 68, 80, 102–103, 121, 123; and political order, 2, 4, 46–47, 61–64, 118, 154–155
Mass culture, 20–21, 32, 150–151, 171, 210, 215, 219
Maupassant, Guy de, 122–123
Maurice, count de Saxe, 36, 56, 98
Mayeur de Saint-Paul, François, 54, 56
Mégard-Gémier, Andrée, 24
Meilhac, Henri, 137, 191
Melodrama, 6, 13
Mercier, Louis-Sébastien, 64–65, 72, 78, 80, 100, 127
Meyer, Arthur, 161
Michelet, Jules, 3
Mille-Noé, H., 142, 147
Mirbeau, Octave, 222
Mistinguett, 25, 235, 284n
Mistresses, actresses as, 23, 25–26, 190–192; demands by, 51–52, 124; expectations about, 2–3, 106–108, 118–120; practices of, 38–39, 41–43, 47–48, 80, 82
Molière, Jean-Baptiste, 11, 38, 72, 133
Moncelet, Charles, 220–221
Le Monde (high society), 11, 53, 91, 211; rituals of, 34, 42, 48, 100, 119–121; sociability of, 16, 51, 124, 160, 215
Montaland, Céline, 89, 104
Monteil, Edgar, 132–134
Monuments, to actresses, 174
Morny, Charles de, 91, 151, 155
Mounet-Sully, Jean, 171, 193
Muriel, Auguste, 143, 147
Musset, Alfred de, 189, 207

Nana, 141–142, 149, 157–158, 176, 225, 276n
Napoleon I, 13, 81–83, 84, 145, 169–170, 236
Napoleon III, 8, 18, 131, 139–140, 149, 170, 201. *See also* Second Empire
Navarre, Mademoiselle (actress), 36
Nerval, Gérard de, 98, 263n
Newspapers, 6, 15–17, 20, 210, 213, 222–224, 226
New Woman. *See* Feminism
Nicollet, Jean, 11
Notables, 87, 150, 153
Novels: about actresses, 5–6, 54–55, 97–98,

101, 139–142, 170–180, 262n, 272n, 280–281n; about libertinism, 33–35, 50, 53, 118

Odéon theater, 20, 27, 155, 273n
Offenbach, Jacques, 19, 111, 134, 164, 217
Opéra, 11, 14, 30, 54, 67, 100, 131; audiences at, 18, 20, 79, 215. *See also* Dancers
Operetta, 13, 19, 125, 134
Orléanist regime, 3, 14, 84–85, 91, 93–94, 96, 133, 135, 149–150
Otéro, Caroline, 195–196, 224
Ozy, Alice, 149, 187

Palissot de Monteroy, Charles, 72–73
Papillon de la Ferté, Denis, 69–70
Paris, 8, 10–11, 15, 18, 117, 150, 173–174, 214. *See also* Boulevard
Patti, Adélina, 19, 114, 217
Pearl, Cora, 164, 292n
Perrin, Emile, 218
Perrot, Michelle, 95
Peter, René, 110, 162
Photography, 19, 103, 216–219; magazines using, 167–168, 226, 241, 278n
Pierson, Blanche, 89, 104, 165
Plays, about actresses, 6, 95–99, 135–138, 170, 280n
Playwrights, 14, 23, 26–27, 29, 60, 69, 71–72, 121, 142
Polaire (singer), 116, 196, 204, 235
Politics, of actresses, 200–208
Pompadour, Madame de, 56
Porel, Jacques, 172
Pornocracy, 141, 148, 152–153, 157–158
Pouponne, Mademoiselle (dancer), 47
La Press, 16, 213, 223
Prévot, Jules, 144
Prince of Wales, 117, 123
Privatization, of emotions, 42, 46, 52, 125–127
Prostitution, 24, 36, 40, 57, 93, 130, 156; state-sponsored, 131–134, 164
Proudhon, Pierre-Joseph, 95, 148
Provincial theater, 8, 107, 192
Prudhomme, Louis, 79
Public morality, and actresses, 62–67, 76, 99, 124, 133, 153, 155–156, 158
Public sphere, 4, 9; absolutist, 42, 56–57, 59,

67–68, 73–74; democratic, 83, 150, 162, 171; rise of, 52, 61–62, 64, 67, 210, 238. *See also* Civil society
Public women, 9, 239; actresses as, 5, 67–73, 75–78, 81–83, 181, 197–206; attacks on, 145–147, 156, 170–171

Rachel, 30–31, 112, 142, 153, 173, 201–202, 204, 214–215
Racial ideas, 116
Rats. See Dancers
Raucourt, Mademoiselle (actress), 55–57, 75, 78–80, 82, 85, 115
Reading committee. *See* Comédie-française
Réaux, Gédéon Tallement de, 38
Regency, 39, 41
Reichemberg, Suzanne, 218, 286n
Reiffenberg, Frédéric de, 143, 147
Réjane, 21, 122, 204, 225–226, 230, 268n; as star, 30, 103, 117, 224, 230
Renoir, Auguste, 132
Republicanism, and actresses, 62–63, 131–132, 142, 154–156, 158, 159–162, 171–175
Retif de la Bretonne, Nicolas, 65–66, 78, 100
Retz, Mademoiselle (dancer), 44
Revolution of 1789, 3, 8, 10, 13, 59, 87, 95; actresses in, 74–82, 158, 170–171, 238, 240
Revolution of 1830, 14, 87–88, 90–91, 93, 95, 97, 135, 188, 238
Revolution of 1848, 3, 6, 86, 134, 145, 238
Riccoboni, Louis, 59–64, 67, 75
Richelieu, duke of, 41
Richepin, Jean, 221
Rochefort, Henri, 101–102
Rolandeau, Louise, 82
Romainville, Mademoiselle (singer), 49
Romanticism, 13, 140, 156
Rome (ancient), actresses in, 65–66
Roqueplan, Nestor, 17, 101, 107, 114, 119, 122, 148, 247n
Rousseau, Jean-Jacques, 55, 127, 170; ideas of, 3, 5, 62–66, 81, 86–87; influence of, 7, 35, 79, 142–147, 161–162, 239
Russians, and actresses, 90, 100, 103

Sagan, Prince de, 17
Sainte-Croix, de (author), 55
Saint-Huberty, Madame (singer), 30

Saint-Phal (actor), 75
Saint-Victor, Paul de, 123, 189
Salaries, of actresses, 30–31, 67, 142
Salons, 17, 63, 81, 86, 195, 198–199, 210, 285n
Samary, Jeanne, 109, 133–134
Samson, Joseph-Isidor, 170–171
Samuel, Fernand, 166, 193
Sand, George, 21, 36, 93, 115, 136, 188–189
"Sarah Barnum" affair, 221–222
Sarcey, Francisque, 10, 28, 106–107
Scandals, of actresses, 7, 33, 47, 52–54, 60, 75, 195–196, 230–231
Schneider, Hortense, 17, 19, 144, 156
Scholl, Aurélien, 17, 123, 127, 140–141
Scribe, Eugène, 98, 145
Second Empire, 6, 8, 117, 131, 134, 136, 234–235, 238; political culture of, 141, 149–158, 164, 199
Sem (artist), 116
Séverine (journalist), 203
Sexuality, of actresses, 67, 110–111; deviant, 115–116, 122–124, 128, 183; display of, 23–24, 26, 41, 70, 80–81, 104–105, 212–213; expectations about, 1–3, 60, 75, 207, 215
Society columns, 213–215
Sorel, Cécile, 117, 170, 195, 200, 230, 235
Soubise, prince of, 43, 46
Sports, 167–168
Staël, Germaine de, 95
Star system, 18, 20, 28–30, 32, 217, 249n
Stendhal, 2, 101, 104–105
Street names, 173–174

Taglione, Marie, 100
Taillandiera, Mademoiselle (actress), 116
Taine, Hippolyte, 3, 148
Talma, François, 78–79, 170, 174
Le Temps, 18, 165, 214
Tessandier, Aimée, 192–193, 195
Theater industry, 11–13, 18–21, 28–32, 111, 247n
Theatrical agencies, 31–32
Theatrical dictionaries, 211–213
Thénard, Jenny, 198
Théo, Louise, 117, 129
Thérésa (singer), 19, 157

Thibaud, Anna, 25
Third Republic, 3, 8–9, 105, 121, 130–132, 158, 171, 180, 238–239, 241
Ticket prices, 15
Tilly, Count Alexandre de, 47
Tocqueville, Alexis de, 151
Touchard-Lafosse, Georges, 97
Tours, theatrical, 31, 116, 142, 184, 204–205, 219, 221, 278n

Uchard, Mario, 138
Universal Expositions, 18–19, 217
Uzanne, Octave, 107, 122, 164

Variétés theater, 14–15, 119, 129, 193, 203, 247n
Vaultier, Louis, 178
Véron, Louis, 153
Véron, Pierre, 111–112, 116, 133, 221
Verrière, Mademoiselle (actress), 36, 56
Vestris, Gaetan, 210
Vestris, Madame (actress), 76, 109
Vestris, Mademoiselle (dancer), 44, 46
Viardot, Pauline, 115
Viel-Castel, Count Horace de, 153–154, 200
La Vie parisienne, 18, 121–122, 127, 130–131, 164–165, 168–169
Vigny, Alfred de, 189
Villèle, count de, 215
Villemessant, Hippolyte de, 18, 199, 206
Voltaire, 11, 55, 70, 170

Weiss, Jean-Jacques, 135
Window shopping, 15, 216–219
Women: expectations about, 5, 23, 34, 39–40, 68, 88, 238–239; powers of, 2–3, 7, 23, 60–63, 74, 95, 114, 148–149, 194, 214, 236. *See also* Public women
Working class, 6, 15, 18, 21, 32, 91, 93
Worms, Gustave, 17
Worth, Charles, 112, 234, 292n
Writers, 6, 16–18, 120–122, 142, 154, 188–189, 262n. *See also* Boulevard; Novels

Youths, and actresses, 101–103, 106

Zola, Emile, 141–143, 149, 204